always up to date

The law changes, but Nolo is on top of it! We offer several
ways to make sure you and your Nolo products are up to date:

1 **Nolo's Legal Updater**

We'll send you an email whenever a new edition of this book
is published! Sign up at **www.nolo.com/legalupdater**.

2 **Updates @ Nolo.com**

Check **www.nolo.com/update** to find recent changes
in the law that affect the current edition of your book.

3 **Nolo Customer Service**

To make sure that this edition of the book is the most
recent one, call us at **800-728-3555** and ask one of
our friendly customer service representatives.
Or find out at **www.nolo.com**.

please note

We believe accurate, plain-English legal information should help you solve many of your own legal problems. But this text is not a substitute for personalized advice from a knowledgeable lawyer. If you want the help of a trained professional—and we'll always point out situations in which we think that's a good idea—consult an attorney licensed to practice in your state.

1st edition

Divorce Without Court

A Guide to Mediation and Collaborative Divorce

by Attorney-Mediator Katherine E. Stoner

First Edition	MAY 2006
Editor	EMILY DOSKOW
Illustration	SUSAN PUTNEY
Proofreading	ROBERT WELLS
Index	THÉRÈSE SHERE
Printing	CONSOLIDATED PRINTERS, INC.

Stoner, Katherine E., 1947-
    Divorce without court : a guide to mediation and collaborative divorce / by Katherine E.
Stoner ; edited by Emily Doskow.-- 1st ed.
        p. cm.
    ISBN 1-4133-0494-X (alk. paper)
    1. Divorce mediation--United States--Popular works. 2. Divorce settlements--United
States--Popular works. I. Doskow, Emily. II. Title.

KF535.Z9S76 2006
346.7301'66--dc22

                                                                        2006040027

For information on bulk purchases or corporate premium sales, please contact the Special Sales
Department. For academic sales or textbook adoptions, ask for Academic Sales. Call 800-955-4775 or
write to Nolo, Inc., 950 Parker Street, Berkeley, CA 94710.

About Our Cover

Astrid plays an integral role at Guide Dogs for the Blind
(www.guidedogs.com)—her pups become loyal helpers
and confidence-boosters to visually impaired people.
In much the same way, Nolo books and software will
guide you step by step through the unfamiliar legal
tangles of life's big events.

Acknowledgments

Thanks to everyone who helped make the original version of this book, *Using Divorce Mediation*, a reality, especially Martina Reaves, mediator and friend extraordinaire, and Gary Friedman and Jack Himmelstein, colleagues and mentors at the Center for Mediation in Law. Thanks also to Steve Elias and Robin Leonard, editors of the first edition, and to Emily Doskow, who edited the second edition. My continuing gratitude to the following people who generously took the time to critique drafts of various chapters: Dana Curtis, Mary Duryee, Catherine Jermany Elias, Judith Joshel, Patricia McDermott, Kristin Orliss, Maude Pervere, Tony Roffers, and Susan Walker.

Special thanks to the folks at Nolo who played a part in making the book look so great, from layout to cover art and graphics (especially the divorce game board—a picture really is worth a thousand words).

I am forever indebted to Emily Doskow, Nolo editor, for her role in the transformation of the original book to what is found in these pages, for listening to my half-baked ideas, for superb editing, and for keeping me on track—and on time.

Last, but never least, thanks to my partner Michelle Welsh, to Joseph and Christina, and to the rest of my friends and family for their support and encouragement.

Dedication

To my clients, whose courage and commitment to the possibility of resolution have taught me so much.

Table of Contents

2 What Happens in Mediation

3 What Happens in a Collaborative Divorce

4 Deciding to Mediate or Collaborate

5 Proposing Mediation or Collaboration

6 Finding a Mediator

7 Finding a Collaborative Attorney

8 Using Advisers and Doing Legal Research

9 Getting Started on Information-Gathering

10 Preparing for and Making the Most of the First Session

11 Evaluating Your Progress in Mediation or Collaborative Divorce

12 Communicating in Mediation or Collaborative Divorce

13 Negotiating in Mediation and Collaborative Divorce

14 Court-Sponsored Mediation

15 Encountering Difficulties in Mediation and Collaboration

16 Writing Up the Agreement

17 Women and Men in Mediation and Collaborative Divorce

18 Unmarried Couples in Mediation and Collaboration

19 Mediation and Collaboration After Divorce

Appendix

Index

Introduction

I t's happened. The thing you thought would never happen to your marriage. You and your spouse are divorcing. Your friends tell you, "You need protection. Get yourself a good lawyer." You call a lawyer who has been highly recommended. The lawyer wants a $5,000 retainer, payable at the time of the first appointment.

You consider doing your own divorce. You look at a self-help book. The forms and procedure seem overwhelming. Besides, the book says it's only for people who have ironed out their differences. Every time you and your spouse try to talk about how you will divide things up, who will have custody of the children, and how much child support will be paid, you end up arguing without getting anywhere.

Even if you and your spouse can agree on everything, you're afraid you might overlook something. You want some help with the divorce, but you can't afford the huge retainers that lawyers charge. What's more, you're afraid of starting your own personal version of World War III by getting lawyers involved.

If you find yourself in this sort of situation, you will benefit from reading this book. We describe how you can get as much help as you need for the divorce—at a price you can afford—by using a neutral professional known as a mediator or by seeking out lawyers who offer a new approach to resolving the issues in divorce cases, called "collaborative law" or "collaborative divorce." A mediator or two collaborative lawyers, one for each of you, can help you and your spouse reach a complete agreement that will settle your divorce case without a costly legal battle. A mediator does not impose a decision on you. Nor do your collaborative lawyers decide for you. The two of you decide what's best for you, with their help.

What Exactly Is Mediation?

Mediation is a process in which you and your spouse negotiate an acceptable agreement with the help of a neutral third party—the mediator—who assists you in negotiating, but who does not make the decisions for you. If, before reading further, you want to know more about how mediation can work to produce a voluntary settlement between divorcing spouses, skip ahead to Chapter 2 and give it a good browse.

Why Mediate or Collaborate? Consider the Alternative

Deciding whether or not to mediate or collaborate requires that you make an informed choice. While divorce mediation has grown in popularity quite substantially during the past few years, it's still a relatively new concept in many parts of the country. Collaborative divorce

What Exactly Is Collaborative Divorce?

Like mediation, collaborative divorce (also called collaborative law, or collaborative practice) is a process in which you and your spouse negotiate an acceptable agreement with some professional help. Instead of using one neutral mediator, you and your spouse hire specially trained collaborative attorneys who advise and assist you in negotiating the settlement agreement. Ordinarily, both spouses and their attorneys sign a "no court" agreement that requires the attorneys to withdraw from the case if a settlement is not reached and the case goes to court. A collaborative divorce may also involve other professionals, such as child custody specialists or neutral accountants, who are committed to helping you settle your case without litigation. If, before reading further, you want to know more about how collaborative divorce can work to produce a voluntary settlement between divorcing spouses, skip ahead to Chapter 3 for a more complete description of what happens in a typical collaborative divorce.

We live in an adversarial culture, so it's no surprise that our legal system is adversarial as well. If you doubt this, note how the media thrives on reporting conflict in and out of court. In our legal system, every court case is like a war or a duel. The opposing party is an enemy who cannot be trusted. We hire lawyers to attack the other side and "protect" us, our property, and our honor. Lawyers plan their strategies carefully, trying to get the best advantage for their clients and crush the opposition. Often, cases settle at the last minute, with no one feeling very good about it.

If the case doesn't settle, the lawyers do battle in the courtroom before a judge and maybe a jury—although juries are rarely involved in divorce cases. At the end of the case, the judge or jury considers everything that has been presented and decides the outcome. Sometimes there is a clear "winner." Sometimes both sides feel like they've lost. Often, no one feels that justice has been done—mainly because the result has been dictated by laws that seem fair to no one. And, to add insult to injury, when the dust settles both sides realize that whatever money or property they were fighting over has been depleted by legal fees.

Taking a case through an adversarial legal proceeding is called "litigation." Litigation is extremely expensive because of the hours spent by the lawyers in assembling information, investigating, and

is an even newer phenomenon, and it is only just beginning to take hold in many places. As you consider these options, it's important to first understand how divorces have traditionally been handled.

preparing for trial, in addition to the time spent in trial, which can be days, weeks, or even months. Litigation is also very time-consuming and emotionally draining for the parties in the lawsuit.

Litigation is a terrible way to make the personal decisions that a divorce entails—decisions that will affect you, your spouse, and your children for a long time to come. But litigation is the way those decisions will be made if you and your spouse can't come up with an agreement.

When you litigate your divorce, your spouse becomes your intimate enemy. Your adversarial lawyer will probably advise you not to talk to your spouse directly about the issues, but to communicate through your lawyer. Not only is this expensive, but it can lead to serious misunderstandings that further erode trust and respect between you and your spouse. And imagine what harm it can do to your children.

EXAMPLE: Ellen and Joe are getting divorced after 15 years of marriage. They have several mutual funds and other investments that are managed by a financial planning firm called XYZ Company. While their breakup hasn't always been easy, they both want to be fair in the divorce. Following the advice of their relatives and friends, each has hired a lawyer to handle the divorce case.

When Joe moves out of the house that he and Ellen have been living in,

he calls the broker at XYZ Company and leaves a message letting the broker know his new address. The broker's assistant takes the message and puts in for a change of address on all of the mutual funds and other investments jointly owned by Ellen and Joe. Joe is unaware that this has been done.

A month or so goes by and Ellen realizes that she hasn't received statements for the investments. She calls XYZ Company and is informed that Joe changed the mailing address on all the accounts the previous month. Ellen's first impulse upon learning this is to call Joe and demand an explanation. If she did so, she would learn that this was not something Joe did, and the problem would be cleared up.

Instead, following her lawyer's advice, Ellen does not contact Joe but passes the information on to her lawyer.

Ellen's lawyer tells her she needs a restraining order requiring that the addresses be reinstated and preventing Joe from taking similar actions in the future. The lawyer also recommends a court order putting a freeze on all investments and bank accounts. The lawyer fires off a letter to Joe's lawyer and proceeds to file a motion (written request) with the court. Joe's lawyer responds to Ellen's restraining order requests with counterattacks and requests on behalf of Joe. Soon, what could have been a civil and respectful end to the marriage has mushroomed into an antagonistic and expensive court battle.

This scenario, or some form of it, is played out in countless divorces across the country every year. Even though most divorce cases settle before an actual court trial, and even though some lawyers try to downplay the adversarial aspects of a litigated divorce case, many divorcing couples experience the embittering effects that litigation tends to produce as their lawyers spar with each other, often on the basis of incomplete or inaccurate information. Minor misunderstandings that could have been cleared up with a direct conversation, like the change of address snafu in Joe and Ellen's case, instead ignite major conflagrations.

Fortunately, there are alternatives to adversarial divorce litigation. In fact, there are several alternatives, as discussed below. For most people, the best of those alternatives is either mediation or collaborative divorce, or sometimes a combination of the two.

Divorce Decision Continuum

When discussing mediation, legal experts often put it into a category generally referred to as "alternative dispute resolution," or ADR, because mediation is an alternative to adversarial litigation. The D in ADR underscores the problem with using litigation to decide divorce issues. The assumption is that there is a *dispute* that must be resolved, either in litigation or in an alternative process. For most divorcing couples, this assumption is incorrect.

It's true that divorcing spouses have many decisions to make, and they may have different points of view on those decisions. But this doesn't mean that they have an actual dispute that has to be resolved. They may simply need help making the decisions together. Often, the questions are just how much and what kind of help they need. So step away from the adversarial assumptions. Rather than looking at resolving your divorce issues through either adversarial litigation or an alternative to it, consider your options in terms of a continuum (sliding scale) of different ways you and your spouse can make the decisions you need to make in order to get divorced.

As you can see, you retain the most control and spend the least money if you and your spouse do your own divorce from beginning to end. At the other extreme, where you have the least control and spend the most money, is adversarial litigation. In between are several options.

⚠️ **Mediation may not work if there's a power imbalance.** If there is a power imbalance between divorcing spouses,

Divorce Decision Continuum

Most Control Least Expense					Least Control Most Expense
Do your own divorce	Mediation (one neutral person assists you to reach a decision)	Collaboration (collaborative lawyers help you decide)	Nonadversarial (lawyers negotiate —see Chapter 8)	Arbitration (neutral third person decides)	Litigation

doing the divorce without any outside help will be less expensive than litigating. However, it may also mean less control, not more, for the less-powerful spouse, because the other will dominate. This may be a situation in which you will be better off choosing to be represented by collaborative attorneys who can make sure that the power imbalance is addressed. If you have concerns about a power imbalance in your relationship, see Chapters 3 and 15. If the power imbalance is gender-related, take a look at Chapter 17.

Unless you and your spouse feel completely comfortable with your ability to negotiate everything yourselves and do all your own paperwork for the divorce, you will probably want some professional help. Mediation or collaboration is the next-best option on the continuum. It provides the specific help you need while keeping costs down and letting you stay in control of what happens.

Why Mediation or Collaboration Can Be Your Best Option

In mediation, a neutral third party helps you and your spouse negotiate a complete settlement of all the issues that must be decided in your divorce. The mediator does not decide for you, so you have control over the outcome of the case. In mediation, you and your spouse communicate directly as much as possible. Even when you communicate through the mediator, having fewer people involved in the communication cuts down on the chances of a misunderstanding.

In a collaborative divorce, you and your spouse are both represented throughout the entire process by specially trained collaborative lawyers who are committed to helping the two of you make decisions together. You meet separately with your own attorney and the four of you meet together on a regular basis, in "four-way" meetings. Collaborative divorce involves more professionals than mediation. Therefore, it is likely to be more expensive, and the collaborative lawyers need to be skilled in communicating effectively and accurately.

Mediation is informal. You and your spouse, with the mediator's help, set all the ground rules for exchanging information. You control the timing and the scope of the entire process, without having to adhere to elaborate (and expensive) legal procedures. Mediation usually takes much less time than litigation. It can even take place all in one day, although most divorcing couples meet for several sessions on separate days over a period of days or weeks or months.

Collaborative divorce is also informal, although it may be somewhat less flexible than mediation, because there are more people's schedules and perspectives to accommodate.

In both mediation and collaboration, you can still use other advisers, such as child specialists and financial analysts, and if you mediate, consulting divorce lawyers, but you—not your advisers—are in control of the process. They are there to help you successfully mediate your case. The mediator or the consulting lawyers help keep you and any other advisers on track so that things don't spin out of control as they did in Joe and Ellen's case.

Eventually, you will have to have some contact with a domestic relations or family court to get legally divorced. Through mediation or collaboration, you can keep that contact brief and manageable. Once you use mediation to reach agreement on all the issues, you'll make the legal part of the divorce a simple, uncontested procedure that doesn't require a trial or contentious hearings on points of evidence and pretrial maneuvers.

Alas, mediation doesn't work for everyone. Nor does collaborative divorce. Some people need a more structured, less direct way to handle the divorce. Mediation or collaboration can and do work for most people, however.

Getting the Most out of This Book

In the next several chapters, we describe
- how mediation or collaboration fits into the overall divorce process —See Chapter 1
- how to decide whether and when to mediate or use a collaborative process—See Chapter 4
- how to find the right mediator or collaborative lawyer for your situation—See Chapters 6 and 7
- how to get your spouse to agree to mediate or collaborate—See Chapter 5
- how to prepare for mediation or collaborative divorce—See Chapters 9 and 10.

We also give you a description of what happens in a typical mediation, using a hypothetical couple in Chapter 2, and we give a similar description of a typical collaborative divorce in Chapter 3.

You'll learn how to communicate and negotiate effectively in mediation or collaboration and how to deal with problems that arise. We also give you guidelines on selecting and working with other advisers while you are going through the process, and we spend some time looking at how you can write up your settlement in a binding and legally enforceable agreement.

In the latter part of the book, we spend some time on specific issues, including:

- how a spouse's gender may affect the process (Chapter 17)

- how to use mediation or collaboration if you are ending a nonmarital relationship, rather than a legal marriage (Chapter 18)
- how to use mediation or collaboration to resolve postdivorce issues such as changes in child custody and support arrangements (Chapter 19), and
- how to use mediation or collaboration to hammer out a financial agreement with a new spouse or partner (Chapter 19).

To use this book most effectively, first read Chapters 1, 2, 3, and 4. Then, depending on your situation, use the

Your Situation	Read (or Skip)
You and your spouse have agreed to mediate	Skip Chapter 5
You and your spouse have agreed to a collaborative process	Skip Chapter 5
You and your spouse have picked your mediator	Skip Chapters 6 & 7
You and your spouse have picked your collaborative attorneys	Skip Chapters 6 & 7
You are going to your first meeting with your collaborative attorney	Read Chapter 9
You are about to attend your first mediation session	Read Chapters 9 & 10
You need help in communicating and negotiating during the process	Read Chapters 12 & 13
You are using court-sponsored mediation	Read Chapter 14
You want help in selecting and using an adviser	Read Chapter 8
You encounter difficulties while you are mediating or collaborating	Read Chapter 15
You are ready to write up your divorce (separation or marital settlement) agreement	Read Chapter 16
You are interested in reading about gender differences in mediation	Read Chapter 17
You are ending a nonmarital relationship and want to learn how to use mediation in your situation	Read Chapter 18
You are already divorced and want to try mediation to settle a new issue that has come up with your ex-spouse	Read Chapter 19

remaining chapters to help you go through the mediation or collaborative process step by step. The chart above shows which chapters you may want to read (or skip) depending on your situation.

Let your mediator or collaborative lawyer be your guide. If you decide to mediate, use your mediator when you need help. If you choose a collaborative process, seek assistance from your collaborative attorney. We hope you will find this book useful as you consider whether to mediate or collaborate and as you go through the process. But we cannot cover every possible contingency that might arise. So don't be surprised if things happen in your mediation or collaborative divorce that don't look like what we've described in this book. When that occurs, use your mediator or collaborative lawyer to answer your questions. If your mediator or your lawyer tells you something inconsistent with what we're saying here, and if what he or she says sounds reasonable in the context of what you are going through, feel free to ignore our suggestions and go with what your mediator or lawyer tells you.

Definitions

Throughout this book, we'll use certain terms that have specific meanings. We'll try to define them for you when they come up. But there are a few terms we use so often that it makes sense to define them now.

Divorce. We use this word to refer to the legal process of ending a marriage. The technical legal word for divorce in your state might be different, such as "dissolution of marriage." If you are ending a nonmarital relationship, you may think of yourselves as getting divorced, but the law doesn't. In the eyes of the legal system, you're breaking up, or if it gets to court, you're dissolving a partnership, just as if business partners chose to end their relationship. Nevertheless, we use the word divorce to include the end of a nonmarital relationship.

Spouse. We use this term rather than "husband" or "wife" because it can refer to either gender. We also intend it to cover nonmarital partners. Occasionally, when it seems appropriate, we will use the word "partner" in addition to or instead of "spouse."

Fictional characters. To illustrate several of the points in this book, we'll introduce you to several fictional couples. Some will make only a cameo appearance once in the book. Other couples appear a few times. You've already met Joe and Ellen. In Chapter 1, we'll introduce you to Lucinda and Franco, another couple dragged into costly adversarial litigation. In Chapter 2, you'll get an insider's view of Robert and Fran's mediation.

Icons

Look for these icons to alert you to certain information:

 When you see this icon, you can skip information that may not apply to you.

 This icon alerts you to a practical tip or good idea.

 This icon tells you to consider your options carefully before making a particular decision.

 This icon introduces a male/female couple.

 This icon introduces a female couple.

 This icon introduces a male couple.

 This icon alerts you to the fact that you might want help from an adviser other than your mediator.

 This icon reminds you that your mediator is your best source of information about your mediation.

 This icon alerts you to a chart or checklist you can copy and use in mediation or in some other way.

 Following this icon are resources to help you learn more on specific subjects.

Chapter 1

The Role of Mediation and Collaborative Law in the Divorce Process

Getting divorced is a little like taking a long journey to a new country. The traditional way of traveling involves hiring a guide (your lawyer) to get you there. Along the way, there are stops, each of which can be expensive and risky. Ultimately, you'll arrive at your destination, but the trip may have cost you a lot more than you expected. You may not even have all your luggage when you get there. Some of it may never show up.

When you use mediation or collaboration to settle your divorce, you and your spouse hire a different kind of guide (the mediator or the collaborative lawyers, working together). The trip may still be long and arduous. These new guides can't "beam you up" past all the financial and emotional obstacles along the route. But they can help the two of you map out an express route that bypasses the most expensive and risky stops along the way.

More information on mediation and collaborative divorce. If, before going further, you want to know more about how mediation works, give Chapter 2 a good browse. If you are interested in a little more about collaborative divorce, check out Chapter 3. Don't forget to return to read the rest of this chapter.

Mediation or Collaboration: The Express Route to Divorce

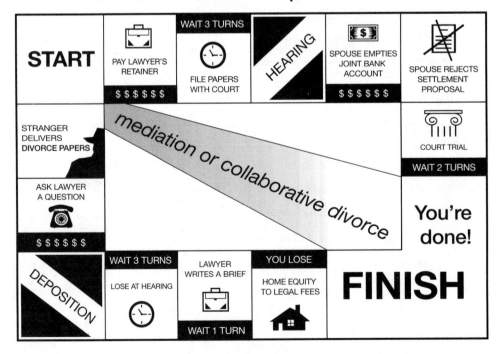

In order to understand how a mediator or collaborative lawyer helps you avoid the pitfalls, you need to know something about the typical divorce process. In this chapter, we first take a look at the divorce process. We then explore how mediation can help you and your spouse control the timing and direction of the divorce so that you make the best of the situation you are in, rather than making things worse.

The Four Divorces

When we use the word "divorce" to describe the official end of a relationship, we are really talking about four different divorces that are taking place: the emotional divorce, the social divorce, the financial divorce, and the legal divorce. Each divorce can affect the others in ways that are either helpful or harmful.

The *emotional divorce* begins with the decision to separate and ends when both spouses accept the fact that the relationship is over. An awareness of where you and your spouse are in the emotional divorce is essential to a successful mediation. An out-of-control emotional divorce can interfere with the smooth progress of the other three divorces and effectively preclude the possibility of a successful mediation. Couples ending a nonmarital relationship also go through the emotional divorce.

In the *social divorce*, you readjust your relationships with other people. Instead of connecting to family and friends as part of a couple, you begin to interact with them as a single person. For their part, family and mutual friends will also have to adjust to your new status. They may even get involved in your divorce process by taking sides with one of you or offering advice. Sometimes this is helpful; sometimes it's not. Either way, it can have an impact on the divorce process and on the success or failure of mediation. Again, couples ending a nonmarital relationship also go through the social divorce.

In the *financial divorce*, the property and debts you have accumulated during your relationship will get divided up. The income you used to support one household will have to somehow stretch to pay for two. Ideally, you and your spouse will find a way to divide things up that works for both of you without spending a ton of money on lawyers' fees and court costs. But this will require cooperation. If you and your spouse are unable to cooperate because of what is happening in one, two, or all three of the other divorces, you will find it hard to make the financial decisions needed to complete the divorce process. Because mediation proceeds in stages that allow you to consider one issue at a time, it provides a format for separating out the financial divorce from the other three divorces so that you and your spouse can focus on financial solutions that work.

Nonmarital couples may or may not go through a financial divorce, depending on whether they acquired assets or debts jointly or shared their incomes and whether they are legally joined in one of the marriage-like relationships available in some states.

The *legal divorce* can be the simplest of the four divorces. Depending on the laws of the state where you live, there may be waiting periods and other formalities to be observed. Certain papers will need to be completed and filed with the court, and eventually a judge will sign your divorce judgment.

As long as the legal requirements of your state are followed, and if the case is uncontested (meaning you have no disagreements that the court needs to resolve), getting a divorce is not all that complicated or expensive. But if you and your spouse get stuck in emotional, social, or financial conflict, the legal divorce can become a battle. And a very long, costly, and painful battle it can be.

It may not be possible for you to avoid a contested legal battle. For example, if one of you refuses to accept the end of the relationship or is so mistrustful or angry that even the most minimal kind of cooperation is impossible, then you may have no choice but to settle everything in a contested court case—unless, of course, you are willing to wait and let time smooth the way. Just how long to wait is covered in Chapter 5 and in Chapter 15, together with ideas for what to do while you're waiting.

The Religious or Cultural Divorce

If you and your spouse belong to a particular religious or cultural community, ending your relationship in the eyes of your community may be a fifth part of the divorce process. Mediation can be especially valuable for you, because it allows you and your spouse to include your religious or cultural values in your divorce agreement.

If you and your spouse both want to settle things but are having trouble doing that on your own, mediation or collaborative divorce can give you a way to keep the legal divorce simple and uncontested. Both mediation and collaborative divorce offer tools to help you and your spouse communicate at a time when things between you may be at an all-time low. With the help of the mediator or your collaborative lawyers, you can assess where you are in each of the four divorces, identify the decisions that you need to make together, and then make those decisions in a way that takes into account what needs to happen in each of the four divorces.

Some nonmarital couples go through a process very similar to a legal divorce (see Chapter 18). Others do not go through a legal divorce. They can use the court system to resolve their disputes if they can't agree on their own or with a mediator, but their legal action is analogous to dissolving a business partnership.

The Emotional Divorce

No matter what caused the breakdown of your relationship, and no matter whose decision it was to divorce, both you and your spouse will go through a period of emotional adjustment to the reality that the relationship is over. Getting at least partway through this period of adjustment is a prerequisite to getting through the rest of the divorce.

Psychologists who have studied divorce believe that ending a relationship means going through a grieving process similar to grieving the death of a loved one. Borrowing from Elisabeth Kubler-Ross's studies of the grief process, psychologists have identified certain emotional stages that everyone grieving the loss of a relationship goes through:

- denial and shock—this can't be happening; sure, our relationship has some problems, but we can work it out; s/he'll come back if I give it a little time
- bargaining—I'll do things differently to make this stop happening
- anger—potential depression or rage
- sadness and guilt, and
- acceptance.

Each spouse goes through this process in a different way. Some people have

a lot more trouble getting through a particular stage, such as denial. Sometimes the process is more like a spiral, and a period of sadness might be followed by a return to denial, bargaining, or anger.

 Getting through the emotional divorce is not easy. There are many good books that can help you get through this time. You might start with *Crazy Time: Surviving Divorce and Building a New Life*, by Abigail Trafford (Harper Collins); *The Good Divorce: Keeping Your Family Together When Your Marriage Comes Apart*, by Constance Ahrons, Ph.D. (Harper Collins); or *Between Love and Hate: A Guide to Civilized Divorce*, by Lois Gold, M.S.W. (NAL/Dutton).

 A good counselor or support group can be very helpful. This is especially true if you are finding it hard to function in your daily life or if you are unable to carry on a civil conversation with your spouse. If you are concerned about the cost of counseling, consider how much you may save in lawyers' fees. For tips on finding a good counselor or support group, see Chapter 8.

Your emotional timing may be very different from your spouse's timing. Making decisions about the divorce without being aware of these differences can lead to trouble.

Terms of Unendearment: the "Leaver" and the "Leavee"

Experts who study divorce have observed that even if both spouses have been dissatisfied in the relationship, one spouse usually starts the process of separation. This person is sometimes called the "divorce seeker," "initiator," or "leaver." The other spouse is referred to as the "divorce opposer," "left," or "leavee." The leavee is often taken by surprise by the leaver's decision to separate. For the leavee, there is still hope—even if there were problems in the marriage. For the leaver, the relationship is beyond repair. The leaver tends to push for the divorce. The leavee tends to resist. Carried to extremes, this can lead to impasse or all-out war. Even in less extreme cases, a spouse's role as leaver or leavee can have an impact on how each spouse approaches negotiating during the mediation. (See Chapter 13.)

If you start to feel stuck in the role of leaver or leavee, consider seeking the help of a trusted friend, adviser, or counselor. A good counselor can help you understand how you got to where you are, and can give you tools for managing the intense feelings—and tough choices—that accompany a divorce. (See Chapter 8.)

For example, if you are the one who initiated the separation, you probably began grieving the loss of your hopes and dreams for the relationship months or years ago. You have probably passed through the denial stage and have experienced at least some of the feelings that go with the later stages. You may feel ready to put the painful past behind you and get on with your new life, while your spouse is just beginning to face the reality of the divorce.

On the other hand, if your spouse has just left you, you are probably in the earliest stage of the grieving process: denial and shock, with moments of intense anger and sadness mixed in. Chances are you will need some time to sort through your feelings about the separation without the pressure of having to be reasonable or fair to someone who has just shattered your dreams.

If you and your spouse are in very different phases of the emotional divorce, allow a little time to pass before attempting to negotiate anything but the most immediate and temporary arrangements. Good advice from counselors and supportive consulting lawyers (or collaborative lawyers, if you choose that route) can help you make temporary arrangements that protect your rights while everyone adjusts to the separation. (See Chapter 7 for more on finding a collaborative lawyer, or to find a consulting lawyer, see Chapter 8.)

This can also be a good time to start the mediation process. The mediator can help you come up with a temporary agreement while laying the groundwork for constructive communication later on. Remember, mediation often occurs in different phases over a period of time, depending on how difficult the issues are and where the parties are in the emotional divorce.

Even after the initial stage of adjustment, there may be times when interactions between you and your spouse are very volatile, depending on where each of you is in the process. This can be true even if you are each making good progress in the emotional divorce. Working together in mediation or in a collaborative setting can allow you to take a "time out" when you need to because of particularly intense feelings, then pick up where you left off when things have calmed down.

The Social Divorce

You and your spouse (and children) may not be the only ones whose lives will be changed by your separation. Other people—family, friends, business colleagues, neighbors—have related to the two of you as a couple. Now they must go through their own period of adjustment to the end of your relationship. Those closest to you may experience a sense of loss and a grieving process of their own. They may take sides and blame the other person for the breakup. They may offer helpful or unhelpful advice. They may feel caught in the middle and avoid contact with both of you.

On your end, you face daily decisions about what to say about your situation, who to confide in, and who to avoid. If you are the one who moved out, you may also be establishing new routines and contacts and leaving behind old ones.

The social divorce process has a ripple effect. Your divorce is like a stone thrown into a group of leaves floating on a lake. You and your spouse (and your children) are in the center, and you experience the first and strongest splashes. Close friends and family feel the ripples next, then neighbors, business colleagues, and so on out into your community. Eventually, the ripples lose momentum, with no sign of them on the lake. The leaves still float, but in a new pattern created by the ripples from the stone.

The Social Divorce: Kids

If you have children, it is especially important that you find ways to handle conflicts with your spouse and avoid a legal battle. Psychologists point out that the children most badly hurt by divorce are the ones whose parents are in "high conflict." These are the "angry associates" and "fiery foes" studied by divorce expert Constance Ahrons. These parents let their anger at one another spill over into their daily lives and relationships, instead of containing the marital conflict. Their inability to control their behavior during angry times can lead to constant court battles, with a devastating effect on the children for years to come.

Fortunately, there is a lot of help out there for you and your children. Establish contact with a good counselor who can give you advice on helping your children through the divorce and handling the conflict with your spouse. Or look for a class for divorcing parents; some classes even include a program for children.

 Read up on postseparation parenting. A classic that never goes out of date is *Mom's House, Dad's House: Making Shared Custody Work*, by Isolina Ricci, Ph.D. (Simon and Schuster). You'll find lots of helpful information, including art and journal entries by children of divorcing families, in *Helping Your Kids Cope With Divorce the Sandcastles Way*, by M. Gary Neuman, L.M.H.C., with Patricia Romanowski (Random House). There is also some good information for parents in *Between Love and Hate: A Guide to Civilized Divorce*, by Lois Gold, M.S.W. (NAL/Dutton). A good book for younger children (age four to eight) is *Dinosaurs Divorce: A Guide for Changing Families*, by Laurene Krasny Brown and Marc Brown (Little, Brown and Company). Older children (eight to 13) may benefit from reading *My Parents Are Divorced, Too: A Book for Kids by Kids*, by Melanie, Annie, and Steven Ford, as told to Jan Blackstone-Ford (Magination Press).

Above all, remember that you, and not your children, are getting a divorce from your spouse.

The Social Divorce: Family and Friends

Even though you and your spouse (and children) feel the most dramatic effects of the divorce, you can't underestimate the impact on family and close friends. Family members especially can have strong feelings about divorce in general and about your divorce in particular. Your family is likely to be supportive and protective of you, while your spouse's family supports and defends your spouse. Family members tend to want to blame someone for the breakup; if you are the leaver, you may even find members of your own family turning against you. Close friends may react like relatives do. You may find that close couple friends who have shared outings and activities with you and your spouse now feel awkward spending time with either one of you alone.

Friends and associates who haven't known you as well may still be affected by your separation. They, too, may have strong opinions about marriage and divorce. Maybe they have been present during emotional encounters between you and your spouse. Perhaps you've confided in a coworker or a neighbor or another parent, and now they feel involved in your process.

No matter how directly or remotely people are connected to you, not only can they be affected by your divorce, but they can also influence it. They may offer advice. If you are lucky, their advice will be helpful—but even well-meaning advice can sometimes make things worse. If they take sides and blame one of you, this will only add to your troubles. If your spouse's family decides to bankroll a costly legal case on your spouse's behalf, you may find yourself getting divorced from the whole family, not just your spouse.

Using Mediation or Collaboration During the Social Divorce

Mediation and collaborative divorce offer you a chance to keep other people's concerns and agendas from controlling what happens in your divorce, because you and your spouse have the final say in any agreements you reach. At the same time, you can discuss concerns about particular family members or close friends in a mediation or collaborative session, even though these kinds of issues could be considered irrelevant in a legal divorce proceeding. It is even possible to include older children or key family members or friends in some of the mediation sessions so they become part of the solution instead of part of the problem, something that virtually never happens in court.

The Financial Divorce

Separating out finances can be hard, even in the best of circumstances. You don't have to be a professor of economics to understand that two households cost more to support than one. Many of us barely live within our means—this may very well describe you and your spouse before you split up. Now, the income that barely paid the bills of one household will, at least temporarily, be expected to cover the expenses of two. This means that you and your spouse have to figure out who pays for what, where to cut back, and how to do it fairly.

Maybe your family has been able to save carefully and build up some investments. Maybe you own a house together and both of you want it. Or maybe one of you wants to sell it and the other one wants to keep it but can't afford a buyout. Maybe you have a good pension plan at your job and your spouse has no retirement. Maybe your spouse's family has helped the two of you to buy a house or pay off debts. Who gets the savings or the pension? Will the house be sold? Will you have to pay back your spouse's parents for the money they lent you?

Sometimes, financial pressures have led to or played a part in the decision to separate. You may face a mountain of debts you don't know how you will ever pay. Will your spouse have to pay some of them? How can you be sure that will happen?

Of course, you can always have the answers to these and other financial questions decided in court, but then you'll be spending your limited funds on the legal process, leaving even less money to go around. You may also find that your lawyer pressures you into agreeing to a financial arrangement you are unhappy with in order to settle the case and avoid the risk of having a judge order something even worse. In all but a relatively few cases, this is exactly what happens as the case gets closer to trial. The pressure to settle gets more and more intense. Settlement judges are prone to engage in serious arm-twisting ("Counsel, if your client doesn't agree to sell the house, I'll seriously consider ordering it sold at auction") in an endless effort to conserve scarce judicial resources. Faced with these threats, the lawyers pass them on to their clients, painting an ever-bleaker picture of the likely outcome in court. Few divorcing spouses can hold firm to their desired course.

Whether you settle or have a judge decide, the outcome of a contested case may not work for you *or* your spouse nearly as well as something you agree on together. For instance, most financial separation arrangements have tax consequences. If you and your spouse work together, you might be able to figure out a way to save taxes for both of you by dividing your assets in a certain way that is different from what a judge is able to do. Or, if you and your spouse

can't agree on whether to sell your house, it may be possible for you to take out a loan against the house together so that one of you has the cash to buy out the other. Or you might agree to go in on a consolidation loan for the bills, so that the monthly payments will be lower. In most cases, if you work together, you and your spouse can be as creative as you want, and your agreement will be legally acceptable.

Finding a financial solution that works for you and your spouse takes cooperation. It may even depend on getting other people to cooperate, like family members or business associates. If your emotional and social divorces are going smoothly, cooperation is a lot more likely. But if you and your spouse are constantly reacting to each other in negative ways, or if family or friends have taken sides, your attempts to negotiate a workable financial settlement may run into heavy interference.

Using mediation or collaboration increases the likelihood of cooperation between you and your spouse. Both approaches give you a forum outside of the legal arena to work out the financial arrangements without ignoring what is going on socially and emotionally.

Information on money and divorce. No matter what method you use to get through your divorce, you can find the answers to most financial issues you are likely to face in *Divorce & Money: How to*

Make the Best Financial Decisions During Divorce, by Violet Woodhouse with Dale Fetherling (Nolo).

The Legal Divorce

Different states have different laws and procedures to be used in a divorce. This means you will need to find out your own state's specific requirements at some point. (Most often this information will come from your mediator, collaborative lawyer, consulting lawyer, or law coach.) But even with these state differences, the basic process is the same in all states: One spouse begins the case by filing certain papers, then decisions about the legal and financial issues are written up in a court order and a judge grants the divorce.

If the case is uncontested, the process doesn't have to take very long or cost very much. You may even be able to handle the divorce yourself, using a self-help book or other resource. If the case is contested, it can take months or even years to complete, at a cost running into the thousands or tens of thousands of dollars and more.

Whether your case will be contested or uncontested depends on whether you and your spouse can come to an agreement on the legal and financial issues in your case. Because of what's going on in the emotional and social divorces, you and your spouse may have trouble doing

this on your own. A mediator or two good collaborative lawyers can help you negotiate the agreement needed to make your case an uncontested one, whether or not you use lawyers to handle the legal divorce.

Keeping It Simple: The Uncontested Divorce

We've all heard of the nightmare divorce cases that drag on for years and bankrupt the participants, leaving them and their children emotionally scarred and embittered. Thankfully, these cases are in the minority, even though they get a lot of attention. Most divorcing couples resolve their divorce issues with little or no courtroom wrangling. They do this by negotiating a settlement out of court on their own or with the help of lawyers, or in collaboration, or in mediation with a neutral person who facilitates the settlement.

The terms of the settlement are written down in an agreement that can be presented to the judge as part of the uncontested divorce. In this book, we refer to the written agreement as the "divorce agreement," although there are many other designations for it, such as "marital settlement agreement" or "stipulated divorce judgment or decree." (See Chapter 16.)

Once you and your spouse write up and sign the divorce agreement, your legal divorce will be uncontested. It typically will require these four steps:

1. **Filing the papers.** You or your spouse files a written request for divorce (called a petition or complaint) with the court, sometimes accompanied by supportive documents required by state or local laws.

2. **Serving the papers.** The spouse who files the papers has them legally delivered to the other spouse—this can be done cooperatively, using the mail or a mutual friend, or it can be done by formal service (having an adult deliver the papers in person to the nonfiling spouse).

3. **Appearing in court (on paper or in person).** You and/or your spouse must appear in court to assure the judge that your marriage really is over and that you have satisfied the basic requirements for a divorce. Some states allow you to avoid an in-person appearance before the judge by filing an affidavit—a sworn statement—asserting the necessary facts. Even if you are required to appear in person, this is a process that typically takes no longer than five to ten minutes.

4. **Entering the judgment.** Your divorce agreement is approved in a judgment, or decree, of divorce signed by the judge. In some states there are two judgments, a temporary or "interlocutory" judgment and a final judgment, granted after a waiting period is over.

That's it. Sometimes, the paperwork might make it seem a little more complicated, but the complications are all on the surface. If you or your spouse is handy with paperwork, you can complete the divorce yourselves. If not, you can pay a reasonable fee to have the papers prepared for you. Even if you or your spouse must make an in-person court appearance, it is almost completely automatic and shouldn't require the services of a lawyer.

If getting a legal divorce is so simple, why do some people experience bitter, expensive divorces that last months or years? Remember, the uncontested divorce can happen *only* if you and your spouse are able to agree on everything.

Beyond the Basics: The Contested Divorce

If you can't agree on some or all of the things that have to be decided, or if you turn your divorce case over to your lawyer before even trying to reach an agreement, you jeopardize your chance of having a meaningful say about the core decisions in your case, and the legal divorce can become immensely more complicated, expensive, and unpleasant. Why? Partly because the legal system is set up in an adversarial, win-lose format. Partly

Why Do They Act That Way?

Lawyers are trained to follow certain standard procedures and rules when they represent someone. If you hire a lawyer to handle your divorce case before attempting to negotiate an agreement with your spouse, your lawyer will probably follow the procedures and rules that apply to your case. Your lawyer may even consider it malpractice not to use every possible legal maneuver in your behalf. Even if you find a lawyer who will consider avoiding unnecessary and costly legal procedures, there is no guarantee that your spouse's lawyer will do the same. Once the case is filed, it can easily take on a life of its own. Instead of four easy-to-handle steps to an uncontested divorce, you have multiple steps, each adding to the expense and hostility typically generated in a contested case.

Unlike lawyers representing clients in a typical contested case, collaborative lawyers take specialized training in negotiating effectively in a collaborative setting, while still protecting their clients' interests. In addition, both lawyers – and the divorcing spouses – sign an agreement committing themselves to work together and requiring the lawyers to withdraw if the case becomes contested.

because of how lawyers are trained and expected to operate in that adversarial system. (See "Why Do They Act That Way?" above.) Partly because even simple communications can easily get distorted by the process of going through the lawyers before they reach you, and each misunderstanding adds to the mistrust and anger between you and your spouse.

In mediation or collaborative divorce, you bypass the worst parts of the legal process. First, both approaches are nonadversarial. Second, you speak for yourself in the negotiations, even if you have a lawyer advising you as you go. In fact, you don't even need to be represented by a lawyer in mediation, although you may find it beneficial to hire a lawyer to advise you and to handle the uncontested divorce. Third, you deal directly with your spouse, supported by the mediator or your collaborative lawyer, cutting down on the risk of miscommunications.

What exactly do you bypass in mediation? Remember the four steps for the uncontested divorce. Triple that (at a minimum) and crank up the intensity several notches, and you begin to get the picture. Below are the typical steps in a contested divorce.

Filing the Papers

This is similar to the first step of the uncontested divorce: One spouse files a petition or complaint with the court.

Some states allow the spouses to file a joint petition, but this is not common. Usually, the person who files pays a filing fee to the court.

The petition typically contains information such as the names of the spouses and any minor children, and significant dates such as the date of marriage, the children's birthdates, and the date of separation.

The petition states the reason ("grounds") for the divorce. If your state has no-fault divorce and the spouse filing the papers opts to elect a no-fault ground, the papers will say something like "irreconcilable differences" or "irremediable breakdown." If your state has fault divorces and the spouse filing the papers opts to elect a fault ground, the petition might accuse the other spouse of mental cruelty, adultery, abandonment, or something similar. In some states, the filing spouse can allege "separation" if the parties have been living apart for the required amount of time—usually at least one year.

Service and Response

This next step starts out like the second step of the uncontested divorce: The petition is served on (received by) the nonfiling spouse. But unlike the uncontested divorce, this can come as a complete surprise to the recipient. Having a stranger hand you legal papers telling you that you are being sued for divorce can be a humiliating and enraging experience. It can undermine trust and communication between you and your spouse. In fact, it can turn a potentially uncontested divorce into a contested one just like that. If you have a choice, don't do it this way.

The spouse who is served usually has a certain period of time to file a response or countercomplaint contesting the allegations and requests in the petition. There's usually a filing fee for the response as well.

Temporary Orders

At the same time or after a petition is filed, either spouse can ask the judge to make temporary orders, called interim or pendente lite (pending the litigation) orders. Temporary orders typically cover things like child support, alimony (also called "maintenance" or "spousal support"), possession of assets (such as cars or the family home), and restraining orders, barring a spouse from doing certain acts such as emptying bank accounts. These orders stay in effect while the divorce case is pending.

If You Litigate

The spouse asking for temporary orders files and serves papers stating the reasons for the request. Sometimes the judge grants emergency orders even before the papers are served. Once served, the other spouse files and serves papers consenting to or opposing the request. In order to convince the judge to agree with them, both sides often make extreme and inflammatory accusations in their papers, causing even more bitterness and mistrust between the spouses.

After the papers are filed, the lawyers will talk to each other about what is likely to happen in court and will try to get their clients to agree to some sort of compromise. If that's not possible, there is a hearing where the judge makes a decision, and one of the lawyers writes it up into an order that the judge signs.

The temporary orders can be changed, or modified, later on by filing more papers and having another hearing. This process of getting or changing temporary orders can continue on for months or years until the whole case is completed.

If You Mediate or Collaborate

The fight over temporary orders is one of the important steps you can bypass in mediation or collaboration. With the help of the mediator or collaborative lawyers, you and your spouse can figure out what needs to be decided on a temporary basis, negotiate something that makes sense to you, and put your agreement in writing. Your temporary agreement might still get filed with the court, but you can do this without filling the court file with angry accusations and counteraccusations. You can also tailor the specifics of your agreement to take into account what is going on in your emotional, social, and

financial divorces in a way that a judge can't.

Discovery

Discovery is a process in which lawyers use certain legal procedures to gather evidence and information from the other spouse to use toward settlement negotiations or trial.

If You Litigate

Discovery can eat up a lot of time, cause hard feelings, and cost a lot of money. Unfortunately, it is often used to intimidate or wear down the other side, not simply to get information. If the lawyers don't agree on what can be asked for, or if a witness refuses to cooperate, then more papers get filed with the court, there are more hearings, and the expense and unpleasantness escalate.

Because discovery consumes so much time on the part of the lawyers *and* the divorcing spouses, it can be one of the most expensive and embittering parts of a divorce.

Take Lucinda and Franco. When Lucinda realized her marriage of nine years was over, she hired a lawyer recommended by several friends and filed for divorce. Franco took the advice of his friends and family and also got a lawyer. During their marriage, Lucinda and Franco both took an active role in handling the finances.

As part of his standard procedure, Lucinda's lawyer has served Franco's lawyer with written questions, called interrogatories, about the finances and other details of the spouses' lives. The questions must be answered in writing within 30 days. Franco and his lawyer spend many hours going through the questions, deciding which ones to answer and which ones to refuse to answer. (State laws on discovery typically allow parties to refuse to answer certain types of questions involving confidential communications and privacy.) When Franco and his lawyer finish, the lawyer's secretary types the answers, Franco proofreads and signs them, and his lawyer sends them back to Lucinda's lawyer.

Meanwhile, Franco's lawyer has mailed to Lucinda's lawyer an extensive list of documents, called a subpoena duces tecum or an inspection demand, to be produced in 30 days. Lucinda spends hours going through boxes and files, then her lawyer spends hours looking at all the documents, then the lawyer's paralegal makes copies and sends them to Franco's lawyer, who spends hours looking at them and making notes.

After this, Franco's lawyer schedules a deposition of Lucinda, and Lucinda's lawyer does the same with Franco. This procedure is a lot like court testimony, only it takes place in one of the lawyers' offices. A court reporter is there to make an official record. The witness (Lucinda or Franco) swears to tell the truth. Then the lawyers ask questions about the facts of the case. Because the lawyers don't finish their questions by the end of the day, the depositions are carried over to additional days, until all the questions are answered.

Lucinda and Franco's lawyers also subpoena other people—bank representatives, business associates, friends, family—to produce documents or to appear at a deposition to answer questions.

Lucinda, Franco, and some witnesses give incomplete answers or don't produce all the documents requested, or their lawyers don't agree on whether certain questions have to be answered; Lucinda and Franco end up paying their lawyers to get court orders requiring more information or preventing improper questions.

By the time they get to their divorce trial, Lucinda and Franco have between them run up over $50,000 in legal bills to get information that could have been exchanged informally and that may not even be important to the case. In addition, Lucinda and Franco are furious at each other for the time and money they've had to spend in complying with the discovery procedures, and are depressed because they realize that almost all the equity they have in their house will go to pay legal bills they ran up in the course of "discovering" what one or both of them already knew.

If You Mediate or Collaborate

In mediation or collaboration, you can eliminate the need for expensive discovery by agreeing to give each other any and all information you have about your finances and other matters that need to be decided. If you agree to exchange information that needs to be kept confidential, you can make a nondisclosure agreement between yourselves and have it filed as an uncontested "protective order" (an order requiring that certain documents or information be kept confidential and be treated by the spouses and the court in a manner designed to protect that confidentiality).

Expert Opinions

Sometimes, spouses disagree about a particular issue, such as the value of a piece of real estate or a family-owned business, whether the children are better off with one parent or the other, or how much money one of the spouses really earns (or is capable of earning).

If You Litigate

If you litigate your divorce, the lawyers may hire expert witnesses to study the situation and prepare written reports. Sometimes both sides agree to use one expert and split the cost. Sometimes the judge will appoint an expert and order the spouses to share the cost. But more often, each side has his or her own experts. Naturally, experts are paid handsomely to render their opinions. And their fees go up if they must testify at a deposition or in court.

If You Mediate or Collaborate

You can save a lot of money in expert witness fees by agreeing in mediation or collaboration to get neutral professional opinions on certain issues. Experts who know that spouses have jointly hired them to give an opinion that will not end up in court often will give a preliminary report at a fee greatly reduced from what they would charge for a more complete, formal report. This may be all you need to negotiate an acceptable compromise.

Settlement Conference

As mentioned earlier, most divorce cases—even those that are hotly contested—settle before trial. The obvious aim of mediation is settlement of the issues.

If You Litigate

If your case is ready for trial and hasn't been settled by negotiations between the lawyers, the judge will often order everyone to come to court for a mandatory settlement conference. The lawyers may be required to file settlement conference statements ahead of time. These can be quite lengthy, and in them the lawyers can take extreme positions on the issues in the case, which may further alienate the spouses and make them even less likely to settle.

At the conference, the judge usually starts by meeting with both lawyers in the judge's office, called the chambers. Each lawyer will lay out the strong points of his or her case for the judge while poking holes in the other side's position.

After listening to the lawyers, the judge will make suggestions for compromising the case, based on the strength of each party's legal position. The lawyers take the suggestions back to the spouses, who have been waiting around, wondering what is going on. Each lawyer tries to convince his or her client to agree to what the judge has proposed by pointing out the weaknesses in that spouse's case. This may be the first time the spouse has heard of these weaknesses, having been convinced by the lawyer that his or her position was a winner. Spouses who agree to a settlement under these circumstances often feel later that their lawyers forced them into an unacceptable compromise.

If the lawyers persuade the spouses to agree, then the judge will probably come into the courtroom so the agreement can be read out loud—"put on the record"—and approved by the judge. This may be the first and only time the spouses ever see the judge. The lawyers and the judge's clerk take notes on the agreement, and a court reporter makes a record of the agreement for later reference. One of the lawyers is given the task of writing up the agreement, and everyone leaves. The spouses may be so dazed and overwhelmed by this experience that they don't know what they agreed to or why.

Even after the settlement is agreed to, it can take many back-and-forth drafts between the lawyers to agree on the precise wording, adding another layer of expense. Sometimes the lawyers do not agree on what the settlement was, or they think of an item or issue that was left out. This can mean filing more papers, more hearings and discussions, and more legal fees.

If You Mediate or Collaborate

When you settle your case in mediation or collaboration, the mediator or your collaborative lawyer works with you to make sure all your concerns are discussed. Even though you may have to compromise on some things, you have a chance to explain your point of view and your feelings and, hopefully, to find a solution that both of you can live with.

If you mediate, the mediator prepares the divorce agreement, or a very thorough written summary of the points agreed on, for you. If you collaborate, one of the collaborative lawyers writes up the agreement, with input from you, your spouse, and the other lawyer. Then you all review the divorce agreement (or summary) together, and use mediation or collaboration for any necessary changes, additions, or corrections. This cuts down on the need for numerous drafts and redrafts going back and forth between lawyers.

Trial

Before the court can grant a divorce judgment, the facts supporting the request for divorce and the evidence relating to any issues that haven't been settled must be presented to the judge at a trial or hearing, unless the case is completely uncontested and the state laws allow the necessary facts to be presented in an affidavit.

If You Litigate

Most contested cases are settled before trial. The prospect of adding to an already-enormous legal bill and the fear of losing in court are enough to convince most people to take the best deal they can get at that point. If the case doesn't settle, there will be a trial. In almost every state, the case will be decided by a judge, not a jury.

Lawyers spend many hours preparing for a trial. They will go over documents, meet with witnesses, take copious notes, file written statements called briefs, prepare charts and summaries, do legal research, and run up very large bills.

At the trial, the spouses must take the witness stand to answer questions from their own lawyers and the lawyers for the other side. Other witnesses, including expensive experts, might testify, and the lawyers will object to questions, make

arguments, and do many of the other things we've seen them do in courtroom dramas in movies and on TV.

The judge will listen, occasionally ask questions, and take notes. If a lawyer objects to a question asked by the other lawyer, the judge will decide whether the question has to be answered.

At the end of the trial, the judge can announce a decision right then and there or send everyone home and issue a written decision in a few days, weeks, or months. Most judges opt for the latter approach.

If You Mediate or Collaborate

If you mediate or collaborate your case, there is no trial. At most, you will make a brief—five- or ten-minute—court appearance to present the uncontested judgment. You and your spouse decide on how to handle all the legal and financial issues. The mediator or collaborative lawyer offers suggestions and keeps the negotiations going, but the professionals do not make the decisions for you; you have the final say in what happens.

Judgment

Once the judge has decided how to rule in the case, or has approved the settlement agreement, the judge will sign a court order spelling out the terms of the divorce. This is the judgment—or decree—of divorce.

If You Litigate

As soon as the judge decides the case, the written judgment is prepared by one of the lawyers. The lawyers send drafts of the judgment back and forth, trying to make the wording of the judgment most advantageous to their clients. If they don't agree on the wording, they may be back in court, arguing their cause to the judge.

Eventually, the judge will sign the written judgment. At that point the divorce will be official. In some cases, if there has been a long delay since the decision was made and the spouses need their divorce date to be earlier because of taxes or in order to remarry, the judgment might backdate the divorce to an earlier date; this is called a nunc pro tunc (now for then) judgment.

In many states, there are two parts to the judgment: an interlocutory or temporary judgment, and a final judgment that gets filed once the required waiting period ends.

Some states also allow for bifurcated, or partial, judgments so that different issues get decided at different times. For example, a bifurcated judgment on marital status can grant the divorce, ending the marriage itself, but leave the financial and child custody issues to be decided later. This may be done to allow the spouses to file as single taxpayers or to remarry. It can also affect insurance benefits, pension rights, and other things that depend on marital status and, therefore, can be another source of contention between the lawyers if one spouse wants the bifurcation and the other doesn't. Even so, bifurcation can be a good way to put emotions to rest by obtaining closure on the marriage before taking up the more difficult issues.

If You Mediate or Collaborate

A divorce that is mediated or collaborated is uncontested; this means you and your spouse agree upon the form and timing of the judgment in advance. The process of getting it filed with the court takes very little time and effort.

Postdivorce Procedures

Even after the judgment is signed and filed, there can be more disagreements about what the judgment means.

If You Litigate

These disagreements are especially likely if the case was litigated instead of settled. For example, if the judge orders the house sold and the sales proceeds divided, imagine the later arguments: whether to list the house with an agent, whom to list it with, what price to ask, what repairs should be made and how to pay for them, what offers to accept or reject, and so on. The lawyers might take these questions back to the judge to be answered. Or one spouse might appeal to a higher court the decision to sell the house.

Either situation means more papers filed, more hearings and legal arguments, and astronomical legal fees that cut even further into your equity in the house or your savings.

Even if you don't disagree on the correctness of the judgment or what it means, certain decisions, such as child custody and visitation, child support, and sometimes alimony, can be changed if circumstances change. If the original case was contested, any revisited issue is likely to be contested, too. This can lead to more papers being filed, more hearings, and, of course, more legal fees.

If You Mediate or Collaborate

If you mediate or collaborate, you will have thought carefully about the decisions in your divorce agreement before agreeing to them, so new disagreements about those decisions are unlikely. Your divorce agreement is also more likely to cover how to handle certain situations that might come up in the future. And even if something that you didn't expect comes up, you'll be able to ask your mediator or collaborative lawyers to help you negotiate an agreement on the new issues.

Long-Term Effects of a Contested Legal Divorce

The legal system is equipped to deal only with legal and financial issues. It often provides no help with the emotional or social divorces. When spouses can't coordinate the emotional and social divorces with the financial and legal divorces by working out a settlement, their lives are likely to be affected for years to come.

Going through a litigated divorce may have a disastrous effect on the spouses' ability to heal from the trauma of the divorce, even if the judge's decision is financially and legally correct. The effect on their children's lives can be equally destructive. Relationships with family, friends, and business associates can also be harmed. The contested legal divorce may cause conflicts and bitterness that last for years, long after the divorce itself has ended.

Mediation and Collaboration: A Different Way to Divorce

Mediation and collaborative divorce are not quick fixes for all the problems you will go through during your divorce. They won't turn your spouse into a different person, solve your financial woes, or undo the pain you've suffered. But it can be a way for you and your spouse to make the best of a bad situation by working together to avoid the worst pitfalls of the legal divorce.

There are five ways that mediation or collaboration can cut down on the acrimony and expense of divorce, while getting results that are at least as good as what you'd get in court. Through either of these approaches, you and your spouse can:

- stabilize the situation through a temporary agreement
- exchange all necessary information voluntarily
- agree on legal procedures that minimize expense and streamline the process
- negotiate a settlement that works for you, and
- decide how to handle postdivorce decisions.

Whether you and your spouse use mediation or collaboration from the very beginning of the divorce process or only for part of it, you will save time and money. Perhaps just as important, you will more likely get through the divorce with your privacy and dignity reasonably intact.

■

Chapter 2

What Happens in Mediation

In deciding whether to mediate your divorce, you'll probably want to get a sense of what happens in a typical mediation. This chapter takes you through the stages of a typical mediation, from the first session to the point where you and your spouse reach an agreement. To demonstrate what a mediation process looks like, we'll follow the mediation of a fictional couple, Robert and Fran.

 You don't have to read this chapter to succeed in mediation. We hope that this chapter will give you a good idea of what might happen in your mediation. But if you don't feel this material will be helpful, skip all or any part of this chapter.

 Each situation is different. Every mediator has his or her own approach, and every couple is unique. If our explanation of mediation doesn't describe what's happening in your mediation, don't worry. As long as you're comfortable with your mediator and you seem to be making progress, that's what's important.

An Overview of Mediation

In mediation, you and your spouse work with a mediator to negotiate a legally binding divorce agreement. If the mediation is successful, the agreement will be one that you and your spouse will abide by after it's been signed.

Mediator's Job

The mediator's job is to structure the mediation in a way that optimizes the chance of successfully negotiating a divorce agreement. A key difference between mediation and one-on-one negotiations is the organization, or structure, provided by the mediator. For this reason, mediation is often referred to as a structured negotiation. (Collaborative law is similar in that it provides a structure, but the structure is provided by the spouses's attorneys working together, as described in Chapter 3.)

Structure of a Typical Mediation

Mediation usually consists of five stages. These stages usually occur in sequence, one after another, although sometimes you will cycle back through earlier stages before reaching a complete agreement on all issues. And some mediations have a life of their own, where it's hard to discern any stages at all. Still, you should find it helpful to look at what happens in each stage of a typical mediation, given that every mediation will have the essential features of each stage, even if the features don't appear in the typical order.

In single-issue mediations—for example, a mediation to determine the amount of money to be paid to compensate someone for injuries caused by a car accident—all five stages might occur in just one or two sessions. Most divorce mediations take more sessions to complete all five stages, however, because of the many different issues—property division, debt allocation, alimony, child custody and support—that need to be addressed.

The five stages of a typical mediation are:

1. introductory
2. information gathering
3. framing
4. negotiating, and
5. concluding.

Mediation: An Insider's View

If you're interested in eavesdropping on some real mediations, take a look at *A Guide to Divorce Mediation,* by Gary J. Friedman (Workman Publishing Company). This book includes detailed accounts of six different mediations drawn from the author's extensive mediation experience. Each account is presented as an edited transcript, giving you a realistic picture of how things can go in mediation.

Using the Law in Mediation

As you read our description of a typical mediation, you'll notice that we don't talk

a lot about the law or legal rights. You may wonder where the law fits in, given that divorce is, after all, a legal event. What about your legal rights to property? What about the laws governing child support, custody, and other legal issues? Aren't these important? Yes and no.

One of the great features of mediation is that you and your spouse get to decide what's best for you, even if it's different from what the laws provide. There are a few things you cannot legally agree to—such as giving up the right to receive child support—but these are rare. Other than the few exceptions, you are free to make whatever agreement is best for you.

Being free to decide the terms of your settlement doesn't mean that the legal rules aren't significant. If you want your agreement to withstand the test of time, you should know how it compares to what the law would dictate. What are your legal rights? Which ones are you compromising? Do you have a good reason for compromising them? How does your overall agreement compare to the likely result if you went to court? Asking—and getting answers to—these questions will guide you in negotiating the right settlement.

How to learn about the particular laws that apply to your case, and how to include consideration of the legal issues in your negotiations, depends on how your mediation is structured. Mediators vary in their approach to this question, so it is something for you to raise in the first session. We give you an idea of how to talk about the law in the mediation sample in this chapter; more information on applying it to your own mediation is in Chapter 10.

Finding and Using a Consulting Lawyer

You may find it very helpful to consult with a lawyer from time to time during the mediation. A good consulting lawyer can help you understand your legal alternatives early on so that there are no surprises during the mediation. Your lawyer can coach you through the negotiation stage and help you evaluate your options as the mediation progresses. And your lawyer can review the divorce agreement when you finally reach a settlement.

You may be concerned that consulting a lawyer will be unnecessarily expensive and adversarial. That is a risk if you don't lay the proper groundwork for the consultation or if you aren't careful in selecting a consulting lawyer. You can eliminate the risk, however, by following some simple guidelines:

- Select a consulting lawyer who understands and supports mediation.
- Schedule an initial consultation with a consulting lawyer as early as possible.
- Consult with your lawyer as needed as the mediation progresses.

- Make sure the lawyer charges you an hourly fee for meeting with you that is comparable to the hourly fees charged by similarly experienced lawyers in your community. Do not pay a large up-front retainer.
- Always remember that your lawyer works for you. His or her job is to give you advice and feedback on the agreement you are negotiating for yourself; the decisions are up to you.

More information on lawyers. Before you begin mediation, and before you select a consulting lawyer, read Chapter 8, *Using Advisers and Doing Legal Research*. There, we explain in more detail the points outlined above. If you follow our approach, you'll be better informed during the mediation and you'll ensure that you and your lawyer can work as a team.

Introductory Stage

In this first stage, the mediator works with you and your spouse to lay a foundation for the rest of the mediation. You give the mediator background information about your situation, and the mediator explains how the mediation will be conducted. Depending on how well you and your spouse communicate and what the issues are in your case, the mediator suggests an approach that should optimize the chances of reaching an agreement.

Typical Mediation

The introductory stage begins when you first contact the mediator's office for an appointment and provide the mediator with preliminary information. Most of the work done in this stage, however, takes place during the first session. Depending on how your mediator works, he or she will meet jointly with both you and your spouse, will meet separately with each of you, or will combine the two approaches.

The mediator explains the mediation process and discusses with you the ground rules of the mediation. The mediator gives each of you an opportunity to present background information and to ask questions about the mediation.

During this stage, the mediator begins to observe how you and your spouse interact and communicate. This helps the mediator work with the two of you in a way that encourages constructive communication. (For tips on communicating constructively during mediation, see Chapter 12.) You will also give the mediator an idea of the issues on which you agree and disagree. This will help the mediator develop an agenda for the rest of the mediation.

During this first stage, consider discussing with the mediator whether and how much you will consider the legal rules that a judge might apply to your case. As mentioned earlier, it is our view that having this kind of information is essential to making informed choices about settlement. What a judge would do isn't necessarily the best solution for your case, and the beauty of mediation is that you can design your own solutions without having to follow those rules—but knowing the rules can be helpful. Not all mediators think alike on this question. The first session is the time for you to see if you've picked the right mediator. No matter how carefully you've gone about selecting this mediator, you won't know whether you've got the right fit until you spend some time observing and interacting with the mediator. In Chapter 10, we give tips on what to look for during the first session in order to decide whether to proceed with this mediator.

In the first session, you'll also get a sense of whether negotiating directly with your spouse without a lawyer by your side is likely to be effective, or whether you would be better off with a collaborative process and the added buffer of having your own lawyer present for the negotiations.

At some point during the introductory stage, you'll want to discuss whether to sign a written agreement to mediate. A written agreement spelling out the ground rules for the mediation can be important. Not only does it protect the privacy of your mediation, it also avoids later misunderstandings about things such as the mediation fees and the mediator's role.

Some mediators ask you to sign an agreement to mediate before the first session; others have you sign it at the first session; still others discuss its contents at the first session and then send out the written agreement after the session. However your mediator handles this, be sure to discuss any questions you have about the topics covered in the agreement before you sign it. Chapter 6 covers the essential points that should be included in an agreement to mediate. Do not proceed to the second stage of mediation until you have an agreement to mediate (written or unwritten) that you understand and with which you are comfortable.

If you have confidentiality concerns. In some states, and in some situations, things said in mediation can be reported to governmental agencies or used as evidence in future court proceedings. If you have any concerns about the confidentiality of what you might say in the mediation, discuss this with your mediator at the first opportunity. For more on this subject, see Chapter 6.

Robert and Fran's Mediation

Robert and Fran have been separated for several months. Robert is a supervisor in a midsized manufacturing company. Fran works part-time as a registered nurse and earns much less than Robert. They have two children: Brian, age 20, and Julie, age 16.

Fran and Robert have seen friends of theirs go through bitter divorces, and they both want to avoid that if possible. A friend of Robert's suggests mediation and Robert brings up the idea with Fran, who agrees to give it a try. The mediator they choose is a lawyer who practices mediation exclusively.

Prior to meeting with Robert and Fran, the mediator sends each of them a brochure describing mediation and detailing information about the mediator's practice and fees. When Robert and Fran arrive for their first session, they are greeted by the mediator's assistant, who offers them their choice of tea, coffee, or soft drinks and asks each of them to fill out a form with basic personal information.

After a few minutes, the mediator arrives, introduces herself to each of them, and invites them into her office—a large room with three comfortable chairs arranged in the middle and a table off to one side. A large pad of plain paper stands on an easel near the chairs. The mediator invites Robert and Fran to take their seats and joins them in the remaining chair.

The mediator begins by explaining that the purpose of the meeting is to get acquainted and to discuss how to use the mediation process to come up with a settlement agreement. She reminds

Robert and Fran that mediation is a voluntary process and that they can stop the mediation at any time. She tells them that any statements they make during the mediation are confidential under the law of their state. The mediator briefly explains that she will try to help Robert and Fran reach an agreement, but that she will not make any decisions for them. She then asks each of them to give her some background about their situation and the issues that need to be decided.

Robert: "Well, why don't I begin. We've been married for almost twenty-two years. Our son Brian is a sophomore in college, and our daughter Julie is a junior in high school. We've already agreed that Julie will live with her mother until she graduates. Julie comes over to my place, or we go out somewhere, at least once or twice a week. Fran and I tried marriage counseling last year, but things just haven't worked out, and I think we both know it's time for us to take the next step and get divorced. We need to decide what to do about the house and our other property. We've also got some debts, and Fran has been running up the credit cards since I moved out, so we have to somehow get a handle on our finances."

When Robert finishes, the mediator summarizes Robert's points and asks if she has heard him correctly. When Robert nods, the mediator turns to Fran and asks if she has background information to add.

Fran: "I have been using the credit cards to live on. Robert has no idea what it takes to run this household. He thinks I am a spendthrift, but I would like to see him do a better job. Our daughter is in her junior year of high school. This whole separation has been hard enough on her and Brian without telling them they have to cut back on their expenses just so Robert can have a new life."

Robert (interrupting): "Fran, you're going to have to start being more realistic. You don't need to take Julie out every weekend and buy her designer clothes. There is no reason why Brian can't take out a student loan for part of his expenses. If you want to keep that house until Julie graduates, we're going to have to find some other areas to cut back on."

Fran (to mediator): "Do I have to listen to him patronize me like this?"

Mediator: "Well, our goal in mediation is to come up with a settlement agreement that will work for both of you. In order to help you do that, we'll need to look at your financial situation in some detail. In addition, I will want to hear from each one of you about your priorities and concerns. I can see already that you have different points of view on some things. I am going to want to know a lot more about how you see things. That doesn't mean I'm going to decide who's right. It just means I want to know as much as I can about where you agree and where you have differences. I need to know this in order to help you come up with an acceptable settlement agreement without asking either one of you to give up your different points of view. Unlike a legal case, mediation is a voluntary process that you both control. So, you don't have to stay here if the process isn't working for you. However, I encourage you to give it a try."

The mediator then proposes that Robert and Fran speak in turn, without interrupting each other, so that each of them gets a chance to express fully his or her point of view. She reminds them that listening to each other doesn't mean that they agree with what is being said, and she tells them that disagreement can be a valuable basis for making decisions. Although they are skeptical, Robert and Fran agree to give it a try.

After Fran and Robert each say a little more about themselves, the mediator explains that the mediation will proceed in stages, starting with assembling information, then looking more specifically at how each spouse views the issues, and eventually negotiating a settlement. She tells them that it will be important that each of them understands the legal rules applicable to their case as part of the information to consider in coming up with a settlement. Both Fran and Robert agree that they would like to know the legal rules as they consider their settlement, and they ask the mediator whether she can help with this.

The mediator explains that because she is a lawyer, she has the knowledge and experience to make sure they cover all the basic legal points, but as a neutral mediator, she can't give them separate advice. She encourages each of them to consider finding a legal adviser, or consulting lawyer, to get some advice before they begin negotiating and again when the written divorce agreement is ready to be reviewed. That way, they can be assured that they are fully informed as they shape and finalize their agreement. She offers to give them referrals to lawyers who understand and support mediation and who will charge a reasonable hourly fee for the consultation, instead of a huge advance retainer fee. They take her up on this offer.

The mediator, Fran, and Robert spend the rest of the session talking about how the mediation will work, addressing Robert and Fran's concerns, and beginning to identify the issues that will need further development and discussion.

The mediator gives Robert and Fran a written agreement for mediation and reviews it with them. They sign the agreement and schedule another appointment for the following week. The mediator gives them each financial worksheets to complete and bring with them to the next session.

Information-Gathering Stage

In order for the mediation to be successful, you, your spouse, and the mediator need to be as fully informed as possible about the facts of your case. This is the information-gathering stage. Sometimes it begins during the first session; sometimes it starts after that session.

Typical Mediation

Once the mediator is familiar with the background of your situation and everyone is clear about the ground rules for the mediation, the mediator will go over the facts in detail to make sure that the mediator has—and you and your spouse agree on—all the information necessary to complete a settlement. It may happen that you and your spouse disagree about something that took place in the past. Except in the rare situation where you need to decide about the truth of a past event in order to resolve a current issue, the mediator may encourage you to agree to disagree about the past and focus instead on current facts and information. You'll see an example of this in Robert and Fran's mediation as they discuss what to do with their home and they remember past conversations about it differently.

If information that you and the mediator need is unavailable or in dispute, the mediator will try to help you find ways to get it or to determine what is correct. For example, you might need the policy number and other details of a life insurance policy. If you can't locate your copy of the policy, the mediator might suggest ways to get this information, such as contacting the broker who sold you the policy or writing to the insurance company. Or perhaps neither you nor your spouse knows what a certain piece of property is worth or you disagree about the value of the property. The mediator might help you decide on a tiebreaker to use in the mediation, such as looking up blue book figures for vehicles or obtaining a binding or nonbinding valuation from a neutral appraiser.

The mediator may first begin to discuss the general legal rules that might apply to your case. This can include the laws of your state dictating how a judge would divide your assets and debts, how child custody and child support would be decided, when and how alimony can be ordered, and laws dealing with related issues like taxes and life and health insurance. This general legal information will help you decide how to approach the issues in your case. As you progress with the mediation, you may come back to some of the legal rules and discuss them in more detail as they apply to your particular case. For example, you might review the state child support guidelines early on. During a later stage, you might discuss how the guidelines would impact your cash flow when your take-home income is compared to your expenses, or how the law deals with child support if your income or other circumstances change.

During this stage, the mediator will probably ask you and your spouse to bring in financial documents such as tax returns and bank and mortgage statements. If you haven't already prepared worksheets like the ones we provide in Chapter 9, the mediator may ask you to do so.

Having Qualms About Disclosure?

You might have reasons for holding back certain information during the mediation—for example, if disclosure would mean sharing sensitive business information. If you are concerned about confidentiality, discuss with your mediator what can be done to protect your privacy. If there is information you don't want your spouse or the mediator to know, bear in mind that the odds of reaching a solid agreement in mediation are greatly diminished if you withhold essential information. Not only is the agreement possibly vulnerable to legal attack, but it won't be as workable as one that takes into consideration all of your circumstances.

As you progress, the mediator will summarize the information being assembled. If you agree that additional research is needed or a neutral expert is to be consulted, that will go on a "to do" list. Some mediators use a flip chart or white board for summaries and lists. Other mediators prepare a file summary to refer to in future sessions.

Some mediators conduct all or a part of the information-gathering stage of the mediation in separate meetings, or caucuses, with each spouse. If the mediator uses joint meetings instead, the mediator will monitor the communications between you and your spouse and give suggestions for improving the quality of those communications. This will help you build confidence and skills for the later stages of negotiation, when heightened intensity can make it harder to communicate well. (For more on communication techniques, see Chapter 12.)

This second stage of the mediation can span two or more sessions, especially if you need to do outside work to obtain additional information or appraisals. If you feel that you already know enough about your situation and have definite ideas on how to work out a settlement, you may find yourself impatient with this stage and anxious to move ahead with the negotiations.

Even though you may want to rush on, the mediator's job is to make sure that both you and your spouse have all the facts and information you need to negotiate an agreement that is legally binding and that you won't regret having signed. There may be information you (or your spouse) are unaware of that would make a difference in what you agree to. If so, it's much better to find out before you sign the agreement than afterward, when it's too late. Also, your spouse may not be as well-informed or well-prepared as you are, and may need to go slower in order to negotiate from a position of knowledge. It's also important that the mediator have a good grasp on your situation in order to be effective in helping you negotiate. So be patient with this stage and your patience will pay off in a well-considered, solid agreement.

During this stage, you may find it helpful to take your own notes of the agreed facts, missing and disputed information, and agreed research assignments or expert opinions to be obtained. You can use the Mediation Progress Notes form in the appendix.

Robert and Fran's Mediation

In Robert and Fran's case, the information-gathering stage begins with their second joint session. They have brought with them the completed financial questionnaires that the mediator gave them during the first session. Using these questionnaires, the mediator reviews with them the information that each has put down about their assets and debts. As they go through the worksheets, the mediator asks clarifying questions. The mediator summarizes the facts relating to each item on a flip chart, noting areas of agreement and disagreement and places where additional facts are needed. For

example, the mediator notes that Robert and Fran have already agreed to divide one bank account. Neither Robert nor Fran is certain about the current value of their house, however, nor do they agree what to do with it. Robert thinks they should sell it; Fran would like to keep the house, if at all possible. The mediator puts question marks for these points on the flip chart.

During the discussion of the house, Robert says that Fran has always complained about the house: It is too small, the kitchen isn't convenient, they need another bathroom. Fran hotly denies this, saying she has always loved the house. After listening to this exchange, the mediator observes that Robert and Fran, like most divorcing couples, have very different understandings of things said in the past. She suggests that it is not necessary (or even possible) to decide who is right in order to make a decision now about the house. She asks whether they are willing to agree to disagree about what Fran thought of the house in the past and turn their attention to solving the current problem. They both nod their agreement.

When they have gone through all of the assets and debts, the mediator uses the notes on the flip chart to prepare a list of additional information that is needed. This includes values of the house and the two cars, details of the life insurance policies, and values and projections for Robert's retirement plan and Fran's deferred compensation account.

The mediator then helps Robert and Fran figure out how to get the necessary information. After some discussion, they agree that the mediator will contact a qualified neutral appraiser to obtain a nonbinding opinion of the value of the house. Robert volunteers to get *Kelley Blue Book* values for the two cars. Fran will call the life insurance agent and get printouts of the policy information. Robert and Fran will each contact their own employer to obtain current information regarding their retirement and deferred compensation plans.

Next, the mediator reviews the income information with Robert and Fran. Each has brought current pay stubs and tax returns for the last three years. As they go through this information, the mediator stops frequently to clarify issues. Fran finds this especially helpful, because she has never been a numbers person and has always felt at a disadvantage when talking about financial matters with Robert. Working through the information with the mediator helps Fran feel more confident in her ability to read the tax returns and understand the concepts being discussed. The mediator summarizes the income information on a new page of the flip chart.

When the second session ends, the mediator reviews with Robert and Fran the list of information each of them is going to obtain for the next session. They agree to begin the next session

by reporting on these before looking at Robert and Fran's lists of monthly expenses, which they weren't able to get to in this session.

Before adjourning this session, the mediator reminds Fran and Robert that they agreed in the first session to discuss the legal rules as part of their mediation. The mediator suggests they have this discussion at their next session, after reviewing the monthly budgets. They schedule the third session for three weeks later to give everyone time to get the additional information required and to give Fran and Robert time to find and make appointments with consulting lawyers.

At the third session, Robert and Fran report on the information they have obtained regarding the values of the cars, the life insurance policies, and their retirement benefits. The mediator reports on the appraisal of the house. Robert and Fran agree to use these figures as working numbers for their discussions.

The mediator then takes Robert and Fran through a review of their monthly expense budgets. Together they make adjustments where needed. The mediator summarizes the expense information on a flip chart and lists the issues that need to be resolved during the mediation, using the summaries as a reference. These include what to do with the house and the retirement benefits, child support, payment of college expenses, and alimony.

The mediator then leads a discussion of the possible legal rules on each of these issues. Because Robert and Fran have each had a chance to discuss the legal rules with a consulting lawyer, this is more of a review than new information to them.

As they go through the legal options, they begin to see that the legal outcome is clear-cut on some issues but not others. For example, the range of child support that might be ordered by a judge is pretty predictable, due to inflexible state guidelines. But there is less certainty about what a judge would do about the house, payment of the children's college education, or alimony. By the end of this discussion, Fran and Robert feel comfortable about their grasp of the legal rules and how they could apply to their particular situation. They also have a better idea of some of the limitations of the legal rules in providing answers.

The mediator finishes this discussion by reminding Robert and Fran that they do not need to follow the legal rules, but that their understanding of the rules will help them evaluate their options when they get to the negotiating stage.

Robert and Fran conclude the session by scheduling another session the following week. They agree that they will spend time at the next session exploring with the mediator their needs and concerns and any other factors that might influence their settlement.

Framing Stage

In the framing stage, the mediator helps each spouse outline his or her reasons for wanting certain outcomes in the settlement. These reasons consist of individual concerns, priorities, goals, and values. They are often referred to by mediators as "needs and interests." In this book, we use the broader term "interests."

Typical Mediation

Identifying interests helps to frame the core goal of the mediation: finding a resolution of the issues that successfully addresses each spouse's most important interests. In most divorces, many issues need to be examined in light of each spouse's interest. These include property and debt division, child custody, child support, and alimony. For a complete list of the kinds of issues that might be discussed, see Chapter 9.

In the case we are following in this chapter, one issue is what to do with the house. Robert wants to sell it. When the mediator explores with Robert why he wants this outcome, she discovers that the reasons include Robert's desire to buy a place of his own, his desire to have cash to help put the children through college, and his concern that there be enough money left over to pay the credit card debts. These are some of his interests.

Fran's reasons for wanting to keep the house include her desire to own a home instead of renting, her attachment to this particular house and neighborhood, and her concern for Julie's stability while she finishes high school and begins college. These are some of her interests. Once these interests are identified, the possibility of finding acceptable settlement options that address all or most of them increases.

Often, spouses' interests will overlap. This is especially likely if the interests involve a concern for other people, such as children. Robert shares Fran's desire to avoid disrupting their daughter in her last two years of high school, if possible, and they both want to see that their children get a college education. When an overlap like this occurs, it increases the likelihood of finding settlement options that address their common concerns.

Of course, it's not always possible to negotiate an agreement that satisfies fully all of the interests of the disputing parties. Some interests may have to be compromised, especially in divorce, where limited resources must be divided between two households. But if the focus is on identifying and addressing each person's most important needs and interests, the resulting compromises will be ones that both spouses can live with.

Interest-Based Negotiation

Using interests to resolve disputes is known as interest-based negotiation. It forms the basis of most successful mediations. Interest-based negotiation is the subject of the classic bestseller *Getting to Yes*, by Fisher, Ury, and Patton (Penguin 2nd Ed. 1991).

If you want to know more about using interest-based negotiation in your mediation, take a look at Chapter 13, where the subject is covered in more detail.

Some mediators prefer to conduct the framing stage in separate sessions, as they believe it better prepares each of you for the next stage: negotiating. Other mediators favor joint sessions because they believe that hearing your spouse formulate his or her interests with the mediator's help lays a better foundation for the give and take of the negotiation stage. Either way can work, although separate sessions make the mediation cost a little more and take a little longer, because anything important said in the separate session will have to be repeated to the other spouse.

As you and your spouse describe your respective interests, the mediator may summarize them on a flip chart or central list. This list can be referred to later on in the mediation when you are trying to determine whether a proposed solution adequately addresses your needs and interests.

Recycling Back to the Information-Gathering Stage

Sometimes, the process of identifying issues and interests leads to more questions about the facts. That may require a return to the information-gathering stage. If this happens, you may feel frustrated and impatient to move on. Just remember, you can't negotiate a successful settlement with incomplete information. Even if it seems like you're going backward, you are actually making progress toward your goal of settlement by filling in important information gaps. In addition, you're not going to be able to go any faster than the slower party feels comfortable going. To efficient, get-down-to-business people, this can seem like foot dragging, whereas efficiency can feel oppressive and overwhelming to a more deliberate person. If you're the efficient type and your spouse is not, recognize that part of the price of reaching an agreement is adapting your tempo to that of your spouse.

Robert and Fran's Mediation

Because the mediation has gone relatively smoothly up to this point, the mediator proposes to conduct the framing stage in a joint session—her preferred approach—rather than using separate sessions. But she tells Fran and Robert that they can request separate sessions at any time if they feel they need to.

The framing stage begins for Fran and Robert with the fourth joint session. Using the process of speaking in turn that they agreed to at the first session, Robert and Fran explain to the mediator how they feel about what should happen to the house. Robert says that he would like to see Julie be able to stay in the house until she finishes high school. But he really wants to have enough cash to pay off the credit card debts and make a down payment on a house of his own. At the very least, he wants to live in a nicer place than the small apartment he's been renting since he and Fran separated.

Fran, in turn, states her desire to maintain the home for their daughter, at least until after her high school graduation that summer. Fran also expresses her fear that if the house is sold, she won't be able to buy a home of her own in the neighborhood where she lives now, while she believes Robert, with his higher income, will easily be able to go out and obtain financing for a new home.

As Robert and Fran speak, the mediator summarizes their main concerns on the flip chart. By the time each spouse has finished, the mediator has listed their interests on each of the issues. She then points out to Robert and Fran some interests that overlap, such as their desire to maintain the house for Julie until she graduates from high school and the importance they both place on helping each of their children through college. She reminds them that these overlaps can help form a foundation for a settlement between them.

As the session concludes, the mediator asks Robert and Fran to be prepared to brainstorm options for settlement at the next meeting.

Negotiating Stage

Once the mediator has helped the spouses frame the issues and interests clearly, it is time to negotiate an acceptable settlement. This usually begins with an exploration of possible options. With the mediator's help, the spouses discuss and evaluate the options, until eventually they narrow down the options to the ones that work best for both spouses. Getting to the final combination of options will involve compromises and concessions on both sides.

Typical Mediation

Most mediators will emphasize the problem-solving aspect of negotiation at this stage. The problem to be solved is finding settlement options that address each spouse's most important interests as fully as possible. With this focus, you'll be able to negotiate by trading off acceptable options instead of getting locked into zero-sum bargaining, where one spouse's gain is the other spouse's loss.

To begin the negotiating stage, you decide, with the mediator's help, which issue or combination of issues to work on first. This will depend on the circumstances of your particular case. For example, if one main issue is the key to the whole case and everything else depends on it, you probably want to start with that issue. But if communications between you and your spouse have been difficult to this point, your mediator might encourage you to warm up by tackling some easy issues first. Whatever you start with, you will probably end up considering several issues at a time, and possibly even reconsidering issues you already talked about once you start looking at how they all fit together.

Once you've picked an issue or set of issues to start with, your mediator will probably help you develop a list of as many different settlement options as you can think of. This is often done through a process called brainstorming (see "Brainstorming: A Creative Way to Expand the Pie," below).

Brainstorming: A Creative Way to Expand the Pie

Just about every negotiation involves some compromising—what experts refer to as dividing the pie. Mediators try to find ways to "expand the pie" before dividing it, so that each side gets as much as possible from the settlement. Often, the best way to expand the pie is to find an option that is different from what either side is asking for but that meets both sides' interests at least as well. Mediators use the technique of brainstorming to generate new settlement options.

In brainstorming, the goal is to come up with as many ideas as possible, so that all possibilities are on the table. It is called brainstorming because you use the part of your brain that is creative rather than the analytical part. To ensure success in keeping the ideas flowing, you agree to list every idea that comes to mind without judging any of the ideas right away. Judging an idea too soon engages the analytical part of your brain and can shut down the creative process prematurely. Analyzing the good and bad points of an option will come later, when brainstorming is completed.

After you have generated a list of possible options, you'll probably find a few that are obviously unworkable or unacceptable. Those get eliminated. With the rest, you'll need to examine them one by one and start testing them out. In order to be acceptable, an option has to address a need or interest of at least one spouse while not interfering with any important need or interest of the other spouse.

After you've weeded out clearly unacceptable options, your mediator will help you zero in on the options that appear most promising. As you go through this process for each issue, you'll begin to see the possible tradeoffs that can balance out the overall settlement. For example, an option for settling one issue might work better for your spouse than for you, but there may be an option you find attractive on another issue. In that case, you might be willing to trade one for the other to arrive at a balance that seems reasonably fair. You'll repeat this process with different combinations as you go through your entire list of issues. Sometimes, you'll rearrange earlier tradeoffs as you see better combinations emerge.

As you examine and reexamine options, your mediator will help you keep focused on the options that best match the interests that you and your spouse identified during the framing stage.

Recycling Back to the Information-Gathering or Framing Stage

This is another place where you might need to go back to an earlier stage in order to move forward. For example, you might need more information in order to know whether an option being considered is realistic, so you go back to Stage Two, information gathering. Or, there might be an option that seems to meet the criteria of addressing a need or interest, but it doesn't feel right to one of you. Chances are it clashes with a need or interest you haven't put your finger on yet, so the mediator may want to go back to the framing stage in order to uncover that need or interest before moving on. Don't lose hope at this point: Sometimes a step back is just what's needed in order to take two steps forward.

For example, one option Robert and Fran come up with is remodeling the basement of their house to make it a rental. Considering this option causes Fran to express a desire to have the use of the basement for crafts and sewing as well as her reluctance to share the house with strangers. These are interests of hers that were not yet expressed. Making the basement a rental might also be restricted by local building or zoning codes, so considering this kind of option means finding out about legal requirements, as well as the feasibility of financing.

Take your time. After you've sorted through all the options and come up with a tentative settlement, you may stop to consider if the overall balance feels okay. If it doesn't, you might need to back up a little and figure out what adjustments can be made. If the overall balance seems right, then you're ready to go on to the final stage: concluding the agreement.

Robert and Fran's Mediation

When Fran and Robert arrive for the next session, the mediator has tacked up on the wall the summaries of basic financial information and the lists of Robert and Fran's interests prepared during previous sessions. The mediator begins with a review of the posted lists. She asks Robert and Fran if they have anything to add. Fran nods and says that their son Brian has just learned the amount of his financial aid package for the following year. The mediator notes this new information on the summary.

After Robert and Fran confirm that the information on the summaries is current and complete, the mediator explains the negotiating process. The first step will be to brainstorm as many options as possible. There will be no evaluating or negotiating of options until as many as possible have been written down.

They begin with the house. At first, the obvious options go on the list: sell the house, Fran buys out Robert, Robert buys out Fran. Then, less obvious options emerge: Fran keeps the house and rents out rooms, Robert and Fran refinance and remodel the basement into an apartment that can be rented out, Robert and Fran take turns living in the house for six-month periods, Robert and Fran co-own the house for a while with plans to sell it later. At times, both Robert and Fran jump in with a "no way" or "yes, but," and the mediator reminds them that all options, even obviously impossible ones, should go on the list for now.

When they can't think of any more options about the house, they repeat the process with each of the other issues. Sometimes, options on issues they have already discussed come up, and those get written down, too.

When they have brainstormed as many options as possible, they consider the options one at a time. Any option that is totally impossible or absolutely unacceptable is eliminated. The remaining options are then examined to see how they match with Robert's and Fran's lists of interests.

As they go through this process, Robert and Fran begin to see possible trade-offs that might work for them:

Robert: "Maybe we can refinance at a lower interest rate and pull out enough money for me to make a down payment on a small condo. If I had the write-off from owning a place of my own, I could probably afford to pay more child support."

Fran: "I might be willing to do that, but I would need to know that the house payments won't go up too much. Also, the roof really needs to be replaced. We would need to use some of the refinance money for that. And I was thinking of renting out a room or two so I'd have a little more cash, but I wouldn't want that to mean you'd pay me less monthly support."

As this discussion continues, Robert and Fran exchange ideas, suggest compromises, and eventually come up with a proposed agreement that seems acceptable.

As the mediator reviews the proposed agreement with Robert and Fran, she points out that it is based on some assumptions that they will need to check on. They are planning to refinance and will need to look into available loans and rates to make sure they qualify and that the house payments won't increase beyond a certain limit. They agree that a refinance in Fran's name only would be preferable, but Robert is prepared to participate in a joint refinance if Fran can't qualify on her own. There are also tax questions about the support arrangement that they'll need to check out. They decide that the mediator will draw up a settlement agreement based on their discussion at the session, but that it will be tentative only until they have had a chance to double check these questions. They agree that they will meet again to discuss any changes after they have each reviewed the draft with their advisers.

Concluding Stage

In this stage, the tentative settlement agreement is put into writing and circulated to both spouses for review with their advisers.

Typical Mediation

If the issues in your case are simple, the mediator may prepare a memorandum outlining your settlement and give you an opportunity to sign it before you leave the mediation session in which you finished up your negotiating. The memorandum can summarize the essential points of agreement and can be used as a basis for preparing a formal settlement agreement that will be filed with the court as part of the now-uncontested divorce case.

 The memorandum indicates your commitment to the settlement. It carries weight, even though it isn't the actual document that gets filed with the court. It may even be used as legal evidence of your agreement if you later change your mind. In some circumstances, you may have a legal right to a certain length of time (a rescission period) after signing to change your mind. Sometimes, your mediator will include a rescission period in the actual memorandum. But if there's no rescission period, you should hold off on signing the memorandum if you have any doubts at all about the settlement. Take whatever time you need to review it carefully.

Many mediators, especially those who are also lawyers, will prepare the written settlement agreement that will be filed with the court. This document is likely to include some "boilerplate" language, that is, standard legal language that goes into every agreement of its kind. In addition, the agreement will spell out all the terms of your settlement in greater detail than in a memorandum. Because of this, take the time to review the written settlement agreement carefully and thoroughly before signing it. Most likely, you will want to have a consulting attorney review the agreement before you sign it. For more about who prepares the divorce agreement and what it should include, see Chapter 16.

Using a Consulting Lawyer

Earlier, we suggested that you find a consulting lawyer as soon as possible in the mediation process. If you haven't already done this, now is a good time to seriously consider using one to review the written memorandum or settlement agreement.

A good consulting lawyer can help ensure that the wording of the agreement is clear and unambiguous. The last thing you want is to find out months or years later that the wording of the written agreement has a different legal meaning from what you intended. Think of this review as legal proofreading: a double check to be sure the agreement says what you, your spouse, and the mediator intend it to say.

In addition, if you haven't yet discussed the laws in your state, a consulting lawyer can explain your legal rights regarding property, alimony, child support, and custody. There is nothing wrong with agreeing to a settlement that calls for you to give up certain things to which you might legally be entitled. In fact, your settlement probably won't look just like what you'd get if you went to court, because you have spent time during the mediation customizing the settlement to your own situation. But, ideally, the settlement should meet your goals and objectives at least as well as what you could get in court. A consulting lawyer can help you make that determination.

You may be concerned that involving a lawyer at this point could undermine the progress that's been made in mediation. You can minimize the risk by selecting a mediation-friendly lawyer early on and following the other guidelines discussed in this chapter and Chapter 8.

Revising the Written Agreement

Quite often, the written agreement will need to be revised before it can be signed. There are three types of revisions. The first type consists of correcting typographical errors such as misspellings, incorrect dates and account numbers, and other factual information.

The second type consists of rewording any parts that are ambiguous, unclear, or different from what was agreed on. These types of revisions don't involve any renegotiating and are often taken care of through brief phone calls or letters among you, your spouse (or your consulting lawyers, if you agree to work through them for the review process), and the mediator.

The third type of revision involves changes or additions to what was agreed on during the mediation. This can occur if new information that puts things in a different light becomes available during the review process or if an issue that needs to be resolved was left out during the negotiations. Or, sometimes, a spouse sees the proposed agreement differently once it is set down in black and white.

Whatever the reason, if you or your spouse requests a revision that changes the settlement terms, this will almost always require further discussion in mediation. Depending on the issue, you may need to return to the information-gathering stage or the framing stage before the issue can be resolved. This may make you feel like you're going backwards, especially if you aren't the one who suggests the change. But remember that the goal is a written agreement both of you can live with, so you are actually moving closer to that goal by catching and working through any potential problems *before* the agreement is finalized.

Concluding the Mediation

After the written agreement has been prepared, reviewed, and revised as needed, you may find it helpful to have a brief final session with the mediator to go over and sign the agreement. This can provide a sense of closure. It also gives you a chance to reaffirm your choice of resolving your case amicably through mediation and to underscore your commitment to abide by the terms of the agreement.

Robert and Fran's Mediation

In Robert and Fran's case, they find out that they can refinance their mortgage as they had hoped, and their accountant confirms that the child support and alimony arrangement they are thinking of will generate the tax savings they were expecting. Robert's lawyer reviews the settlement agreement, as does Fran's lawyer. In a letter to the mediator, Fran's lawyer requests some minor wording changes. In a telephone conference Robert, Fran, and the mediator agree that the proposed changes help clarify the agreement. The mediator makes the changes and sends a final draft to Robert and Fran and their lawyers. The mediator suggests a brief meeting to go over the agreement together and sign it.

At this final meeting, the mediator tells Robert and Fran that she appreciates their hard work and efforts in settling their case. Fran thanks the mediator for her help in negotiating a fair agreement. Robert confesses that he was skeptical that he and Fran could ever reach an agreement

and says he will recommend mediation to his friends. The mediator gives Robert the signed original agreement to take to his lawyer, because Robert and Fran have agreed that Robert's lawyer will process the uncontested divorce. As Robert and Fran leave, they discuss arrangements for their daughter's upcoming prom. While neither Robert nor Fran is completely over the hurt and disappointment of ending their marriage, the experience of mediation has helped them develop constructive and respectful ways to communicate when they need to.

Assessing the Cost of Robert and Fran's Mediation

Now that you've had an opportunity to follow a hypothetical couple through a fairly typical divorce mediation involving the family home, retirement benefits, child support and alimony, and college expenses, you may be curious about what this would have cost. The example below is our best estimate, assuming the mediator charges $200 an hour.

So that is mediation in a nutshell. Will your mediation look just like this? No. But we hope this whirlwind description gives you an idea of the possibilities and, most of all, the belief that with the help of a good mediator, you and your spouse can negotiate a divorce agreement that works for you.

Mediation vs. Litigation Expenses

MEDIATION EXPENSE
(One mediator at $200 per hour)

Introductory—1 hour **200**
Information gathering—6 hours 1,200
Framing—3 hours 600
Negotiating—4 hours 800
Concluding and agreement preparation—4 hours ....<u>800</u>
Subtotal Mediation Component **3,600**

Legal Expenses and Filing Fees
Consulting lawyers 1,000
Real estate appraisal 450
Tax consultation 500
Signature session 200
Uncontested divorce 500
Filing fees to court ....<u>500</u>
Subtotal Legal Costs and Filing Fees Component **3,150**

GRAND TOTAL **$6,750**

This may seem like a lot, but consider the following conservative estimate of what it would cost Robert and Fran to litigate their case in court, even assuming that it settles prior to trial.

LITIGATION EXPENSE
(Two lawyers at $250 per hour each)

Prefiling analysis and preparation—20 hours **5,000**
Filing fees 550
Prepare and attend initial hearing—12 hours 3,000
Formal discovery (interrogatories, depositions, etc.)—80 hours 20,000
Costs (additional fees for filing papers, expert witnesses,
          appraisals, court reporter, etc.) 20,000
Pretrial preparation and meetings—40 hours 10,000
Settlement—40 hours 10,000
Agreement preparation—20 hours ....<u>5,000</u>

GRAND TOTAL **$73,550**

Not only is mediation a far less expensive approach to divorce, but it takes much less time and leaves the divorcing couple in much better shape, both psychologically and financially.

Chapter 3

What Happens in a Collaborative Divorce

Before deciding whether collaborative divorce is right for you, it may help to read a bit about how a typical collaborative case proceeds. This chapter follows a fictional couple, Cole and Traci, through the stages of a typical collaborative divorce, from the first meeting with a collaborative attorney to the final settlement., The stages of a collaborative divorce are similar to a mediation, so you might find it helpful to read Chapter 2, What Happens in Mediation, before you read this one.

 You don't have to read this chapter to succeed in a collaborative divorce. This chapter should give you a good idea of what might happen in your case if you choose the collaborative route. But if you don't feel this material would be helpful, skip any part or all of this chapter.

Each case is different. Even if you decide to collaborate, this chapter may not describe your experience of the collaborative process. If that's the case, don't worry. As long as you're comfortable with your collaborative lawyer and you seem to be making progress, that's what's important.

An Overview of Collaborative Divorce

Collaborative divorce, like mediation, puts the emphasis on reaching a settlement without acrimonious and costly court battles. In a collaborative divorce, both spouses hire attorneys who know how to handle the divorce in a nonadversarial way. The spouses and their attorneys work together in "four-way" meetings, often without the assistance of a mediator.

The Collaborative Team

Collaborative divorce frequently involves other professionals who work with the attorneys in the collaborative process and who provide support or expert analysis on financial issues or what's best for the children. For example, each spouse might have a "coach"—usually a mental health professional—to help them deal with their emotions and participate constructively in the four-way meetings. If there are children, the spouses might decide to hire a counselor to assess the children's needs and help reach agreements that address those needs. An accountant or financial planner is sometimes brought in to analyze the finances and present mutually beneficial settlement options. The lawyers and other professionals working on the case are sometimes called the "collaborative team."

The Team Approach Can Be Cost Effective

While it may seem counterintuitive, using a "team" of professionals can actually make the divorce cheaper. Lawyers—even good ones trained in collaborative divorce—don't have some of the specialized skills you might need to move things along. Even if they did, their hourly rates are often significantly higher than the rates charged by coaches, child advocates, and financial specialists. As long as these services are coordinated to avoid duplication, you'll probably save money in the long run.

The Collaborative Agreement

The spouses and their collaborative attorneys usually sign a "no court" collaborative divorce agreement at the beginning of the case, committing themselves to work collaboratively toward a mutually acceptable settlement, and requiring both attorneys to withdraw from the case if either spouse ends the process and goes to court. In some places, the agreement is submitted to the court and becomes a court order.

Typically, the other collaborative professionals also sign "no court" agreements that commit them to working toward settlement and require them to withdraw if the case becomes contested. The "no court" agreement is a strong incentive to follow through with the collaborative process. If your lawyer and other professional advisers are all required to withdraw from the case, going to court will require you to hire a new team and get everyone up to speed for the litigation. This will be enormously expensive and time-consuming. See "Collaborative Divorce Is Controversial," below.

Collaborative Divorce Is Controversial

Collaborative divorce is a relatively new phenomenon and it is meeting with resistance from some lawyers and judges. They question the wisdom of the "no court" agreement requiring the attorneys and other professionals to withdraw if the case doesn't settle. They argue that this not only poses a financial risk to spouses who would have to pay even more money to bring new lawyers up to speed, but it requires a spouse to start all over building a relationship with a new lawyer at a time of emotional stress. These critics also worry that the "no court" agreement actually increases the risk that a spouse will be coerced into accepting an undesirable settlement by threats that the other spouse will end the collaborative process and go to court.

Additionally, some in the legal profession posit that attorneys in a collaborative setting might not advocate for their clients as zealously as they should because of the commitment to work toward common solutions and because of their ongoing collegial relationships with other collaborative attorneys. Finally, they suggest that a failed collaboration could engender even greater contentiousness between the spouses if they give up on collaboration.

Proponents of collaborative divorce point out that in general, attorneys are trained and conditioned to use adversarial tactics, including threatening to take the other party to court. They contend that the requirement that collaborative lawyers withdraw before going to court is essential to prevent attorneys from engaging in adversarial tactics in an ever-escalating, unproductive, and damaging battle during the collaborative process. Besides, they say, it's not as if these things don't happen in spades in a traditional divorce negotiation—at least collaborative divorce holds out a possibility that the negotiation will proceed in a more civil and constructive fashion. This makes the risk of having to start over worth the gamble. In addition, there can be much to salvage from a failed collaborative process—information exchanged, partial agreements reached, and insight into the other spouse's concerns—thus moving the case forward so that the spouses will not really be starting over.

As for the other criticisms, collaborative lawyers argue that all of these risks are potentially present in any divorce case, and that collaborating decreases the chances that they will negatively affect the divorce process.

A copy of the collaborative divorce agreement signed by Cole, Traci, and their attorneys is found at the end of this chapter.

The Collaborative Divorce Meetings

Most of what happens in a collaborative divorce takes place in meetings. The first meeting will be between each spouse and his or her own collaborative attorney. After that, both spouses and their attorneys attend four-way meetings from the beginning of the case until a settlement is reached. Along the way as needed, the spouses will again meet separately with their attorneys. Other members of the collaborative team may attend selected four-ways when necessary. In addition, the spouses and various members of the collaborative team sometimes meet without the attorneys in order to develop necessary information or prepare for four-way meetings.

In between meetings, the spouses may have "homework" to do just like spouses in mediation, such as completing worksheets and assembling information and documents needed for the meetings.

The Stages of a Collaborative Divorce

A collaborative divorce, like a mediation, is a structured negotiation that proceeds in stages. These stages are designed to minimize adversarial posturing and to maximize the potential for a mutually acceptable settlement.

There are five stages of a typical collaborative divorce:

1. introductory
2. information-gathering
3. framing
4. negotiating, and
5. concluding.

The first three stages—introductory, information-gathering, and framing—prepare the way for a successful negotiation. Collaborative attorneys, like mediators, are trained to conduct these preparatory stages in a respectful and thorough way. This lays a solid foundation for approaching the negotiation with complete information and a clear understanding of the concerns that will have to be addressed in order to reach an agreement.

Using the Law in Collaborative Divorce

In a contested divorce case, a great deal of emphasis is placed on what each spouse is "entitled to" and on the legally correct result of any disputed issue. The lawyers argue with each other about the law. They try to persuade the judge of the correctness of their respective interpretations of the law as it applies to the case. What is fair, practical, or in the best interests of the spouses and the children tends to get lost in the shuffle.

In a collaborative divorce, as in a mediation, the law is still important, but it is just one factor to consider in deciding what is best for you, your spouse, and your children. Other factors—such as your individual goals and priorities—are just as important. The collaborative process is designed to examine all the angles, so that you end up with an agreement that is equitable and workable, even if it doesn't look just like what a judge would order.

A collaborative approach without the "no court" agreement may not look like this. You and your spouse might decide to work with lawyers who offer a collaborative approach to negotiating a settlement without having you sign an agreement requiring them to withdraw from the case if you litigate. If so, what happens in your case may not look much like what we are describing here. If that's the case, and if you're comfortable with how things are going, use what's useful in these pages and feel free to ignore the rest.

Introductory Stage

The introductory stage of a collaborative case consists of your first meeting with your collaborative attorney and the first four-way meeting between you, your spouse, and the two collaborative attorneys. If you and your attorney decide it would be helpful for you to work with a coach, your first meeting with your coach will likely take place during the introductory stage—most likely before the first four-way.

Typical Collaborative Case

Most collaborative divorces follow a similar pattern. We'll outline that pattern and then give an example of a typical case.

You Meet With Your Collaborative Attorney

The introductory stage begins with one or more meetings between you and your collaborative attorney to discuss the collaborative process and to prepare for the first four-way meeting.

When you meet with your attorney for the first time, you will be asked to give some background about yourself, your spouse, the circumstances of your separation, and other details relevant to your case. The two of you will also likely spend some time discussing the pros and cons of using a collaborative process.

Once you decide to go forward with a collaborative divorce, either at the time of the first meeting or in a prior meeting, you and your attorney will work on preparing for the first four-way meeting.

Typically, there are six areas to address in preparing for the first four-way meeting:

- Identifying your short-term and long-term goals
- Understanding the collaborative process
- Reviewing the collaborative agreement
- Assessing your readiness for the meeting
- Identifying ways to improve your readiness for the meeting
- Making a plan for assembling necessary financial and other information (see Information-Gathering Stage, below).

The Attorneys Meet

The introductory stage often includes a "pre-meeting" between the collaborative attorneys, at which you and your spouse are not present. Many collaborative attorneys believe that having a pre-meeting lays a foundation for a more productive and efficient four-way meeting. At this pre-meeting the attorneys discuss any unique features to your case that might require special attention or sensitivity. They establish a proposed agenda for the first four-way meeting, and divide up responsibility for leading the discussion that will take place at the time of the four-way. They agree on a time and place for the four-way, as well as any other necessary logistics.

You Meet With a Collaborative Coach (Optional)

If you are having an especially hard time with the emotional aspects of the divorce, or if you and your spouse have trouble being civil to one another when you are together, your attorney may suggest that you get some coaching from a trained collaborative coach before the four-way.

This will involve an initial meeting with your coach, and maybe one or two follow-up meetings to get you ready for the four-way. If your spouse is also working with a coach, the two of you may also attend a four-way meeting with both coaches to help you prepare for and make the most of the first four-way with the collaborative attorneys.

The First "Four-Way"

The first four-way meeting—attended by you, your spouse, and your respective attorneys—is also part of the introductory stage. At this meeting, the four of you will get to know each other and develop a plan of action for handling your divorce.

Typically, the first four-way meeting will include the following elements:
- Review the collaborative process
- Identify collaborative team members
- Review and sign the collaborative documents
- Identify shared and individual short-term and long-term goals that establish a process for making an interim agreement
- Agree on process for future meetings.

Traci and Cole's Case

Traci and Cole have been married for 15 years. They have two children, a son Kyle, age 12, and a daughter Nicole, age eight. Cole is a firefighter. He makes good money and has excellent benefits through his union. Traci is a bookkeeper. She stopped working when Kyle was born, but went back to work for a local accountancy firm about three years ago. Her work involves lots of overtime during tax season, and fewer hours in the summer. She is paid by the hour and has no benefits.

Traci and Cole started having marital problems about a year and a half ago. Cole moved out of the family home five months ago and has been living with his parents. Traci and Cole tried marital counseling. When it became clear that they would be divorcing, their counselor recommended the collaborative divorce process. He gave them a brochure about collaborative divorce that included the names of local attorneys trained and experienced in the collaborative divorce process.

Traci and Cole Meet With Their Collaborative Attorneys

Traci makes an appointment with Glenda McAdams, one of the collaborative attorneys listed on the brochure. Cole selects collaborative attorney Sam Shaw, who was also listed on the brochure.

Traci meets with Glenda McAdams twice. In the first meeting they discuss Traci's situation and the state laws that apply to property division, child support, alimony, and other issues likely to come up in a contested case. They discuss the pros and cons of mediation or collaborative divorce as opposed to a contested court case. Traci is interested in a nonadversarial approach like mediation or collaborative divorce. She feels intimidated by Cole, especially lately, so she likes the idea of having her own attorney by her side when she meets with Cole to discuss the divorce. Brenda informs Traci that they may be able to accomplish a settlement in collaborative four-way meetings with Cole and his attorney. If they run into problems in the four-way meetings, they can consider hiring a mediator to facilitate the process

at a later point. Glenda gives Traci some financial worksheets and a questionnaire about the children to complete and bring back to their next meeting. Glenda also gives Traci a retainer agreement explaining what Glenda's role would be in the collaborative divorce process and spelling out Glenda's fee arrangement with Traci.

After her first meeting with Glenda, Traci tells Cole that she is interested in the collaborative divorce idea. Cole makes an appointment with attorney Sam Shaw. Cole's appointment with Sam is similar to Traci's first appointment with Glenda. Sam gives Cole basic information about the laws that would apply to the case and they discuss Cole's questions about collaborative divorce. They also spend time talking about what is likely to happen at the first four-way meeting and they agree that, unless Cole thinks of other questions, they don't need to meet again until after the first four-way meeting.

With Cole's permission, Sam contacts Glenda to let her know that Cole has agreed to try the collaborative divorce process. Sam and Glenda arrange a date to meet and discuss preparations for the first four-way meeting. Glenda then makes another appointment with Traci to go over any follow-up questions of Traci's and to prepare Traci for the first four-way meeting.

At Traci's second meeting with Glenda, Traci signs Glenda's retainer agreement after they discuss a few questions Traci has. They talk about Traci's concerns about meeting with Cole and his attorney. Traci gives Glenda the completed financial worksheets and the completed parenting questionnaire. They go over the information together. Glenda gives Traci copies of the standard collaborative divorce agreement to look at before the four-way meeting. They agree that Glenda will call Traci to discuss final details about the four-way meeting after Glenda meets with Cole's attorney Sam.

The Attorneys Meet

About two weeks later, Glenda and Sam meet at Glenda's office. Glenda tells Sam that Traci wants the collaborative process to be a success, but Traci is apprehensive about meeting with Cole, because he tends to "blow up" whenever he doesn't get his way. Traci is worried that this could happen during a four-way meeting. Sam says that Cole is also concerned that the four-way meeting will turn into a shouting match and go nowhere. Sam and Glenda know that concerns like these are common for divorcing couples. They have learned how to structure four-way meetings to increase the chances of productive communication. They also agree that it might be helpful for Cole and Traci to have their own coaches to help them prepare to communicate effectively before the first four-way meeting. Glenda and Sam agree that the first four-way meeting will take place at

a neutral location (the conference room of a collaborative colleague). They also agree on the agenda for the four-way and they schedule a tentative date about four weeks later, to give Traci and Cole time to meet with their collaborative coaches first.

After the meeting between the attorneys, Glenda calls Traci to fill her in on what was discussed at the meeting. Glenda gives Traci the names of two experienced collaborative coaches and Traci agrees to make an appointment as soon as possible. Sam has a similar telephone conversation with Cole.

Traci and Cole With Their Coaches

Cole selects Dan Baker as his coach. When they meet, Dan works with Cole on effective communication techniques and they go over what is likely to happen in the first four-way and how to respond to challenging interactions with Traci at the meeting. Dan gives Cole some tips for "keeping his cool" if he starts to get upset with Traci at the meeting.

Meanwhile, Traci works with her coach, Paul Gates, on ways to avoid going into "emotional overwhelm" at the four-way meeting.

The First Four-Way

On the day of the first four-way, Traci meets Glenda at her office and they walk the short distance to the meeting place. They arrive just as Sam is pulling into the driveway. A few minutes later, Cole arrives. The receptionist shows them all into the conference room, which is stocked with coffee, tea, and soft drinks. Sam has brought some pastries from a nearby bakery. Everyone introduces themselves and they sit at the table, Traci next to Glenda and Cole next to Sam. As agreed in advance, Glenda begins the meeting by handing out a draft agenda approved by her and Sam. The agenda includes these items:

- Introductions and overview
- Concerns and questions about the process
- Ground rules
- Short-term and long-term goals (Traci, Cole)
- Review and sign collaborative agreement.
- Time frame and schedule of meetings.

Glenda asks whether anyone has any questions, or if anything should be added to the agenda. Cole says he is concerned about cash flow, and wonders whether there will be time to talk about how the bills are being paid. Sam replies that he and Glenda both recognize the importance of addressing this question as soon as possible, and that they have some ideas on how this might be done. He suggests adding this to the agenda right before the last item (time frame and schedule of meetings). Glenda says, "I agree with this approach, if it makes sense to the two of you," looking at Traci and Cole. They both nod their agreement. "Good, then. Let's begin," says Glenda.

The meeting then continues, as Traci, Cole, Sam, and Glenda converse informally about the collaborative process and how to address some of the concerns previously raised by Traci and Cole.

As the conversation continues, both Traci and Cole discover that it is not as hard as they had thought to talk about their case in each other's presence. Both of them feel that the presence of the lawyers is helpful in keeping things calm and productive. By the time they sign the collaborative agreement, each of them feels more confident that they might be able to resolve their case amicably.

Next, they tackle the issue of interim agreements. Glenda tells Traci and Cole that she and Sam see this as a "dress rehearsal" for negotiating the divorce settlement itself.

Sam adds, "This is why it is important for us to spend some time on talking about how we will reach any interim agreements."

Glenda says, "First, let's agree that anything decided on a temporary basis will not be considered a waiver of any legal rights either of you may have. In other words, temporary agreements will not set a precedent, and they can be retroactively modified if it turns out there are other factors we failed to consider when we first made the agreements. In an ideal world, we would not negotiate even temporary agreements until we had completed the information-gathering stage. But, obviously, you both have bills to pay and schedules to arrange for yourselves and your children. So there have to be some interim decisions made. What we want to do is make sure that those temporary agreements don't put either of you at a disadvantage."

The conversation then continues with a discussion of Traci and Cole's specific situation. At this point, the four-way meeting has shifted from the introductory stage to the information-gathering stage. Read on.

Information-Gathering Stage

This is the stage in which you and your spouse work with your collaborative attorneys to prepare detailed information about yourselves, your finances, your children, and any other aspects of your case that are important to take into consideration in reaching a settlement.

Typical Collaborative Case

This stage often overlaps the introductory stage, given that you and your collaborative attorney will probably begin discussing the factual information involved in your case and the legal aspects of it during your first meeting. Your attorney will probably give you detailed questionnaires or worksheets to complete, and ask you to provide copies of various documents pertinent to your case. For examples of the kinds of information you might be

asked to provide, see Chapter 9, Getting Started on Information-Gathering.

Once you have assembled the necessary information, you and your attorney will go over it together and the two of you will decide how put it into a format that can be shared with your spouse, your spouse's attorney, and any other members of the collaborative team who might need it.

As you are gathering factual information, you will begin to discuss the legal significance of the information, first with your attorney, and then in the four-way meetings. Knowing what could happen in your case if you went to court instead of collaborating will be important when it comes time to negotiate an agreement.

In all likelihood, you will continue to work on information-gathering, including discussions about the legal aspects of your case, well after the first four-way meeting.

Traci and Cole's Case

When Traci and Cole each meet with their attorneys for the first time, they are given confidential questionnaires, detailed financial worksheets, and parenting questionnaires to complete and fill out. These worksheets and questionnaires have been developed by the local collaborative practice professional group to which both attorneys belong.

Before the first four-way meeting, Traci's attorney Glenda McAdams reviews all of the information with Traci. Glenda then prepares a detailed summary of information to be shared at the four-way meeting. Cole and his attorney Sam Shaw confer by phone. Sam asks for additional documentation regarding Cole's work schedule, his earnings, and his retirement benefits. Cole promises to forward the information to Sam in time for Sam to include it in the packet he is preparing for the four-way meeting.

At the first four-way Sam and Glenda exchange packets containing the information and documents they've compiled along with their clients Traci and Cole each receive copies of the packets, too.

In discussing their short-term and long-term objectives at the first four-way meeting, Traci and Cole identify two short-term needs they want to address soon. Cole wants to move into a place of his own so that he can spend more time with the children on a regular basis. That will mean using some of his income to pay rent. Since the separation, he has been depositing most of his paycheck into the joint account and Traci has been paying all of the family bills from that account. For her part, Traci wants to be assured that she will have enough money to pay household expenses. She also has some concerns about Cole's proposed plan to spend equal time with the children after he moves into a new place.

Sam suggests having a child advocate meet with Traci, Cole, and their children, Kyle and Nicole, to assess the children's

needs regarding time-sharing and other parenting issues that might come up. Glenda agrees that this would be a good idea. She and Sam come up with the names of three local counselors they agree would be good choices. One of them, Ric Nachez, is on the list of approved providers for the family health plan offered through Cole's employment, so they select him.

The financial information complied by Traci and Cole includes details of their respective incomes, copies of their pay stubs and recent tax returns, and detailed budgets. Everyone spends some time during the first four-way meeting going over this information and discussing it, without making any decisions about the short-term issues yet. They agree to schedule another four-way meeting in approximately three weeks. At that meeting, they will invite Ric Nachez to be present and report on his assessment of issues regarding the children. They will also use that meeting to discuss possible options for a temporary support agreement that will enable Cole to move into a place of his own and still cover all necessary bills.

Between the first four-way and the second one, Cole and Traci work with their attorneys to study the cash flow information further and discuss possible options for support payments. Because some of the options involve tax consequences, Sam suggests to Cole that the spouses hire a designated accountant to act as a neutral financial analyst for both sides. With Cole's permission, Sam contacts Glenda, who recommends to Traci that this would be a cost-effective way to obtain the necessary tax information. With everyone's okay, Sam and Glenda arrange to hire CPA Maya Martin.

Later, after the temporary agreements are made, Traci, Cole and their collaborative team will turn their attention to the long-term issues, including how to divide up their property. That involves additional research and analysis. For example, they hire a neutral appraiser to give an opinion on the value of the family home, and a neutral actuary to value Cole's retirement benefits. Deciding what information is needed and how to get it is the subject of several discussions at the ongoing four-way meetings over the next couple of months.

Framing Stage

As in a mediation, the information-gathering stage gives way to a framing stage, in which you, your spouse, and the collaborative team focus on your respective points of view on the issues to be addressed in the settlement.

Typical Collaborative Case

Once all of the essential information has been gathered, exchanged, and analyzed, the focus shifts to considering how you and your spouse view the issues in your case. In particular, what are your needs, priorities, and goals? These are what negotiators call your "interests."

An understanding of your interests—and the interests of your spouse and your children—is essential to reaching an agreement. In a contested court case, the outcome of a particular issue, such as child support or property division, is dictated by the law, regardless of what you or your spouse might need or want. The collaborative divorce process, like mediation, shifts the decision-making emphasis from legal rules to interests. For example, the question of child support would be examined from all parties' standpoints, including your children's, and then you would attempt to negotiate a child support agreement that addresses everyone's interests in a mutually-balanced way. This is what's known a "interest-based negotiating." For more on interest-based negotiating, see Chapter 13.

Traci and Cole's Case

About three and a half months after the first four-way meeting, all of the necessary data and legal analysis is completed. Traci, Cole, and their collaborative team decide that it is time to frame the issues and interests to be addressed in the final settlement negotiations.

With the help of the child advocate Ric Nachez and the attorneys and coaches, Traci and Cole have come up with a workable process for communicating about the children and scheduling time-sharing, using email and a website where they can post their work schedules, the time-sharing calendar, and other pertinent information. They also agree to meet with Ric and the coaches once a year (or more frequently if necessary) to evaluate and adjust this process.

The remaining issues to be decided are financial, including property division, debt payments, child support, alimony, college education costs, health insurance, and life insurance.

The family home is the main asset. It has been appraised at $700,000. The current balance on the mortgage is $100,000, leaving equity of $650,000. There is a small savings account in addition to the household checking account and the parties have two vehicles.

The actuary hired by the collaborative team has placed a current value of between $200,000 and $250,000 on Cole's pension. In addition, Cole has a deferred compensation plan worth $80,000.

One area of contention involves numerous antiques now furnishing the family home. Cole says that these antiques, which came from his family, were an advance on his inheritance. Traci believes that the antiques were given to the two of them as gifts by Cole's family over the years.

With these issues in mind, Traci, Cole, and their attorneys agree to spend time talking—first with Traci speaking, and then with Cole—about their respective views on these issues and the things that will be important to them in considering options for settling the issues.

Traci's attorney, Glenda, asks Traci to talk about her view of what should happen with the house. Traci says that she would like to stay in the house until both children graduate from high school. Glenda asks Traci to elaborate on her reasons for this. Traci explains that the house is in a good neighborhood, near the children's school and friends. She says that she and Cole chose that house as a good place to raise the children. If she and Cole were to sell the house, she is pretty sure she would not be able to afford to buy a place in that neighborhood. She also sees the house as a good long-term investment for her. She is afraid she would lose the opportunity to invest in real estate if she had to start over.

Sam, Cole's attorney, then asks Cole to talk a little bit about his view of what should happen with the house. Cole says his main problem with Traci keeping the house is that he doesn't think she can afford to buy him out for his share of the equity. Even though Cole is now living in a place of his own (a rental), it is not big enough for the children to have their own bedrooms. Besides, Cole says he would like to have his own place to start a new life in and to build up equity. In addition, renting doesn't give Cole the tax write-offs that home ownership would.

Traci and Cole then go on to explain their perspectives on the retirement accounts. Cole would like to keep his pension. He says he worked hard for it and wants to know that it's there for him when he is no longer able to continue working as a firefighter. Traci is also concerned about her retirement future. She has taken time off over the years to take care of the children, and she feels that she will need a share of Cole's retirement benefits. Besides, she says that she too made sacrifices to support Cole's career, and she wants her contributions to be acknowledged.

With regard to child support and alimony, Traci wants to know that she'll be in a position to pay her bills and set aside some savings for contingencies. She wants to continue to work part-time, or at least on a flexible schedule so that she can be available to the children when they are not in school. She is interested in taking some courses to upgrade her bookkeeping and tax preparation skills, with the hope of eventually starting her own tax and bookkeeping business.

For Cole, it's important that he and Traci pay off their credit card debts. He wants to be in a position to live within his means and not run up new debt in order to pay his bills. He would like to have as little financial interaction with Traci as possible, since he feels this puts pressure on their relationship as coparents. He wants to know that there will be an end to alimony at a specified time in the future.

As Cole and Traci discuss what is important to each of them—their "interests"—the attorneys use a flipchart to keep a running list of the interests. This list will be referred to later during the negotiation stage in order to determine how well certain options will meet Traci's and Cole's interests.

Negotiating Stage

Once the essential information has been gathered, exchanged, and reviewed, and you have framed the issues and interests, you are ready to begin the negotiating stage.

Negotiating in a collaborative divorce, like negotiating in mediation, starts with the assumption that any agreement reached must be satisfactory to both spouses. To accomplish this, the negotiation is structured in a way that maximizes the potential to find solutions that benefit both of you.

Typical Collaborative Case

In the negotiating stage, you will have one or more four-way meetings with your collaborative attorneys. Depending on the issues being negotiated, you may have other members of the collaborative team present at these four-way meetings. For example, if you are negotiating the financial aspects of your case, you may have a financial planner or accountant present. If you are working on a parenting agreement, you might invite the child advocate who knows your children to attend.

The first step in the negotiating phase is to identify as many options as possible for the issue you are discussing. This is done through a "brainstorming" session in which you, your spouse, your collaborative attorneys and any other members of the collaborative team who are present participate. For more on brainstorming see Chapter 2, "Brainstorming: A Creative Way to Expand the Pie."

Once you have come up with a list of all the possible options, you and the collaborative team members examine them in light of your interests, consider their feasibility, and develop a short list of the most promising options.

Divorce is almost always a package deal in which an agreement about one issue has an impact on all the other issues. You may start with one issue, but eventually you'll need to determine whether the overall package seems balanced and fair. One common way to do this is to take the most promising options for resolving each issue and put together proposals for settlement of the entire case. This can involve trade-offs in which one of you agrees to accept a less desirable option in one area in exchange for a more desirable option in the other area.

Your collaborative lawyers and the other members of the collaborative team will be there to help you decide how best to proceed with the actual negotiation and coach you to consider all of the relevant factors as you move toward making decisions.

As you examine each option, you'll be assessing its feasibility, given that any settlement must not only address your interests, but must also be workable.

Often this involves consulting with experts, like a financial advisor or tax specialist. At the end of the negotiating phase, the attorneys will probably summarize the agreed terms on a flip chart, legal pad, or computer printout.

Traci and Cole's Case

After framing the issues and interests, Traci and Cole and their attorneys schedule another four-way meeting to brainstorm options for settling the financial aspects of their case. At this short four-way meeting, the focus is to come up with as many ideas as possible for what to do with the house, the retirement benefits, child support, alimony, and the other financial issues. On a flipchart, Sam makes five columns, one for each of these issues and one labeled miscellaneous. As an idea is mentioned, Sam writes it down in the appropriate column.

Next, the four of them review the lists and pick three or four ideas from each category that seem most promising. It is agreed that these top ideas will be given to the collaborative financial analyst, CPA Maya Martin. She will analyze them and bring spreadsheets with her to the next four-way meeting.

At the next four-way, everyone reviews Maya Martin's spreadsheets. She explains how different options interrelate and answers questions.

As the meeting progresses, it becomes clear that Traci and Cole are most interested in an option that would involve having the two of them purchase a condominium for Cole to live in. They would co-own the family house and the condominium for six years. At that time, their son Kyle would be finishing high school and their daughter Nicole would be entering high school. Traci would have the right to refinance and buy out Cole's share of the family home at that time or the home would be sold and Traci would take her share of the proceeds to purchase a new home. In determining Traci's share of the equity in the family home, she would receive credit for the equity in the condominium occupied by Cole, and it would be transferred to Cole. Cole would keep all of his deferred compensation plan, and Traci would get a percentage of Cole's union pension, to be paid directly to her by the plan when Cole reaches retirement age. Traci's share of the deferred compensation plan would also be credited to her in calculating her share of the equity in the family home.

Maya Martin's spreadsheets show how Cole and Traci can structure the child support and alimony to minimize income taxes for each of them. Traci and Cole decide that the money they save by doing this will be deposited each year into college savings accounts for Kyle and Nicole. They agree that alimony payments will stop in six years, after the house and the condo are bought out or sold, unless Traci becomes disabled and cannot work. Cole will keep the children on his health insurance plan and he will pay half of the cost of new health insurance coverage for Traci for three years following the divorce. They agree that the antiques from Cole's family will stay in the family home until Traci buys Cole out or it is sold. At that time, Cole will take half of the antiques and Traci will keep the other half. If one of them decides to sell an antique, it will be offered first to the other party. Each of them agrees to make a will leaving the family antiques in his or her possession to the children. Cole agrees to keep Traci and the children as the only beneficiaries of his life insurance coverage. When alimony ends, the children will be the sole beneficiaries until Nicole reaches the age of 22.

As the outlines of this agreement are worked out, Glenda records them on her computer. At the end of the meeting, she prints out the list of agreed terms and Sam offers to prepare the settlement agreement, using Glenda's printout as a guide.

Concluding Stage

Once a tentative agreement is reached, the agreed terms are put into a written settlement agreement, which is thoroughly reviewed, revised if necessary, and signed. Other documents needed to complete the divorce are also prepared and signed during this stage.

Typical Collaborative Case

The attorney designated to draft the settlement agreement prepares a formal document that will be accepted by the court in the uncontested case. In addition to the specific provisions you've negotiated, the settlement agreement typically includes "boilerplate," that is, standard legal language that goes in all settlement agreements.

The draft agreement is circulated to the spouses and the other attorney for a careful review.

Because the attorney preparing the agreement was present at the four-ways, the chances of a misunderstanding about the terms of the agreement are low. Still, putting things in writing sometimes highlights a difference in interpretation or turns up a new issue that no one thought of. If so, there may be a follow-up meeting to clarify any questionable items.

After the agreement has been revised and finalized, you may have a final meeting to sign the agreement and any accompanying documents needed to complete the contested case. Otherwise, the documents will be circulated for separate signature, and copies will be provided after everyone has signed.

Traci and Cole's Case

As agreed, Sam writes up the draft settlement agreement. Two weeks after the last four-way, Sam completes the draft and sends it to Cole for a preliminary review. He and Cole discuss the draft in a telephone conference and he makes a couple of minor changes. He then forwards the draft to Glenda. Glenda sends the draft to Traci and they review it together in an office conference. Glenda then contacts Sam to arrange a four-way to go over some questions she and Traci have about the draft.

At the four-way, everyone agrees that the draft needs some clarifying language regarding the potential buyout or sale of the family home and the transfer of the condominium to Cole. There are additional guidelines developed for the college savings accounts. Sam agrees to make these changes.

Sam's revisions to the draft are circulated and approved. Traci and Cole meet one last time with their collaborative lawyers in a four-way meeting at which they sign the agreement, together with other documents to be filed with the court to complete the divorce. To celebrate their success, Sam brings a cake and Glenda brings sparkling cider to pour into champagne glasses.

The Role of Law in Collaborative Divorce

As you read our description of a typical collaborative divorce, you'll notice that we don't talk much about the law or legal rights. The lawyers may discuss the law at their initial meeting, and it may come up here and there as a reference point, but it is not the basis of most decisions. You may wonder where the law fits in, given that divorce is, after all, a legal event. What about your legal rights to property? What about the laws governing child support, custody, and other legal issues? Aren't those important? Yes and no.

One of the great features of collaboration, like mediation, is that you and your spouse get to decide what's best for you, even if it's different from what the laws provide. There are a few things you cannot legally agree to—such as giving up the right to receive child support—but these are rare. Other than the few exceptions, you are free to make whatever agreement is best for you.

Being free to decide the terms of your settlement doesn't mean that the legal rules aren't significant. If you want your agreement to withstand the test of time, you should know how it compares to what the law would dictate. What are your legal rights? Which ones are you compromising? Do you have a good reason for compromising them? How does your overall agreement compare to the likely result if you went to court? Asking—and getting answers to—these questions will guide you in negotiating the right settlement.

In a collaborative process your lawyer is likely to tell you how the law might apply to your situation, especially if the law is in your favor and you're considering moving in a direction other than what the law might provide. But how much you actually use the law in your decision-making process is up to you and is something you'll work out with your collaborative lawyer.

After Traci and Cole sign, Sam and Glenda congratulate them on their accomplishment. As they say goodbye, Traci jokes that she is going to miss these meetings. Cole says, smiling, "I won't miss paying the bills."

"True," says Traci, "but think of all the money we've saved not going to court."

"Not to mention our sanity," says Cole. With that, everyone shakes hands and says goodbye.

A few weeks later, the judge signs the uncontested judgment of divorce. Traci and Cole receive copies from their attorneys. It is a bittersweet moment. The journey from separation to divorce has not been easy, but they know that they chose a route that minimized emotional and economic costs to themselves and their children.

Assessing the Cost of Cole and Traci's Collaborative Divorce

Now that you've followed Traci and Cole through a typical collaborative divorce involving the family home, retirement benefits, child support, and alimony, you may wonder what all this would have cost. Here is our best estimate.

Litigation vs. Collaborative Divorce Expenses

LITIGATION EXPENSE
(Two lawyers at $250 per hour each)

Prefiling analysis and preparation—20 hours 5,000
Filing fees.. 550
Prepare and attend initial hearing—12 hours....................................3,000
Formal discovery (interrogatories, depositions, etc.)—80 hours 20,000
Costs (additional fees for filing papers, expert witnesses,
      appraisals, court reporter, etc.)...20,000
Pretrial preparation and meetings—40 hours...10,000
Settlement—40 hours 10,000
Agreement preparation—20 hours..5,000

GRAND TOTAL **$73,550**

Not only is collaboration a far less expensive approach to divorce, but it takes much less time and leaves the divorcing couple in much better shape, both psychologically and financially.

COLLABORATIVE DIVORCE EXPENSE
Attorneys' fees ($250 per hour)

Introductory—

Traci—3 hours 750

Cole—2 hours 500

One four-way—2 hours..1,000

Information-gathering—

Traci—4 hours 1,000

Cole—4 hours 1,000

Three four-ways – 6 hours..3,000

Framing—

Traci—1 hour 250

Cole—1 hour 250

One four-way—3 hours..1,500

Negotiating—

Traci—1 hour 250

Cole—1 hour 250

One four-way—3 hours..1,500

Concluding and agreement preparation

Traci—2 hours 500

Cole—5 hours 1,250

Two four-ways—3 hours 1,500

Subtotal attorneys' fees 14,500

Other Expenses and Filing Fees

Traci's coach—6 hours @ $60..360

Cole's coach—6 hours @ $60...360

Child specialist—8 sessions @ $25 copay.......................................200

CPA—10 hours @ $85...850

Real estate appraisal 450

Pension evaluation..375

Filing fees to court 500

Subtotal Other Expenses and Filing Fees 3,095

GRAND TOTAL $17,595

While this is considerably more than the typical cost of a mediation
(see Chapter 2), it is only a fraction of what it could cost Traci and Cole to
litigate their case in court, even if they were able to settle prior to trial.

Traci and Cole's Divorce Agreement

Here is the "no court" collaborative agreement that Traci and Cole sign at the first four-way meeting.

COLLABORATIVE DIVORCE AGREEMENT

This agreement is entered into by Traci Waxner (Traci), her attorney, Glenda McAdams (McAdams), and Cole Waxner (Cole), and his attorney, Sam Shaw (Shaw).

INTRODUCTION

A.   Traci and Cole (" the spouses") are currently married to each other. The spouses have separated. A proceeding for divorce will be filed by one of the spouses. The spouses want to negotiate a settlement agreement that resolves all of the issues raised by their separation and dissolution of their marriage.

B.   McAdams represents Traci. Shaw represents Cole. The attorneys are referred to in this agreement as "the collaborative attorneys." The collaborative attorneys are members in good standing of the Main Street Collaborative Practice Group.

C.   In negotiating a settlement, we all want to proceed in a collaborative manner. We want to avoid an adversarial litigation approach to problem solving, if at all possible. We believe that this is in the best interests of the spouses and the minor children. We understand that working together collaboratively means that each of us will look for solutions that work for the whole family, not just for one spouse. Unlike a traditional litigation, in which the lawyer for each spouse advocates only for the interests of his or her client, the lawyers in a collaborative divorce focus on the interests of both spouses and the children.

AGREEMENT

1.   Commitment to Work Collaboratively.

We agree to treat all aspects of the divorce case as a collaborative case. We commit ourselves to working together to find mutually acceptable solutions to all issues that may arise in the case. We agree to devote our efforts to reaching a negotiated settlement in an efficient, cooperative manner in accord with the terms of this agreement. We agree to work together in collaborative meetings until a complete settlement is reached or until the collaborative process is terminated in accordance with this agreement.

As used in this agreement, the term "collaborative meeting" refers to any meeting of two or more people held in person, or by electronic media, in order to further the objectives of this agreement. A collaborative meeting of the spouses and the collaborative attorneys is referred to as a "four-way meeting."

2.   Agreement to Exchange Information Informally.

Except for requests to provide information required by state law, all requests for information and documents shall be made and complied with informally. No formal discovery request (as defined by state law), nor any motion to compel or for sanctions for any discovery requests is required or available during the collaborative process.

Responses to all requests for information or documents shall be as thorough as possible and shall be provided within a reasonable time.

To reassure the spouse requesting information that the responding spouse has provided full and complete disclosure, the responding spouse shall verify the accuracy of any information or documents produced under penalty of perjury whenever possible. If verification under penalty of perjury is not possible, the spouse will provide an explanation of the reason why verification is not possible.

3.   Commitment to Good Faith and Integrity.

Each of us shall uphold a high standard of integrity in the collaborative process. We agree not to take advantage of any inadvertent mistakes or miscalculations by another participant, but shall disclose them and seek to have them corrected.

4.   The Collaborative Attorneys May Not Represent the Spouses in Contested Litigation.

Except as provided below, the collaborative attorneys, and any attorney who is a partner, employee, employer, or otherwise in association with the collaborative attorneys, are hereby disqualified from ever appearing as attorneys of record for either spouse in any contested case, whether in the divorce case or in any other litigation in which the spouses are adverse parties.

If the spouses enter into an agreement or stipulation regarding any or all issues in the divorce case, the collaborative attorneys named above may appear as attorneys of record in any uncontested portion of the case for purposes of filing the agreement or stipulation and any judgment or order based on the agreement or stipulation, as well as any necessary document directly related to the agreement or stipulation.

5.   **Agreement Not to Use Court.**

As long as this agreement is in effect, we agree that neither spouse nor his or her attorney file any pleading or other document requesting intervention by the court in this case other than an agreement or stipulation signed by both spouses and the collaborative attorneys.

6.   **Other Professionals.**

When appropriate, we will use the services of one or more of the other professionals to support the collaborative process, including divorce coaches, a child advocate, or a financial analyst (collectively referred to as "collaborative professionals"). When a collaborative professional is engaged, we agree that the collaborative professional and the collaborative attorneys, as well as any other collaborative professionals already involved in this case may communicate with each other as necessary for resolution of the case. A separate retainer agreement will be signed with each collaborative professional.

When appropriate, we use neutral experts to help us resolve any disagreements regarding essential facts in the case, such as the valuation of assets. Before retaining an expert, we will sign a written agreement as to how the fee charged by the expert will be paid. Unless we agree otherwise in writing, any report prepared by the expert will be covered by the confidentiality provisions of this agreement.

7.   **Confidentiality of the Collaborative Process.**

a. All Statements Made During Collaborative Meetings Are Confidential

Except as provided below or upon written agreement signed by the spouses and their collaborative attorneys, all statements made by anyone during collaborative meetings shall be deemed in the nature of settlement conferences. Therefore, all such statements shall be confidential and inadmissible in evidence for any purpose in any court proceeding between the spouses.

b. All Documents Prepared for the Collaborative Process Are Confidential

Except as provided below or upon written agreement signed by the spouses and their collaborative attorneys, all documents prepared for the collaborative process, other than the disclosure declarations required by law, shall be deemed to have been prepared for purposes of settlement and shall be confidential and inadmissible in evidence for any purpose in any court proceeding between the spouses.

The documents deemed confidential under this agreement include all notes, work papers, summaries, and reports prepared for the collaborative process by any professional person or firm.

c. Exception for Threats

Oral or written statements made by either spouse or any attorney or other collaborative professional, threatening to conceal the whereabouts of the children, or change the residence of the children without the other parent's consent, or to commit irreparable or substantial economic damage to either participant, or to violate any agreed-upon restraining orders, are not confidential and such statements shall be admissible in evidence.

8. Limitations of the Process.

In choosing the collaborative process, we understand that there is no guarantee that the process will be successful in resolving our case. We also understand that the collaborative process cannot eliminate concerns about any disharmony, distrust, or irreconcilable differences in the spousal relationship.

The spouses understand that they are expected to assert their own needs and interests and that their respective collaborative attorneys will help each of them do so.

We further understand that each of the collaborative attorneys has a professional duty to represent his or her own client, and is not the attorney for the other party, even though the attorneys are committed to the collaborative process.

9. Termination of Collaborative Law Process.

Either spouse may unilaterally and without cause terminate his or her participation under this agreement by giving written notice of such election to the other spouse and the collaborative attorneys and professionals involved in this case.

This agreement will be deemed automatically terminated if either spouse or an attorney acting on his or her behalf, takes any unilateral step to use the court for resolution of any issue in this case in violation of the provisions of this agreement. This clause does not apply to any step the spouses jointly take to file a stipulation, judgment, or other jointly signed or prepared pleading.

When the collaborative process is terminated, each collaborative attorney and collaborative professional involved in the case shall be disqualified from taking any further action in the case, except such actions as are necessary to implement or confirm the termination, or to transfer the spouses' matters to new attorneys or professionals.

10.   <u>Withdrawal of Attorneys.</u>

Any collaborative attorney may withdraw from this matter unilaterally by giving ten (10) days' written notice of withdrawal to both spouses and the other collaborative attorneys and professionals involved in this case. A notice of withdrawal by a collaborative attorney does not necessarily terminate the collaborative law process. Upon the written agreement of the remaining participants in the collaborative process, the spouse who has been represented by the withdrawing attorney may continue in the collaborative process without an attorney, or may retain a new collaborative attorney who agrees in writing to be bound by this agreement.

11.   <u>Transfer of Case to Successor Counsel.</u>

Upon termination of the process or withdrawal of an attorney, a withdrawing attorney shall promptly cooperate with his or her client to facilitate the transfer of the client's matter to a new attorney selected by the client.

12.   <u>This Agreement Is Binding Even If Not Filed With the Court.</u>

This agreement is binding when signed by both spouses and their collaborative attorneys. It need not be filed with the court in any divorce action in order to be binding.

By Signing This Agreement, each of us acknowledges that we have read this agreement, understand the terms of this agreement, and agree to comply and be bound by its terms.

Date:_____   Date:_____

_____   _____

Traci Waxner   Cole Waxner

_____   _____

Glenda McAdams   Sam Shaw

Chapter 4

Deciding to Mediate or Collaborate

By now you may be saying to yourself, "Mediation and collaborative divorce sound great, but how do I know that a nonadversarial approach like mediation or collaboration will work for my spouse and me? We didn't get along all that well before our separation. Now things are even worse. Besides, which of the two approaches is better for us?" This chapter will help you answer both of these questions.

Is Mediation or Collaboration Right for You?

Will It Play in Peoria?

You won't know for sure whether you can successfully handle your divorce with a nonadversarial approach like mediation or collaboration unless you try it. Mediation or collaboration can work for most people who try it, so chances are one of them will work for you. Everyone's situation is unique, however, and some people's circumstances can make it difficult or impossible to negotiate an agreement, even with the help of a mediator.

So is there a way to figure out whether your circumstances favor—or disfavor—an approach like mediation or collaboration?

There is no clear test for what makes for a successful or unsuccessful mediation or collaboration, but certain factors can be good indicators. The section that follows looks at these factors and gives you an opportunity to test your own readiness (as well as your spouse's) for using a nonadversarial approach to your divorce. We also offer some tips for enhancing your (or your spouse's) readiness if certain factors present problems.

Evaluate Your Situation: Are You Ready for Mediation or Collaboration?

To start thinking about your readiness for mediation or collaboration, take the self-test that follows. While it won't give you a scientifically based assessment of your potential for success in mediation or collaboration, it will give you a handle on the kinds of factors to consider.

In the test, you are asked to respond to 12 statements. Circle 4 if you strongly agree with the statement, 3 if you somewhat agree with the statement, 2 if you somewhat disagree with the statement, and 1 if you strongly disagree with the statement. If you want to test your spouse's readiness, make a copy of the test before you write in your answers.

For Each Statement, Circle One

Statement	Agree Strongly	Agree Somewhat	Disagree Somewhat	Disagree Strongly
1. The decision to divorce was mutual.	4	3	2	1
2. I have no desire to reconcile.	4	3	2	1
3. It is important that I stay on good terms with my spouse.	4	3	2	1
4. I don't blame my spouse for our separation.	4	3	2	1
5. My spouse has not lied to me about anything important.	4	3	2	1
6. I can disagree with my spouse without saying or doing things I later regret.	4	3	2	1
7. I am in good physical and mental health.	4	3	2	1
8. I understand our financial situation.	4	3	2	1
9. I am not easily intimidated by my spouse.	4	3	2	1
10. Physical violence is not an issue in our relationship.	4	3	2	1
11. Alcohol or drug abuse is not an issue in our relationship.	4	3	2	1
12. (If you have children) My spouse is a good parent.	4	3	2	1

Now figure your total score by adding up the numbers you've circled. The lowest possible score is 12 and the highest is 48—or 11 and 44 if you don't have children. Also note whether you've circled a 1 in response to any of the statements.

A total score of 20 or lower indicates that emotional issues or relationship dynamics, such as a power imbalance, could interfere with your ability to mediate until those issues or dynamics are addressed. Conversely, a total score of 36 or higher indicates the absence of serious emotional stumbling blocks and relationship hurdles to overcome before beginning. A score in between (21–35) can warrant some close attention to your situation before going ahead with mediation. A circled 1 in response to any statement might be a red flag in that area and might require some attention before mediating, even if your overall score is pretty high. Of course, these numbers are only rough indicators designed to get you thinking about your readiness to mediate. Ultimately, you'll be the best judge of whether or not you're ready.

 A marginal score may point to using collaboration instead of mediation. If your score is low and you still want to move forward, you might find it easier to work with the hands-on assistance of a collaborative lawyer—and possibly a collaborative coach—by your side. Collaborative divorce is designed to ensure that professionals on both sides are involved every step of the way, whereas in mediation you and your spouse may choose to work alone with the mediator for some or all of the process. If there are factors in your situation that are too challenging for you to handle on your own, you might want the support of a collaborative professional to help you through. See *Mediation vs. Collaboration: Factors to Consider in Choosing The Right Approach*, below.

Shall We Dance: Is Your Spouse Ready?

Whatever your score on our test, neither mediation nor collaboration can happen unless your spouse is willing and able to participate, too. In Chapter 5, we explain how to persuade your spouse to give mediation or collaboration a try, but before we do that, it would be nice to know where your spouse may fall on the ready/not-ready continuum.

If you're on speaking terms with your spouse, and if your spouse is willing, ask him or her to take the test you just completed.

Even if your spouse doesn't take the test, you can get some idea of your spouse's readiness by imagining yourself in your spouse's shoes and responding to each of the statements as honestly as you can from your spouse's point of view. For this test to be of use to you, you must respond to each of the statements as you truly think your spouse would.

Score your spouse's test the same way you scored your own. Don't compare the scores until you have completed both tests. And don't be alarmed if your spouse's scores are different from yours for many of the statements in the test. This doesn't mean you can't do well in mediation or collaboration. It just means you and your spouse see things differently, which isn't a surprise, given that you're getting a divorce. What does matter is how you deal with your differences. The mediator or your collaborative lawyers can help you with that.

Facing the Music: Factors in a Successful Mediation or Collaborative Divorce

Even if you (and/or your spouse) scored low on the mediation readiness test, when you consider the financial and emotional costs of a contested divorce, you might want to get out on the dance floor and give mediation a try. But before you do, there may be steps you can take to improve your chances of success.

The test you just took is intended to highlight not just the circumstances of your current situation, but also certain attitudes and behavior that can either promote or interfere with a mediated settlement. These are things you might be able to change. Let's take a closer look at each statement and see how changes might be made.

The Decision to Divorce Was Mutual

Sometimes, the decision to divorce is mutual: Both spouses come to the conclusion, more or less at the same time, that the marriage is over. For other couples, the decision is more one-sided: One spouse decides that a divorce is necessary, while the other spouse is unprepared for, and perhaps opposed to, the idea of getting divorced.

When the decision to divorce is mutual, spouses usually find it easier to begin working together on a settlement in mediation or collaborative divorce than they would if one spouse initiates the divorce. Where one spouse makes the decision to divorce, it is natural for the other to resist cooperating with any requests to move along in the process, including a request to mediate or collaborate. This usually changes with the passage of time, so factor timing into your assessment of your readiness. (See Chapter 5 for more on timing.)

Is breaking up hard to do? If you and your spouse are in the roles of leaver and leavee (see "Terms of Unendearment: the 'Leaver' and the 'Leavee'" in Chapter 1), expect weeks or even months to pass before negotiating anything but the most urgent matters. If you are the leaver, prepare to be patient, and let your spouse know you're willing to wait until he or she is ready. Check with a lawyer knowledgeable about mediation or collaboration to make sure essential matters that can't wait get handled in the meantime. (See Chapter 8.)

If you are the leavee, don't be afraid to ask for time to adjust to what's happening. Let your spouse know you're not ruling out the possibility of mediation or collaboration when the time comes. If you're having trouble making the emotional adjustment, consider getting help from a counselor. (See Chapter 8 for advice on finding a counselor.)

You Have No Desire to Reconcile

If you and your spouse have accepted (however reluctantly) the reality of your separation being permanent, and if neither one of you has an overwhelming desire to reconcile, then the odds are that each of you has reached a point in the emotional divorce (Chapter 1) when mediation or collaborative divorce can be productive. This doesn't mean you must rule out the possibility of reconciliation. But you do have to be ready to focus on what happens if you and your spouse don't get back together.

You cannot accept that it's over. If either your or your spouse cannot accept the end of your marriage and think constructively about making arrangements for your separate futures, it might be useful to spend some more time, either separately or together, and preferably with the help of a wise friend or counselor, resolving the question of whether or not your relationship is truly over. You and your spouse can still use mediation or collaboration as a way to negotiate a temporary agreement to stabilize your situation while you figure out the future of your relationship.

It Is Important That You Stay on Good Terms With Your Spouse

Spouses who want to remain on good terms with each other, either because they have children together or because of their own values, can use this motivation to get through the rough spots in negotiating and compromising during mediation. It is not essential to good mediation or collaboration, but it certainly helps.

If you don't care to stay on good terms. Check yourself to see whether you have a high level of animosity toward your spouse that could undermine mediation. If so, you might find it helpful to work with a counselor on ways to keep this animosity in check while you go ahead with mediation or collaboration. Another option is to find a mediator who will conduct some or all of the mediation in separate caucuses so that you don't have to deal directly with your partner. Remember that this approach can be expensive, however, as the mediator must repeat everything important that gets communicated in a separate session. There is also a risk that emphasizing separate sessions can make the mediation more adversarial by minimizing opportunities for you and your spouse to deal directly with each other. Still, mediation under these circumstances is almost always preferable to full-blown engagement in the legal system.

Joint Sessions vs. Separate Sessions

One good feature of both mediation and collaboration is that they give you and your spouse the chance to work directly with each other (with the support of your mediator or collaborative lawyers) to come up with an agreement that will work for both of you. This is especially important if you have children and want to continue to parent them in a coordinated way. The best way to work directly with each other is to proceed by way of joint sessions in which both you and your spouse – and the mediator or your collaborative attorneys – are present. In joint sessions you and your spouse can practice constructive ways to communicate and make decisions. Later on, you'll be able to draw on this experience.

Joint sessions (called "four-ways"), are an essential feature of collaborative divorce. You will have some separate meetings with your own collaborative lawyer – or other advisors – in between the four-ways, but the point of collaborating is to use face to face meetings to bridge differences. If the two of you can't be in the same room, even with your lawyers by your side, you can't take advantage of this feature of collaboration. You may still be able to hire collaborative attorneys to negotiate a settlement of your case. But if the negotiation takes place entirely in separate meetings, many of the benefits of collaborative divorce will be lost to you.

On the other hand , mediation may still be possible when joint sessions are out of the question—for example, one spouse agrees to mediate but refuses to be in the same room with the other, or there is current domestic violence in the relationship. If that is the case, you may choose to mediate in separate sessions (called caucuses). Caucusing can be more expensive than meeting jointly, because a lot of information imparted in caucuses must be repeated. For example, if you give the mediator information about your finances privately, the information can't be used in negotiating a settlement until it is repeated to your spouse. And if your spouse raises questions about the information, the mediator will have to go back to you to get the answers. This is much more time-consuming than having one conversation with all three of you present.

In addition, the fact that you and your spouse communicate and negotiate indirectly—through the mediator— means that you don't get the chance to practice better ways to deal with each other. In fact, mediating in caucuses can make it very easy to maintain an adversarial attitude toward your spouse. This can actually inhibit the development of a positive relationship as parents.

Nevertheless, mediating in caucuses, or using collaborative law without four-way meetings, is preferable to the ravages of all-out litigation. If meeting separately in caucuses is the only way you and your spouse will be able to use a nonadversarial process, then seriously consider the option.

You Don't Blame Your Spouse for Your Separation

It's natural at times to blame your spouse for things that went wrong in your marriage or for making the decision to divorce. But if you feel that your spouse is entirely, or almost entirely, to blame, you might find it hard to make an agreement in mediation that your spouse considers acceptable. And if you want your spouse to acknowledge and pay for his or her wrongdoing in some way, such as giving you the bulk of the marital property, mediation may not succeed, because your spouse may not be prepared to accept any blame, let alone pay for it in some tangible way. If your state's laws allow you to prove fault as a ground (reason) for the divorce, and you have the emotional and financial resources for it, maybe a contested divorce is the right approach for you.

 Mediation or collaboration can work even if you blame your spouse. If you gave yourself a low score on this but want to try mediation or collaborative divorce, you have several options:

- You can raise the issue of fault in a mediation session or four-way, and see whether your spouse will negotiate an agreement that compensates you. It's not likely, but depending on your relationship, it may be worth a try.
- You can work with a counselor on understanding your own role in your breakup and on forgiving your spouse for his or her part in it.
- You can make your feelings known in the mediation or four-way while acknowledging that you're willing to reach a settlement that won't be one-sided in your favor, but will take your spouse's interests into account, too.

Your Spouse Has Not Lied to You About Anything Important

If your spouse has lied to you in the relationship, you may need to take a close look at whether you can trust your spouse to be truthful and sincere during the mediation or collaboration.

 Lying once doesn't have to mean lying always. If your spouse has lied to you about an affair, you may be afraid to believe anything your spouse tells you, especially if you only recently discovered the deceit. But this doesn't necessarily mean that your spouse will lie about other crucial aspects of the relationship, such as finances and property. You might try asking a supportive friend or counselor to help you deal with the emotional betrayal separately, so that you can still work with your spouse on the financial and property issues in mediation or collaboration. Asking for verification of all the facts and figures—such as voluntary exchange of documents—is often part of the process.

If your spouse has lied to you about property or finances, you have a different problem. It might not be wise for you to rely on the voluntary exchange of information to find out the facts. You may want to consider ways to verify important facts independently. You may even need to ask a lawyer to conduct legal discovery of the facts and records to give you a complete financial picture before attempting to negotiate a settlement. It may also be important to work closely with your lawyer or financial adviser to develop settlement options that don't rely on your spouse to provide information in the future. For example, you may be better off being bought out of a joint investment than co-owning it with your spouse, or arranging a cash buyout of property instead of accepting a promise of future payments.

You Can Disagree With Your Spouse Without Saying or Doing Things You Later Regret

If this statement is true, you have the ability to stand up for yourself during a conflict with your spouse without losing control of your own behavior. You don't need to score a perfect 4 to have a good experience in mediation or collaboration. After all, helping you communicate

constructively about a problem you and your spouse disagree on is one of the main jobs of the mediator or collaborative lawyer. But if your emotional reactions to your spouse are so strong that even attempting this seems impossible, then mediation or collaboration may not be the right thing for you just now.

You may need a cooling-off period. If certain issues need to be discussed and decided immediately, ask to limit the discussions to those items, and negotiate a definite time to resume the mediation or collaboration after you've gotten over the worst upset. Read Chapter 12 for suggestions on improving communication. And try working with a counselor on ways to make your reactions to your spouse less volatile. (See Chapter 8.)

You Are in Good Physical and Mental Health

Mediation and collaboration are not always easy. They are structured negotiations that at times can be quite strenuous, emotionally and mentally. If your stamina is depleted by poor physical or mental health, mediation or collaboration could be counterproductive.

Talk to your treating doctor. Ask your doctor to assess your condition and its effect on your ability to engage in mediation or collaboration. If you have a short-term health problem, consider waiting to start mediation or collaboration until you return to good health. If your condition is chronic or long-term, your doctor may suggest ways to structure the mediation or collaboration so you can participate, such as limiting the length of each meeting, adjusting the physical environment (chairs, ventilation), meeting separately (caucusing), or having a support person accompany you to mediation sessions. (See Chapter 8.)

You Understand the Financial Situation

Financial issues are a big part of any divorce. In order to negotiate a good financial settlement, you need to understand the financial realities of your marriage. The mediation or collaboration process can help you get a better handle on your financial situation and the options presented by it, but the more you know to start with and the more comfortable you are talking about financial matters, the more confident you will be and the fewer surprises you'll encounter. Also, if you know very little about your joint finances and your spouse is very knowledgeable, you may feel at a disadvantage. Once you've begun a mediation or collaborative divorce, you can ask your mediator or collaborative lawyer to help you get the financial information you'll need to feel like you're on a level playing field with your spouse. But you can start this process even before mediation or collaboration begins.

 Educate yourself! If you gave yourself a low score on statement number 8, find out as much as you can about your finances before starting mediation or collaboration. Try putting together some of the information outlined in Chapter 9. If you're comfortable working with your spouse on this, try doing it together. This is good practice for mediation or collaboration. If you feel you lack financial expertise, try working with a friend who is good at these things or with a financial planner, an accountant, or some other professional adviser who can help you learn what you need to know to be comfortable talking and thinking about your financial future. (See Chapter 8.)

You Are Not Easily Intimidated by Your Spouse

In mediation or collaboration, you will speak for yourself and negotiate your own agreement. If you find yourself easily intimidated in your spouse's presence, speaking up may be hard for you. Practicing with the coaching and support of a mediator or collaborative lawyer (and possibly a collaborative coach as well), can help you get better at this (see Chapter 13), but you'll need a minimum level of self-confidence just to start the process.

 Ways to work in mediation or collaboration. If you are uncomfortable with the idea of talking to your spouse directly, even with a mediator or your collaborative attorney there, you may need to delay the process until you feel more comfortable. But there are several things you can do right away to foster the chances of success in when you do begin:

- Before you start mediation or collaboration, practice expressing what's important to you, with the help of a good friend or counselor.
- Look for a mediator who offers the option of separate caucuses, where you and your spouse each meet alone with the mediator. As we've noted earlier, this can increase the cost and

might perpetuate adversarial posturing. But these disadvantages may be outweighed by the benefits of being able to mediate at all.

- Consider working with a support person you can bring with you to mediation, at least at first. (See Chapter 8.)

Physical Violence Is Not an Issue in Your Relationship

If physical violence is part of your marriage, it may not be possible to keep the playing field level and tempers cool enough to negotiate an agreement directly in mediation or collaboration.

 Mediation or collaborative divorce often isn't appropriate in an abusive relationship. Attempt mediation or collaboration only after you and your spouse have at least begun to get a handle on the root causes of the violent behavior through counseling or support groups. Before you enter mediation or collaboration, ask about the availability of separate sessions. If the primary issue relates to the custody of your children or other parenting issues, seriously consider the structure and safety offered by separate sessions with a court-sponsored mediation program. (See Chapter 14.)

Alcohol or Drug Abuse Is Not an Issue in Your Relationship

An alcohol or drug problem can impair a person's ability to think clearly and make sensible decisions. It can also lead to out-of-control behavior. This can undermine the success of any negotiation, whether it is conducted between lawyers acting on behalf of absent clients or during mediation or collaboration.

 A recovery program is a must. Any alcohol or drug problem must be dealt with in an effective recovery program if you expect mediation or collaboration to be productive. Recovery experts say that the most effective programs depend on the active participation of the whole family, so contact a recovery counselor now if you haven't already done so. If you've already begun a recovery program, work with your counselor to arrange the details of the mediation or collaboration so it will succeed. This might mean adjusting the timing of the meetings, selecting a mediator or collaborative attorneys sensitive to recovery issues, including a recovery counselor in some of the sessions, or doing other things that adapt the process to your particular situation. You'll find that mediation or collaboration can even be an important part of the recovery process, because it gives you and your spouse an opportunity to rebuild self-esteem by making your own choices and being responsible for them.

(If You Have Children) Your Spouse Is a Good Parent

Mediation or collaborative divorce is usually considered one of the best ways for divorcing parents to negotiate agreements about their children. You can talk, parent to parent, about what is best for your children, rather than leaving the decisions up to strangers. Differences in parenting styles or the amount of time each of you spends with your children *can* be addressed in mediation. But if either you or your spouse believes the other is not capable of caring for the children, you may not be able to negotiate an acceptable custody arrangement until that issue is fully evaluated. This is especially true if the problem you are concerned about is so serious as to constitute child abuse.

 Use mediation or collaboration to agree to an evaluation. You and your spouse might be able to agree in mediation or collaboration to get a parenting evaluation done. For example, you could mutually select a child psychologist or custody investigator to evaluate each of you and make recommendations. You could agree in advance on how to split the cost of the evaluation and even to keep the results confidential.

⚠ Confidentiality and accusations of abuse. If one of you is accused of child abuse, you may not be able to keep the evaluation confidential. Most states require any allegation of child abuse to be reported to child welfare authorities. This is a time when competent legal advice is essential. (See Chapter 8.)

If your disagreement about parenting issues is so pervasive that you cannot agree about how to proceed, you may need to get things started through the court. Even so, you might be able to use mediation or collaborative divorce to negotiate an agreement after the evaluation phase is completed. In fact, you may be required by the laws of your state to attend mediation in a court-sponsored program before a judge will even hear your case. (See Chapter 14.)

It Takes Two to Tango

If your spouse was willing to take the test we have included above, be sure to share with him or her the comments and tips in "Facing the Music," above. If you had to guess at your spouse's responses to the test because you don't communicate well, *don't* try to tell your spouse what to do to get ready for mediation or collaboration. This will almost certainly backfire. The fact that communication between you is poor indicates a potential for overreactions. The last thing you need

is to turn your spouse off to the idea of mediation or collaborative divorce by being pushy. There may be another opportunity to get this information to your spouse in a way that will be better received when you propose mediation or collaboration. (See Chapter 5.) For now, be aware that a low score on the test for your spouse may mean putting up with some delays and adjustments.

This section has focused on things that can prevent you from having a satisfactory experience in mediation or collaboration. We've done this so that you can spot any big problems and take steps to fix them before you start. Don't be discouraged from giving mediation or collaborative divorce a whirl. The most important thing is your willingness to try. If it turns out that mediation or collaboration won't work, you'll have lost very little in time or money, compared to starting out with contested litigation. And if it does work, you will have saved much, much more than money and time.

Comparing Mediation and Collaborative Divorce

Once you've decided that a nonadversarial approach to settling your divorce is worth a try, you'll need to figure out whether to try mediation or collaboration. Mediation and collaborative divorce are "cousins" in the world of nonadversarial dispute resolution. They share many similarities, but they are also different. Each offers some distinct advantages and disadvantages. This section describes the features of each approach—and its pros and cons—so that you will have a basis for choosing the right place to start.

Key Features of Mediation

In mediation, you and your spouse hire a neutral person—the mediator—to help the two of you negotiate a settlement of your case. The mediator assists you, but does not have any power to decide what the settlement will be. Mediation is informal and flexible. It is up to the two of you and the mediator to decide what happens when. Many divorcing spouses use mediation without ever consulting a lawyer. Others use lawyers or other professionals to advise them in between mediation sessions or to review the settlement agreement. Still others hire lawyers or other professionals to accompany them to the mediation sessions. Mediation is almost always less time consuming and less expensive than contested litigation. For a more complete description of what typically happens in mediation, see Chapter 2.

To reiterate, these are the important features of mediation:

- Neutral person (mediator) helps you negotiate
- Mediator has no power to decide the case
- Informal

- Flexible
- No obligation to hire a lawyer or other adviser
- Efficient—less time consuming than litigation
- Inexpensive—compared to litigation

Key Features of Collaborative Divorce

In collaborative divorce, you and your spouse hire collaborative attorneys committed to settling the case without resorting to adversarial tactics and without using contested court proceedings. The four of you sign a "no court" agreement that requires the attorneys to withdraw from the case if the collaborative process ends without a settlement. Collaborative divorce involves separate meetings with your own lawyer and "four-way" meetings with your spouse and both attorneys. Like mediation, collaboration is informal and flexible. The four of you decide when and how to proceed, subject to any guidelines your attorneys may have agreed to if they are members of a local collaborative group. The attorneys may also recommend that you agree to hire other collaborative professionals— such as appraisers, tax or financial specialists, or child specialists—to assist with aspects of the case. Collaborative divorce is generally less time consuming than contested litigation. Even with the ongoing involvement of attorneys, collaborating is usually significantly less costly than a contested case. For a more complete description of what typically happens in a collaborative divorce, see Chapter 3.

Again, a recap of the important features of collaborative divorce:

- Spouses are represented by collaborative attorneys
- Spouses and attorneys sign "no court" agreement (attorneys must withdraw if case goes to court)
- Spouses and attorneys negotiate in "four-way" meetings
- Attorneys may recommend involving collaborative professionals
- Informal
- Flexible (subject to agreed local procedures)

More efficient than litigation

Less expensive than litigation

Mediation vs. Collaboration: Factors to Consider in Choosing the Right Approach

Neither mediation nor collaboration is necessarily going to be the best—or worst— choice in all cases. Some people will do better with one approach, while some are better served by the other. Some will do just fine with either. Which approach to use is determined by the unique circumstances of your case, your individual preferences, and the availability of good mediators or collaborative attorneys. Here are the most common factors that may influence your choice.

Factors Favoring Collaboration

Need or desire for separate legal representation

If you need the guidance of an attorney looking out for your interests every step of the way, you might find collaborative divorce a better option than mediation. For example, your case might involve some complicated legal or financial issues that you don't feel competent to negotiate. Or you may just be more comfortable with the idea of having a professional to confer with at every turn. In collaborative divorce, the two attorneys guide every aspect of the case, so this approach would address your need for representation throughout the process.

Power imbalance in your relationship

If there are long-standing dynamics in your relationship with your spouse that leave one or both of you feeling at a distinct disadvantage in conversations about difficult subjects, you might want the added insulation and structure provided by collaborative divorce. Having a good collaborative attorney at your elbow can sometimes give you more confidence in expressing what's important to you, even in the face of your spouse's disapproval. Or if you know you have a tendency to "take over" in conversations with your spouse, you might find it helpful to have a supportive attorney there to nudge you into respectful silence when necessary.

Downsides to Collaboration

The primary downside to collaboration is that if it doesn't work, your collaborative lawyer is required to withdraw, and you have to start all over with a new lawyer and possibly new experts and advisers. This means a lot of expense and delay while you get your new lawyer up to speed and retain new professionals. Some lawyers are critical of collaborative divorce for this reason.

In addition, some lawyers argue that collaborative law blurs the role of your attorney, who is expected to look for compromises and solutions acceptable to the other side while at the same time representing you and your interests. (See Collaboration: Captial "C" or Lower-case "c"? below). Of course, this criticism ignores the fact that if you have chosen to collaborate, *you* have decided that it is in your interests to find mutually acceptable solutions.

Another argument that can be made against collaboration as opposed to mediation is that because lawyers are more involved in the negotiating process than they generally are in mediation, you may be less likely to arrive at creative solutions—solutions that are outside what the law might prescribe (for example, trading payments for education or job-training now for a shorter period paying alimony in the future). One of the strengths of a nonadversarial process is that the law is only a guidepost, not a prescription, and you are free to decide what actually will work for you. The more lawyers are involved in the process, the argument goes, the less outside-the-box thinking will be applied.

Finally, as in the case of an unsuccessful mediation, there is some risk that a case can become very adversarial if collaboration fails, since at that point there can be a tendency to give up on ever reaching a reasonable settlement. A solution to this problem is to spend time developing an "exit plan" if it looks like collaboration is not working. (See Chapter 15). However, this may not always be possible.

Factors Favoring Mediation

Flexibility and control over the process

Mediation is potentially more flexible than collaboration. For starters, you only need three participants for mediation to take place: you, your spouse, and the mediator. There's nothing to stop you from adding other people to the process if and when you need them, but you're not required to have attorneys—and possibly other professionals—actively involved in the process.

Mediation is also likely to be more flexible than collaboration when it comes to the procedures you will follow. Most collaborative attorneys belong to a collaborative group comprising local attorneys and other professionals trained and experienced in handling collaborative

Collaboration: Captial "C" or Lowercase "c"?

Collaborative Law Is Controversial in the Legal Profession. Many lawyers and judges are enthusiastic about collaborative law. They see it as a potential benefit for divorcing couples—for all the reasons we discuss here. Others take a more critical view. They see collaboration as a potential danger for unwary couples. Their concerns are twofold.

First, critics of collaborative law point to the financial risk of having to start over with new lawyers if collaboration fails. They argue that this is unnecessary and unfair, especially to a spouse who has participated in the collaborative process. Proponents of collaborative law argue that the requirement of withdrawal is necessary to keep the attorneys—and the spouses—from threatening or even initiating litigation every time the negotiations hit a rough spot. They content that the risk of starting over is more than outweighed by the promise of a mutually satisfactory process and settlement.

Secondly, some lawyers feel that collaborative divorce blurs the role of the attorney, who is expected to be your advocate but also to work cooperatively with the attorney who is advocating for your spouse. Lawyers in the collaborative law community work together frequently, which can be an advantage or a disadvantage—they may know and trust each other, and be able to work out difficult issues in your case, but they also may be so comfortable with each other that they don't want to debate much, and instead propose compromises that you might not want to make. Collaborative attorneys counter that it is the attorney's job make sure that you look for options that work for everyone and that don't do anything against your own interests—collaboration does not mean capitulation.

Some lawyers are sympathetic to the idea of collaboration but are uncomfortable with the requirement to withdraw if the case goes to court or with the potential loyalty conflict between representing a client and belonging to a collaborative group. These lawyers have resolved this dilemma by offering to negotiate for their clients with a "collaborative approach." They oppose using a "no court" agreement that mandates withdrawal of the attorneys if the case doesn't settle. This approach is sometimes referred to as collaborative law with a lowercase "c," as distinct from what has come to be known as collaborative divorce or collaborative law (collaborative law with a capital "C"). If you decide to hire an attorney who offers a collaborative approach without the "no court" commitment— and if your spouse does the same— you may still reap the benefits of collaborating. Just be aware that your case may not look much like what we describe in this book.

cases. To ensure that the process will go smoothly in all cases, most collaborative groups have developed their own "protocols"—or rules—that will apply to cases handled by members of the group. This can be a good thing, because it minimizes the possibility of miscues between the professionals. But the trade-off is that you may have less input than you would like in how and when things happen in the case. This won't happen in mediation, where you work directly with the mediator on deciding both the process and the substance of your case.

Efficiency and cost savings

Mediation is potentially more efficient and cost-effective than collaboration. Just from a logistical standpoint, coordinating the calendars of four or more people, at least two of whom are busy professionals, is a time-consuming endeavor, one that can add to the cost of the process. In addition, the active participation of two attorneys, and possibly other professionals, makes the cost almost certain to be higher than a mediation in which the two spouses meet alone with the mediator, even if they consult with lawyers and other experts from time to time.

Confidentiality

At least one state (California) has laws in place to protect the confidentiality of statements made during a mediation. No such laws have yet been enacted to protect the confidentiality of

collaboration. You do share attorney-client confidentiality with your own collaborative lawyer, but the four-way meetings are not considered "confidential" settlement discussions, and the laws protecting settlement discussions are far from absolute. While you can—and should—sign a confidentiality agreement if you choose collaborative divorce, the enforceability of such an agreement may be subject to exceptions. If confidentiality is important to you, and if you are in a state with strong laws protecting mediation confidentiality, you might be better off mediating.

Downsides to Mediation

If you aren't able to reach a settlement through mediation, you may have to start over, and you will have "lost" the money you spent on the mediation process. In some cases, your consulting lawyer might not be a litigator, forcing you to start over with a new lawyer for the contested case that could be your next step. (If you are concerned that mediation might not work, you should ask your consulting lawyer whether he or she is willing to work with you on a contested case, so that you can be sure you hire someone who can go the distance with you.)

In addition, if mediation doesn't result in an agreement, there is a temptation to completely abandon the idea of coming to a mutually acceptable settlement. If so, your case could become highly contentious.

These downsides are fairly minimal, though, because the cost of mediation is generally so reasonable. Also, you may be able to shift over to a collaborative process or another nonadversarial process rather than going into all-out litigation. (See Chapter 15).

 The availability of competent mediators or collaborative attorneys is a factor in choosing your process.

Ideally, you will have access to well-trained, experienced mediators *and* collaborative attorneys in your area. If so, your choice of one approach over the other will be based on factors other than availability of qualified professionals. If the choices in your area are more limited, don't let the lack of availability of mediators or collaborative attorneys deter you. Both mediation and collaborative divorce are preferable to contested litigation in most instances. So if you locate a good mediator but can't find any attorneys practicing collaborative divorce, it may be worth giving mediation a try even if collaboration is your first choice. Conversely, if you would rather mediate, but can only find collaborative attorneys, give serious consideration to collaboration.

Mediated Collaborative Divorce: An Emerging Option

Using mediation to settle divorce cases began in the late 1970s as an alternative to adversarial litigation. More recently, collaborative divorce has developed as a middle ground between litigation and mediation—for divorcing spouses who want the comfort of attorneys to represent them in nonadversarial negotiations and for divorce attorneys who seek a better way to help their clients reach settlement. In theory, the collaborative attorneys replace the mediator in helping spouses negotiate a settlement. In practice, some spouses and attorneys are finding that there are times when a mediator can be very helpful in resolving a collaborative case. As a result, some collaborative attorneys are using a hybrid approach in which a mediator may be asked to facilitate the four-way meetings that are almost always a part of the collaborative process. Be sure to ask potential collaborative attorneys whether this is an option. Although the addition of a mediator can add another layer of expense, it can be money well spent if it leads to a mutually acceptable settlement.

Making Your Choice

Once you've read this far, you may have a good idea of which approach is right for you. If you're still unsure, try using the simple test outlined below.

STEP ONE: Assess Factors Favoring Collaboration

On a scale of 1 to 5, how important to you is each of the factors in this group? FOR EACH FACTOR, CIRCLE ONE

Less Important			More Important	
Need for separate legal representation				
1	2	3	4	5
Need to deal with a power imbalance in your relationship				
1	2	3	4	5
Desire for predetermined structure in the process				
1	2	3	4	5
Write down the total score in this group: _____				

STEP TWO: Assess Factors Favoring Mediation

On a scale of 1 to 5, how important to you is each of the factors in this group? FOR EACH FACTOR, CIRCLE ONE

Less Important			More Important	
Flexibility and control over the process				
1	2	3	4	5
Efficiency and cost savings				
1	2	3	4	5
Write down the total score in this group: _____				

STEP THREE: Weigh Your Scores From Each Group

Compare the scores from each group. Do the factors favoring collaboration outweigh mediation, or vice versa? If the scores are close, consider the following tiebreakers. (You may have to do a little research to get the answers to these questions. See Chapter 8 for help in researching your state's confidentiality laws and Chapters 6 and 7 for tips on finding mediators and collaborative attorneys.)

Is confidentiality a major concern, and if so, do your state laws provide added protection for mediation that is not available for collaboration? If your answer to this question is yes, score a point for mediation.

Are good mediators available in your area? If your answer to this question is yes, score a point for mediation.

Are good collaborative attorneys available in your area? If your answer to this question is yes, score a point for collaboration.

LAST STEP: Is That Your Final Answer?

Now close your eyes and do a "gut check." Do the results of this little test ring true for you? If so, you probably have your answer. If not, try to identify what it is about the numeric results of the test that seems off to you. It may be that you scored a factor too high or too low the first time. Eventually, you'll figure out where you belong, at least to start. And remember, if you guess wrong, it's never to late to make a course adjustment, if it turns out another approach is better. Chapter 11 shows you how to evaluate, early in the process, whether you've made the right decision.

Chapter 5

Proposing Mediation or Collaboration

I n this chapter, we discuss optimum times for proposing mediation or collaborative divorce and how to make the proposal (or have someone else make it for you) in a way that will work. Even though you've looked at your situation and you want to mediate or collaborate, you need to figure out how and when to get your spouse to agree.

Can you skip this chapter? If you and your spouse have already agreed to mediate or use a collaborative process, you can skip this chapter.

When to Propose Mediation or Collaborative Divorce

It's possible to suggest mediation or collaboration at any time before your divorce is finished. That said, it's true that there are some times during the course of your separation and divorce that may be better than others.

Think back to the discussion in Chapter 1 on the four divorces: emotional, social, financial, and legal. There are points in each of these divorces when your spouse may be more or less receptive to the idea of mediation or collaboration and more or less motivated to make it work.

Optimum Times in the Emotional Divorce

The emotional divorce goes through the stages of denial, bargaining, anger, sadness, and finally acceptance. As discussed in Chapter 1, hardly anybody goes through these stages in a completely linear fashion, but there are times when the feelings of one stage clearly predominate. It helps to be aware of where *you* are in the emotional process, but if you have reached the point where you want to try mediation or collaboration, your emotional state is not likely to be a barrier to beginning it. Your spouse's emotional state may be another story. Depending on where your spouse is in the process, you may find it more or less difficult to get your spouse's attention the first time you suggest mediation or collaborative divorce.

A proposal to mediate or collaborate made to someone in denial may not be well received. Your invitation may be ignored, or your spouse may agree to try the process and then not follow through. If this happens, make a note to try again after your spouse is over the initial shock of the separation.

You may have better luck if your spouse is in the bargaining stage. This tends to be a time when the reality of the situation has begun to sink in and before your spouse has developed any hard-line positions on the divorce issues.

Proceed with caution if your spouse is in the anger stage. If he or she seems incapable of having a civil conversation with you at this time, wait a little longer until the intense anger fades. On the other hand, the anger stage can be a surprisingly good time to bring up mediation or collaboration if your spouse is able to handle his or her angry feelings without acting inappropriately. Anger is often what propels a grieving spouse out of denial and bargaining, providing energy to move forward. Anger can help keep things going as long as it is channeled into constructive activities. At this stage, mediation or collaboration can be an excellent way to focus your angry spouse's energy.

Take Fran, who was introduced in Chapter 2. When her husband Robert told her he was leaving, her world turned upside down and she became, in her words, a basket case. She couldn't sleep, and she lost her appetite and found it difficult to concentrate. If someone had asked her at that point to sit down with Robert and negotiate a divorce agreement, she would have found the mere suggestion overwhelming. All she wanted was for things to be how they used to be. As the weeks and months went by, however, she began to adjust to the reality of her situation. With the help of a supportive counselor, she regained her self-esteem, and she began to allow herself to feel indignant about some of the ways Robert had treated her. She

discovered newfound energy for projects at home and at work. Although angry at Robert, she felt more capable of sticking up for herself in disagreements with him than she had in the beginning. So when he suggested mediation, she was willing to consider it.

During the sadness stage, as in the denial stage, there can be times of emotional paralysis or heightened sensitivity. This can make it difficult to get your spouse's attention; if you do, your offer to mediate or use collaborative lawyers could be misinterpreted and could set off a reaction of anger and distrust. You should be especially careful in communications with your spouse during this time. For Fran, the burst of energy that characterized her angry phase was followed by another low period in her grieving process, when she found herself acutely aware of the pain of losing the family life she and Robert had shared for so many years. She felt very vulnerable around Robert, and she hated the idea of breaking down in front of him. If he had waited until then to propose mediation, she might have angrily rejected the idea, just out of a reluctance to put herself in a new situation where she might fall apart. Fortunately, she and Robert had already begun mediation, and Fran felt comfortable enough with the mediator and the process to know that she could handle her feelings in the mediation sessions.

Sadness will give way to increasingly long times of acceptance, just as clouds give way to periods of clearing at the end of a storm. The road ahead can be seen more clearly during a period of acceptance, which makes it an excellent time to propose and begin mediation or a collaborative divorce process.

Optimum Times in the Social Divorce

The social divorce encompasses the changing relationships among you, your spouse, your family, and your community. One cannot generalize about personal relationships, so you will be the best judge of what time in this process may be the best time to propose mediation or collaboration.

For example, special days such as birthdays, anniversaries, or holidays, may be especially good times or especially bad times to bring up the divorce, including the idea of mediating or collaborating.

If a special day is already prompting painful memories and emotions in your spouse, you may want to wait for another time to bring up anything about the divorce. On the other hand, if the special day is likely to bring out feelings of forgiveness and generosity in your spouse, because of personal, cultural, or religious meanings attached to the day, then that may be a good occasion for suggesting mediation or collaboration, both of which put the focus on resolving your divorce amicably.

Visits from out-of-town friends or family can also present obstacles or opportunities. Some friends and family members may view your separation as adversarial. If you make your proposal to mediate or collaborate when they are around, they may urge your spouse to reject mediation in favor of the "protection" of hiring a strong legal advocate. Even collaborating with the help of a lawyer may seem too conciliatory to folks who view you as trying to take advantage of your spouse. Other friends or family members may be quite supportive of a cost-effective and nonadversarial settlement of divorce, and they may encourage your spouse to try mediation or collaboration. Paying attention to who has your spouse's ear can help you time your proposal for likely acceptance.

Optimum Times in the Financial Divorce

One of the main advantages of mediation is its relatively low cost. Collaborative divorce can be more expensive than mediation, but it is still much less costly than a contested case. From a financial standpoint, getting into mediation or collaboration before either of you has invested a lot of money in legal fees will keep the cost of your divorce at a minimum. Because the focus of the financial divorce is on how to divide up your limited resources, mediation—or if you need representation, collaborative divorce—is a logical choice for accomplishing this from the very beginning. There may be things going on in the emotional or social divorces that require you to hold off, but in general, the sooner the better when it comes to proposing mediation or collaboration during the progress of the financial divorce.

Optimum Times in the Contested Legal Divorce

People studying mediation have observed that there are times during a lawsuit—including divorce cases—when people are especially receptive to the idea of mediation. There is every reason to think this is true of collaboration too (although it is still new enough that not many studies on collaboration have been done).

The prospect of going to court can be emotionally and financially threatening. A mediation or collaboration proposal made before filing the legal papers to begin the actual divorce is often accepted, because it offers an inexpensive and less-threatening alternative to court. If the process results in a complete agreement, then the entire divorce case will be uncontested. And, even if only a partial agreement is reached in mediation or collaboration, that much of the divorce will be uncontested.

Even after a contested case is started, a proposal to mediate is more likely to be accepted if it is made *before* some legal procedure that is likely to be expensive or risky. Proposing collaboration after the case is underway can be trickier, because you and your spouse would in all likelihood need to switch to collaborative attorneys, unless the lawyer who has been representing you practices collaborative law too, or is at least supportive of collaborating. However, shifting to a collaborative approach—even if you keep the same attorneys—is still possible, if that is what you and your spouse both want and if your attorneys have experience in working collaboratively.

For example, if it is early in the case, you can suggest mediation or collaboration to work out a temporary support agreement before you and your spouse pay the lawyers to file the paperwork needed for a court order. Even after the papers are filed, your spouse may agree to mediation or collaborative divorce in order to avoid the stress and risk of going to a court hearing. In that instance, the lawyers could ask the judge to continue, or postpone, the hearing while you attempt to work out an agreement.

A stitch in time. Hido and Tashira separated on fairly good terms. They both realized that they had grown apart over the years. Their children were grown now, and divorce seemed like the right thing to do. Hido proposed that they divide their accumulated assets equally and get an uncontested divorce. He even offered to pay the legal fees. But Hido was outraged when Tashira asked for spousal support (alimony).

Tashira had heard about mediation and suggested it to Hido, but he would have none of it unless Tashira abandoned her request for spousal support. So Tashira hired a lawyer and filed for divorce, requesting temporary spousal support. When Hido received Tashira's papers, he hired his own lawyer to contest Tashira's request for spousal support.

After reviewing the case, Hido's lawyer advised him that the judge would probably order him to pay Tashira $1,200 per month as temporary spousal support plus Tashira's attorney fees of $2,500. Shortly before the hearing, Tashira's lawyer proposed mediation to Hido's lawyer. This time, Hido readily agreed.

During the discovery, or information-gathering, phase of the case, a good time to propose mediation is before answers to written questions, called interrogatories, are due or before you are asked to provide copies of certain documents. Another good time is before a spouse's deposition (oral testimony). These procedures tend to be very time-consuming, stressful, and expensive, so a more direct and inexpensive process like mediation or collaboration may suddenly appear more attractive.

Just before any mandatory court settlement conference is another good time to suggest mediation. By then, most or all of the necessary information about the case has been exchanged or obtained, and both sides are prepared to discuss settlement.

Settlement, Collaborative Style. Geri and Kyle both hire lawyers to handle their case. The lawyers file papers, exchange disclosures and conduct depositions and other "discovery" (formal procedures to get information from the opposing party). When the court sets the date for a trial, preceded by a mandatory settlement conference, Kyle's attorney tells him the attorney fees to prepare for and attend the mandatory conference and trial will be $25,000 or more, not counting Geri's attorney's fees, which Kyle might also have to pay. With Kyle's consent, his attorney, who also practices collaborative law, proposes to Geri's attorney that they schedule a collaborative four-way meeting before the settlement conference. Geri and her attorney agree. The case is settled at the four-way without the expense and anxiety entailed in gearing up for and attending a court-mandated settlement conference. Although a formal "no court" agreement is not signed in this case, since neither Geri nor Kyle want their attorneys to withdraw if the case doesn't settle, the attorneys are able to use a collaborative, nonadversarial approach to the settlement process.

If a mandatory settlement conference came and went without settlement, you can propose mediation or a collaborative approach as a last-ditch means of avoiding the risk and expense of a trial. As with the temporary orders stage, the lawyers can request a continuance of the settlement conference or the trial pending the outcome of mediation.

Finally, if your case seems stalled at any point, with no progress in sight, mediation or collaboration may be just the jump-start needed to get things moving in a positive direction.

Who Should Propose Mediation or Collaboration?

Ideally, you will be the one to propose mediation or collaborative divorce to your spouse. After all, the whole idea of mediation or collaboration is to work cooperatively with your spouse in settling your divorce, and you can get off to a good start by having a civil exchange about how to go about reaching a settlement. So, if you are on pretty good speaking terms with your spouse, plan to make the proposal yourself.

If You Want to Mediate. If you are already working with a lawyer, discuss with your lawyer whether to propose mediation directly to your spouse or

Using Bifurcation to Pave the Way

Bifurcation offers an exception to the general rule that mediation should be proposed before a legal procedure. The word "bifurcate" is a legal term for cutting a case into two parts—in this instance, separating the part of the divorce that ends the marriage from the part that settles property division, custody, and support. Many states allow spouses to obtain a bifurcated judgment of divorce once the legal waiting periods have expired, if settling the other issues is going to take longer.

If the emotional divorce seems at a standstill and is hanging you up from even talking about how to reach a settlement with your spouse, you may be able to nudge yourself and your spouse closer to an emotional resolution by going ahead with the divorce. Find out if bifurcation is possible in your state. A proposal to mediate or collaborate that your spouse would have rejected before the bifurcated divorce judgment may be received more favorably after the dust of the divorce has settled. But bifurcation can have some significant legal, financial, and tax implications, and it can backfire if proposed too soon. So, consider the angles carefully with the help of a good legal adviser before proposing bifurcation.

How Far You Are Into Litigation Can Affect Mediation or the Collaborative Process

Most of our descriptions of mediation or collaborative divorce refer to a process that begins before a legal case is underway. If you start mediation or collaboration during litigation, some of the things we've described in a typical mediation or collaboration may not occur. For example, you may have done a lot of legal discovery during the litigation, so information-gathering in mediation or collaboration won't take long. You may also have developed an idea of what your realistic chances are in court, which helps prepare you to negotiate. On the other hand, you and your spouse may have burned some bridges in making decisions that can't be undone. So, if you're entering mediation or collaboration midstream, prepare to be especially flexible, and don't be surprised if the whole process is quicker.

to have the lawyer do it. Some lawyers believe it is inappropriate for a client to communicate directly with the other spouse, especially if the other spouse also has a lawyer.

And, if you don't have a lawyer but your spouse does, you may find your efforts to contact your spouse rebuffed or ignored, if your spouse is being advised not to talk to you. In that case, you may have to communicate with your spouse's lawyer or hire a lawyer to make the mediation proposal for you.

If You Want to Use Collaborative Divorce. If you have already selected a collaborative lawyer, discuss with him or her whether to propose collaboration directly to your spouse or to have the lawyer do it. Some lawyers believe it is inappropriate for a client to communicate directly with the other spouse, especially if the other spouse also has a lawyer. If that is the case, your lawyer may want make the proposal directly to your spouse (if your spouse does not yet have an attorney) or to your spouse's attorney.

If you don't have a lawyer but your spouse does, you may find your efforts to contact your spouse rebuffed or ignored, if your spouse is being advised not to talk to you. In that case, you should hire a collaborative attorney to make the proposal for you.

If your relationship with your spouse is strained, but minimal communications are possible, you could let your spouse know in writing that you are interested in mediation or collaboration.

If you are proposing mediation, you can say in your letter that you've asked a mediator or mediation service to contact your spouse to explain the process from a neutral point of view. Mediation services are usually happy to have a staff member do this in a separate telephone conversation or face-to-face meeting. Many private mediators avoid advance meetings or telephone conversations with one party, because this could give an impression of lack of neutrality, but they usually have written material on mediation that they are willing to provide to you and your spouse.

If you are proposing collaboration, consider contacting a local collaborative group and finding out if a brochure on collaborative divorce is available to enclose with your letter.

If communications between you and your spouse have broken down to the point where anything you suggest is going to be met with a knee-jerk rejection, then you might be better off having someone else present the idea of mediation. Perhaps you can enlist the help of a trusted mutual friend or relative, or your family accountant or financial adviser. Counselors, spiritual advisers, and other people your spouse respects are also potential intermediaries. And if you and your spouse have already begun the legal process and are represented by lawyers, you can ask your lawyer to propose mediation or collaboration.

How to Propose Mediation or Collaborative Divorce

If you have decided to propose mediation or collaboration to your spouse, spend some time figuring out what you will say and how you will say it. Below are some suggestions, as well as some dos and don'ts to keep in mind. At the end of this chapter is a checklist of points to make about mediation when promoting the idea to your spouse or partner, along with a sample letter you can refer to if you decide to make your proposal in writing.

Consult your adviser first. If you are going to make the proposal yourself but are working with a lawyer or other adviser, find out if he or she has additional suggestions based on the knowledge of your particular circumstances.

Skip ahead if someone else will make the proposal. If the suggestion to mediate or collaborate will be made by your lawyer or other intermediary, that person will have his or her own ideas about how to make the proposal. In that case, you can skip the rest of this chapter.

Proposing Mediation Orally or in Writing

If you and your spouse communicate pretty well face to face or on the telephone, you may be able to make the suggestion to mediate or use collaborative law in an informal and nonthreatening way by just talking to your spouse about it.

If your spouse has a way of reacting negatively to your ideas and suggestions during conversations, or if you and your spouse aren't on speaking terms, then make the proposal in writing.

 Think about past communications. If you can't decide whether to talk to your spouse about mediation or write a letter, think about whether your communications so far have been mostly oral, mostly written, or a combination of both. If you and your spouse have been talking about things as you go along, your spouse might be alarmed or offended to suddenly get a letter from you. If your communications have been mostly in writing or even partly in writing, then a note from you probably won't set off any alarms and would give your spouse time to reflect and get advice from other people before responding.

Knowing What to Say

Whether you make the proposal in person, over the phone, or in writing, present mediation or collaborative divorce in a way that is neutral and nonthreatening. Provide your spouse with information about the mediation or collaboration process without making your spouse feel like he or she is being coerced or sold a bill of goods.

This is going to take some planning and practice. If you are proposing mediation, read Chapter 6 so you have a better idea of how to pick a mediator. If you can, talk to people who have experience with mediation. You may even want to contact potential mediators or mediation services to find out their charges and requirements.

If you are proposing collaborative divorce, and if you haven't picked a lawyer to represent you yet, read Chapter 7 so you'll have an idea of how you and your spouse should go about selecting attorneys.

If you propose mediation or collaboration in writing, consider writing a draft letter and having a trusted friend or adviser look it over before sending the final product to your spouse. (The checklists and sample letters at the end of this chapter can help.)

If you make the proposal in person or on the telephone, plan ahead what you will say, and write down some notes about it. Consider practicing with a friend to make sure you set the right tone and cover all the points you need to make. (The checklists at the end of this chapter have ideas on the points to cover.)

Offering Brochures and Other Materials

If you have brochures or other printed materials explaining mediation, consider giving them to your spouse to review. If you have more than one or two, you might want to pick out a couple of the best ones and let your spouse know you have more if she or he is interested. You could even offer to lend or give a copy of this book to your spouse. That way, both of you would be using the same frame of reference as you discuss whether, how, and with whom to mediate.

Proposing a Specific Mediator

Chapter 6 covers finding and selecting a mediator for your case. Depending on your circumstances, you may want to start that process before you suggest mediation to your spouse, or you may want to wait until your spouse can take an active role in the selection process.

If you are proposing mediation through a court-sponsored service, you may not have a choice about the specific mediator. (See Chapter 14.) In most other cases, it is a good idea to give your spouse a list of mediators, with information about their charges and procedures, and then let your spouse choose from the list. This gives your spouse the message that you are willing to share information and let your spouse have a say in what happens. That way, the mediation is more likely to start off on a cooperative note.

Should you contact the potential mediators in advance? The answer depends on whether your spouse will view this as an attempt on your part to sway the mediator to your side rather than a neutral request for general information. If you are in doubt about this, it might be best to avoid prior contact with the mediators you want to propose. As we discuss in Chapter 6, you can usually find out something about mediators in your area without speaking with them directly. Then you can tell your spouse what you've found out and assure your spouse that you haven't compromised the mediator's neutrality by making the initial contact.

If your spouse is likely to view with suspicion anyone you suggest, propose mediation in general terms and offer to consider a mediator suggested by your spouse. You can still check out potential mediators in the area so that you can make an informed decision on your spouse's suggestion, but you can avoid giving your spouse the feeling of being railroaded or dictated to.

Avoid Proposing Specific Collaborative Attorneys Unless Asked

If you are proposing collaborative divorce, and if neither you nor your spouse has retained an attorney, there's nothing wrong with giving your spouse a brochure or other information listing local attorneys with experience in collaborative practice. However, avoid suggesting particular attorneys for your spouse, unless your spouse specifically requests this.

Dos and Don'ts of Proposing Mediation or Collaboration

However you decide to go about proposing mediation or collaborative divorce, it is important to convey to your spouse your willingness to consider his or her point of view on whether, when, how, and with whom to start the process. This sets the stage for successful negotiations once you get started. Here are seven simple rules to remember:

- *Do* your homework. Find out about mediation or collaboration, how it works, what it costs, and who offers it in your area. Read Chapters 2, 3, 4, 6, 7, 9, and 10. Talk to people knowledgeable about mediation and collaboration.

- *Do* give neutral reasons to mediate or collaborate. Point out that mediation or collaboration is inexpensive for both of you and that it will help you come up with a fair and amicable settlement.

- *Do* offer to share information. Tell your spouse about this book. Offer to lend or buy your spouse a copy. Tell your spouse what you've learned about mediators or collaborative lawyers in your area. If you have brochures or other printed materials from potential mediators or collaborative professional groups, offer copies to your spouse.

- *Do* give your spouse choices. Demonstrate your willingness to be flexible from the beginning by asking your spouse's opinion about your proposal. If you are proposing mediation, ask your spouse to suggest a mediator with whom he or she would be comfortable or by giving your spouse a list of several mediators to choose from.

- *Don't* try a hard sell. Give your spouse a short summary of why you think using mediation or collaboration is a good idea, offer to share the information you have, and give your spouse the choice of mediators. Then back off and wait for your spouse's answer. Your spouse is more likely to participate fully in the mediation or collaboration if he or she doesn't feel pressured into doing it.

- *Don't* threaten or patronize. It's one thing to say that mediation or collaboration will cost less and be less acrimonious than litigation. It's quite another to say that you will take your spouse to court and leave him or her penniless if your offer to mediate or collaborate is turned down. Remember, mediation and collaborative law are voluntary. Show your spouse you understand this by avoiding ultimatums. And try not to sound like an expert on the subject when you share the information you've collected. Mediation—or collaboration—is a negotiation between equals. You don't want your spouse thinking you feel superior before you've even started.

- *Do* try again. If your spouse doesn't respond to your proposal, or if he or she turns you down, don't give up on the idea. Your spouse may need a reminder, or the time may not be quite right. Look for an opening and ask again. No matter how far along you are in the process of getting a divorce, mediating an agreement on the remaining issues— or settling them collaboratively— can save time and money.

Below are two lists. One lists things to say when proposing mediation, including points you can make about mediation that may convince your spouse to try it. The second is a similar list of points to make about collaborative divorce. Refer to the appropriate list when you talk to your spouse or when you sit down to write your letter proposing mediation or collaboration.

Concepts to Consider

A Guideline for Proposing Mediation

Points about mediation:

❑ Mediation is a private negotiation conducted with the assistance of a neutral third party called a mediator.

❑ Mediation is inexpensive compared to paying lawyers to do the negotiating or to fight in court.

❑ You and your spouse decide how fast or slow the mediation goes.

❑ Mediation allows you to settle your case fairly and amicably.

❑ To protect your rights, you can each have any agreement reached in mediation reviewed by your own lawyers before you sign it.

❑ Because mediation is voluntary, neither of you has to agree to anything you consider unacceptable, and either one of you can leave the mediation at any time.

❑ If a settlement is reached in mediation, the divorce will be uncontested.

❑ If you have children, mediation allows you to decide what's best for your children and protects your children from the trauma of a contested court case.

Information you can share:

❑ Give references, such as who told you about mediation—a trusted mutual friend or adviser, this book, or someone else.

❑ Encourage your spouse to check with your references—the mutual friend, or this book—or to do his or her own research.

❑ Summarize what you've found out about mediators in your area—names, fees, and procedures. (See Chapter 6 for hints on questions to ask potential mediators.)

❑ Offer copies of brochures and other printed materials about mediation.

Extending the invitation:

❑ State your willingness to negotiate a fair agreement in mediation.

❑ Ask your spouse to give mediation a try.

❑ Invite your spouse to choose a mediator or to join you in interviewing and selecting a mediator.

❑ Ask (don't demand) that your spouse let you know if he or she is interested, or has any questions, within a specific period of time. Unless your circumstances make getting started more urgent, two or three weeks is usually a good time frame. If you don't hear back by then, make a note to follow up when the time seems right.

Additional points of interest—aspects of mediation that may apply, depending on the laws of your state and other circumstances. You can mention them to your spouse as things to clarify with the mediator.

❑ Mediation is usually confidential, meaning what is said in mediation can't be used against either party in court. (See Chapter 10 for more on confidentiality.)

❑ Mediation is usually voluntary. In some states, however, you can be ordered to attend mediation, especially if you don't agree on custody of and visitation with your children. (See Chapter 14.)

A Guideline for Proposing Collaborative Divorce

Points about the collaborative process:

❏ Collaborative divorce (sometimes called collaborative law or collaborative practice) is a private negotiation in which divorcing spouses, their lawyers, and possibly other professionals work together—usually in "four-way" meetings—to reach a settlement without resorting to adversarial tactics or contested court procedures.

❏ Collaborative divorce is inexpensive compared to paying adversarial lawyers to take hard line positions or to fight in court.

❏ You, your spouse, and your collaborative attorneys decide the pace of the process.

❏ Using collaboration allows you to settle your case fairly and amicably.

❏ To protect your rights, you have a collaborating attorney by your side to advise you and to review any agreement before you sign it.

❏ Because collaborating is voluntary, neither of you has to agree to anything you consider unacceptable, and either one of you can end the process at any time (the attorneys must withdraw if collaborating ends without an agreement).

❏ If a settlement is reached in collaboration, the divorce will be uncontested.

❏ If you have children, collaborating allows you to decide what's best for your children and protects your children from the trauma of a contested court case.

Information you can share:

❏ Give references, such as who told you about collaborative divorce—a trusted mutual friend or adviser, this book, or someone else.

❏ Encourage your spouse to check with your references—the mutual friend, or this book—or to do his or her own research.

❏ Summarize what you've found out about collaborative divorce in your area—the name of a local collaborative group, fees, and procedures. (See Chapter 7 for hints on questions to ask potential collaborative lawyers.)

❏ Offer copies of brochures and other printed materials about collaborative divorce.

Extending the invitation:

❏ State your willingness to negotiate a fair agreement through the collaborative process.

❏ Ask your spouse to give collaboration a try.

❏ Invite your spouse to consult with advisers about using collaborative law.

❏ Ask (don't demand) that your spouse let you know if he or she is interested, or has any questions, within a specific period of time. Unless your circumstances make getting started more urgent, two or three weeks is usually a good time frame. If you don't hear back by then, make a note to follow up when the time seems right.

Sample Letter Proposing Mediation

When Robert decided to suggest mediation to his wife Fran, he had a feeling she'd respond better if he put his proposal in writing. Here is the letter he wrote.

Dear Fran,

I've been thinking about how we can get through this divorce without spending a lot of money we don't have on lawyers' fees and court costs. I also want to try to agree on a fair settlement without the bitter court fights we've seen some of our friends go through. I know that neither one of us wants to put the kids through an ugly court battle, either.

I ran into Charlie Walters a few weeks ago. He said his sister Anita and her husband are getting divorced, and they're doing it through a mediator. He said we really should consider it, too.

According to Charlie, you meet in private with a neutral mediator and negotiate an agreement that seems fair to both of you. Before we sign the agreement, we can have lawyers look it over to make sure our rights are protected. We would be paying only one mediator instead of hiring two lawyers to negotiate the agreement for us. Then we can use the agreement to get an uncontested divorce, which will save us a lot of money in court costs and lawyers' fees.

I've been reading a book called *Divorce Without Court*, which has a lot of good information about mediation. (The book also describes collaborative divorce, where people hire lawyers to help them negotiate a settlement, but I don't think we need the added expense of having lawyers there all the time — I think we can just consult lawyers when and if we need them.) I'd be happy to give you a copy if you're interested.

From what I've found out about mediation, I'd like to try it. Unfortunately, Anita and her husband are out of state so we can't use their mediator. But I've checked around, and it seems like there are a lot of good mediators in town for us to choose from. I haven't talked to any of them directly yet. I thought I'd wait and see if you're interested in the idea.

I did call the local community mediation service, and they sent me a brochure and information sheet. I'm enclosing copies for you. They charge a sign-up fee of $125, and then we pay a sliding scale between $100 and $275 for each two-hour session, depending on our family income. I think that it would work out to about $175 a session for us. They said it usually takes three to eight sessions, so we might be able do this for around $650 to $1,400. Their caseworker would meet with each of us first, and then they would assign us to one of their mediators. The only problem is that we don't get to choose the mediator assigned to our case, and they aren't lawyers, so the legal agreement would have to be done separately. But you might want to call them yourself and see what you think.

I think it might be better to use a private mediator. They charge more than the community service, but we could pick the person we want instead of having someone assigned to us. A lot of private mediators are also lawyers, so that would help us make sure the legal part gets done right. I'm enclosing a list of several mediators I've heard are good, along with their telephone numbers, so you can check them out.

I think we should probably get going on this pretty soon. I know we've both been putting off doing anything about the divorce, but it seems like it's time. Could you please let me know in the next couple of weeks if you're interested in mediation and whether you have some idea of who would be a good mediator? Hopefully we can find someone we both feel comfortable with.

Thanks,
Robert

Sample Letter Proposing Collaborative Divorce

Shawn and Tanya recently separated. Shawn's coworker, Abe, used collaboration to negotiate a settlement agreement. Abe tells Shawn about collaborative divorce and convinces Shawn that he and Tanya should try collaboration. Shawn sends Tanya the following email.

Tanya,

I know we've had a hard time talking lately so I'm sending you this email. You mentioned seeing a lawyer – I'm not sure where you're at with that, but here's an idea I'd like you consider. You remember Abe Johnston. He got divorced last year. He and his wife wanted to get a settlement without paying a ton of money to the lawyers and putting themselves and the kids through all that. So they did this thing called collaborative divorce.

They each had a lawyer, but they signed an agreement that they would all cooperate and stay out of court. If anyone tried to go to court, the lawyers couldn't take the case to court and they would have to start over with new lawyers. So they had these meetings called "four-ways" where Abe and his wife and the lawyers got together and cut through all the bs to come up with a fair settlement. I think they got advice from an accountant about some tax angles of the settlement. Sometimes they met just with the accountant, sometimes with all of them. Anyway, Abe's sold on it. He says he and his ex-wife Christie are still on good speaking terms, thanks to the way they handled their divorce. In fact, he said you can contact her if you want her take on how it went. Her email is cdef@ isp.xxx.

Abe says there's a group of lawyers in our county who have all been trained in collaborative divorce. His attorney and his ex's attorney are members of that group. He gave me a brochure that I'll send you. I also found a book describing collaborative divorce. It's called *Divorce Without Court*. It talks about mediation too, but I think you said you're more comfortable having an attorney represent you. That's why I was thinking collaborative divorce might be the way to go. Let me know if you want to borrow the book.

There's a list of collaborative lawyers in the brochure I'm sending. I haven't contacted any of them. If you're interested in talking to one of them, you can have first choice.

Think about it. I think it makes sense to stay out of court if we can. I want to be fair and I want you to feel like your rights are protected, so this seems like a good option. Plus it would be so much better for the kids if we can work something out.

I'm not in a big rush. Take your time. I know it's a big decision. Maybe you could get back to me in a few weeks. If that's a problem, just let me know.

Shawn

Chapter 6

Finding a Mediator

Let's assume that you've decided that mediation is the way you want to go. At some point, either before you propose mediation to your spouse or after the two of you have agreed to mediate, you will need to find a good mediator. Where do you begin?

In order to find the right mediator for you, you need to know the answers to these three questions:

- What makes someone qualified to mediate your case?
- How do you find mediators who are qualified to handle your case?
- How do you know when you've found the right mediator?

This chapter helps you answer the first two questions and gives you a start on answering the third. In Chapter 11, we'll help you answer the last question by suggesting ways to make sure that the mediator (and the process) you've picked is the right one for you.

Can you skip this chapter? If you've already selected a mediator with whom you are comfortable, or if you've decided to use a collaborative process instead of mediation, you can skip this chapter. Chapter 7 gives you advice on how to find a good collaborative attorney.

Do you have a lawyer? If you are working with a lawyer or other adviser, you might ask that person to help you find and select a mediator. In that case,

use this chapter as a general reference. Read the parts that are helpful, and skip any parts that don't seem to apply. (See Chapter 8 for more on working with a lawyer and other advisers.)

Shortcut to Finding the Right Mediator

The best way to find a good mediator is to ask people you trust—relatives, friends, colleagues, and professionals you know—to refer you to mediators who have the background and experience necessary to help you settle the issues in your case. A mediator whose name comes up again and again is probably the one you want. See how you feel about your initial contacts with the mediator and his or her staff. If your impression is positive, and if your spouse agrees, make an appointment. Use Chapter 11 to help you assess your experience at the first session, and you're on your way. You won't need to read anything else in this chapter.

Check for conflicts of interest. Ask the mediator whether he or she has a prior or existing relationship with your spouse. If so, find out whether the mediator thinks the relationship would compromise neutrality in your mediation. You can then decide whether you feel comfortable proceeding with this mediator.

Qualified Mediators: What to Look For

Mediation is more of an art than a science, so it can be hard to say just what makes a good mediator. Still, there are some traits that most good mediators possess.

Basic Qualifications

First and foremost, a good mediator is skilled at listening, communicating, and helping people work through their conflict to a satisfactory resolution.

In addition, a good mediator should be knowledgeable about the subject matter of your case. Most professional divorce mediators have a background in law or mental health—specifically, family and child psychology. Occasionally, you'll run across a mediator whose background is in finance and accounting. Sometimes you'll find a mediator with a background in more than one of these areas. You should work with a mediator whose background fits the issues to be negotiated in your mediation.

For example, if you need to settle issues regarding your children, choose a mediator who has expertise in handling child custody and support. If your concerns focus on financial matters, your mediator needs to have a background in property settlements to help you figure out the best options. If you will be negotiating a variety of issues, including property and parenting, your mediator should be conversant in all of them—or consider using two or more mediators. (This option is covered below.) For now, remember that the mediator must be able to understand and handle the kinds of issues you will be talking about.

Using a Lawyer-Mediator

As we have said, most divorce mediators have a background in law, mental health, or, occasionally, finance and accounting. Is it best to use a mediator who is also a lawyer, given that your goal is to negotiate a legally binding divorce agreement?

While the art of mediation doesn't depend on legal expertise, using a lawyer who is also a skilled mediator can save you from discovering unexpected legal complications at the end of the mediation. Here are some things to consider.

Advantages of Using a Lawyer-Mediator

Lawyers with experience in divorce law are familiar with all the legalities that go into making a divorce agreement complete and workable. Their knowledge usually extends to tax matters and other financial issues. They are well-versed in domestic relations law and are familiar with local court practices.

If you negotiate a settlement with the help of an experienced lawyer-mediator, your settlement will probably cover all the necessary legal issues.

A lawyer-mediator can also prepare the written divorce agreement to submit to the court in the uncontested divorce case that is the end result of a successful mediation. This saves the added expense and possible delays and misunderstandings that can occur if you have someone other than your mediator prepare the divorce agreement.

Disadvantages of Using a Lawyer-Mediator

There are a few possible disadvantages to using a lawyer-mediator. The person may be less sensitive to interpersonal issues that come up between you and your spouse, and less practiced in dealing with difficult dynamics between the two of you. (However, many lawyer-mediators are trained to deal with these dynamics—it's something to check out when you interview the mediator.) A lawyer-mediator may tend to push the negotiations in the direction of the standard legal outcome instead of being open to more creative options. And a lawyer-mediator may charge considerably more than a nonlawyer mediator.

Making the Decision

All things being equal, you're probably best off using a lawyer-mediator who can make sure you cover all the legal issues and who can write the divorce agreement for you. But if you are prepared to handle

the legal work some other way, if the financial and property issues in your case are not complicated, if dealing with the emotional issues between you and your spouse in the mediation is important, or if the main issues relate to child custody and other parenting concerns, you might benefit from working with a nonlawyer mediator who has a mental health background. Or, if your only issues are financial and you've found an experienced mediator who is a financial professional especially qualified to help with your issues, you may choose that person over a lawyer-mediator.

If you choose a nonlawyer mediator. Plan on working closely with a consulting lawyer who can make sure you're covering the legal bases as you go through mediation. (See Chapter 8.)

If you choose a lawyer-mediator, you can work separately with a counselor to help defuse volatile emotional interactions between you and your spouse as you go through mediation. And you can make sure special tax or financial questions are handled by consulting an accountant or financial adviser when necessary.

Some people solve the lawyer/non-lawyer dilemma by working with comediators—one lawyer and one nonlawyer. An obvious downside of this approach is that the cost can be steep, because you're paying two professionals instead of one. Some comediators discount their fees to compensate for this, and some couples feel the benefit of having two mediators justifies the additional cost.

In addition, comediation requires more coordination, and that could prolong the process, unless the comediators are experienced at working together.

If you're interested in using comediators, make sure the ones you consider charge fees you can afford and they have worked together before. We've addressed this concern in Worksheet 1—Questions for Potential Mediators, found in the appendix.

Professional Licensing

Although the idea of asking a third party to help settle a disagreement has been around for centuries, the profession of divorce mediation is still relatively new. Because of this, divorce mediators in most states are not subject to licensing requirements that set minimum levels of training or experience for mediators. But this is changing as state lawmakers become aware of the need for it.

From your standpoint, a license may give you some assurance that your case will be handled competently. So find out whether your state has a licensing law, and, if so, be sure to find out whether any mediator you consider has the necessary license.

To find out whether your state has a mediator licensing law, you can ask the mediator you are considering or ask your lawyer (if you have one). You can

also check with your local law library or public library reference librarian, local bar association, or state department of consumer affairs for the latest information. Or you can contact one of the professional mediation organizations listed at the end of this chapter for information about mediator licensing in your state.

Whether or not mediators are required to be licensed in your state, you can reasonably expect your mediator to hold a license in a related field, such as law, mental health, or accounting. Working with someone who calls himself or herself a professional but who has no license even in a related field means taking a big risk that the mediator won't adhere to minimum standards of competence and professionalism that a license imposes. Why take that chance if licensed professionals are available?

Adherence to Voluntary Standards of Conduct

Some national and local mediation organizations have developed voluntary standards of professional conduct for mediators. These cover issues like confidentiality, conflicts of interest, and maintaining neutrality. Regardless of whether your state has licensing requirements, you can ask whether a potential mediator is familiar with or subscribes to any voluntary standards for mediators. We address this topic in

Worksheet 1—Questions for Potential Mediators, found in the appendix.

Training in Mediation Techniques

Training in mediation techniques is widely available. The typical introductory training program consists of 35 to 40 course hours, so this should be the absolute minimum amount of mediation training your mediator has completed, unless he or she has many years of experience to make up for the lack of formal training. At least some of the training should be geared specifically to divorce mediation. Questions about training are included in Worksheet 1— Questions for Potential Mediators, found in the appendix.

If the mediator completed the initial mediation training more than a year before your interview, ask about continuing education. Ordinarily, you should expect a mediator to have completed five to ten additional hours of continuing education within the last year. Again, some of these hours should be devoted to divorce issues.

Mediation Experience

In addition to inquiring about a potential mediator's training, find out the extent of his or her experience in conducting actual mediations. There may be reasons to choose a less-experienced mediator over a more-experienced one, such as cost, availability, or special expertise. Special circumstances aside, however, an experienced mediator is more likely to know how to smooth out what can be a bumpy road through the mediation process.

It is also important to find out how much of a mediator's experience has been devoted to divorces, because mediating divorces is quite different from mediating other kinds of disputes. A good rule to go by is that at least 50% of the mediator's recent caseload should be divorces.

When considering a mediator's experience, look at both the number of years of experience and the average number of active cases mediated. For example, a mediator who has been mediating 30 divorce cases a year for three years has more depth of experience than someone who has been mediating five divorce cases a year for five years. Another way to gauge the mediator's caseload is to look at the number of sessions per month. An average case might require five to six sessions, so ten cases a year would mean an average caseload of four or five sessions per month, and so forth.

The mediator's experience should be recent. Mediation skills get rusty without practice, so look for someone who has been actively engaged in mediating divorces within the last six months to one year.

How much experience is enough? There is no precise answer to this question. But unless your case is so simple that you're willing to take a chance on a beginner, you probably want someone who has been mediating for at least one year at the rate of at least ten divorce cases a year (four to five sessions per month).

If you find a mediator whose background matches your needs, does it matter whether that person focuses exclusively on mediation or offers mediation services in addition to continuing work in another field? Probably not. As long as a potential mediator conducts a reasonable number of divorce mediations on a regular basis and is qualified in other ways, it shouldn't matter whether you use a part-time or full-time mediator.

Reputation

As we said above, the single most effective way to know whether a potential mediator will do a good job for you is to talk to people who are familiar with the mediator's work and reputation: your friends and acquaintances, or professionals or counselors who have worked with the mediator. (Because of confidentiality, the mediator may not be able to give you names of former clients as references to talk to, but you can ask if anyone has given permission for this.) The more often a mediator's name comes up in positive comments about his or her skill, ethics, and experience in divorce

mediation, the more likely it is that this reputation is well-deserved, especially if the comments come from a variety of unrelated sources.

Finding the Right Fit

Determining a mediator's basic qualifications may not be enough. You also need to consider whether there is anything unique about your case or your mediator that would make a particular mediator the right (or wrong) choice for you.

First, find out whether anything in the mediator's background would compromise his or her neutrality in working with you and your spouse. Next, look at your situation and see whether you need a mediator with special skills or expertise or whether other circumstances might mean selecting a particular mediator.

Neutrality

To be effective, a mediator must be neutral. She or he must not have any preexisting relationship with either or both of you that would create a conflict of interest. Furthermore, the mediator should conduct the mediation without taking sides. You'll get an idea of how a mediator avoids taking sides once you spend time in a session with the mediator. Meanwhile, you can find out ahead of time whether the mediator has a conflict of interest.

When you call to make an appointment, ask whether the mediator has any prior or current relationship with either you or your spouse that could be viewed as a conflict of interest. Most mediators keep records that allow them to check for conflicts of interest, and they will be happy to tell you.

Even if one or both of you have a connection with the mediator, you may decide to go ahead with the mediation after discussing it with your spouse and the mediator. Sometimes a mediator who knows one or both of you can actually do a better job for you than someone who doesn't know you at all. The key is that no one—you, your spouse, or the mediator—should feel that the preexisting relationship will impair the mediator's neutrality.

Special Skills or Expertise

In addition to verifying the mediator's neutrality, consider whether your case has any of the following characteristics:

- You and your spouse disagree on one major issue (such as child custody, a complex tax question, or a special business or real estate matter) that requires specialized knowledge to understand. You agree on all other issues.
- You and your spouse need help settling a variety of issues, including some that require special expertise.

- There is a significant power imbalance between you and your spouse; one of you tends to be easily intimidated or overwhelmed by the other.
- There have been incidents of domestic violence in your relationship.
- You or your spouse has a substance abuse history or is in a recovery program that needs to be supported during the mediation.
- You have cultural or religious concerns or other unique circumstances.

If your case falls into one or more of the categories described above, you may want a mediator with experience dealing with situations like yours. Before you decide whether that's necessary, let's examine each of these situations more closely.

One-Issue Cases

If there is really only one bone of contention between you and your spouse, you might choose a mediator with experience dealing with that kind of issue.

Disagreements about children. The most common single-issue cases involve disputes over child custody or other issues concerning the children. Spouses often can resolve their financial issues without much difficulty but have a hard time agreeing on what's best for their children. If this is true for you, you might be able to resolve these questions

Help in Making Decisions About Your Children

If you and your spouse are having trouble making or keeping agreements about child custody and time-sharing, there are a few things you can try that might get you back on track.

First: Do some reading up on child custody and time-sharing. You'll find that you are not alone in having trouble sorting through the decisions that need to be made and that there are ways to prioritize and resolve your differences with your spouse if you focus on the important things your children need.

Mom's House, Dad's House: Making Two Homes for Your Child, Revised Edition, by Isolina Ricci, Ph.D. (Simon and Schuster), is a comprehensive guide for divorcing parents. *Helping Your Kids Cope With Divorce the Sandcastles Way,* by M. Gary Neuman, L.M.H.C., with Patricia Romanowski (Random House), offers practical suggestions based on the author's experience running programs for children of divorcing families. Another helpful book is *The Good Divorce: Keeping Your Family Together When Your Marriage Comes Apart,* by Constance Ahrons, Ph.D. (Harper Collins).

Second: Enroll in a class for divorcing parents. You can do this together if your spouse is willing, but even if your spouse won't go, you'll find it helpful to attend on your own. These classes are offered in many communities. Some are sponsored by the court; others are offered by private agencies or groups. To find out whether such a class is offered in your area, check with the local divorce court, bar association, or community counseling or mediation center, or some of the other referral sources we've listed at the end of this chapter. If a class isn't an option, consider consulting a parent education specialist such as a marriage and family counselor. Again, it's best to do this together with your spouse, but even going on your own will help. (See Chapter 8.)

Third: Spend some time reflecting and organizing your thoughts about what's best for your children. If possible, coordinate this with your spouse. Use the workbook *Building a Parenting Agreement That Works: How to Put Your Kids First When Your Marriage Doesn't Last,* by Mimi Lyster (Nolo), to help you organize your thoughts, or try the exercises in Worksheet 7—Exercise: Assessing Your Children's Needs, found in the appendix.

After you've gone through these three steps, try sitting down again with your spouse to talk about time-sharing and custody. Chances are the communications will go much more smoothly once you've both spent some time learning more about what children in general, and your children in particular, need in this situation.

yourselves with a little help. (See "Help in Making Decisions About Your Children," above.) If that won't work, you might want a divorce mediator with special training and experience in child development and custody matters.

Complex tax or legal issues. If the only real issue in your case involves unusual or complex tax or legal matters, you might be best off with a mediator who has expertise in that area. For example, if you are involved in a dispute with the IRS over liability for back taxes, and the major issue in your divorce is how to deal with the potential liability, consider a mediator who has special tax expertise. Or perhaps you or your spouse is considering filing for bankruptcy. You may want a mediator who understands the intricacies of both bankruptcy and divorce law.

Unique property issues. Sometimes, the main disagreement is over a specialized asset, such as a certain kind of business, unique commercial real estate, or international property or investments. If this seems familiar, ask yourself whether your situation is so specialized that someone with general knowledge would have a hard time understanding it. If your answer is "yes," then look for a mediator who has the specialized expertise you need in addition to the general qualifications you want.

What if you can't find a qualified mediator who also has the special expertise you're looking for? (This is quite possible, given that mediation as

a professional discipline is still relatively new.) If you are in this situation, it's probably best to select a qualified general purpose divorce mediator and then ask the mediator to include nonmediator specialists in the process as needed.

Multi-Issue Cases

In most divorce cases there's a variety of issues that need to be addressed. For example, many divorcing spouses need help in negotiating about children *and* property *and* child support or alimony *and* related tax issues. If that's your situation, look for a mediator who is generally qualified in divorce mediation, rather than a specialist.

A good divorce mediator should have some experience in all financial and nonfinancial issues that commonly arise in a divorce. Ideally, this includes a basic familiarity with financial and legal documents such as deeds, appraisals, account statements, and tax returns. The mediator will help you assess when and if it is necessary to consult with an expert in a particular field. The consultant works with you and the mediator to help develop any information that might be needed in order to negotiate a satisfactory agreement about the issue. For example, you and your spouse might decide to have a neutral accountant study the possible tax consequences of selling or dividing certain real estate so that you will be able to choose what works best for you.

Significant Power Imbalance

If you or your spouse feels intimidated by the other or feels overwhelmed in interactions between you, there's a chance you need more time for healing and strengthening after the trauma of the separation before beginning mediation. (See Chapter 4.) If you think you're ready for mediation, but you're concerned that the patterns of communication between you and your spouse create an ongoing power imbalance, consider a mediator who has a reputation for being able to deal effectively with such situations.

When seeking referrals, ask about potential mediators who have experience with situations like yours. If you get conflicting information about potential mediators on this point, or if your referral sources can't address this question, don't worry. Once you've got a list of qualified potential mediators and make an appointment with at least one of them, you'll have a chance to see how things actually go in a mediation session. If you don't find the first session helpful in addressing the power imbalance, you can try a different mediator before making your final selection. (See Chapters 10 and 11.)

How to deal with power imbalances in mediation, especially between men and women, is the subject of ongoing debate among mediators and critics of mediation. If you want to read more about this, see Chapter 17.

Domestic Violence

If interactions between you and your spouse have included pushing, shoving, hitting, or other physically aggressive behavior, you need to think very carefully about whether and under what circumstances you should be mediating your divorce. As we discuss in Chapter 4, do not consider mediating in this situation unless both you and your spouse have moved beyond the violence and are involved in ongoing counseling that can help support you through the process.

If you are in counseling and can interact without the threat of physical aggression, then you might be able to mediate. Be sure to find a mediator who is experienced in working with couples who have a history of domestic violence. The term "domestic violence" can include the whole spectrum of aggressive acts, from threats of chronic battering to violence to occasional shoving. Inform the mediator ahead of time about your particular circumstances.

Depending on the severity of the abuse, you may need to make arrangements for separate meetings with the mediator, or you might include a friend or advocate for one or both of you in the mediation. In some cases, you may even need to have the mediation take place in a facility that has security personnel available. Court-sponsored mediation services almost always have this feature available. (See Chapter 14.)

If you still have questions about whether and how to mediate because of violent incidents in your relationship, you may want to take a look at our more detailed discussion of this subject. (See Chapter 4.)

Substance Abuse or Recovery

If problems with alcohol or drugs have been an issue in your relationship, it may be difficult to mediate unless the problems are being addressed in an ongoing program of recovery that both you and your spouse actively support. Without an effective recovery program in place, you may find that your efforts to mediate will be met with active or passive resistance and that the person with substance abuse issues won't follow through on the agreements you make.

If you do have a good recovery program in place, then look for a mediator who is familiar with, and experienced in, dealing with people in recovery. And be sure to inform the mediator of your situation so that what you do in mediation will be congruent with the recovery effort.

Other Special Circumstances

Other unique circumstances might influence your choice of a mediator. We discuss some of the most obvious ones in this section, and include a space to note your particular concerns in Worksheet 1—Questions for Potential Mediators, found in the appendix.

As we've said about other special criteria, make sure your mediator has the basic qualifications for a divorce mediator in addition to any special qualifications you want to add. If you can't find someone who fits the bill, go with a qualified divorce mediator who can help you address your special concerns by using a consultant or comediator, or by adapting the process in some other way that works for you.

Cultural or Religious Concerns

You or your spouse may consider it important to work with a mediator who understands your cultural norms and values. Or you may want to find a mediator who will support your religious values. Or perhaps you and your spouse have very different cultural or religious backgrounds and you need a mediator who is experienced in mediating between people with cultural or religious differences. If you want to make sure your mediator has this kind of background, ask ahead of time.

Same-Sex Relationships

Mediation works just as well in dissolving nonmarital same-sex relationships as it does in dissolving traditional marriages—but if you are dissolving a same-sex relationship, you will want to make sure you find a mediator with background in that area. Even in states where same-sex couples can marry or enter into marriage-like relationships, ending a same-sex relationship can involve special laws and court procedures. Traditional marital attorney-mediators can certainly mediate these cases, but do make sure you find someone who has experience with the special issues involved for same-sex couples. Chapter 18 has more about this.

For more on the legalities of same-sex relationships, check out *A Legal Guide for Lesbian & Gay Couples,* by Hayden Curry, Denis Clifford, and Frederick Hertz (Nolo).

Long-Distance Mediation

What happens if you and your partner don't live in the same geographic location? Can one or both of you telecommute to mediation sessions?

Most mediators believe that a successful mediation depends on good communication between the mediator and the partners. Mediators depend on the nonverbal cues and body language of face-to-face encounters to help them establish good communications with you. So your mediator may be reluctant to conduct telephonic mediation, especially at the beginning stage.

Recognizing the realities of our mobile society, however, some mediators offer teleconference mediation services or Web-based real-time mediation. Another approach is email, with which some mediators are experimenting. Some mediators also consider videoconferencing as a way to solve the long-distance dilemma. It allows the mediator

and each spouse to use visual cues to enhance the spoken word. As this technology becomes more widely available and affordable, it is likely that more mediators will offer this option to spouses separated by great distances.

Some mediators require in-person attendance at first but consider such things as teleconferencing during later stages of the mediation, after the relationships between each of you and the mediator are well-established.

If you find yourself physically distant from your spouse, it won't hurt to ask whether the mediator offers an alternative to in-person attendance at mediation sessions.

Special Needs

Perhaps some other circumstance makes it important to find a mediator with a particular background or mediation format. An obvious example is language proficiency. If you or your spouse is uncomfortable speaking English, you'd probably prefer to find a mediator who speaks your language of choice or who offers translation services. Or if one of you uses a wheelchair, you need a mediator who can provide an accessible meeting place.

If you are ending a same-sex relationship, you'll need a mediator who has experience in helping same-sex or unmarried couples mediate. (See Chapter 18 for more on how to find the right mediator for that type of case.)

These are just a few examples of special circumstances that might warrant trying to find a mediator with certain skills, background, or resources. Be sure to ask about the mediator's ability to meet your criteria when you are doing your search.

Who Provides Mediation Services

Mediation services can be obtained from several different sources.

Mediation Agencies

Depending on your community, you may have the option of mediating your divorce through a local mediation agency or center.

Community mediation agencies usually offer mediation services for many different kinds of disputes, such as landlord-tenant problems, neighborhood issues, business disputes, and other general community problems, as well as divorces. They often, but not always, rely on volunteers to conduct the mediation. Each agency has its own criteria for qualifying and training volunteers or paid staff who mediate for them.

Volunteer mediators come from a variety of backgrounds. Some are newly trained mediators who want to gain experience in a structured setting before going into private practice; some are professional mediators who agree to conduct some mediations pro bono (for free or for a greatly reduced fee); some are individuals who believe mediating is a good way for them to serve their community. If the agency has affiliations with a law school or university, the mediators may include student interns. Because of this, you'll want to ask carefully about the qualifying criteria used by the agency as well as the qualifications of the individual mediator(s) to be assigned to your case.

Mediation agencies often arrange for an initial in-person or telephone interview with each spouse to take down basic information about the case and answer questions about the mediation process. The actual mediation might be conducted by a single mediator or by comediators. The comediation approach—two or more mediators working together on one case—is frequently used by agencies to train new mediators and student interns—this allows the less-experienced mediator to practice under the supervision of a more-experienced mediator. This can be okay, if the supervising mediator is well-qualified and also experienced at supervising new mediators, but find out about this ahead of time.

Some mediation agencies offer you a choice of mediators, but many do not. Be sure to ask.

Many mediation agencies receive public or private funding, so their fees may be lower than the fees charged by private mediators. (See "Private Practice Mediation," below.) Some agencies offer sliding-scale fees. Some agencies charge a one-time setup fee, while others offer the initial meeting at no charge.

When you mediate through an agency, the agency may limit the amount of time or number of sessions devoted to your case. If so, you might decide to use a private practice mediator who is available to spend more time working with you and your spouse if necessary.

Mediation agencies offer little law. Many mediation agencies rely on nonlawyer mediators and don't allow the mediators to discuss the law, because they believe this would amount to giving legal advice without a license. As with a private practice mediator who isn't a lawyer, this means you'll have to get your understanding of the law from an outside resource such as a consulting attorney or your own research. For these reasons, you may be better off with a lawyer-mediator who can help make sure that you end up with a legally binding agreement. As we explain in Chapter 2, and Chapter 10, omitting any consideration of the legal rules can be a real disadvantage in trying to come up with an agreement that is comprehensive, fair, and balanced. Even though the law is not always precise, you will want to use your judgment about what should happen in your case. The law gives you and your spouse certain legal rights based on what lawmakers in your state consider fair and just. A mediator who omits any consideration of the law from the negotiations doesn't give you a chance to weigh the legally defined options against the other alternatives before agreeing to give up something to which you would be legally entitled. So your best bet is to use a mediator who will discuss the law but who won't get hung up on the law when it comes to helping you figure out what's fair.

If you're interested in exploring the option of using a mediation agency or center, find out whether there is one in your area. Check out how they work, who their mediators are, and what they charge. Worksheet 1—Questions for Potential Mediators, includes a set of questions to ask about mediation agencies. Worksheet 1 is in the appendix.

Web-Based Mediation Services

For most divorces, in-person meetings with a mediator and your spouse will be the most effective way to reach a settlement. Although Web-based mediation services are emerging as a tool for settling commercial cases, they usually focus on the amount of money that will change hands, and may not be appropriate for most marital mediations. If you are interested in exploring Web-based negotiation, make sure that any service you consider using provides live mediators for real-time Web meetings, and not just formulas for entering numbers and coming to a compromise.

Court-Sponsored Mediation

Another choice you might have is court-sponsored mediation. Divorce courts in most states offer some mediation services. In most states, the service is limited to issues involving custody and visitation of minor children. A few states offer mediation for the financial issues, too. Some state courts charge a fee; others provide the service for free; still others provide referrals to a panel of approved mediators providing reduced-fee services for a specified number of sessions, with the option to continue longer at a higher rate. In many states, there has to be a court case filed before you can use the mediation service. Mediation for disputed child custody issues is mandated by law in some states.

Because of its close connection to the court system, court-sponsored mediation is an option to consider carefully before choosing it. What you say and do in a court-sponsored mediation could affect your court case if you can't reach an agreement, because many court mediators must report the results of their mediations to the court. Before agreeing to use court-sponsored mediation services, read Chapter 14.

Private Practice Mediation

Your third option is to use a mediator in private practice. As the idea of using divorce mediation has gained acceptance, more and more professionals from a variety of backgrounds offer their services as mediators. Depending on the issues in your case, you can select a mediator, or even a team of mediators (comediators), whose background and training are best suited to help you with the decisions that need to be made. Scheduling meeting times that are convenient for you and your spouse may also be easier with a private mediator than one from an agency or the court system, and you can take whatever time or number of sessions you need to reach a complete agreement.

Fees for private practice mediators will vary, depending on the experience, training, and reputation of the mediator.

Retired Judges and Mediation

Some judges who have retired from sitting on the bench offer their services as private mediators. Usually they work through an agency such as the American Arbitration Association. Occasionally they are in private practice.

A retired judge can be very knowledgeable about the legal rules and outcomes and may be able to draw on a wealth of experience from years on the bench. But being a judge who decides things for people doesn't necessarily teach a person how to be a mediator who helps people make their own decisions. Additionally, retired judges often charge higher fees than other mediators. But if you want the atmosphere of authority that a retired judge can provide, and if you can afford the fees, this might be an option to consider.

Market conditions and the cost of living in your community can also affect mediators' fees. For example, in some areas of the country, fees may range from a low of $20 or $30 per hour to $150 per hour or more. In other places, the range may start at $150 per hour or more and go up from there.

Most private mediators charge by the hour for mediation services. Others charge a flat rate for each session. Some offer the first session at no charge or for a reduced fee.

Lawyer-mediators usually write up the divorce agreement, either for a flat rate or for an hourly fee. If the mediator writes up a settlement memorandum instead of the actual divorce agreement, the fee may be included in the per-session fee, or it may be a separate charge.

If you are considering using comediators, find out how the fees are billed as well as the qualifications and experience of the comediators.

The best way to get an idea of the range of fees and pricing options in your area is to ask about fees when you are discussing mediation with friends and other referral sources and when you are screening potential mediators. We include specific questions about fees in Worksheet 1—Questions for Potential Mediators, found in the appendix.

Making a List of Potential Mediators

We've said it before but it bears repeating: The single best source of names of good mediators is personal referrals. Folks who have successfully mediated their divorces may be more than happy to recommend their mediator. Other professionals, such as lawyers, accountants, and counselors, may be able to refer you to mediators who have worked well with their clients. Once you start asking, you are likely to get at least a few names to put on your list. You may even find a certain name

What Price Justice?

When you first start looking into fees charged by mediators in your area, you may experience a touch of sticker shock at the hourly rates being quoted. Most qualified mediators are professionals who will charge a substantial fee for their services. But when you consider how much you would be spending on lawyers' fees and other court costs if you used the court to resolve your disputes, you will most likely see that mediation is still quite a bargain. For a quick take on how mediation compares with litigation in terms of the potential cost, revisit the Robert and Fran divorce in Chapter 2.

Divorce can be expensive, even if you mediate, but mediation gives you a much better chance to keep the cost to a minimum.

coming up again and again, which can be a good indicator of that mediator's ability.

If your search for personal referrals comes up short or you want to expand your list, many local, regional, and national organizations may be able to provide you with additional names of mediators in your area. We provide a suggested list of organizations at the end of this chapter, including contact information for national organizations.

Checking It Twice: Screening and Interviewing Potential Mediators

Once you have a list of potential mediators, find out as much as you can about them before narrowing down your choice to two or three to seriously consider.

If you and your spouse are coordinating your search for a mediator, arrange to share and compare your lists so you don't duplicate your efforts. Then agree on who will contact which mediators, unless you decide to both contact each mediator and compare notes.

Once you've figured out who you will contact—or if you are not coordinating the search with your spouse—find Worksheet 1 in the appendix and make enough copies so you have one for each mediator or agency you plan to contact.

Write down the name and address of each mediator or agency on a copy of Worksheet 1, along with where you got the mediator or agency's name and anything else you know about the mediator at this point. Then decide whether your first contact with each one will be by phone, mail, email, or in person.

Start with the mediators or agencies you're most interested in, and work your way through the stack. After verifying the name and contact information, ask whether the mediator or agency has a brochure to give you. If so, you might want to look at it before going on with the rest of Worksheet 1, because it may answer many of your questions.

Take notes on Worksheet 1 as you go so you'll have something to refer to when you get to the point of choosing. The last section of Worksheet 1 lets you jot down your thoughts and impressions about the mediator. For example, you might call one mediator who sounds just like your Uncle Bert. Or maybe a mediation office you visit has a friendly feeling to it. These comments can be especially useful when you're trying to decide among equally qualified mediators, so take a moment to make a note or two before you go on to the next one.

Worksheet 1 is as thorough as we can make it, but you might think of things to ask we haven't included. Or you might want to skip some questions that don't seem important to you. Feel free to make it work for you.

You may find that some mediators will talk to you and answer your questions themselves. If so, that's great, because you'll get a sense of their personal style as you talk to them. Usually they'll be willing to spend some time talking to your spouse, too, if your spouse is interested.

Many mediators believe that talking to one spouse alone before the sessions begin might give the impression that the mediator is not impartial. These mediators have receptionists or assistants who will answer your questions. Your interaction with the mediator's assistant can tell you quite a bit about the mediator's background and approach, and how comfortable you will feel working with his or her staff, but you'll have to wait until you actually meet with the mediator before getting a sense of his or her personal style. Make notes about as much as you can, so you can decide whether this mediator might be one for you and your spouse.

After you've found out as much as you can about each mediator, try narrowing your list to a few—more than one and fewer than five—who are your top choices. You may do this on your own or with your spouse. Either way, the goal is to have a short list from which to make your final selection.

Once you've compiled your short list, rank the mediators on it by first choice, second choice, and so forth. If you and your spouse are doing this together, do your rankings separately, and then compare notes. This is good practice for some of the decision making you'll be doing in mediation. You may disagree on some of the rankings. That's perfectly okay. If you disagree or if you're doing this part on your own, let your spouse have the choice between the qualified mediators on your short list. This way, you let your spouse know that you are willing to consider his or her wishes, which sets a good tone for the rest of the mediation.

Interviewing and Selecting a Mediator

Once you and your spouse have picked your first choice, you will need to spend some time with the mediator before you can know whether you will both be comfortable working with that person. Some mediators, especially new mediators trying to build their practices, offer an introductory session at no charge. Others may offer a reduced rate for the first mediation session.

Regardless of whether you are meeting in a free introductory session or paying a fee, use this first session as a chance to get to know the mediator and answer any questions you have about the process.

Before you first meet with the mediator, read Chapters 9 and 10. These will help you get the most out of your first meeting.

After the first session, use the tips in Chapter 11 to help you reflect on your feelings about the mediator and his or her approach. Did the mediator put you at ease and answer your questions? If your answer is not an unqualified "yes," consider making an appointment with another mediator whose name is on your short list before you decide. Remember, the success of your mediation will depend partly on good chemistry with the mediator. A highly qualified mediator may work very well with another couple but be the wrong match for you. If you or your spouse has misgivings about a particular mediator, don't be shy about meeting with someone else. The time and money you invest in finding the right mediator will pay off in a settlement agreement that both you and your spouse can live with.

Where to Look for Potential Mediators

	Name of mediator	Phone number

Personal Referrals

friends

financial advisers/accountants

lawyers (be sure the lawyer is
   familiar with and supportive of
   mediation)

therapists/counselors

spiritual advisers (minister, priest,
   rabbi, etc.)

Local Professional Associations

local bar association

local chapter or association of
   accountants, financial planners,
   therapists, or other professionals

Local Agencies and Institutions

lawyer referral panel

legal aid office

military legal aid (for military
   personnel and dependents)

local university or junior college
   (law school or prelaw dispute
   resolution program)

community mediation service or
   center

Local Directories

telephone directory (check
   "Mediation," "Dispute Resolution,"
   "Divorce," or "Divorce Assistance")

	Name of mediator	Phone number

***Online Directories/Websites
With Referrals***

mediate.com

divorcenet.com

acresolution.org

Other:

National Organizations

**Association for Conflict Resolution
(includes Academy of Family Mediators)**
1015 18th Street, NW, Suite 1150
Washington, DC 20036
Voice: 202-464-9700
Fax: 202-464-9720
Website: www.acrnet.org

**American Arbitration Association
(AAA)**

1633 Broadway, Floor 10
New York, NY 10019-6708
Voice: 212-484-4181
Fax: 212-246-7274
Website: www.adr.org

**Judicial Arbitration and Mediation
Services (JAMS)**

Home office:
1920 Main Street, Suite 300
Irvine, CA 92614
Voice: 949-224-1810
Fax: 949-224-1818
Website: www.jamsadr.com

	Name of mediator	Phone number
National Organizations, cont.		
Association of Family and Conciliation Courts		
6525 Grand Teton Plaza		
Madison, WI 53719-1085		
Voice: 608-664-3750	_____	_____
Fax: 608-664-3751	_____	_____
Email: afcc@afccnet.org	_____	_____
Website: www.afccnet.org		

Finding a Collaborative Attorney

At some point, either before you propose using collaborative lawyers or after you and your spouse have agreed to do so, you will need to find a good collaborative lawyer. Where do you begin?

In order to find the right attorney, you need to know the answers to these three questions:

- What makes someone qualified to represent you in a collaborative divorce?
- How do you find lawyers who are qualified to handle your case?
- How do you know when you've found the right lawyer?

This chapter helps you answer the first two questions and gives you a start on answering the third. In Chapter 11, we'll help you answer the last question by suggesting ways to make sure that the lawyer—and the process—that you've picked is the right one for you.

➡ **Can you skip this chapter?** If you've already selected a collaborative lawyer with whom you are comfortable, you can skip this chapter.

Shortcut to Finding the Right Collaborative Attorney

In the chapter on finding a mediator, we advise using personal contacts to find referrals to potential mediators.

You can try that when you go looking for a collaborative lawyer, but because collaborative law is relatively new, you may not have a lot of success. (Of course, if your cousin just went through a collaborative divorce and thinks the world of his or her lawyer, that's a great start.)

Instead, consider first whether you know other attorneys whom you like and trust. Perhaps you've worked with a business lawyer in connection with your small business, or maybe one of the soccer moms on your son's team is a lawyer. Check with those folks about whether they are familiar with collaborative law and whether they know anyone who practices it. If they don't, the next best thing would be for them to give you a referral to a family law attorney, whom you can then call and ask for some advice on finding a collaborative lawyer.

Another avenue is to do some research into local collaborative law organizations. An Internet search might yield information about a local group of attorneys who practice collaborative divorce law. There's more about this below.

If you try a couple of different methods and find one attorney's name coming up again and again, that lawyer may well be the one you want. See how you feel about your initial contacts with the attorney and his or her staff. If your impression is positive, make an appointment. Use Chapter 11 to help you assess your experience at the first meeting, and you're on your way. You won't need to read anything else in this chapter.

Qualified Attorneys: What to Look For

Because collaborative law is relatively new, it's difficult to measure what makes someone a good collaborative lawyer. However, it's fair to say that it may be a combination of the characteristics that make a good mediator and those that make a good lawyer.

Basic Qualifications

Both mediators and collaborative attorneys need to be good listeners and clear communicators. In addition, a good collaborative lawyer should be knowledgeable about family law. Some family law attorneys also have some background in psychology, and some have financial or tax backgrounds. You should look for a collaborative lawyer whose background and skills fit your particular situation—for example, if you know there will be a difficult negotiation over various pension plans, a lawyer with a background in finance might be perfect for you. And if you need to settle issues regarding your children, the lawyer should have expertise in handling child custody and support.

If you will be negotiating a variety of issues, including property and parenting,

your lawyer should be conversant in all of them. (This option is covered below.) Remember, though, that most collaborative divorce lawyers use a team approach. You're likely to be using an actuary to evaluate your pension plans, and meeting with a counselor to discuss a parenting plan. So while the lawyer should be familiar with the rules that apply to your case, don't make yourself crazy trying to find someone who's an expert on every single issue.

Certified Specialists

Some states have standards for certification of family law specialists. This means the lawyer has the experience, skills, and respect from his or her colleagues that the state requires. Usually the lawyer must have completed a large number of cases, practiced for a significant period of time, and passed a written exam designed to measure legal knowledge. In most states, standards for certification are tough, so a certified family law expert is most likely a very skilled lawyer. If you're interested in finding a certified famiy law expert, first check to make sure that your state offers certification. If it does, ask potential lawyers whether they are certified.

Of course, this doesn't mean that noncertified lawyers aren't good too! Some lawyers who are very skilled and experienced might not be certified. Don't use certification as a litmus test.

A Collaborative Approach May Not Equate to a Collaborative Divorce

Some lawyers endorse many of the principles of collaborative law while remaining critical of the "no court" agreement that requires withdrawal if the case doesn't settle. You may find such a lawyer who offers to handle your divorce "collaboratively" and still be available to represent you if you end up with a contested case. If your lawyer is skilled in collaborative negotiating and if your spouse hires an equally skilled lawyer, the four of you may negotiate a settlement satisfactory to both of you, even if the process doesn't follow the format we're calling collaborative divorce. If you are considering this avenue, you and your spouse should coordinate your search efforts to ensure that neither one of you ends up with an attorney who engages in adversarial tactics that sabotage any attempt to proceed collaboratively.

Training in Collaborative Techniques

Training in collaborative practice is now available in many places. Because collaborative law is a relatively new way of practicing divorce law, you definitely want to find a lawyer who has been trained to practice collaborative law. The typical introductory training program consists of 12 course hours, so this should be the absolute minimum amount of training your lawyer has completed. Most collaborative professional associations also require their members to complete a 30–40- hour program in mediation or dispute resolution, too. Questions about training are included in Worksheet 2—Questions for Potential Collaborative Attorneys, found in the appendix.

If the lawyer completed his or her initial training in collaborative law more than a year before your interview, ask about continuing education. Ordinarily, you should expect a lawyer to have completed five to ten additional hours of continuing education within the last year.

Experience

In addition to inquiring about a potential lawyer's training, find out the extent of his or her experience in collaborative law cases. However, because the process is so new, you shouldn't necessarily reject a lawyer who hasn't done very many collaborative cases. Unless you live in a major metropolitan area, you'll have a hard time finding a lawyer who has done many collaborative cases. Instead, focus on the lawyer's experience as a family lawyer, on his or her collaborative divorce training, on your own intuition—how you feel about the lawyer when you meet him or her—and on how comfortable the lawyer seems with discussing the concepts of collaborative divorce. There may also be other reasons to choose a less-experienced lawyer over a more-experienced one, such as cost, availability, or special expertise.

How much divorce experience is enough? There is no precise answer to this question. But unless your case is so simple that you're willing to take a chance on a beginner, you probably want someone who has been in practice for at least one year and has handled at least ten divorce cases.

Reputation

As we said above, the single most effective way to know if a potential collaborative lawyer will do a good job for you is to talk to people who are familiar with the lawyer's work and reputation: your friends and acquaintances, or professionals or counselors who have worked with the lawyer. Because of confidentiality, the lawyer may not be able to give you names of former clients as references to talk to, but you can ask if anyone has given permission for this. You might also ask for the names of lawyers who have represented the other spouse in collaborative divorce cases, who might provide valuable references. No matter what other information you get, the more often a lawyer's name comes up in

positive comments about his or her skill, ethics, and experience in divorce law, the more likely it is that this reputation is well-deserved, especially if the comments come from a variety of unrelated sources.

Finding the Right Fit

Determining a lawyer's basic qualifications may not be enough. You also need to consider if there is anything unique about your case that would make a particular lawyer the right (or wrong) choice for you.

First, find out if anything in the lawyer's background would compromise his or her ability to work with you, your spouse, and your spouse's attorney. Next, look at your situation and see if you need a lawyer with special skills or expertise or if other circumstances might mean you should select a particular lawyer.

Conflicts of Interest

To be effective, a lawyer must not have any conflicts of interest—meaning, he or she must be able to work for the interests of the client without interference from other interests. In most cases, this will mean that your lawyer cannot have any preexisting relationship with your spouse that would create a conflict of interest.

You can usually find out ahead of time whether the lawyer has a conflict of interest. When you call to make an appointment, ask whether the lawyer has any prior or current relationship with your spouse that could be viewed as a conflict of interest. Most lawyers keep records that allow them to check for conflicts of interest, and they will be happy to tell you. If your spouse has already contacted this particular lawyer and has given the lawyer confidential information about your marriage, the lawyer should tell you that he or she is unable to represent you, and you will be spared the trouble of even making an appointment.

Even if your spouse does have a connection with the lawyer, you may decide to go ahead anyway, after discussing it with your spouse and the lawyer. Especially in a collaborative divorce, where there's a commitment to negotiating a solution, a lawyer who knows one or both of you can actually do a better job for you than someone who doesn't know you at all. The key is that no one—you, your spouse, or the lawyer—should feel that the preexisting relationship will impair the lawyer's ability to support your interests and advise you about the best course of action.

Special Skills or Expertise

In addition to verifying that there are no conflicts of interest that will get in the way, consider whether your case has any of the following characteristics:

- You and your spouse disagree on one major issue (such as child custody, a complex tax question, or a special business or real estate matter) that requires specialized knowledge to understand. You agree on all other issues.
- You and your spouse need help settling a variety of issues, including some that require special expertise.
- There is a significant power imbalance between you and your spouse; one of you tends to be easily intimidated or overwhelmed by the other.
- There have been incidents of domestic violence in your relationship.
- You or your spouse has a substance abuse history or is in a recovery program that needs to be supported during the mediation.
- You have certain cultural or religious concerns or other unique circumstances.

If your case falls into one or more of the categories described above, you may want a lawyer with experience dealing with situations like yours. Before you decide whether that's necessary, let's examine each of these situations more closely.

One-Issue Cases

If there is really only one bone of contention between you and your spouse, you might each want to choose a lawyer with experience dealing with that kind of issue.

Disagreements about children. The most common single-issue cases involve disputes over child custody or other issues concerning the children. Spouses often can resolve their financial issues without much difficulty but have a hard time agreeing on their children's needs. If this is true for you, you might be able to resolve these questions yourselves with a little help from collaborative lawyers who have some background in handling custody issues. If the issues to resolve require more specialized help, your collaborative lawyer may suggest including a child specialist in the collaborative process. (For tips on resolving child issues see "Help in Making Decisions About Your Children," in Chapter 6.)

Complex tax or legal issues. If the only real issue in your case involves unusual or complex tax or legal matters, you might be best off with a lawyer who has expertise in that area. For example, if you are involved in a dispute with the IRS over liability for back taxes, and the major issue in your divorce is how to deal with the potential liability, consider a lawyer who has special tax expertise. Or perhaps you or your spouse is considering filing for bankruptcy. You may want a lawyer who understands the intricacies of both bankruptcy and divorce law.

Unique property issues. Sometimes, the main disagreement is over a specialized asset, such as a certain kind of business, unique commercial real estate, or international property or investments. If this seems familiar, ask yourself whether your situation is so specialized that someone with general knowledge would have a hard time understanding it. If your answer is "yes," then look for a lawyer who has the specialized expertise in addition to the general qualifications you want.

What if you can't find a qualified collaborative lawyer who also has the special expertise you're looking for? (This is possible, given that collaborative law as a professional discipline is still relatively new and even very experienced family law attorneys may not be trained in the collaborative process.) If you are in this situation, it's probably best to select a qualified general purpose collaborative lawyer and then use other advisors and specialists in the process as needed. This is very common in collaborative divorce cases in any event.

Multi-Issue Cases

Most divorce cases involve a variety of issues that need to be addressed. For example, many divorcing spouses need help in negotiating about children and property and child support or alimony and related tax issues. If that's your situation, look for a lawyer who has broad experience in family law and has collaborative divorce training, rather than someone with a special focus.

A good divorce lawyer should have some experience in all financial and nonfinancial issues that commonly arise. Ideally, this includes a basic familiarity with financial and legal documents such as deeds, appraisals, account statements, and tax returns. Your lawyer will help you assess when and if it is necessary to consult with an expert in a particular field. The consultant works with you, your lawyer, your spouse, and your spouse's lawyer to develop any information that might be needed in order to negotiate a satisfactory agreement about the issue. For example, you all might decide together to have a neutral accountant study the possible tax consequences of selling or dividing certain real estate so that you will be able to choose what works best for you.

Domestic Violence

If interactions between you and your spouse have included pushing, shoving, hitting, or other physically aggressive behavior, you are probably making a good choice in picking collaborative divorce over mediation. As we discuss in Chapter 4, most people should not consider mediating in a domestic violence situation unless both partners have moved beyond the violence and are involved in ongoing counseling. This is true for collaborative divorce as well—if you are not moving past the domestic violence issues, then you most likely will want a lawyer who will look only at your interests and will keep you insulated from your spouse. In fact, even collaborative

divorce is unlikely to be successful unless you and your spouse are addressing the conditions that gave rise to the violence with professional counseling.

If you are going forward with a collaborative process, be sure to find a lawyer who is experienced in working with couples who have a history of domestic violence. The term "domestic violence" can include the whole spectrum of aggressive acts, from threats of chronic battering to violence to occasional shoving. Inform the lawyer ahead of time about your particular circumstances.

If you still have questions about whether and how to proceed with your divorce because of violent incidents in your relationship, you may want to take a look at our more detailed discussion of this subject. (See Chapter 17.)

Substance Abuse or Recovery

If problems with alcohol or drugs have been an issue in your relationship, it may be difficult to use a collaborative process unless the problems are being addressed in an ongoing program of recovery that both you and your spouse actively support. Without an effective recovery program in place, you may find that your efforts to use a cooperative process will be met with active or passive resistance and that the agreements you make aren't followed through.

If you do have a good recovery program in place, then look for a lawyer who is familiar with, and experienced in, dealing with people in recovery. And be sure to inform the lawyer of your situation so that the divorce process will be congruent with the recovery effort.

Other Special Circumstances

Other unique circumstances might influence your choice of a collaborative lawyer. We discuss some of the most obvious ones in this section, and include a space to note your particular concerns in Worksheet 2—Questions for Potential Collaborative Attorneys, found in the appendix.

As we've said about other special criteria, make sure your lawyer has the basic qualifications for a divorce lawyer in addition to any special qualifications you want to add. If you can't find someone who fits the bill, go with a qualified divorce lawyer who can help you address your special concerns by using a consultant or advisor, or by adapting the process in some other way that works for you.

Cultural or Religious Concerns

You may consider it important to work with a lawyer who understands your cultural norms and values. Or you may want to find one who will support your religious values. Or perhaps you and your spouse have very different cultural or religious backgrounds and you need a lawyer who is experienced in working on cases where cultural or religious

differences are an issue. If you want to make sure your lawyer has this kind of background, ask ahead of time.

Same-Sex Relationships

Collaborative law can work just as well in dissolving nonmarital same-sex relationships as it does in dissolving traditional marriages—but if you are dissolving a same-sex relationship, you will want to make sure you find a lawyer with background in that area. Even in states where same-sex couples can marry or enter into marriage-like relationships, ending a same-sex relationship can involve special laws and court procedures. Traditional marital attorneys can certainly take on these cases, but do make sure you find someone who has experience with the special issues involved for same-sex couples. Chapter 18 addresses this in more detail.

For more on the legalities of same-sex relationships, check out *A Legal Guide for Lesbian & Gay Couples,* by Hayden Curry, Denis Clifford, and Frederick Hertz (Nolo).

Long-Distance Divorce

If you and your partner don't live nearby anymore, you can still use collaborative law to resolve the issues in your divorce. Although it's common in collaborative cases to have at least one joint session where both partners and their lawyers are present, and for the partners to meet together with advisors at various points, you can probably make adjustments to account for the distance. Telephone conferences, Web-based real-time conferences, or videoconferencing can solve the long-distance dilemma. In particular, as videoconferencing technology becomes more widely available and affordable, it is likely that more lawyers will use it in collaborative cases.

Special Needs

Perhaps some other circumstance makes it important to find a lawyer with a particular background or mediation format. An obvious example is language proficiency. If you are uncomfortable speaking English, you'd probably prefer to find a lawyer who speaks your language of choice or who offers translation services. Or if one of you uses a wheelchair, you need a lawyer who can provide an accessible meeting place.

If you are ending a same-sex relationship, you'll need a lawyer who has experience in helping same-sex or unmarried couples mediate. (See Chapter 18 for more on how to find the right person.)

These are just a few examples of special circumstances that might warrant trying to find a lawyer with certain skills, background, or resources. If you find yourself in a situation like this, you should be sure to ask about the lawyer's ability to meet your criteria when you are doing your search.

What Price Collaboration?

Fees for private practice lawyers will vary, depending on the experience, training, and reputation of the lawyer. Market conditions and the cost of living in your community can also affect attorney fees. For example, in some areas of the country, fees may range from a low of $100 or $125 per hour to $350 per hour or more. In other places, the range may start at $150 per hour or more and go up from there.

Most lawyers charge by the hour. On occasion, you might find one who charges a flat rate a divorce, but this will be a rarity. Some lawyers offer the first meeting or consultation at no charge or for a reduced fee.

The best way to get an idea of the range of fees and pricing options in your area is to ask about fees when you are talking friends and other referral sources and when you are screening potential lawyers. We include specific questions about fees in Worksheet 2—Questions for Potential Collaborative Attorneys, found in the appendix.

Making a List of Potential Lawyers

We've said it before but it bears repeating: The single best source of names of good divorce lawyers is personal referrals.

Folks who have successfully used collaborative divorce may be more than happy to recommend their lawyer, or even the lawyer who was on the other side. Other professionals, such as lawyers, accountants, and counselors, may be able to refer you to lawyers who have worked well with their clients. Once you start asking, you are likely to get at least a few names to put on your list. You may even find a certain name coming up again and again, which can be a good indicator of that lawyer's ability.

If your search for personal referrals comes up short or you want to expand your list, local, regional, and national organizations may be able to provide you with additional names of collaborative lawyers in your area. We provide a suggested list of organizations at the end of this chapter, including contact information for national organizations,

Checking It Twice: Screening and Interviewing Potential Lawyers

Once you have a list of potential lawyers, you'll want to find out as much as you can about them before narrowing down your choice to two or three to seriously consider.

First, find Worksheet 2 in the appendix and make enough copies so you have one for each lawyer you plan to contact. Write down the name and address of

each lawyer on a copy of the worksheet, along with where you got the referral and anything else you know about the lawyer at this point. Then decide whether your first contact will be by phone, mail, or email, or in person.

Start with the lawyers you're most interested in, and work your way through the stack. After verifying the name and contact information, ask if the lawyer has a brochure to give you. If so, you might want to look at it before going on with the rest of Worksheet 2, because it may answer many of your questions.

Take notes on Worksheet 2 as you go so you'll have something to refer to when you get to the point of choosing. The last section of the worksheet lets you jot down your thoughts and impressions about the lawyer. For example, you might call one lawyer who reminds you strongly of someone. Or maybe a law office you visit has a casual feeling to it that you like. These comments can be especially useful when you're trying to decide among equally qualified lawyers, so take a moment to make a note or two before you go on to the next one.

Worksheet 2 is as thorough as we can make it, but you might think of things to ask we haven't included. Or you might want to skip some questions that don't seem important to you. Feel free to make it work for you.

You may find that some lawyers will talk to you and answer your questions themselves. If so, that's great, because you'll get a sense of their personal style as you talk to them. Some lawyers might have a receptionist or assistant who will answer your questions. Your interaction with the lawyer's assistant can tell you quite a bit about the lawyer's background and approach, and how comfortable you will feel working with his or her staff, but you'll have to wait until you actually meet with the lawyer before getting a sense of his or her personal style. Make notes about as much as you can, so you can decide whether this lawyer might be one for you.

After you've found out as much as you can about each lawyer, try narrowing your list to a few—more than one and fewer than five—who are your top choices. Once you've compiled your short list, rank the mediators on it by first choice, second choice, and so forth. Then you can move on to the final step.

Interviewing and Selecting a Collaborative Lawyer

Once you have picked your first choice, you will need to spend some time with the lawyer before you can know for certain whether you will both be comfortable working with that person. Some lawyers, especially lawyers who are new

to collaborative law and are trying to get clients to try it, offer an introductory session at no charge. Others may offer a reduced rate for the first visit if it's intended to be mostly a getting-to-know-you session.

Regardless of whether you are meeting in a free introductory session or are paying a fee, use this first session as a chance to get to know the lawyer and answer any questions you have about the process.

Before you meet with the lawyer for the first time, read Chapters 2, 3, and 4. These will help you get the most out of your first meeting.

After the meeting, reflect on your feelings about the lawyer and his or her approach. Did the lawyer put you at ease and answer your questions? If your answer is not an unqualified "yes," consider making an appointment with another lawyer whose name is on your short list before you decide. A highly qualified lawyer may work very well with another person but be the wrong match for you. If you have misgivings about a particular lawyer, don't be shy about meeting with someone else. The time and money you invest in finding the right lawyer will pay off in a process that's comfortable for you and in which you feel secure that you are getting the best representation possible.

Where to Look for Potential Collaborative Lawyers

	Name of mediator	Phone number

Personal Referrals

friends

financial advisers/accountants

lawyers (be sure the lawyer is
familiar with and supportive
of mediation)

therapists/counselors

spiritual advisers
(minister, priest, rabbi, etc.)

Local Professional Associations

local bar association

local chapter or association of
accountants, financial planners,
therapists, or other professionals

local association of collaborative
lawyers and related professionals

Local Agencies and Institutions

lawyer referral panel

legal aid office

military legal aid (for military
personnel and dependents)

local university or junior college
(law school or prelaw dispute
resolution program)

Local Directories

telephone directory (check
"Collaborative Law," "Collaborative
Divorce," "Collaborative Practice,"
"Dispute Resolution," "Divorce," or
"Divorce Assistance")

	Name of Lawyer	Phone number
Online Directories/Websites With Referrals		
Collaborativepractice.com	_____	_____
Collaborativedivorce.com	_____	_____
mediate.com	_____	_____
divorcenet.com	_____	_____
acresolution.org	_____	_____
Other:	_____	_____

National Organizations

International Academy of Collaborative Professionals

145 Wildhorse Valley Road
Novato, CA 94947
Phone (415) 897-2398
Email:
paula@collaborativepractice.com _____   _____
Website:
collaborativepractice.com _____   _____

Association for Conflict Resolution(includes Academy of Family Mediators)

1015 18th Street, NW, Suite 1150
Washington, DC 20036
Voice: 202-464-9700 _____   _____
Fax: 202-464-9720 _____   _____
Website: www.acrnet.org _____   _____

Chapter 8

Using Advisers and Doing Legal Research

In addition to the mediator, you may want or need to work with one or more outside advisers, such as people in your circle of intimates, legal advisers, counselors or therapists, financial advisers, or other specialists. In a collaborative process, you're even more likely to use outside specialists. However, in that context it's likely that your collaborative attorney will make recommendations about which advisers you need to use, and even suggest whom you should select in these roles. This chapter, then, is directed primarily toward those who will be using mediation. A mediator may also recommend that you and your spouse use a jointly selected adviser for certain purposes. It's also likely, though, that you'll want to select your own advisers who will work only with you while you are in the mediation process. For those situations, this chapter helps you:

- assess whether and when to use an adviser
- understand the types of advisers
- find various types of advisers, and
- maximize the benefits of working with an adviser while minimizing the costs.

This chapter also provides some tips on doing your own research on divorce issues.

 You might skip this chapter or read certain sections. If you aren't going to use any outside advisers, if you've already selected advisers, or if you're using a collaborative process in which the lawyers recommend advisers that you and your spouse will consult jointly, you can skip this chapter. If you know what type of advisers you need, read the rest of this section and then the sections on the kinds of advisers you are considering. If you are using a collaborative process, you can still review this chapter to get an idea of what kinds of advisers are out there and how you might use them.

How and When to Use Advisers in Mediation

Outside advisers are not always necessary while going through mediation. If you work with a lawyer-mediator who can explain the legal rules, prepare the divorce agreement, and help you with the other legal paperwork for the uncontested divorce, it is quite possible to mediate your divorce with just the help of the mediator.

But there may be times when consulting an adviser is a good idea. For example, if your mediator is not a lawyer you may want a legal adviser who can fill you in on the divorce laws of your state and translate any agreement you reach into an acceptable court document.

In various parts of this book, we suggest that you consult an adviser if certain kinds of questions arise—such as a financial adviser who can help you to understand the tax implications of a proposed settlement. Your mediator may also suggest this if the circumstances call for it. Realize that using an adviser while you are in mediation has both potential benefits and potential costs, however. You will need to weigh these benefits and costs to decide what's best for you.

Benefits of Using Advisers	Costs of Using Advisers
valuable advice on an issue being mediated	fees charged by the adviser
help in analyzing information or proposals	advice inconsistent with other advice
constructive settlement suggestions	advice inconsistent with goals of mediation
personalized support during the process	possible confusion

First and Last Stop: Your Mediator

Think of your mediator as a kind of adviser. He or she should be the first person you talk to when questions come up during the mediation. If you wonder whether you should consult an outside adviser, ask your mediator. If you need referrals to an adviser who understands and supports mediation, ask your mediator. If you don't know what you should ask the adviser to do for you, ask your mediator. Using the mediator's help

at these times ensures that involving an adviser moves things forward instead of hanging them up.

If you decide to use an adviser, inform your mediator. And if you get inconsistent or confusing information from your adviser, ask your mediator to help you sort things out. Doing this lets the mediator coordinate what is going on outside the mediation with what is happening in the mediation.

Same Adviser—Different Hats

The kinds of advisers you are likely to use fall into certain categories. First, there are family, friends, and acquaintances. In addition, you may want the help of a legal adviser, a counselor or therapist (including, perhaps, a spiritual counselor), or a financial adviser. At some points in the mediation, you might also want to work with a negotiation coach, a parenting coach, a mediation support person, or a professional who deals with specific issues such as an appraiser, an actuary, a pension expert, or an insurance agent.

You may be thinking, "Wait a minute. What started out as a simple matter of sitting down with my spouse and a neutral person to settle our divorce is turning into a three-ring circus!"

We're not suggesting that you would use all or even most of these advisers— and especially not at the same time. But depending on your needs, you might

How Mediators Can Help You Find and Work With Advisers

How can your mediator respond to your questions and requests for referrals and still be neutral? This is a question that is regularly debated among professional mediators. While mediators differ in their opinions about how best to maintain neutrality while being as helpful as possible, most will agree that it is quite possible to stay neutral while helping one party or the other as long as both parties have the same access to the mediator's help and the help is about the process (the how) and not the content (the what) of the mediation. Mediators often describe themselves as neutral on the issues but *not* on the process. The process, or how, of the mediation, is what you pay the mediator to take care of.

When you ask the mediator to help you find a good lawyer or even what kinds of questions to ask the lawyer, that is a question about the how of mediation: how to get the advice you need from a lawyer in order to proceed with the mediation. Or if your spouse is confused about a complicated financial worksheet and the mediator suggests that your spouse work with a financial planner, this is a suggestion for how your spouse can be better informed about the financial decisions that need to be made. Don't worry about trying to tell a how question from a what question. That's your mediator's job. If you ask a question that would affect the mediator's neutrality, he or she will turn it into a how question by suggesting a way for you to get it answered by someone else.

---

have a brief consultation with one or more advisers during the course of the mediation.

When and if you look for an adviser, it's possible you'll find one who can help you on more than one front. For example, you may find a legal adviser who can also act as your negotiation coach and mediation support person. Or, it may be that your counselor can also act as a parenting coach.

So that you will know what to look for and expect in your unique circumstances, we describe each type of adviser and tell you how to work with each one. Then you can ask your mediator to help you pick the best adviser for your circumstances, when and if you need one.

Don't Be Penny-Wise and Pound-Foolish

A major consideration in using outside advisers is the cost. Most advisers we discuss are professionals who charge hefty fees for their services. So you'll want to think carefully before consulting an adviser.

But don't let the cost alone deter you from getting valuable advice when you need it. The overall cost of the mediation, including the advice, will still be far less than what you'd pay in a contested court case. And once you make the decision to consult with an adviser, don't let the fees charged be your sole criteria in selecting an adviser. You may think you're saving money by picking a low-cost adviser instead of an experienced specialist who charges a higher hourly fee. But the high-paid specialist might spend less time—and therefore charge you less—giving you more solid advice than the cut-rate adviser who lacks the expertise to give you the succinct help you need.

So find out about a potential adviser's background, experience, and qualifications, as well as the fees charged, before plunking down your hard-earned cash for an hour or two of time and advice.

Beware of Adversarial Advisers

Mediation is nonadversarial. The mediator helps you approach the decisions that need to be made in mediation from a neutral, problem-solving point of view. The goal is to find solutions that are mutually satisfactory. An outcome that is great for you but terrible for your spouse might be fine in the adversarial setting of contested litigation but has no place in mediation.

Some professionals, especially those with little or no experience with mediation, may offer you advice that is highly adversarial. Adversarial advice focuses exclusively on what is to your best advantage, regardless of the potential disadvantages to your spouse and regardless of the effect that taking such a position might have on the negotiations.

An adversarial adviser might even try to talk you out of mediating at all, warning you that you are sure to be taken advantage of and implying that he or she can do better for you in an adversarial negotiation or contested court case.

Beware of these adversarial advisers. Unless you are prepared to resist their extreme approach by listening to their advice and then evaluating it from a more objective standpoint, keep looking until you find someone with a nonadversarial approach.

Friends, Romans, and Countrymen

By now, you have probably sought the advice of friends, family, and acquaintances. And, even if you haven't asked for it, you've probably been offered a ton of unsolicited advice.

While your friends and family play an important, even crucial, role in supporting you through this difficult time, you should not use them as advisers except in very limited circumstances. Why? Because you need your friends and family for listening and supporting. To paraphrase Julius Caesar, they can lend their ears.

But friends and family are rarely objective enough to give you the kind of hard-headed advice that you are going to need in order to make decisions on the important matters you face. Furthermore, unless your friends and family happen to have professional expertise in the areas of law, counseling, or finance, they won't be in a position to advise you accurately. In fact, the ones with professional expertise may decline to advise you, recognizing the inherent difficulty of being your supportive friend and giving you objective advice at the same time.

Be especially wary of advice from people who want to tell you horror stories about their own bad experiences or, worse yet, about the bad experiences of their friends, or even friends of their friends. Advice of this kind is likely to suggest that you take aggressive or inflammatory actions that could undermine a successful mediation. Even if you listen to their advice, don't follow it without at least getting a second opinion from a more neutral adviser.

Beyond listening and supporting, there are a couple of ways your family and friends can help. First, they can often be a good source of referrals to mediators and professional advisers. Second, if you are fortunate enough to know someone who has had a positive experience in mediation, that person can give you a personal account of the process that will help you be better prepared for it.

In general, however, recognize that your friends and family are your support system. To expect them to be more than that is unfair to them and to you.

Legal Adviser

When we use the term legal adviser, we are really talking about a special type of lawyer—one who is willing to consult with you as an integral part of the mediation process. While business lawyers have long served the role of consultant to their clients, divorce lawyers are accustomed to taking over and handling the entire case. For this reason, many lawyers who have special expertise in the divorce area are unwilling to stay on the sidelines as a consultant. As mediation is used by more and more divorcing couples, however, the need for consulting lawyers also increases. In addition, many divorce lawyers are becoming mediators as the demand for divorce mediation grows, and these lawyers usually are happy to work as consulting lawyers on cases they aren't mediating.

What About Nonlawyers as Legal Advisers?

In every state except Arizona, it is illegal for a nonlawyer to provide the type of information you would want from your legal adviser. For instance, in a number of states, independent paralegals provide divorce services directly to the public. These services are limited primarily to secretarial tasks, however. While some independent paralegals may be very knowledgeable about the law (indeed, many are former legal secretaries who have decided to branch out on their own), they aren't supposed to deliver their expertise to the public; only lawyers have that privilege.

If you do ultimately use a nonlawyer for your legal coach, be aware that the individual most likely is exceeding the limits of what's permitted by your state's law.

Why Consult a Legal Adviser?

At some point before you firm up any settlement agreement in mediation, you may want to consult with someone about your legal rights. While you can learn a lot about your rights from doing your own legal research (see "Finding Answers to Legal Questions," below), consulting with an actual legal adviser can help you get answers that are more specifically tailored to your case.

Your legal adviser can also help predict the range of possible legal outcomes if you were to go to court and the cost of paying a lawyer to fight for them—your BATNA-WATNA (to learn more about BATNA-WATNA, see Chapter 13, which discusses negotiation in mediation and collaborative divorce). Knowing your BATNA-WATNA can be integral to a successful negotiation. A good legal adviser can coach you in negotiating techniques and can help you think up creative solutions to propose in the mediation that are better than or at least as good as the court outcomes.

 Make sure your adviser is familiar with contested divorce cases. As we discuss later in this section, it is important to find a legal adviser who will give you a realistic idea of what you would get from a contested court case, including the cost of the litigation. All too often, a lawyer will describe an extreme adversarial position and lead you to believe you're entitled to something you'd probably never get in court.

Your legal adviser can also act as a law coach on an as-needed basis during the mediation. Even before the mediation, your legal adviser/law coach can help you evaluate the option of mediation, select a mediator, and persuade your spouse to mediate. Between sessions, you can consult with your law coach to clarify questions and prepare for negotiations. If you are participating in court-sponsored mediation, it is especially important to have a knowledgeable law coach guiding you through the process. (See Chapter 14 on court-sponsored mediation.)

Your legal adviser can review any written agreement prepared by the mediator to make sure that what is written down says what you want it to say and will be legally binding once signed.

Finally, your legal adviser can help you prepare the papers needed for an uncontested divorce once your settlement agreement is signed, if it's not part of your mediation agreement to have your mediator do that for you.

When to Consult a Legal Adviser

Once you find a legal adviser who understands and supports mediation, it is a good idea to have a brief consultation early on during the mediation process. Not only will this give you important information about your legal rights, but it will also allow you to begin building a good working relationship with your legal adviser.

If you wait until you've already negotiated an agreement to consult a legal adviser, you may be in for some surprises about your legal rights that could undermine your commitment to the agreement you've just negotiated. Going back to mediation and trying to renegotiate the agreement at that point is often disastrous.

If you instead start out the process with solid legal information about your personal situation, you can negotiate an agreement that takes into account all your legal rights. This makes it much less likely that the mediation will fall apart at the last minute.

As your mediation progresses, you should feel free to consult with your legal adviser on an as-needed basis in between mediation sessions, whenever you have questions about your legal rights or the legal process.

Qualifications of a Legal Adviser

As we mention, your legal adviser will most likely be a lawyer licensed to practice law in your state. But there are some more specific qualifications that you will want to look for.

A lawyer who advises clients going through mediation is often referred to as a consulting lawyer. Just finding someone licensed to practice law is not enough. You want a lawyer who has significant experience in the area of divorce law. In some states, lawyers can obtain certification as specialists in certain fields of the law. If this is true in your state, consider looking for a certified specialist in divorce law, family law, or matrimonial law. This may sound extravagant, but many certified specialists are quite knowledgeable about mediation and experienced as consulting lawyers. Their high hourly fee is often justified by the quality and efficiency of their advice.

In addition, your consulting lawyer should have a good reputation for competence, honesty, and respectful treatment of clients. Ask your referral sources about these qualities.

It is also critical that your consulting lawyer be experienced in and supportive of mediation. A consulting lawyer who is ignorant of or hostile to mediation can undermine everything you are trying to accomplish in mediating your divorce. For example, a lawyer who doesn't approve of mediation or who thinks mediation is a good idea but doesn't know enough about it could easily advise you to take a position that is legally correct but extremely adversarial. What you want is advice designed to inform you of your legal rights and to help you promote a reasonable settlement. There's a list of suggested questions below that may help you find the right consulting lawyer.

Fees

Most divorce lawyers charge an hourly fee. Most of them also expect to be paid an initial large retainer (advance deposit) of several thousand dollars to cover the cost of beginning a contested case. Many consulting lawyers will charge by the

hour instead of charging a large retainer, so look for a consulting lawyer who will charge you by the hour. Even so, be prepared for the hourly fee to range as high as $250 to $500, especially in major metropolitan areas. When you do find a consulting lawyer who charges by the hour without requiring a retainer, it's a good idea to confirm the fee arrangement in writing.

Controlling Legal Fees

Most likely, you will be paying your legal adviser by the hour. Often this means that you'll get billed for each portion of the hour that the lawyer is spending on your case, rounded upwards. For instance, if your legal adviser is charging you $200 an hour, you may get billed at the rate of $20 for every six minutes (that is, for each tenth of an hour) or for any part of that period that the lawyer's attention is focused on your case. So, a one-minute phone call might be rounded up to the full six minutes and cost you $20. To keep yourself from getting billed a full hour for a bunch of short calls that total less than an hour of the lawyer's time, carefully plan your calls to fill up the billing interval—that is, to get your money's worth.

Negotiating Legal Fees

Sometimes, lawyers agree to take certain cases pro bono—free of charge—such as when the client is referred by a low-income legal service. In addition, some lawyers agree to reduce their rates for clients who are members of prepaid legal plans with which the lawyer has a relationship. But, in general, most lawyers will expect to charge their normal hourly fee to every client.

If you want to negotiate a lower fee, ask about the availability of a free consultation, sliding scale, or other reduced-fee arrangement when you set the appointment. If this option is available, great. If not, you can ask if the lawyer might make an exception to the regular rate in your case. If the answer is "no," don't try to negotiate a special arrangement with the receptionist or legal assistant setting the appointment. He or she will have no authority to lower the fee without the lawyer's approval.

Once you're face to face with the lawyer, it won't hurt to ask again if he or she will give you a reduced fee for consulting services. But don't be surprised if you're turned down, and do be ready to pay for whatever time you spent at the previously quoted rate, unless you've arranged something different in advance.

Locating a Good Legal Adviser

The best way to find a good legal adviser is through referrals. Your mediator may be able to give you a list of potential consulting lawyers he or she knows. Or if you are working with a counselor, or a financial or other adviser, you may be able to get referrals that way. You may have come across the names of good consulting lawyers in your search for a mediator. Many lawyer-mediators offer their services as consulting lawyers, too. This is also where friends, family, and acquaintances can help, especially if they have been through mediation themselves and understand how helpful a good consulting lawyer can be.

In addition to referrals, you might try contacting your local bar association, professional mediation association, or mediation center (See Chapter 6.) Finally, you can get listings of lawyers by geographical area in *Martindale-Hubbell*, a national lawyer directory available in many public libraries and law libraries and on the Internet at www.martindale.com.

Interviewing and Selecting a Legal Adviser

Once you have a list of names, first contact the one who seems best. Or if you can afford it, consider meeting with the top two or three candidates in order to select the one you want to work with. It may seem like a waste of money, but considering the cost of adversarial litigation, paying a few hundred dollars to find a good consulting lawyer you're comfortable with is a bargain.

Concepts to Consider

Questions to ask potential consulting lawyers:

❑ How many years have you practiced divorce law?

❑ How much of your practice is devoted to advising clients in mediation?

❑ Have you had any training in divorce mediation?

❑ What kind of help can I expect from you while I am in mediation?

❑ Will you review any written agreement prepared by the mediator?

❑ Will you prepare a written agreement if the mediator doesn't?

❑ What would you look for in a settlement agreement? (The answer should give you some idea of the adviser's attitude toward creative approaches to settlement versus strict adherence to legal rules.)

❑ What do you charge for your services?

❑ Do you require a retainer in this situation?

❑ Other: _____

_____

If you are uncomfortable with how things went in the interview, continue looking. To make the most of time spent with a consulting lawyer, it's important to find someone you feel good about.

Working With a Legal Adviser

You can expect some basic things from your legal adviser. And you can take some actions to make the most of the time and money you spend on consulting with your legal adviser.

Communication

First, your legal adviser should communicate clearly and in plain English. By the same token, you'll need to take responsibility for your end of the communications. If you don't understand something, say so. Be persistent. Ask questions until you are sure you get it. Your adviser should be open to your questions.

Responsiveness

Expect your legal adviser to respond to your telephone calls or letters within a reasonable time, usually two or three days for nonurgent phone messages and a week or so for letters. You are not your legal adviser's only client, so there will be times when you can't reach your adviser right away. You can and should expect to hear back within a reasonable time, however. If a special urgency or deadline arises, include that information in your message. If you don't get a return call or a letter within the times we've suggested, call and find out the reason for the delay.

Questions

Before meeting with your legal adviser, write down your questions and concerns. Leave room to jot down your adviser's answers and note what you plan to do next. You can use Worksheet 13 in the appendix.

Bring your list or Worksheet 13 with you to the appointment. Tell your adviser that you have a list of questions, and double check the list at the end of the meeting. Write down notes of your adviser's answers as you go along. Go as slowly as you need to.

Support Persons

If you're having trouble focusing and find it difficult to remember your questions or the answers, consider bringing a support person—a friend or family member—with you. Be sure to clear this with your adviser ahead of time. Ask your support person to take notes for you during the meeting. Some people find it helpful to tape-record their meetings with their legal adviser. If you think this would be useful, be sure to discuss it with your adviser in advance.

Before You Leave

Before you leave, go back over what's been discussed and ask your adviser to help you come up with a plan of action based on the advice you've been given. This might consist of getting certain information together or having a plan for things to say and questions to ask at the next mediation session. Write down notes of your plan of action.

Using the Advice

Take seriously the advice you get. You are paying a professional to give you advice you wouldn't think of on your own. Make sure you understand the advice and the reasons for it. Consider it carefully before accepting or rejecting it.

Bear in mind that you may not always like what you hear from your legal adviser. Some legal rules may not seem fair to you. You still need to know them in order to maintain a realistic approach in the mediation.

If Problems Arise

Three kinds of problems can arise when working with a legal adviser:

- communication problems
- unhappiness with the advice, or
- fee disputes.

Communication Problems

If the problem is in the communications between you and your adviser, try letting your adviser know. Sometimes that's all it takes to get back on track. If that does not work, consider seeking the assistance of a counselor or therapist. Maybe the problem is something you can fix on your end. If all else fails, you may need to look for a new adviser whose style of communication is more consistent with your own.

Unhappiness With the Advice

If you are confused by the advice you're getting or if you disagree with it, talk with your adviser. Ask his or her reasons for giving you this particular advice. Ask what other options might be available to you. Then decide for yourself whether you want to follow the advice, disregard it, get a second opinion, or ask your mediator for help in deciding what to do.

A different but related problem arises if your legal adviser tells you something about the law that seems to contradict what you've heard in mediation, or vice versa. For example, the mediator reviews the child support guidelines with you and your spouse and comes up with a child support amount. Your adviser tells you that under the guideline, child support should be twice that much. What's going on? Perhaps the legal guidelines aren't clear and the mediator and adviser interpret them differently. Maybe they are using different factual information in their calculations. Or one of them might be wrong about the law. Ask your adviser to help you sort out the reason for the discrepancy. If there seems to be a disagreement about the law, consider getting a second opinion. (In addition, Chapter 15, about dealing with difficulties, discusses suggestions for dealing with disagreements about the law.)

You Are in Charge of Your Life

Always remember that you are free to make decisions that make sense to you, even if they contradict the advice you are given. For example, if you will pay or receive alimony, your adviser might discourage you from agreeing to a lump sum payment instead of the more traditional arrangement of ongoing payments. Your adviser might be concerned about the risk that future developments could prove the lump sum amount to be higher (or lower) than what would have been paid in monthly alimony payments. But if you and your spouse want to avoid the unpredictability and ongoing entanglement of alimony payments, and you're confident that you understand the tax ramifications, you might reasonably choose to disregard your adviser's recommendation and go ahead with the lump sum payment.

Fee Disputes

Avoid problems about fees at the outset by making sure you have a written agreement with your legal adviser covering how fees will be charged, when you will be billed, and other details. If you do not pay as you go, insist upon receiving a detailed monthly bill, and call any problems to your adviser's attention as soon as you are aware of them.

Keep your sense of perspective when it comes to fees. Many a great working relationship has been poisoned by disagreements over relatively minor fee amounts. If you are otherwise pleased with your adviser's performance, consider cutting your adviser some slack when it comes to the fees.

If you end up with a significant dispute about fees and if talking about it doesn't resolve the problem, you may be able to get help from your local or state bar association. Often, there is a panel of volunteer lawyers available to review the situation and to give an advisory opinion about the fee dispute.

 Visit Nolo's website for more information about working with your lawyer. Go to the Rights & Disputes section at www.nolo.com.

Counselor

Going through a separation and divorce can be an emotionally traumatic experience. While you might be tempted to tough it out, you'll do yourself a tremendous favor if you seek the help of a psychological counselor or therapist in getting through the rough times.

Why Consult a Counselor?

A good counselor will help you cope with the emotional trauma you are experiencing. In addition, your counselor can advise you on how best to communicate with your spouse, both in and out of the mediation sessions. Your counselor may also be able to act as a negotiation coach during the mediation. If you have children, your counselor can help you with the parenting decisions you will need to make now that you and the other parent are no longer in the same household.

Affording counseling. If you don't think you can afford a counselor, consider looking for an individual counselor or an agency, such as a local counseling center or clinic that offers an ongoing group you can join. This is often a very cost-effective way to get the help you need.

When to Consult a Counselor

You may have already consulted a counselor early on in your separation. If you haven't, you can wait until it seems to you that a consultation would be helpful.

How often you see your counselor is a highly individual matter. Some people need the support and assistance of a counselor on a weekly basis or even more frequently. Others find that regular sessions on a less-frequent basis are

Working With a Spiritual Counselor

If you are affiliated with a religious or spiritual community, you may ask a spiritual counselor to help you through the separation and divorce. The process of finding and working with a spiritual counselor is a matter of personal, religious, or spiritual preference, so we won't attempt to tell you how to go about that. But be aware that a spiritual counselor doesn't necessarily have the training and experience to act as a psychological counselor. If you need psychological counseling—for example, to deal with chronic depression or to work on troublesome behavior in yourself that you'd like to change—be sure to ask about your spiritual adviser's expertise in this area before relying on him or her for that kind of help.

sufficient. Many people consult with counselors only on an as-needed basis. It will be up to you and your counselor to decide what is best for you.

Qualifications of a Counselor

Counselors in most states are required to be licensed. The types of licenses available vary from state to state. The typical categories include licensed clinical psychologists, psychiatrists, marriage and family counselors, and licensed social workers. If you have been diagnosed with a serious psychological or psychiatric condition, you will probably be under the care of a licensed psychologist or psychiatrist. Otherwise, consider choosing a marriage and family counselor or social worker, because their fees will generally be lower.

Usually, the more experienced your counselor is in working with people going through separation and divorce, the better. It also is very helpful if your counselor understands mediation and has experience in helping people who are going through mediation.

Fees

Counselors usually charge a per-session fee, typically $60 to $125. Many insurance companies will cover part of the expense of counseling—called psychotherapy. It is worth checking to see if at least a portion of your counseling expense can be covered. Some insurance companies require that you get a referral from a medical doctor or use counselors on certain preapproved lists.

Avoid problems over fees by having a clear agreement, preferably in writing. Call any billing problems to your counselor's attention immediately.

Locating a Good Counselor

As with other advisers, your best source of potential counselors is personal referrals. Look for names that come up again and again. Your mediator, legal adviser, or financial adviser may be a good source of referrals. If your community has a college or university offering a degree in counseling or a related field, you might be able to obtain referrals that way (and it also might be a good resource for low-cost counseling).

If referrals aren't generating enough options, consult some local professional organizations of psychologists or counselors, as well as the Yellow Pages of your local phone book. Look under counseling services, psychotherapy, psychologists, marriage and family counselors, or social workers.

Interviewing a Counselor

The relationship between client and counselor is very personal. Beyond general questions of education, training, and experience, the only way to interview a prospective counselor is to spend some time in a counseling session and see how you feel about the connection between you and the counselor. You should feel comfortable enough with your counselor to entrust him or her with your most intimate thoughts and feelings. But this does not mean that you want a counselor who simply makes you feel good when you're in session. In fact, the opposite is true. You want a counselor who will challenge you when necessary—who will help you do the hard and sometimes painful work of looking honestly at yourself and your circumstances.

Working With a Counselor

Good communication is as essential to the counseling process as it is to working with any other adviser. Expect your counselor to speak to you in simple, clear language that you understand. You should feel comfortable asking questions when you need to. Counselors have varied approaches to the counseling process; ask your counselor about his or hers.

Be honest with your counselor. If you are smarting from the pain and disappointment of a marital separation, it is especially tempting to exaggerate the faults of your spouse and minimize your own. Don't do this. The point of seeking the help of a counselor is to find better ways to cope with your situation. You can't control what your spouse does, nor can your counselor. What you can and should control is how you behave and what steps you take to improve your situation. Your counselor is there to help you do this. If you don't give your counselor an accurate picture of the problem, he or she is not going to be able to help you very effectively.

Your counselor will probably suggest steps for you to take or exercises for you to try in between sessions. If you don't understand the suggestions, let your counselor know so that he or she can help you understand your task better. If you don't agree with a suggestion, say so. Once you've agreed to try something suggested by your counselor, follow through and report the results accurately at your next session. After all, you are paying your counselor good money to advise you. If you don't intend to follow through, you are wasting your counselor's time and your money. And if the suggestions don't work despite your committed follow-through, your counselor needs to know this in order to make adjustments.

If Problems Arise

If the problem is in the communication, first try bringing it to your counselor's attention. If that doesn't work, you may need to look for someone with whom you can more easily communicate. If you don't like the advice you are getting from your counselor, and if talking about it doesn't change anything, try a session or two with a different counselor. Maybe your counselor's approach just isn't the right one for you.

Financial Adviser

Many of the decisions made during divorce—including dividing assets, allocating debts, and paying or receiving alimony or child support—have financial consequences. If you wait until after your divorce to understand the impact of the divorce on these issues, it may be too late to avoid serious financial ramifications.

Why Consult a Financial Adviser?

As you begin to discuss various financial options in mediation, you might want a financial planner to help you assess the financial implications of the proposed divorce settlement and make wise investments.

In addition, you may want to consult with someone who can help you with tax questions. Many decisions involving property settlement, child support, or alimony have tax consequences. You may have questions about filing joint or separate returns, allocating income and deductions between you, and claiming the children as dependents. If your mediator can't help you with these questions, a knowledgeable tax adviser can explain your options and help you plan accordingly.

To keep your costs down, look for a financial planner who can double as a tax adviser. It may be that your financial planner will refer you to a tax adviser for a brief consultation on a specific tax question, but many times this is not necessary.

Money Matters

Getting divorced can involve many financial decisions. Here are some of the things a good financial adviser can help with:

- assessing cash flow resources and needs
- deciding which assets to keep or sell in your property settlement
- selecting options regarding retirement plans, including Keoghs and IRAs
- evaluating income tax filing and deduction options
- assessing tax consequences of a proposed property settlement
- planning for children's college expenses
- assessing life insurance needs
- evaluating your current investments
- developing a long-range investment plan, and
- choosing estate planning options.

If you don't think you can afford a financial adviser, or if you just want to understand better what your financial adviser is telling you, take a look at *Divorce & Money: How to Make the Best Financial Decisions During Divorce*, by Violet Woodhouse with Dale Fetherling (Nolo). It's full of helpful information and tips.

When to Consult a Financial Adviser

It's a good idea to have at least a short consultation with a financial adviser early on in your separation. That way you can be alerted to any immediate issues and take steps to avoid problems later on.

Once you've made the initial contact, plan to consult your financial adviser before agreeing to any property settlement. Other consultations should be on an as-needed basis.

Qualifications of Financial Advisers

There are two types of financial advisers you might need to work with: a financial planner and a tax adviser. Sometimes you can find one person who is good at both. Sometimes you'll need to consult with two different people in order to get the help you want.

Qualifications of Financial Planners

Good financial planners come from a variety of backgrounds. Some limit themselves exclusively to financial planning and take advantage of a certification process available for financial planners. Others offer their financial planning services as part of a broader-based business, such as an insurance brokerage, stock brokerage, or real estate practice. Two credentials to look for when considering a financial planner are CFP (Certified Financial Planner) and ChFC (Chartered Financial Consultant). Both indicate that the planner has undergone a required course of study in order to earn the credential.

Because you are less likely to find consistent certifying standards on which to rely, it is especially important that you get personal referrals for any financial planner you are considering working with.

Try to find a financial planner who has experience in advising people who are mediating their divorce and, if possible, select one who has worked with your mediator before. While this isn't always possible, it's an added bonus that will help things go more smoothly.

Qualifications of Tax Advisers

Look for a tax adviser who holds some professional license or certification letting him or her prepare tax returns. These include certified public accountants (CPAs), tax attorneys, and enrolled agents (people qualified to appear before the IRS). This will ensure that the person you consult has some degree of competence in tax matters.

In addition to general tax background, it is important that your tax adviser have knowledge of and experience with the tax consequences of separation and divorce. A surprising number of tax experts do not. Be sure to ask. And if possible, find someone with experience advising people in mediation, preferably people who used your mediator.

Fees

Unless you have access to a qualified financial adviser who will assist you without charge, expect to pay a reasonable fee for the financial advice you get—usually, but not always, an hourly rate.

Financial Planners' Fees

Some financial planners charge by the hour, with the amount depending upon their training, expertise, and experience. Typical fees for a complete financial analysis range from $2,000 to $5,000, with hourly rates for consultations between $75 and $200. Other financial planners charge a commission, typically 3%–5%, on investments you purchase through them. Some stockbrokers and insurance brokers will offer financial advice without charge if you maintain accounts with them. Others will expect to charge an hourly fee.

Obviously, you need to find out the fee arrangement at the beginning and decide what's best for you. A commission arrangement can create a conflict of interest for the financial planner, who may be motivated to recommend certain investments because of the commission involved. Still, some commission-only planners give good advice despite this potential conflict.

Tax Advisers' Fees

Tax advisers generally charge by the hour. Tax attorneys will usually charge at the highest rate: $200 to $500 per hour. CPAs generally charge between $75 and $250 per hour, while enrolled agents will charge less, usually $40 to $60 per hour.

Unless you have a particularly complex problem, you probably don't need to spend the extra money on a tax attorney. If you're lucky, you'll find an enrolled agent with experience in the tax aspects of separation and divorce. If not, your best choice is a CPA. Even if you choose a relatively expensive CPA, one or two consultations may be enough. So, the overall cost may not be too high, and the potential tax savings, not to mention the piece of mind from having solid advice, means your money will be well spent.

Locating a Good Financial Adviser

For both tax advisers and financial planners, referrals are your best source of good prospects. Cross-check referrals carefully, and look for names that come up again and again. The recommendations of other professionals—your legal adviser, mediator, and counselor—can be important here.

Interviewing a Financial Adviser

As when selecting other advisers, there is no substitute for a personal interview with a potential financial adviser to see if this is the right person for you to work with. Use the interview as an opportunity to gauge your comfort level with the adviser's communication style. Expect your financial adviser to communicate with you in language that you understand. This does not mean that you have to become an expert in the tax code. But you should be able to follow enough of what your adviser is saying that you can actually communicate meaningfully about taxes and financial matters during your mediation.

Working With a Financial Adviser

When working with a tax adviser, think prevention. Ask for advice in advance. Expect your adviser to give you various options from which to choose, and to illustrate these options with specific examples. Ask questions when you don't understand something.

Keep the fees down by doing your own homework in advance. Before you meet, give your adviser a written list of the questions you need answered. Ask for a list of documents or information you need to bring with you, then follow through. For example, if you want advice on whether to file a joint or separate tax return, tell your adviser. Your adviser can tell you what information he or she will need to give you the best advice. Be sure to have the information written down and organized so that you and your adviser can make the best use of time spent together.

If you are working with a financial planner, the same considerations apply. Make sure that your financial planner communicates with you clearly and in understandable terms. Ask questions when you need to. Find out what information your financial planner needs from you in advance, and assemble it in an organized way.

If Problems Arise

If communications aren't good between you and your adviser and talking about it hasn't cleared up the problem, try finding someone else with whom you can more easily communicate.

If you aren't confident in the advice you're getting, get a second opinion and maybe even a third. You can avoid problems over fees by having a clear written agreement up front.

Specialized Advisers

In addition to counselors and financial and legal advisers, you may consult others to help assure the success of your mediation. This section explains a few of the more common types of additional advisers.

Negotiation Coach

You may not need a negotiation coach. Your mediator will be coaching you and your spouse during the actual negotiations, and that might be enough to keep you on track. Sometimes, however, a little extra personalized assistance can boost your confidence and help you get the most out of the mediation. For example, if you feel unsure of your ability to handle the give-and-take of negotiating with your spouse, a negotiation coach can give you tips and ways to practice that will boost your confidence. Or, maybe you've come away from a mediation session where you negotiated some point and you're confused about what happened or afraid you conceded too much. An hour spent with a negotiation coach between sessions may be all you need to get your bearings again.

Ideally, your legal adviser, counselor, or financial adviser can fill this role so that you don't have to go out and hire a separate professional. The best way to find this out is to ask. Have a candid discussion with each of your advisers. Ask about their knowledge and expertise in negotiation theory and techniques. Talk about their philosophy of negotiation. Hopefully, you'll work with someone who adheres to the principles of interest-based negotiation. Discuss with them the principles of good negotiation outlined in Chapter 13 and ask whether they think they can help you stay on track.

Then pick the one who seems the most comfortable and proficient.

If none of your advisers has the background necessary to act as your negotiation coach, ask your mediator for a referral to someone who can assist you. Discuss with any potential negotiation coach his or her negotiating approach, background, and experience with mediation and with interest-based negotiating before selecting the one to work with.

Be sure to have a clear agreement about fees for this service.

Parenting Coach

If you have children, you are probably making some adjustments in how you parent. You may have questions about what to say to them about the divorce. You might want help in making decisions about the time-sharing schedule and other matters affecting them. This is an ideal time to get some professional help from a parenting coach.

You may not need to hire a separate professional for this. If you are already working with a counselor, you can ask him or her to help you with these questions. If your counselor doesn't feel that this would compromise the individual work you are doing, you won't need to look for a separate parenting coach.

Another option is for you and the other parent to consult a parenting coach together, if you agree about the basic parenting issues and want help in dealing with your children. If you don't agree with each other on parenting issues, then you probably need a mediator rather than a parenting coach, since you'll want to work with someone who knows how to help people resolve their differences in addition to understanding parenting issues.

Classes for divorcing parents exist in many parts of the country. Some are offered through the courts, some are offered by community or private organizations. Some classes even include the children in their program. Ask your mediator or other advisers if such a program exists in your area. You will probably have the option of attending by yourself or with your spouse.

Mediation Support Person

If you really like the idea of mediating your divorce but are having trouble sticking up for yourself during the mediation, either because you get overwhelmed by the process or you feel intimidated by your spouse, consider hiring a mediation support person.

A mediation support person actually accompanies you to the mediation sessions to help you fully participate. He or she is there to answer questions, take notes, remind you of things you wanted to say, and even speak for you if you're having trouble saying things in a constructive manner.

Obviously, you'll need to arrange for this with your mediator and your spouse in advance. Most mediators will welcome the participation of a mediation support person. If your spouse is reluctant to agree, your mediator can help explain the benefits of using a support person and allay your spouse's fears.

If you are working with a legal adviser, counselor, or financial adviser, one of them might be the logical choice for a mediation support person. If you are not sure, ask your mediator for a referral.

Single-Issue Advisers

At some point during your mediation, a question may come up about a particular issue, such as the value of an asset, how to divide a pension, or options for health insurance or life insurance. Typically, your mediator will help you resolve these questions by arranging to consult with neutral experts who work on behalf of both you and your spouse. When this happens, you might want to get a second opinion from an independent adviser. As with other advisers, you'll want to be sure that whoever you select understands the process of mediation and supports your participation in it. The best way to find someone is to ask for referrals from one of your other advisers or from the mediator.

Be sure to clarify your expectations and the fee to be charged in advance.

Coordinating Your Advisers

If you work with more than one adviser, you will want to make sure their efforts on your behalf are coordinated so they do not offer inconsistent advice. In other words, you want them to work as a team on your behalf. To make sure this happens, tell your mediator and each adviser that you are working with others. Offer to sign releases so they can talk to each other when dealing with the same issues.

If you get advice that seems inconsistent, let your advisers know your questions and concerns. Often, the inconsistencies are based on misunderstandings about either the information you have provided or your goals. Spending some time clarifying your concerns will usually straighten things out. If not, ask your mediator to help you sort through the information so that you can make sense of it.

Finding Answers to Legal Questions: Legal Research Online and Off

In the course of the mediation process, you may want to get some information about the laws of your state as they affect mediation or regulate what happens in a divorce. While this information may be available from your mediator or from a consulting lawyer, it's also possible for you to do your own research in a law library or on the Internet, where you can find:

- state statutes—the source of law that most often governs the legal issues involved in a divorce mediation, and
- general background information prepared by family law experts.

If you want to go beyond the state statutes or general background information and, for example, study what the courts have said on a particular issue, this section identifies some good resources that can show you how to do basic legal research.

Law Libraries

Here, briefly, are the basic steps to finding state laws and general background information in a law library.

Finding a Law Library

First you need to find a law library that's open to the public. Public law libraries are often housed in county courthouses, public law schools, and state capitals. If you can't find one, ask a public library reference librarian, court clerk, or lawyer. If there's no public law library in your area, your local public library may have enough basic legal materials to get you started.

Finding State Laws

Most aspects of a divorce—including how property is divided and how kids are cared for—are regulated by state laws called statutes. Mediation-related issues—such as confidentiality and the role of a court-appointed mediator—are also typically addressed by state statutes, if they are addressed at all.

To find the statutes relevant to the issue you're concerned with, you will use a multivolume set of books called the "state code." State codes are divided into titles, with each title relating to a different topic. Most states divide their titles by number; a few states divide them by subject, such as the civil code, family law code, or finance code.

If you already have a reference to the statute—called the citation—finding the statute is straightforward. If you don't have a citation, you can find the statute by looking at the index in the code you're using. If need be, the reference librarian in the law library will direct you to the appropriate code and to the particular part of the code that contains the statutes relevant to your issue.

After you read the statute in the hardcover book, turn to the back of the book. There should be an insert pamphlet (called a "pocket part") for the current or previous year. Look for the same statute in the pocket part to see if it has been amended since the hardcover volume was published. If you don't see a pocket part insert, look on the shelf near where you found the hardcover book. Some inserts are too large to fit in the "pocket" of the hardcover volume and are contained in separate paperback volumes.

Statutes can be hard to read or difficult to interpret. Sometimes they are badly written, and sometimes they are part of a larger set of statutes, called a statutory scheme or an act, that work together as a whole. But interpreting the code shouldn't be impossible. In most codes you'll find in a law library, the statutes are followed by single-paragraph summaries of court cases interpreting one or more parts of the statute. It's always a good idea to browse these summaries, as they may shed light on what a particular word or phrase means. If you want to go further and actually read a case that is summarized, the resources listed below tell you how.

Finding Background Information

Background information—general information about a legal subject—should never be mistaken for the law itself. The law consists of statutes, court decisions, and regulations. But if you want to do your own legal research, it is always a good idea to read some background information first—to get the lay of the land, so to speak.

If you want to research a legal question related to family law but don't know where to begin, one of the best resources is the *Family Law Reporter*, published by the Bureau of National Affairs (BNA). This very thorough, four-volume publication covers all 50 states and the District of Columbia and is updated weekly. It highlights and summarizes court cases,

new statutes, and family law news. It also includes a guide to tax laws affecting family law, a summary of each state's divorce laws, and a sample divorce agreement. Most law libraries carry the *Family Law Reporter*. If, however, it's not in your law library, ask the reference librarian to steer you toward the books that are used for general family law background information by the lawyers who frequent the library.

Additional Legal Research

If your research needs take you beyond looking up a statute or general background information, you will need some guidance in basic legal research techniques. For detailed but user-friendly instructions on legal research, see *Legal Research: How to Find & Understand the Law*, by Stephen Elias and Susan Levinkind (Nolo). If the law library you are using offers an Internet connection, visit Nolo's website at www.nolo.com, click on the site map, and then on the heading "Help With Legal Research."

Other good resources that may be available in your law library are:

- *Legal Research Made Easy: A Roadmap Through the Law Library Maze*, a legal research video by Robert Berring (Legal Star Video)
- *The Legal Research Manual: A Game Plan for Legal Research and Analysis*, by Christopher and Jill Wren (A-R Editions)

- *Introduction to Legal Research: A Layperson's Guide to Finding the Law*, by Al Coco (Want Publishing Co.), and
- *How to Find the Law*, by Morris Cohen, Robert Berring, and Kent Olson (West Publishing Co.).

Legal Research on the Internet

A growing number of basic legal resources are available online through the Internet. This section will get you started searching online.

Finding State Statutes

You can use the Web to find state statutes by visiting FindLaw at www.findlaw.com. Choose "State Law Resources" from the FindLaw homepage. This takes you to a page with a list of all 50 states. Click on the state you want. This will take you to a page that, for most states, offers a "primary materials" link. That link takes you to a page with links for the primary resources for that state—statutes, court decisions, and regulations. Click the link for "statutes" (remember, sometimes they're called "codes"), and away you go.

Online collections of state statutes vary considerably in both their presentation and the means for searching them. Some sites provide several search tools, such as a keyword search, a section-by-section list of the statutes according to topic, and a feature that lets you search by statute number or section. Other sites only offer

one or two of these search utilities. Some sites are meticulously kept up to date, whereas some require you to visit another site—the one maintained by the state's legislature—to bring yourself completely up to date. Few of the sites are official in the sense that the state stands behind their accuracy. But accuracy has not, so far, proven to be a problem.

If you are looking for a brand-new state statute, you may need to use the link to "legislation" rather than the link to "statutes" or the "code," as there is often a delay between when a statute is passed and the time it is worked into the overall compilation of laws.

Unlike the codes found in the law library, the online statutes don't come with summaries of court interpretations. To find out what a court has had to say about a statute you find online, you'll need to engage in a more sophisticated form of research. See "Additional Legal Research on the Web," below.

Finding Pending Legislation

Almost every state legislature maintains its own website for pending legislation. These sites contain not only the most current version of a bill, but also its history. To find the pending bill for your state, go to "State Law Resources" from the FindLaw homepage. This takes you to a page with a list of all 50 states. Click on the state you want, then choose the link for legislation.

Finding Background Information

Remember, background information is general information about a legal subject. One excellent place to look for background information about family law is the Nolo website at www.nolo.com. This resource provides up-to-date, plain-English information about a wide variety of legal topics—including mediation and family law. For example, the family law section includes:

- informative and topical articles about various family law issues
- a bookstore detailing Nolo's family law books
- an update service for Nolo products
- definitions of family law terms, and
- links to other useful online law sites.

Probably the best online site that is purely dedicated to family law is Divorce Helpline Webworks, a website located at www.divorcehelp.com. This site offers:

- an excellent tutorial called a "Short Divorce Course" that helps people think intelligently about divorce and the typical issues that arise
- articles about all facets of a divorce
- a registry of 350 professionals, including attorneys, paralegals, mediators, and mental health professionals, available to help people who are doing their own legal work
- forms to help divorcing couples sort out their situation

- a bookstore that offers a wide selection of family law books, and
- links to other online family law resources.

Other websites that may prove helpful include:

- Divorce Online: http://divorce-online.com
- Divorce Support Page: www.divorcesupport.com
- DivorceInfo: www.divorceinfo.com
- Partners Task Force for Gay and Lesbian Couples: www.buddybuddy .com
- American Bar Association: www.abanet.org

Other divorce websites:

- www.divorcenet.com
- www.smartdivorce.com.

Additional Legal Research on the Web

If you need to do more than look up a statute or some general background information on the Web, you will need some guidance in basic Internet legal research techniques. Nolo's *Legal Research: How to Find & Understand the Law*, by Stephen Elias and Susan Levenkind, shows you step by step how to find legal information on the Web.

Final Thoughts

As you can see, there is a wealth of information and expertise available to help you successfully mediate your divorce. You don't have to become an instant expert on every aspect of your divorce in order to take charge of what is happening. Using advisers from time to time when you need them is a good way to make sure you are making the right decisions without giving up control over what is happening to you.

Chapter 9

Getting Started on Information-Gathering

One of the first things you'll spend time on in mediation or collaborative divorce is getting together all of the information that will be needed in order to negotiate an agreement. You should plan to work closely with your mediator or collaborative attorney in assembling the necessary information. This chapter suggests some things you can do to get ready for the information-gathering stage.

Follow your mediator's—or collaborative attorney's—instructions. If your mediator or collaborative attorney has asked you to do certain things to get ready, then by all means do them. Our suggestions are intended to supplement what your mediator or attorney is having you do. But if what we say is inconsistent with what they tell you, feel free to ignore what's here. For example, we give you worksheets to fill out in advance. If you are mediating, your mediator might prefer to meet with the two of you in the initial session first and then decide together what information to gather and how to do it, so that the entire process, including information gathering, is agreed upon in mediation. Similarly, your collaborative attorney may want to discuss how to go about getting information together before you begin. In that case, don't bother with our worksheets unless you find them helpful for your own use.

You may be able to skip material. Take a look at the table of contents for this chapter. If there are things you've already done, or sections that don't apply to you, skip those and read only the parts that seem new and applicable.

Settling a divorce usually involves making decisions about many interrelated issues, including division of assets and debts, child custody and support, and alimony. (You will find a more complete list of the most common issues included in the divorce agreement in Chapter 16.) The first few steps we outline in this chapter are designed to get you started thinking about the information you'll need in order to address the issues in your case.

Step One: Remember Vital Statistics

In every divorce, the mediator or collaborative attorneys will want to start with some basic information. You probably have this information in your head, but if you don't, you might want to go through the list below and jot down facts and dates.

The basic information you should have ready, if it applies, includes

- date of marriage
- date you began living together (if different from date of marriage)

Coordinating With Your Spouse

The lists and worksheets referred to in this chapter are intended for you to use on your own. One of the most important things you and your spouse can do to prepare for mediation or collaboration is to assess independently all aspects of your situation, without any influence or interference from the other. This will help each of you focus on workable solutions when you begin the mediation or collaboration process.

If you think you'd like to work together with your spouse in gathering the necessary information, check with your mediator or collaborative attorney first. Chances are, he or she will encourage you to try working together if you both are comfortable doing so.

After consulting with your mediator or attorney, if you decide to sit down and complete the worksheets together, we suggest you start by working on them separately. Once you have gone through everything on your own, compare results with your spouse. The two of you can then identify items you agree on, and you can separate out disagreements that you might need help with in the mediation or collaborative four-way meeting. If you spot gaps in your own knowledge when going through the worksheets alone, see if your spouse has the missing information. If not, the two of you can decide how to get it, or you can agree to ask for the mediator's help in figuring out a way to get it.

If your spouse chooses not to gather information on his or her own, or is uncomfortable talking to you about it, then it is best not to insist on sharing the information even after you have gone through everything yourself. Your spouse's reaction may come from insecurity or a lack of confidence. Your preparedness might only aggravate your spouse's feelings. In that case, it's best to wait and let the mediator or the collaborative attorneys assist in exchanging information in a way that will neutralize any imbalance between you and your spouse.

- date you started living separately
- full names, ages, and birth dates of your children
- your age and occupation
- your spouse's age and occupation.

Step Two:
Assess Your Children's Needs

If you don't have children. Skip ahead to Step Three if you don't have children.

If you and your spouse have children together, your life ahead will involve coordination and cooperation as parents. It's a good idea to anticipate the parenting issues by spelling out guidelines and ground rules in a written parenting plan. A parenting plan goes beyond the brief custody terms spelled out in a divorce agreement. The plan outlines your agreements about the times your children spend with each of you; holiday arrangements; responsibility for medical and dental care; how to handle schooling, discipline, and extracurricular activities; and a variety of other issues that may come up.

If you want to spend time in mediation or collaboration developing your custody agreement and parenting plan, first take some time to assess your children's needs and consider how you and the other parent can best meet those needs. This is especially important if you will be using court-sponsored mediation, which usually offers a limited time for working things out.

Your mediator or collaborative attorney may have a format for you to follow in getting ready to talk about parenting issues. If so, use that format instead of ours.

If your mediator or attorney hasn't suggested an approach, you may want to look at the Nolo book on parenting plans. (See "Putting Your Children First," below.)

Putting Your Children First

Your children's welfare will be a top priority in your divorce agreement. This means coming up with a parenting plan that works for you and your spouse and, more important, for your children. An excellent resource for preparing for and negotiating a parenting agreement is *Building a Parenting Agreement that Works: Putting Your Kids First When Your Marriage Doesn't Last,* by Mimi Lyster (Nolo).

This book includes forms, worksheets, and step-by-step instructions to take you through all the issues and decisions that must be included in an effective parenting agreement. You can use the book with your spouse, on your own, or in conjunction with your mediation.

For a simple way to get started, complete Worksheet 7 in the appendix.

Step Three: Locate and Copy Important Documents

During the course of the mediation or collaboration, you may find it helpful to refer to various financial and legal documents of the types listed below. Now is a good time to locate them. You might make a complete set of copies for your own reference, or you might agree with your spouse to share one set of documents. As you go through the list below, make a note of which documents you have and which ones you are missing.

If you don't have some of the documents, don't worry. What's important at this point is to get a handle on what's there. So when you come to a document you don't have, just make a note of it and move on.

When you've finished going through the list and you and your spouse compare your results (if you are communicating well with each other), you may find that you have just about everything between you. If something is still missing, wait until the first mediation session or collaborative four-way meeting to find out whether it's important enough to try to locate.

Some people find it helpful, even reassuring, to locate and assemble significant documents. Others find it a chore. If you don't want to go to the trouble of collecting the documents we list here, skip ahead to Step Four, below.

Here's a list of the main documents you might need. You may think of others—if so, add them to the list. Make a note of where each document is located for future reference. If you want a complete set of documents, make copies as you find them. You might want to organize your copies according to the categories listed below, with a separate folder, envelope, or binder section for each category.

Documents	Location
❏ real estate documents (deeds, purchase agreements, escrow instructions, mortgages, documents showing improvements, etc.)	
❏ tax returns (joint or separate) for the past 3–5 years	
❏ title, registration, and insurance certificates for vehicles, boats, trailers, etc.	
❏ bank statements, canceled checks, check registers, and passbooks for the past 1–2 years	
❏ life insurance policies, including amendments and the most recent premium notice	
❏ investment records (statements for brokerage accounts, mutual funds, stock or bond certificates, etc.)	
❏ retirement/pension plan records (most recent statements)	
❏ promissory notes, IOUs, or other loan records showing money owed to you and/or your spouse by other people	
❏ partnerships or small business certificates or statements of ownership	
❏ wills, trusts, or other estate planning documents	

If You Own and Operate a Business

If you or your spouse (or both of you) owns and works in a partnership, sole proprietorship, limited liability company, closely held corporation, or other business, how to value the business or compensate a nonowning spouse may be an issue in negotiating a settlement.

You can hold off on assembling business documents until you meet with the mediator or your attorney and decide whether any specific documents are needed. Or you can get a start on the process now. Here is a list of basic business documents to look for:

- a recent financial statement, such as a balance sheet, statement of assets and liabilities, profit and loss statement, income statement, or income and expense statement
- recent tax returns for the business
- any partnership agreement and amendments, and
- any articles of incorporation or articles of organization, bylaws, operating agreement and shareholder certificates, or other documents showing ownership of shareholders or members.

Step Four: Inventory Your Assets and Debts

Once you've located any documents you think you'll need, use Worksheets 3 and 4 in the appendix to prepare a complete inventory of your property (assets) and debts.

 This section, like the others, is optional. You may not feel it's necessary to use our worksheets. Maybe you've already agreed on dividing up your property. Maybe your spouse has all the information. Or maybe your mediator or attorney has given you a different questionnaire or worksheet to use. Whatever the reason, it's okay to skip this section. Use it only if you find it helpful.

There are two worksheets for this part:
- Worksheet 3—Assets (Property)
- Worksheet 4—Debts.

To help you make the best use of these worksheets, we'll describe each one and then show you how they would be filled out by a fictional couple.

 Rachel and Aaron have been married for six years. They have two children, David and Danielle. Aaron also has a daughter, Sarah, from his first marriage. Aaron is a bookkeeper for a small business.

Rachel is assistant branch manager at a bank. Rachel moved out a few months ago and is renting an apartment. Aaron and the children are living in the home he and Rachel own together.

Worksheet 3—Assets

This worksheet consists of three parts— or more, if you need to add pages to list additional items. Part 1 contains instructions and asset categories for you to check off. Part 2 is a blank form for you to make a few copies of and list your assets on. Part 3 gives you spaces to list household furnishings, appliances, and tools if you and your spouse need help in dividing them up; you can make extra copies of this page, too, if you need more room. A blank tear-out copy of these forms is in the appendix.

The Eye of the Beholder

You'll notice that on Worksheet 3 we leave room for you to write down your estimate of the value of each asset. You may not know the value of an asset, or you and your spouse may disagree about the value of a certain asset. If so, your mediator will try to help you and your spouse decide on the best way to settle on the value. This might mean asking a neutral third party, such as an appraiser, accountant, or other professional, to value the asset.

You might be tempted to contact someone on your own to obtain a preliminary opinion of value of a particular asset. But if you do this, your spouse might question the neutrality of that person's opinion. It is best to hold off on contacting third parties for opinions on values until you and your spouse – and your attorneys, if you are collaborating – make a joint decision whether to hire someone to appraise the item in question.

Worksheet 3—Assets (Part 1)

Asset Category	Include in Description on Worksheet	Attach to Part 3 of This Worksheet
☑ Real estate	Address and assessor's parcel number	Copy of deed(s), property tax bill
☑ Household furnishings, appliances, tools, and equipment (from Part 3)	To be divided on our own	
N/A ☐ Art, antiques, and collections		
N/A ☐ Collections	Coins, stamps, etc.	
☑ Vehicles	Year, make, and model	Copy of title certificate or registration
N/A ☐ Boats and trailers	Make, model, and size	
☑ Bank and credit union savings, checking, certificate of deposit accounts	Name and branch, type of account, name of account holder	Copy of latest statement(s)
N/A ☐ Other cash	Location	
☑ Tax refunds	Tax year and whether state or federal	
☑ Life insurance	Name of insured, insurance company, face amount, any cash value	
N/A ☐ Stocks, bonds, mutual funds (nonretirement)	Name of investment and account number	Copy of latest share certificate
☑ Retirement plans, pensions, IRAs, Keoghs, 401(k) plans	Name of owner, type of plan	Copy of latest statement
N/A ☐ Money owed to you (notes, accounts receivable)	Name of debtor and purpose of loan	Copy of note, invoice, etc.
N/A ☐ Partnerships, other business	Business name, form of ownership interests, and percentage owned	
N/A ☐ Other		

Worksheet 3—Assets (Part 2)

Make extra copies if you need them. List in order of categories shown in Part 1.

Asset Category	Asset Description	Date Acquired	Joint or Separate	Estimated Current Value	Balance Due on Mortgage or Lien

Worksheet 3—Assets (Part 3)

Household Goods, Art, Antiques, and Collections

❏   We have divided these items to our satisfaction.

☑   We plan to divide these items between us without help. If we need help later, we will complete this worksheet.

❏   We can't agree on who gets some items or we can't agree on values. The items we can't agree on are listed below.

Group items when appropriate—for example, Dining Room Set, Flatware, etc.

The value is your best estimate of what this item would sell for in its current condition. If you prefer to use the cost paid, put "C" beside the cost, or for replacement cost, put "R."

Make extra copies of this page if you need them.

		VALUES	
	Who Gets This Item (If Agreed)	**Furnishings, Appliances, Tools and Equipment**	**Art, Antiques, and Collections**
SUBTOTALS (THIS PAGE)			
TOTALS (LAST PAGE ONLY)			

Worksheet 4—Debts

This worksheet consists of two parts. Part 1 contains instructions and categories. Part 2 is a blank form with spaces for you to fill in. Make a couple of copies to start with so that you will have plenty of room to write down everything. A blank tear-out copy of Worksheet 4 is in the appendix.

Below is Worksheet 4, filled in by Rachel.

Step Five: Summarize Your Income and Make a Budget

In addition to addressing children's needs and dividing up property and debts in your divorce agreement, you will need to agree on child support if you have children, and to decide whether alimony (also called spousal support or maintenance) will be waived or paid. Worksheets 4 and 5 will help you prepare to discuss these issues.

 If you don't have children and you know that neither of you will request alimony, you can skip this section. You can also skip it if you feel you don't have enough information to complete the worksheets or if your mediator or attorney has given you different forms to use.

There are two worksheets for this part. Blank tear-out copies are in the appendix.
- Worksheet 5—Your Income
- Worksheet 6—Your Monthly Expenses.

On these worksheets, you put down your income and expenses, but not your spouse's. When you and your spouse compare your information, this information will make it easy to see what each of you has in available cash and what you will need in order to maintain your own households.

Worksheet 4—Debts (Part 1)

- Use one or more copies of the attached pages to list all debts owed by you or your spouse in the order of the categories below; skip the categories that are not applicable.
- Use one row for each debt.
- If you don't know the balance due on a debt, put "Unknown."
- Check off each category as you finish it, or, if it doesn't apply, write "N/A" or "None."
- Attach a copy of the latest statement for each debt showing current balance due, if available.

Debt Category	Include in Description on Worksheet (Part 2)	Attach to Worksheet
❑ Taxes owed N/A	Tax years	
☑ Secured debts (debts tied to collateral such as mortgage, car loan, 401(k) loan, home equity loan)	Account number and description of collateral securing the debt (such as 19xx Ford)	Copy of latest statement
❑ General unsecured debts (including personal loans from friends or family members) N/A	Creditor name and reason this debt was incurred	Copy of promissory note or latest statement
☑ Credit card debts	Account number	Copy of latest statement
❑ Student loans N/A	Account number	Copy of latest statement
❑ Support arrears (child support or alimony/spousal support) N/A	Names of child/children, if child support	
❑ Overdue bills (not monthly household bills that are current) N/A		Copy of invoice or statement
❑ Other debts (not included above) N/A		

Worksheet 4—Debts (Part 2)

Debt Category	To Whom Owed	Description	Date Incurred	Balance Owed at Separation	Current Balance Owed
Secured Debts	Best Bank Best Bank	Mortgage Car Loan	1996 1998	$101,500 $15,500	$100,050 $15,000
Credit Cards	MBNA	MasterCard (joint)	varies	$1,000	$950
Credit Cards	Best Bank	Visa (Rachel)	varies	$300	$0
Credit Cards	Macy's	(Rachel)	varies	$250	$0

Math Anxiety?

If you're a person who is comfortable working with financial figures and budgets, you may find this part of the process fairly easy. On the other hand, if figures and budgets make you fidget, if your spouse is the one who has handled the finances, or if you've lost your usual facility with numbers because of your current emotional state, you may find this part a bit overwhelming. Don't push yourself to do more than is comfortable for you. Many people find that this is a time when it is helpful to work with a friend or adviser who is good at this kind of thing. Or you can wait and ask for help with it as part of the mediation or collaboration process.

Worksheet 5—Your Income

In the top part of this worksheet, write in your gross (pretax) annual income from the last calendar year. Include all income earned or received by you individually, plus your half of any joint investment income. Do not include income earned or received by your spouse. If you had no income of your own last year, skip this section of the worksheet.

To complete the top part, you can copy the annual income amounts from your last tax return. If you don't have a copy of your tax return or if you haven't filed yet, you may need to do a little more research or just skip this part. After you total last year's income, divide by 12 to get a monthly average.

Fill in your current monthly income in the bottom part of Worksheet 5. This may be the same as your monthly income from last year, or it may be different if you've changed jobs, received a raise, or changed your hours. If your income fluctuates from year to year, you can write in an average based on more than one year. Finally, write down monthly deductions from your paycheck if you are a wage earner.

If you are not employed outside the home and have no income of your own, use the bottom part of Worksheet 5 if you plan to obtain employment soon and you know what your monthly income will be.

Below is Worksheet 5, filled out by Rachel.

Worksheet 5—Your Income

List gross (before-tax) income earned or received by you in previous calendar year. Specify source of income: wages, self-employment, interest, dividends, commissions, annuities, etc. Do *not* include your spouse's income.

Your Gross Taxable Income   **Annual Amount**

_____Salary_____ $___39,800_____

_____ $_____

_____ $_____

_____ $_____

_____ $_____

Total Taxable Income $ ___39,800___ ÷ 12 = $___3,317.00_____
                                                    Monthly Amount

Your Gross Nontaxable Income
Specify source: tax-free interest, disability, etc.

_____ $_____

_____ $_____

_____ $_____

Total Nonaxable Income $ _____ ÷ 12 = $_____
                                                      Monthly Amount

Total Monthly Gross All Income $___3,317.00_____
Add taxable and nontaxable amounts.   Total Monthly

If different from the above, your *current* gross (before-tax) $___Same_____
monthly income (use an average if you need to).   Taxable

                                                                 $_____
                                                                 Nontaxable

Do you pay: State income tax? ☑ yes ☐ no   FICA/Medicare? ☑ yes ☐ no

Regular monthly deductions from your paycheck (attach a copy of a current pay stub):

Federal Tax: ___382.00_____   Mandatory Retirement:_____180.00_____

State Tax: ___120.00_____   Voluntary Deductions: _____

FICA/Medicare: __45.00_____   Health Care, Day Care: _____

Health Insurance: ___30.00_____

Union Dues:_____   Total Deductions: ___757.00_____

Worksheet 6—Your Monthly Expenses

This worksheet helps you put together a monthly budget of your living expenses separate from your spouse's. Having a good idea of your ongoing monthly expenses—including which ones are essential and which ones are discretionary—will help you understand your choices when negotiating a specific financial arrangement. If you and your spouse still live together, or if you've only recently separated, doing a budget may involve a certain amount of estimating and guesswork. If you have access to financial records such as check registers and credit card statements, use them to help make your estimates as accurate as possible.

In the upper half of Part 1, we've tried to include as many categories of expenses as possible, so there's little chance of leaving something out. We also provide space to put down annual figures for expenses such as clothing or vacations, which aren't the same every month. That way, you can divide the annual amount by 12 to arrive at a monthly average.

If you and your spouse have children who spend time in your household, include general expenses such as food, rent, and utilities for the whole household, but don't include expenses that are unique to each child—such as medical and dental expenses, day care, activities, lessons, and private school.

Those go in the bottom part of Part 1. If other children or adults live with you, include their expenses and show any contributions you receive for their expenses at the bottom of Part 1. (We show you an example of this at the end of this section.)

Part 2 is an optional attachment where you can list any monthly installment payments you regularly pay, such as credit cards. Be sure to include the total from Part 2 in the appropriate space on Part 1.

If you don't have all the information you need to complete Worksheet 6, don't worry. This is just a preliminary worksheet to help you assess your own financial reality. If your figures are incomplete or rough, you can use the mediation or collaboration process to fill in the details.

If you have enough information to complete this worksheet, you might discover that your separate monthly expenses far exceed your separate monthly income. While this can be depressing, don't panic. This is important information that will help you negotiate a divorce agreement that is realistic and as fair to you as to your spouse.

We have included an example of Worksheet 6, completed by Aaron.

Worksheet 6—Your Monthly Expenses (Part 1)

Names of all persons in your household whose expenses are included on this worksheet:

Aaron, Sarah, David, Danielle

- List the average monthly expenses for the household in which you live. Do not include your spouse's expenses if you are living separately. Do not include any special expenses for your children (see below).
- Include all expenses that apply. Refer to your records to be as accurate as possible.
- If monthly amount varies, indicate annual amount and divide by 12 for monthly average.
- Put an * next to expenses on which you've had to cut back since your separation.

Item	Annual	Monthly	Item	Annual	Monthly
rent or mortgage		665	life or disability insurance		45
property taxes		50	your education		
owner/renter insurance		40	entertainment		60
maintenance	1500	125	car registration/insurance	500	42
cleaning/yard service/pool			car gasoline and oil		30
water softener/bottled water			car repairs/auto club	600	50
food and household supplies		600	car parking		
food: eating out		75	car payment		250
utilities		200	gifts, donations		
telephone		50	dues/subscriptions		15
laundry/dry cleaning			vacations		
clothing (yourself)	300	25	haircuts, personal hygiene		25
health insurance			pets (food, vet, etc.)		15
unreimbursed medical	100	8	accountant		
unreimbursed dental	75	7	unreimbursed business exp.		
unreimbursed psychotherapy			installments (Part 2)		50+
unreimbursed prescriptions	35	3	other (specify)		
			Total Monthly		$2,4304

Does anyone else contribute to the above expenses? ☑ yes ☐ no

If so, who and how much? _Sarah's mother-child support $150/month_

Worksheet 6—Your Monthly Expenses (Part 1) cont.

Special Expenses for Children

Names of Children: _Sarah, David, Danielle_

Item	Annual	Monthly	Item	Annual	Monthly
health insurance			day care		350
unreimbursed medical	200	17	tuition		
unreimbursed dental	200	17	school lunches, supplies		25
orthodontia			activities/lessons		40
clothing	800	67	other (specify)		
			Total Monthly		516

Does anyone else contribute to the special expenses for children? ☑ yes ☐ no

If so, who and how much? _____

Step Six: Pause to Reflect

When you've worked through the five steps outlined above, stop for a moment and check to be sure you haven't overlooked something. Then ask yourself whether there is any information we haven't mentioned that you think might be important to have available when you meet in mediation or collaboration. If there is, and if the information is readily available, consider having it ready, just in case. If you don't have the information you're thinking of, just make a note of it now, so that you can bring it up with the mediator or your attorney later.

Once you have completed these steps, you'll have a head start on the information gathering stage of mediation or collaboration.

■

Chapter 10

Preparing for and Making the Most of the First Session

You've decided to mediate or collaborate. You and your spouse have selected your mediator or collaborative attorneys. You have gathered your information, using the suggestions in Chapter 9 or instructions from your mediator or collaborative attorney, and you are about to go to the first mediation session or collaborative four-way meeting. How do you to prepare for the first session or four-way? This chapter suggests some things you can do to get ready.

is inconsistent with what your attorney tells you, feel free to ignore what's here. For example, we give you suggestions for communicating with each other. Your attorney will have his or her own way of helping you focus on good communication techniques. If it's confusing to try to follow our suggestions and those of your attorney, just focus on what your attorney is saying. Good teamwork between you and your collaborative attorney is the priority.

 If you are mediating, follow your mediator's instructions. If your mediator has asked you to do certain things to get ready for mediation, by all means, do them. If our suggestions help to supplement what your mediator is having you do, great. But if what we say is inconsistent with what your mediator tells you, feel free to ignore what's here. For example, we suggest some ways you can prepare mentally for the mediation. Maybe your mediator has given you specific exercises to use before the meeting. If so, follow your mediator's lead, and don't bother with our suggestions unless they help too.

 If you are collaborating, follow your attorney's instructions. If your attorney has asked you to do certain things to get ready for the first four-way, by all means, do them. If our suggestions help to supplement what your attorney is having you do, great. But if what we say

Getting Ready

Step One: Read Up on What to Expect

The First Mediation Session

Before you go to mediation, get a preview of what can happen at the first session. Read (or reread) the description of the first session found in Chapter 2. Then review the second part of this chapter for more information about what to expect. We give you a list of questions to ask during the first session.

The First Four-Way

Before the first four-way meeting, get a preview of what can happen. Read (or reread) the description of the first four-way found in Chapter 3. Supplement this with any materials your attorney may have given you.

Brush Up on Communicating and Negotiating

Whether you have chosen to mediate or collaborate, you will benefit from browsing Chapter 12, which outlines the basic techniques of good communication. You'll have a jump-start on a successful mediation or collaboration if you familiarize yourself with these techniques.

An optional but worthwhile thing to do at some point early in the process is to read Chapter 13, which explains the fundamentals of effective negotiating in mediation.

Step Two (Mediating Couples Only): Consider Consulting a Mediation-Friendly Lawyer

You may already have consulted a lawyer for advice about your legal rights and options, and you may have spoken with the lawyer about what will happen in mediation. If not, seriously consider doing so now. Divorce laws vary quite a bit from state to state, and laws and practices regarding mediation can vary, too. A good lawyer who supports mediation can be very helpful in guiding you through the preparation process. He or she can alert you to specific questions to ask during the mediation and can help make sure that you understand the legalities of issues that can arise during the mediation.

As we explain in Chapter 11, most consulting lawyers who support

mediation will meet with you for an hour or so to explain the basics and will charge only for the time spent, rather than insisting on the usual divorce retainer of several thousands of dollars (or more). Paying for an hour or two of time with a competent consulting lawyer before the mediation begins is not only a good investment, it may actually save time and money by helping you stay focused on the important issues during the mediation.

If you're thinking of eventually having your divorce agreement reviewed by a lawyer before you sign it, establishing contact with the reviewing lawyer now will give him or her a sense of your concerns and priorities. When it comes time to review the agreement, your lawyer will be more likely to understand what is important to you. And if you have a lawyer lined up from the beginning, it will be easy to consult with your lawyer from time to time between mediation sessions to answer questions that come up and to brainstorm ways of structuring the agreement that will accomplish your goals.

⚠️ **Avoid mediation-hostile lawyers.** Working with a lawyer who does not understand and support mediation can be a disaster. Lawyers are trained to be advocates, first and foremost. As adversarial advocates, their job is to represent their clients and their clients only, to the full extent of the law. A consulting lawyer needs to go beyond his or her training as an advocate. He or she must be aware of and concerned with your legal rights and at the same time supportive of the goal of mediation, which is to find solutions that work for both you and your spouse and for your children. We suggest you read Chapter 8 before making an appointment with a consulting lawyer.

Step Three: Prepare Yourself Mentally

For this final step, take a few deep breaths, sit back, and prepare yourself mentally and emotionally for the mediation or collaboration process.

Remember that the goal is to come up with an agreement that works for both you and your spouse and that is at least as good for each of you as what you would get in court—taking into account what court would cost as well as the likely outcome. This means that you need to approach the mediation or collaboration with a forward-looking, positive attitude, and a willingness to be realistic about what can be accomplished.

If you find that intense emotions of anger or a desire for revenge interfere with your ability to function or think clearly about your situation, seek the help of a counselor in working through your feelings and finding effective ways to deal with them before beginning the mediation or collaboration. If you find yourself so depressed that you can't focus on anything for very long, this also is a sign that you should get professional help from a counselor. For more on finding and working with a counselor, see Chapter 8.

Even if you feel you are able to function reasonably well, spending an hour or two with a counselor or collaborative coach recommended by your attorney can be an excellent investment of your time and money and can help you stay focused during mediation sessions or collaborative four-ways.

Regardless of whether you decide to prepare with the help of a counselor, here are some tips that will help you keep your focus:

Prepare to listen while your spouse talks. To help you and your spouse negotiate an agreement that is acceptable to both of you, the mediator or your attorneys will need to understand how each of you sees things. You may find it difficult to sit and listen to your spouse or your spouse's attorney say things that you disagree with or experienced differently. You may become concerned that understanding what your spouse says will make the mediator or the attorneys agree with your spouse instead of you. Remind yourself now that the point is not to decide who is right, but for you and the mediator or collaborative attorneys to listen to both of your points of view so that you can make the decisions you need to make. In understanding how your spouse sees things, a mediator or collaborative attorney is not agreeing with your spouse. The mediator or the attorneys will want to hear from you, too, and will be just as concerned about understanding your point of view.

Listen in order to understand. Often we hear what another person says, but we do not really try to understand, especially if we're in conflict with that person. Again, remind yourself that understanding does not mean you agree. Get ready to use mediation or collaboration to understand as much as you can about your spouse's concerns as well as your own. Understanding how your spouse sees things, especially if you disagree, can be very helpful to you in evaluating possible settlement options. It will give you a good idea of which settlement options are likely to be mutually acceptable.

Focus on the future. Your divorce agreement will spell out what is to happen with your property, your finances, and your children in the future, not in the past. Regardless of what has gone on up to this point, it is important that you keep your focus on future goals, needs, and concerns. You can learn from past mistakes and behavior in assessing what is realistic and appropriate, but do not let your feelings about the past dictate your decisions about the future.

Avoid offering solutions or proposals prematurely. It is tempting to think through everything from your own point of view and come up with what seems to you to be the perfect solution for dividing your property, settling your finances, and, if you have children, arranging things for them. It can be counterproductive to present a solution too soon, however. For one thing, a solution you come up with early on might not take into account things your spouse considers important. This is why you need to listen carefully to your spouse's concerns. And even if your ideas are great, the fact that they come from you could cause your spouse to reject them out of hand. The mediation or collaboration process is designed to neutralize dynamics like this. If you think of solutions during the first session or four-way, make a note of them, but wait until your mediator or your attorney invites you to bring them up.

Watch out for unrealistic demands. Feelings of betrayal or anger may tempt you to make unrealistic demands. For example, your feelings about how your spouse has treated you might lead you to want your spouse to give up all legal claims to property without anything in exchange or to pay more money to you than he or she can afford. Ask yourself whether your demand is realistic from your spouse's point of view. If you're in doubt, ask your consulting lawyer or collaborative attorney, or an adviser who understands at least a little about divorce law and can be impartial. (This means don't ask one of your close friends who is on your side no matter what.) If what you are considering is clearly unrealistic, you can derive some satisfaction from imagining it, but don't plan to propose it.

Beware of nonnegotiable demands. This is a cousin of the premature proposal and the unrealistic demand. While it is important to have a pretty good idea of your bottom line, try not to make proposals that you absolutely won't budge from. This is almost sure to bring the negotiations to a grinding halt. There is almost always more than one way to solve any problem, so allow for that possibility when preparing for the mediation session or four-way.

If you have children, focus on what's best for them. Study after study shows that children whose parents are divorcing do best when their parents can set aside their adult disagreements to focus on what's best for their children. Prepare for the mediation session or four-way by reminding yourself that your children need you to work with their other parent in making decisions that are child-focused. Resist the temptation to see yourself as locked in a power struggle with your spouse. If you and your spouse disagree about what would be best for your children, be open to ways to obtain more information about your children's needs that will allow the two of you to make the right decisions.

Picture yourself successfully concluding an agreement with your spouse. Behavioral psychologists have long known that visualizing a positive outcome can improve performance. Many top athletes regularly visualize themselves in successful competition as part of their training. You can borrow a page from their book by sitting for a few moments once or twice a day prior to a mediation session or four-way and visualizing a respectful process of communicating and negotiating.

Along the same lines, use simple affirmations such as "we can work this out" or "we can come to an agreement that works for both of us," which you repeat to yourself (silently, if you're uncomfortable saying them aloud) a few times a day. Preparing yourself with visualizations or affirmations can give you a reservoir of inner strength to draw on when you come to a tough spot during a session or four-way.

Be patient. It's common to come into mediation or collaboration thoroughly prepared and impatient to get on with the negotiations. As we discuss in the next chapter, you will probably start by going over background information, reviewing property inventories and other financial information, and covering other preliminary matters. The process can also get off to a slow start if your spouse isn't well-prepared or needs to go slowly in order to feel comfortable with what's happening. Prepare for this possibility by remembering that the extra time is well spent. The decisions you will be making in mediation or collaboration will seriously and permanently affect your future. Allow yourself the time necessary to make sure that those decisions are the right ones for you, and give your spouse the time he or she needs to do the same. The time spent carefully considering everything will more than pay off in a solid agreement that both you and your spouse can live with and abide by.

Keep things in perspective. People aren't usually at their best when going through a divorce. Your spouse's negative traits may be exaggerated as you mediate. If so, remember that there's nothing you can do about it except what you are doing— getting divorced in the most sensible way possible.

Recap. Check one last time to be sure you've covered everything in steps one through three that apply to you. If you have, you're about as ready as anyone can be to attend the first mediation session or collaborative four-way. Good luck!

 For collaborating couples only—skip to the next chapter.

The rest of the material in this chapter applies only to couples in mediation. Your collaborative attorney takes over at this point in preparing you for the first four-way. If you haven't had a thorough discussion with your attorney about how to get ready or what to expect, now is the time. Take a moment to jot down your questions. Bring them with you when you meet with your attorney. Ask as many questions as you need in order to feel ready.

The First Mediation Session

The first mediation session is part of the introductory stage of mediation. This is when you'll get some first-hand experience of the mediation process.

Mediators differ in approaches. Each mediator has his or her own way of conducting the first session. Often, the first session consists of a joint meeting with you and your spouse. Other times, the first session might consist of separate meetings with each of you, if the mediator prefers to work that way or your circumstances have prompted you to request separate meetings. You may even be doing the mediation by teleconference.

Concepts to Consider

Steps to take before the first session:

❏ Review Worksheet 8—First Session Checklist in the appendix. Make changes and additions to suit your needs.

❏ Bring Worksheet 8 with you to the session. Make sure the mediator addresses all points you want discussed.

❏ During the session, feel free to ask other questions that occur to you. There is no such thing as a stupid question. Mediators know this and encourage questions.

❏ At the end of the session, don't be afraid to say you need additional time to think before scheduling a second session or agreeing to continue.

On the other hand, if you feel comfortable with the mediator, don't be afraid to agree to a time and place for the next session.

❏ After the session, review your notes and Worksheet 8. Ask yourself again if you are comfortable with this mediator.

❏ Decide whether you want to continue with this mediator. If not, notify your spouse and the mediator. You don't have to give a reason or even speak with the mediator, but at least leave a message as a matter of courtesy. If you still want to mediate, and you want to try a different mediator, arrange for an appointment with another mediator and start the process again.

Each mediator's personal style is unique, as is your particular situation. Because of this, it is possible that what we say here won't apply to your mediation. In that case, rely on your mediator to help you with any questions or concerns, and ignore whatever we've said that is at odds with your own mediation experience.

The goals of the first session of mediation are as follows:

• to give you a good idea of what mediation is and how your mediator plans to approach your case

• to develop a clear agreement (preferably in writing) with the mediator about basic conditions of the mediation, such as fees and billing, confidentiality, and disclosure, and

• to help you decide whether you want to continue with this mediator.

Can't Make Up Your Mind?

It can be frustrating to discover that the first mediator you meet with doesn't work out. It's natural to doubt yourself and to feel discouraged. But making several attempts to find the right mediator can still be worth it, as compared to litigating your divorce or sticking with a mediator who isn't right for you.

Mediator Approaches and Styles

Good mediators vary greatly in their approaches and styles. Their training, background, experience, and personalities all influence how they go about the job of bringing people together to resolve their differences. There is no right or wrong approach or style, but knowing something ahead of time about common approaches and styles can help you get a feel for a potential mediator and whether you'll be comfortable with him or her. Below we highlight some things to watch for during the first session.

Does the Mediator Control the Discussion?

Some mediators keep a tight rein on what happens during the mediation session. They have a clear agenda to follow. They may limit the times that you and your spouse can speak, and they often have ground rules, such as no interruptions, raised voices, or disrespectful behavior, that they will announce at the beginning of the session.

On the other end of the control spectrum are mediators who make a point of *not* taking charge. They let the discussion flow where you and your spouse take it, bringing you back to the topic from time to time, but not insisting on a particular sequence. These mediators are more tolerant of emotional expressions and even outbursts during the mediation session.

In between these two extremes are mediators who allow for some give and take, balancing this against a structured agenda. They are ready to negotiate or impose behavior ground rules when needed.

Which approach is right for you depends on the dynamics of your relationship with your spouse and your comfort level in a more or less structured environment.

If you and your spouse have trouble talking about anything without escalating into nasty verbal attacks, you might prefer a mediator who structures each person's time to talk over a mediator who waits until you're at each other's throats before intervening. On the other hand, if you or your spouse need to vent a certain amount in the mediation, you might find it restricting to be limited by the mediator's rules about when and how to talk.

As the session progresses, note how your mediator handles interactions between you and your spouse—and your reaction to the mediator's method. Are you comfortable or uncomfortable with what's happening? Would you like the mediator to step in more or less? If you're worried about particular interactions that might come up, ask the mediator what he or she would do about them.

Will the Mediator Suggest a Settlement?

Some mediators take a very active role in coming up with the terms of the settlement. Once they know the facts and understand the case, they will tell you how they think you should settle the issues. They will readily say whether what you are considering seems fair, and they will use their expertise to put before you what they believe is the best solution.

Other mediators will encourage you to come up with your own ideas for settlement. They will avoid telling you what they think you should do and will emphasize the importance of working together with your spouse to come up with solutions that are uniquely yours. These mediators may offer their own ideas, but not before you've tried to come up with some of your own.

A less directive mediation style can allow you to explore lots of different options and keep full control over what gets decided. Since these are two of the major benefits of mediation, many people will probably prefer a less directive mediator. But if you believe that the only way the two of you will agree is to hear someone else's idea of what's best for you, a more directive mediator might be what you want.

How Does the Mediator Approach Negotiating?

Mediators have different ways to help spouses develop their own negotiating skills and to keep the negotiations going in a constructive direction. A good mediator should be able to give you a short overview of his or her approach to negotiation, including how best to prepare for the negotiation and what steps the negotiation will follow.

During the first session, ask your mediator how he or she handles the negotiations. (See suggested questions on Worksheet 8 in the appendix.) Listen to the answers carefully, and ask follow-up questions if you need to. Compare the mediator's answers to the information found in Chapter 13.

Is Law Important to the Mediator?

We've discussed the importance of being informed about the legal rules and potential court outcomes in negotiating your settlement. While you should feel free to explore settlement options that are different from what a judge would do, you can and should have legal information available to you as you consider the settlement options. The first session is a chance to find out what your mediator's attitude is toward the legal rules.

Some mediators make a point of measuring any settlement by the legal standards. They believe that the legal rules promote fairness.

Other mediators consider the law unimportant. They believe that it is up to you and your spouse to decide what is right for you without regard to legal rules.

Many mediators are in between. They want you to be fully informed of your legal rights, but they recognize that the legal rules offer a one-size-fits-all approach to fairness—and that approach may not be practical or equitable for you and your spouse. These mediators encourage you to look at many different factors, including the law, in negotiating an agreement.

And Justice for All?

Here's an example of how the mediator's attitude toward considering the legal rules can make a big difference in the settlement.

Marcos and Alicia are getting a divorce after 15 years of marriage. During their marriage, Marcos inherited $20,000 from his mother's estate and Alicia inherited $15,000 from her grandmother's estate. Marcos's inheritance was used for the down payment on the family home. Alicia's inheritance was deposited in the joint account and used to pay bills and expenses.

Marcos and Alicia want to mediate their divorce. Here are three different ways their settlement could turn out, depending on the mediator's approach to the law:

1. Mediator A does not believe in discussing the legal rules in mediation. Although Marcos wants to keep the house, he can't afford to buy Alicia out. So Mediator A helps Marcos and Alicia negotiate an agreement that involves selling the house and dividing the proceeds of $100,000 equally. Several months later, Marcos learns from a friend that under state law he had a legal right to be repaid the amount of his inheritance from the sale of the house before dividing up the remainder of $80,000. If Marcos had known this, he might have been able to afford to pay Alicia $40,000 to buy her out, but by now it is too late to do anything about it.

And Justice for All?, cont.

2. **Mediator B** believes in using the law to determine the settlement. She informs Marcos and Alicia that under state law Marcos has the right to be reimbursed for his inheritance, but that Alicia would not be reimbursed because her inheritance was spent on bills and cannot be traced to a particular asset, such as the house. Mediator B encourages Marcos and Alicia to agree that Marcos will keep the house and pay $40,000 to Alicia. Marcos is satisfied with this result, but Alicia ends up feeling cheated out of her inheritance.

3. **Mediator C** helps Marcos and Alicia figure out how much importance to give to the legal rules in working out their settlement. They agree they want to be fair with each other. They also talk about what's important to each of them. Marcos wants to keep the house. Alicia wants to know that there will be money set aside for their daughter's education. Mediator C tells Marcos and Alicia about the legal rule that gives reimbursement to Marcos but not Alicia, and she reminds them that they do not have to agree to anything that seems unfair to either one of them. After considering everything, Marcos and Alicia agree that Marcos will keep the house and pay Alicia $40,000. In addition, when their daughter turns 18, Marcos will sell or refinance and deposit $35,000—the total of both inheritances—into a fund for her college education. The agreement also includes terms to ensure that the $35,000 will be available when the time comes. Marcos and Alicia both feel satisfied that they considered the legal rules and came up with a settlement that is fair and focused on their concerns, not dictated by the law.

As you might guess, we think it's best to work with a mediator who includes legal principles in the discussion but doesn't let you get hung up on them.

If you decide to use a mediator who ignores the legal rules, then be sure to inform yourself of your legal options by consulting with a legal adviser early on in the process. (See Chapter 8 for tips on selecting and using a legal adviser.)

To help you learn what your mediator's attitude toward the law is, we've included some questions on Worksheet 8.

Does the Mediator Support the Use of Legal Advisers?

Most mediators encourage spouses to consult with lawyers and other advisers while the mediation is pending. A few mediators even insist that you have the written settlement agreement reviewed by a lawyer before you sign it. Use the first session to learn your mediator's attitude about legal advisers.

⚠ Don't be pressured into forgoing legal advice. Some mediators will require that you have a consulting attorney during the process or for the purpose of reviewing a draft agreement when you have reached a settlement. Others will leave it up to you whether you want to consult with an outside attorney. But no mediator should actively discourage you from using a consulting attorney. If your mediator isn't supportive of your desire to use legal or

other advisers, you probably want to find a different mediator.

Does the Mediator Work in Joint Sessions, Separate Sessions, or Both?

The first session is a chance to learn whether your mediator will use joint sessions or separate sessions to help you reach an agreement. In earlier chapters, we discuss the idea of conducting the mediation in separate sessions (caucuses) as opposed to having everyone meet together in joint sessions. This is another area where mediators can differ.

You might be thinking that meeting separately will help minimize the stress, anxiety, and discomfort you feel in the presence of your spouse. And as we mentioned earlier, there may be circumstances where separate sessions are called for—such as cases involving domestic violence or power imbalance.

Barring special circumstances, however, joint sessions are the quickest and least expensive way to mediate a settlement agreement in which both you and your spouse will have confidence. In a joint session, you and your spouse are in the room at the same time, hear the same information, engage in honest discussions about what will and won't work for you, and collaborate to find the best resolution of your case. In contrast, separate sessions take up more time and may heighten any mistrust that exists between you and your spouse.

Separate sessions can be useful if you need individualized help in preparing to negotiate productively, but they are considered by most mediators to be an intermediate step toward the ultimate goal of bringing you and your spouse together to negotiate your divorce agreement. And if you have children, mediating in joint sessions will give you a constructive setting in which to learn how to make decisions together about your children—a skill you will find essential as the years go by.

Some mediators believe that everyone who mediates needs to spend some time alone with the mediator preparing for the negotiations, and so they build this into every mediation. Other mediators will meet separately only rarely or not at all because of their belief that meeting separately breeds mistrust instead of promoting collaboration. Then there are mediators who encourage joint sessions but are flexible enough to use separate sessions when needed. Find out your mediator's approach by asking the appropriate questions on Worksheet 8.

If your mediator will include separate sessions, you will need a clear agreement with your mediator about whether the information discussed in the separate sessions will be private or will be shared with the other spouse. Some mediators will not disclose private information divulged in a separate session unless specifically authorized to do so. Other mediators refuse to keep information private because they feel that keeping secrets from you and your spouse would affect their neutrality. Still others will agree not to disclose nonessential private information but will want to disclose factual information that would make a difference in the negotiations. Be sure to find out your mediator's attitude using Worksheet 8.

Does the Mediator's Style Put You at Ease?

Move beyond the common mediation issues. What about the mediator's style? Is it compatible with your style and preferences? Style is a pretty individual thing. It depends on personality, upbringing, education, and all the other factors that combine to set each person apart as a unique individual.

Try as we might to dissect and categorize people into types and temperaments, it is important to recognize that human behavior and compatibility are not easily explained or predicted. The mediator you've selected may have an appearance or mannerism that just rubs you the wrong way. Or you may feel completely safe and at home with the mediator. The reasons why you react one way or another aren't important. What is important is that you feel relatively comfortable with your mediator. Negotiating with your spouse will be hard enough without adding a mediator whose manner irritates you. So pay attention to your reactions to the mediator, and if you're uncomfortable at all, for whatever reason, look further. The extra effort will be well worth it in the long run.

Mediator Neutrality and Bias

An effective mediator should be neutral. This means that in addition to avoiding any conflict of interest created by a prior relationship with you or your spouse, he or she should avoid taking sides with one of you during the mediation. And while you can agree to waive (ignore) a potential conflict of interest arising from a preexisting relationship, do not ignore obvious signals of bias on the part of the mediator during the mediation.

On the other hand, being neutral is not the same as being uncaring. Mediators are trained to listen to each person carefully and empathetically, *without* taking sides. Just because your mediator listens intently to your spouse, perhaps nodding encouragingly or sympathetically, does not mean that the mediator is no longer neutral. It just means that the mediator is trying to establish rapport with your spouse. The mediator will want a good rapport with you, too, in order to have a solid foundation for assisting both of you through the negotiations.

Being neutral also doesn't mean taking a hands-off approach to the mediation process. Although mediators vary in the degree of control they exercise over the process, every mediator considers it his or her responsibility to make sure that the process is fair and balanced enough for each person to be able to communicate and negotiate freely. If it appears to the mediator that one of you is acting in a way that is interfering with the process, the mediator is likely to do or say something to eliminate or change the disruptive behavior.

Finally, being neutral doesn't mean that the mediator won't ever have an opinion or bias about something in the mediation. Mediators are human, after all. In many instances, the mediator can neutralize an opinion or bias internally, using techniques developed through training and experience. But if this isn't possible, you and the mediator will have to deal with the situation.

Sometimes a mediator will tell you that she or he has a particular bias. Sometimes you will feel that the mediator is biased for or against you, even if the mediator hasn't said anything. If so, bring it up yourself. The mediator's response will tell you a lot about how comfortable you are going to be with that particular mediator. Perhaps just talking about your concern and listening to what the mediator has to say will be enough to allay your concerns. If not, this can be a reason to consider a different mediator.

One form of bias that can come up in divorce mediations is gender bias. Unless you choose to work with comediators, the mediator you select will either be male or female. Should you be concerned about the gender of the mediator? Probably not.

Although there is a potential for a two-against-one kind of alignment (the men against the woman or the women against the man or even a cross-gender bias), in reality it rarely works out that way. For one thing, every mediator worth his or her salt is sensitive to the pitfalls of gender bias and has worked hard to develop techniques to get around them. In addition, many factors other than gender have the potential for a two-against-one alignment. For example, if you are an artist with no financial or business experience and your spouse runs a business, a mediator with extensive business background could appear to you to be aligned with your spouse regardless of the mediator's gender.

Still, gender bias is a topic to consider discussing with your mediator, especially if you have specific concerns. And if you're interested in reading a little more about gender issues in mediation, see Chapter 17.

During the first session, ask about the mediator's attitude toward neutrality. If you didn't address conflicts of interest when you made the appointment, do so now. Use Worksheet 8 to ask how the mediator handles bias and maintains neutrality during the course of the mediation. If the mediator is a lawyer, confirm that the mediator will not represent one of you against the other once the mediation is over, especially if the mediation ends without reaching an agreement.

Confidentiality of the Mediation

If you didn't discuss confidentiality when you made your appointment, consider doing so at the first session. Most mediators consider it their ethical duty not to disclose to third parties any information you provide. But the mediator could still be legally compelled to divulge the information to a court or government agency under certain circumstances, unless a state law or written agreement makes the information confidential. For example, you or your spouse could subpoena the mediator to testify at your divorce trial if the mediation is unsuccessful. Or the IRS could subpoena mediation records as part of an audit of your tax returns.

If you don't care about protecting the confidentiality of what is said in mediation, then don't raise it at the first session. But if you want the mediation to be confidential, ask your mediator what can be done to ensure confidentiality.

In some states, information disclosed in mediation is protected by law from disclosure. In other states, you may need a written agreement. Your mediator should be able to tell you what's needed. An example of a written confidentiality agreement is in the "Confidentiality" section of Worksheet 9—Sample Agreement to Mediate, found in the appendix.

Concepts to Consider

Essential Points of Mediation Agreement

- ❑ the names of the people participating in the mediation— ordinarily you, your spouse, and the mediator

- ❑ the subject of the mediation—your divorce or the specific issues you are mediating

- ❑ the mediator's role and responsibilities—facilitation, neutrality, avoidance of conflicts of interest

- ❑ whether and how legal rights will be considered in evaluating settlement options, including the role of consulting lawyers

- ❑ use of experts during mediation— selecting experts, how fees will be paid

- ❑ confidentiality of statements made and records prepared during the mediation—unless this is covered in a separate confidentiality agreement

- ❑ whether you and your spouse will make full disclosure of financial and other information during the mediation

- ❑ who may attend mediation sessions

- ❑ whether the mediator will conduct separate sessions

- ❑ whether statements made in separate sessions will be confidential

- ❑ whether legal proceedings will be suspended during mediation

- ❑ each party's right to end mediation at any time

- ❑ whether the mediator will prepare a written divorce agreement or memorandum of agreement (see Chapter 16)

- ❑ mediation fees—how charged and who pays, and

- ❑ any special ground rules agreed upon.

Agreement to Mediate

Before moving to the second stage of mediation, you should have a clear agreement with the mediator that covers the basic aspects of your mediation. Ordinarily, the agreement should be in writing, because this cuts down on the possibility of confusion about what was agreed to. Some mediators prefer a more informal approach, however, and if you're satisfied that what's been agreed to is clear, you don't have to insist on a written agreement.

Court-sponsored mediation. If you are participating in court-sponsored mediation, you may have less say over the terms and conditions of the mediation. Be sure to read Chapter 14 before participating in court-sponsored mediation.

Many mediators have a standard written agreement to mediate that they use in every mediation case. Some agreements are in the form of a letter from the mediator to you and your spouse. No matter what the form of the agreement, it must clearly spell out everyone's understanding of what the mediation is about, how it will be conducted, and each person's responsibility. Take the time to read the agreement carefully and ask as many questions as you need to. Compare it to the checklist below to make sure all essential points have been covered. If you think something in the agreement is unclear or needs to be added or changed, say so. A good mediator will welcome your questions and suggestions.

If your mediator doesn't offer a written agreement, you could use Worksheet 9 in the appendix. Or if you don't think a written agreement is necessary, use the checklist below to be sure you've covered the essential points needed to have a clear understanding about the mediation.

Take Time to Make Notes

After the first mediation session, take a moment to jot down your thoughts on the experience while it is still fresh in your mind. This will help you decide whether continuing in mediation is the right course for you. Chapter 11 has more about evaluating your decisions after the first session.

Chapter 11

Evaluating Your Progress in Mediation or Collaborative Divorce

After the first mediation session or collaborative four-way is over, it's a good idea to stop and reflect on your decision to mediate or collaborate. It's never too late to make a change if you need to later on, but a course correction would be easier now, when the time and money you've invested in the process is minimal. If you decide to continue, we recommend that you pause from time to time to assess your progress so that you can make any needed adjustments. This chapter offers suggestions for evaluating the first session or meeting and monitoring your progress after that.

can confirm or cancel once you've made up your mind. Mediators tend to be very understanding about this, although they do appreciate a call if you decide to cancel.

As you reflect on your experience of the first session, use Worksheet 8 and any notes you made immediately after the session to help you focus your thoughts. If you still can't decide, close your eyes, take a deep breath or two, and imagine yourself in another session with this mediator. If you have serious misgivings, maybe this isn't the mediator for you. But if you feel okay about it, then you may as well continue with this mediator.

Evaluating the Decision to Mediate or Use Collaborative Divorce

If You Chose Mediation

Reflect on the Experience

By the end of the first session, you should have a pretty good idea whether you want to continue in mediation and if so, whether you want to continue with this mediator. If you feel very certain that you do, by all means go ahead and schedule an appointment for the next session. If you aren't sure and you want some time to think, leave the scheduling to a later time or make a tentative appointment that you

If You Need a Different Mediator

If you think you want to mediate, but you think you haven't found the right mediator, you'll need to notify your spouse and start the process of scheduling a meeting with a new mediator. It's courteous to contact the mediator with whom you met and let him or her know of your decision. There's no need to give an explanation, unless you want to. Then turn back to Chapter 6 and to your original list of potential mediators, and make an appointment with the next person on your list. Eventually you'll find someone who's right for you. Given the importance of the decisions you'll be making, it's worth the extra time and expense to get the right fit.

What If Your Spouse Likes the Mediator, but You Don't?

Do a gut-check to make sure that you're not rejecting the mediator just to needle your spouse. If you're confident that's not the reason for your discomfort, then you may need to insist that your preferences also be taken into account. No one can make either one of you go to mediation without the other person's consent, so you will need to find someone you both feel comfortable with. That may mean continuing the search until you find someone you can agree upon.

If Mediation Isn't the Right Choice for You

If you have reservations about continuing with mediation, consider whether you and your spouse might be candidates for collaborative divorce instead. Unless the two of you can negotiate a settlement without any outside help, using collaborative divorce is going to be a better option than adversarial litigation. If you decide that collaborative divorce is not an option, try to find a divorce lawyer who will agree to use a cooperative approach to negotiating on your behalf, and encourage your spouse to do the same.

If You Chose Collaborative Divorce

Reflect on the Experience

Once you've experienced the first four-way meeting, you'll be in a good position to assess whether you think the collaborative process could work for you.

Think about what it was like to be in the four-way meeting. Use any notes you made right after the four-way, and if your attorney has given you a form on which to jot down your impressions of the meeting, spend some time completing and reviewing the form. Were there things that happened that made you feel comfortable or confident in the process? Were there things that made you feel uncomfortable or pessimistic about collaborative divorce working for you?

Discuss Your Concerns With Your Collaborative Attorney

Make a list of questions and concerns to discuss with your collaborative attorney and if you haven't already done so, schedule a conference with your attorney to go over those questions. Ask your attorney for suggestions for making the next four-way more comfortable, and make suggestions of your own if you have them. Talk with your lawyer until you have a plan for how to make the next four-way easier for you

Dealing With Doubts About Your Collaborative Attorney

If your experience of the first four-way makes you uneasy about your choice of attorney, don't ignore those feelings. At the very least, this is a signal of problems in your relationship with your attorney that should be nipped in the bud. At worst, it may mean that you should consider retaining a different attorney to help you through the collaborative process.

Start by scheduling a meeting with your attorney. Tell your attorney that you have some concerns about the way you are working together that you'd like to discuss. Before you meet, make a note of the specific things that happened that caused your discomfort. When you meet, bring your notes and refer to them. Have an honest conversation with your attorney about your concerns. Chances are good that this will get things back on track between the two of you, and your partnership at subsequent four-ways will be the stronger for having cleared the air.

If you still feel there's a problem between you and your attorney, consider discussing your reservations with a counselor familiar with the collaborative divorce process, or with another collaborative attorney not involved in your case. You might discover that you have been harboring unrealistic expectations of your attorney, or you may conclude that you and your attorney are the wrong "fit" for each other.

If necessary, you can continue the collaborative process with a new attorney, if your spouse and your spouse's attorney agree to the change. If you hire a new attorney, he or she will help you make the transition.

For more suggestions for dealing with problems in your relationship with your lawyer, see Chapter 8.

If Collaborative Divorce Isn't Right for You

If your experience of the first four-way leads you to conclude that collaborating is not the way for you to handle your divorce, you have a several options, depending on why you think collaboration isn't working.

If the problem is financial, and you think you and your spouse can handle things on your own or with less expensive help, consider suggesting that the two of you meet some of the time without your attorneys, and only use them when absolutely necessary, such as to break an impasse or to put the finishing touches on the terms of the agreement and draw up the papers. Another option might be to try using a mediator, with your collaborative attorneys available as consultants. If your attorneys are open to customizing the process, you may be able to stretch your dollars a little further and still keep some of the benefits of collaborative divorce.

If the four-way meeting degenerated into unproductive and adversarial finger-pointing or stonewalling, you may still be able to salvage the process by agreeing to conduct future meetings with the assistance of a mediator. Mediated collaboration is becoming more common as a way to help spouses and lawyers stay on track in high-conflict cases. If your attorneys are open to this, it is likely to be a better option than abandoning the process altogether.

If you think that collaborating or mediating in any form simply won't work, and if you need help in completing your divorce, you may still be able to use your collaborative attorney to help negotiate an agreement about what the next step will be. See Chapter 15 for suggested exit strategies. Your collaborative attorney can also help you find a new attorney to handle the case after the collaborative process ends. (Remember, the collaborative agreement you signed probably requires your attorney to withdraw.)

Monitoring Your Progress

Your mediation or collaborative divorce will almost certainly consist of more than one session or four-way meeting. It's a good idea to keep track of what has happened and where things are going by jotting down a few notes at the end of each session. This can be especially important if you agree to do something before the next session or four-way. Your notes can be a "to do" list for you, to help make sure your assignment doesn't get overlooked or fall through the cracks. You can keep track of things that your spouse, the mediator, the attorneys, or other professionals have agreed to do, too.

It's also helpful to make note of any agreements reached during the session or meeting. These might be agreements about how you're going to communicate; interim agreements, such as who will pay certain bills or scheduling arrangements for your children; or a tentative settlement on one or more issues. Having notes on these issues will help you keep the mediation or collaboration focused and make it less likely you'll get bogged down in misunderstandings or repetitious negotiations.

You can refer to your notes between sessions and meetings. You can even add items you want to cover in the next session. Review your notes right before the next session or meeting so that you come prepared to make the most of it.

Concepts to Consider

Essential Things to Note During Mediation (you can record this information on Worksheet 10 or on a worksheet provided by your mediator or attorney)

❑ date of the session/meeting

❑ people present

❑ date and time of the next session/meeting

❑ agreed assignments to be completed before the next session/meeting, and responsible person

❑ summary of any agreements made during the session/meeting, including tentative agreements under consideration

❑ topics you expect to cover in the next session/meeting, and

❑ questions or concerns to bring up at the next session or meeting with your attorney.

Chapter 12

Communicating in Mediation or Collaborative Divorce

Failure to communicate has scuttled many a negotiation. Conversely, good communication is the foundation of a good mediation or collaborative process. Clear communication will make the information-gathering and framing stages of mediation go more smoothly and efficiently with fewer misunderstandings. In the negotiation stage, good communication skills will help you negotiate in a respectful and constructive manner.

In a collaborative divorce, good communication between you and your lawyer will support the process and in turn, encourage a respectful, forward-moving negotiation. The presence of lawyers doesn't mean that you and your spouse won't be communicating directly—in fact, one of the things that makes collaborative divorce so attractive to many people is that you have the support and advocacy of an attorney while still remaining involved and working directly with your spouse to reach a settlement. Where there are communication issues that are unique to collaborative divorce, we will say so. Otherwise, you can assume that much of the advice here is relevant to both mediation and collaborative divorce.

As you begin the mediation or collaborative process, communications between you and your spouse may be at an all-time low. Simple communications may be difficult, if not impossible, and you may find it hard to negotiate even the most basic transactions, such as when and where to exchange the children or who will pay this month's electric bill.

This chapter offers some basic tips for communicating to help make the mediation or collaboration more productive. We also show you how good communications start the negotiations off on the right foot.

If your mediator's or attorney's approach differs. Your mediator or collaborative lawyer may have a different approach to helping you communicate. In that case, use the techniques listed here only if they are consistent with your mediator's or lawyer's instructions.

What Is Communication?

There are probably many ways to define communication. Because we are talking about communication that leads to good negotiations, we define communication as a verbal statement made by one person, the speaker, for the purpose of conveying information to another person or persons, the listener.

Using this definition, here are three communications:

"Waiter, there's a fly in my soup."

"I ran into Dave the other day. He's married and has a new baby."

"I can't come to the party because I've got the flu."

In each of these examples, the speaker makes an oral statement that contains information for the listener. Our everyday lives are made up of hundreds of communications like these. In most of our daily communications, the information is accurately expressed by the speaker and understood by the listener. The waiter now knows that there is a fly in the customer's soup; Dave's old friend has learned that Dave is now married and has a child; and the party host knows not to expect the friend who has the flu.

Not all communications go smoothly, however. Sometimes, the information the speaker intends to convey is not the information the listener hears. When this happens, we have a miscommunication, and, if not corrected, this miscommunication can cause problems—sometimes significant ones—later on down the road.

What Can Go Wrong in Communications?

If you examine any communication closely, you will see that it consists of two parts. The first part is the speaker's statement. The second part is the listener's understanding. A problem in either part of the communication can cause a miscommunication.

Suppose Chris and Pat are standing and talking on a city sidewalk, and all of a sudden Chris yells, "Look out, Pat!" Pat looks around, but sees nothing. A few seconds later a cardboard box that was dangling from an overhanging window hits Pat on the head. What turned this attempted communication into a miscommunication? Chris, the speaker, made a statement—"Look out, Pat." Chris intended the statement to warn Pat of the cardboard box falling from the window. But Chris's statement gave Pat only part of the information Pat needed. Chris told Pat to look, but didn't say where or what to look for. The problem with this communication was with the speaker's statement.

Sometimes, the problem is not the speaker's statement, but the listener's lack of understanding or inattention. Ling and Miko are coworkers. Ling stops by Miko's office and says, "The design team meeting will be at 8:00 a.m. tomorrow instead of 10:00 a.m." Miko is in the middle of a project when Ling comes by with this information. Miko nods, but she is only half-listening, and she writes down 9:00 a.m. instead of 8:00 a.m. for the rescheduled meeting. Another miscommunication, this time because Miko, the listener, has not fully paid attention to the information from Ling, the speaker.

Your mediation is going to consist of a series of communications. At any given moment you will either be a speaker or a listener. Depending on which role you are in, you can help avoid many miscommunications by following a few simple guidelines outlined in this chapter. We also provide these on a checklist you can take with you to the mediation.

Boosting Your Communication Competence

Learning the techniques of good communication is only part of being an effective communicator. To use these techniques in your mediation, you need an adequate self-image. Your self-image is the filter through which you see the world around you. A positive self-image lets you communicate effectively even in difficult circumstances.

When you are in times of stress, as is often true during a divorce, you can experience a lessening of your self-image, much like a lessening of your bodily immune system. Paying attention to building up your self-image can be like boosting your immune system with vitamin supplements. The result will be better communications both in and outside of your mediation.

You can work on boosting your self-image with the help of a counselor or one of the many books on self-esteem available. A good resource is *Your Attitude Is Showing: A Primer of Human Relations*, by Sharon L. O'Neil and Elwood N. Chapman (Prentice Hall).

Or try this simple exercise: Make a list of five positive factors in your life, including people, activities, or things you do well. Put the list on your mirror and read it every morning for a week. Then look at the list and make any changes you want, and repeat the process. Do this at least three weeks in a row, and then as many weeks as you want after that.

Tips for Good Communication

Remember, every communication has two components: what the speaker says and what the listener hears. Here are tips for each.

Tips for Speakers

Communication begins with the speaker. These tips can help you convey your message clearly and specifically.

State your intention—to communicate facts, a problem, or both—clearly at the outset. Sometimes, your communication is intended to convey only factual information. Other times, you want to bring up a problem that needs to be solved. Many communications made during mediation contain both factual information and a problem. Sometimes it is hard for the listener to tell from the speaker's words whether the statement is intended simply to convey factual information or is intended to open up a discussion about a problem. Consider the following examples:

Lester tells the mediator, "Our mortgage payment is $1,000 per month."

Shaleh says to Kamel, "Nadio's little league game starts at 4:00 p.m. tomorrow."

These two statements seem to impart some straightforward information. In the first statement, Lester discloses the amount of the monthly mortgage payment. In the second statement, Shaleh tells Kamel what time Nadio's game starts.

Suppose, however, Lester is bringing up the monthly mortgage payment because he wants the mediator's help in deciding who should pay it. If that is Lester's intent, Lester must be aware of this so he can make a statement that will alert the mediator to the problem Lester wants to discuss.

In the second statement, Shaleh may be expecting to start a discussion about the problem of who is going to pick up Nadio and get him to his game. If she knows that that is her intention, she is more likely to make a clear statement to Kamel that will get the discussion going in a positive direction.

So the first step in making any communication is to be aware of what you are trying to convey to your listener.

Be specific and accurate. When your statement conveys factual information, be as specific and accurate as possible.

Shaleh tells Kamel, "Nadio's little league game is after school on Thursday."

Shaleh's statement is accurate as far as it goes, but it isn't very specific. Does after school mean 3:30, 4:00, or 4:30? Is the game this Thursday, next Thursday, or every Thursday? If Shaleh is more specific to begin with, the odds of a clear communication are greatly enhanced.

Lester's statement was, "Our mortgage payment is $1,000 per month."

This is specific, but what if the mortgage has a variable rate that changes every six months? It would be more accurate for him to add, "and the amount changes every six months because we have a variable loan."

Tips for Listeners

The listener's attitude and approach have as much to do with the quality of the communication as does the speaker's delivery.

Give the speaker your full attention. If you're on the receiving end of a communication, one of the most important things to do is to pay attention. Remember the discussion between Ling and Miko earlier in this chapter? Ling tried to tell Miko about a change in an important meeting time, but Miko was not really listening to Ling and wrote down the wrong time. Miko will wish she had listened more carefully when she finds out she missed the meeting.

Listen to the speaker's whole statement and don't interrupt. This sounds simple, but it is harder than you think, especially if what the speaker says elicits an angry reaction on your part, if you think you've heard it all before, or if you're distracted by your own thoughts. Looking the speaker in the eye and waiting until he or she finishes will help focus your attention on the speaker's statement. (If direct eye contact is considered rude and inappropriate in your culture, adapt your behavior to maintain a respectful listening posture.) Pay attention to your body language. If you are fidgeting with papers, looking away, frowning, shaking your head, or gesturing with your hands, you are not listening, and you are probably distracting the speaker.

Use feedback or questions to double-check your understanding. When the speaker is finished, tell the speaker what you heard, and ask whether you heard it right. This simple step makes every communication self-correcting. If there has been any problem in the communication, either in the statement or in the listening, using feedback to double check the meaning gives you a chance to correct any misunderstanding before moving forward.

 Angela says to Richard, "I'll meet you at Dumbo's Restaurant at 6:30 tomorrow night."

Richard might think Angela means the Dumbo's Restaurant downtown, instead of the one on the outskirts of town. If Richard doesn't clear this up, they may be waiting in different Dumbo's Restaurants at opposite ends of town the following evening. But if Richard says, "So I'll see you at 6:30 tomorrow night at Dumbo's Restaurant downtown, right?" Angela can say, "No, I meant the one on the outskirts of town." By using feedback, Richard has averted a potential mishap.

Even if you're sure you know what the speaker means, try putting your feedback into the form of a question. Start with "Are you saying … ?" or "Do you mean … ?" You might be surprised to discover you missed something, and even if you got it right, you'll send the message that you're listening and sincerely wanting to understand. This will encourage a cooperative tone in future discussions.

Tips for Communicating About Problems

Many communications in your mediation, or with your collaborative lawyer and your spouse in a collaborative process, will be about problems or disagreements. The four tips above can begin to help you keep the communication focused and constructive, thereby avoiding misunderstandings. Here are a few more guidelines to ensure a positive result.

Tips for Speakers

Again, let's start with the tips for speakers.

If you are bringing up a problem, remember that it is your problem. If it weren't your problem, you wouldn't be bringing it up. While you can expect the mediator (or your lawyer) and your spouse to listen to what you have to say about the problem, you cannot expect them to read your mind. You will need to describe your problem clearly enough that the listeners can understand what it is that you want and why.

Say, "I have a problem," or "I'd like to discuss what to do about … "

Let's go back to our previous example. Lester wants to discuss who will make the mortgage payment; he should be clear about the problem he wants to talk about.

Lester might say, "The mortgage payment is $1,000 per month, and we have some other bills due at the same time. I want to discuss who is going to pay which bills, since my salary isn't enough to cover the mortgage payment and the other bills."

Avoid blaming. Quite often, it's hard not to see the problem as connected to or even caused by your spouse. Starting out the communication by focusing on your spouse's fault, however, is almost guaranteed not to work. Instead of hearing what you have to say about the problem, your spouse is likely to become defensive. This means your spouse will stop listening or even counterattack. Your goal should be to define the problem clearly before trying to solve it, so you'll want to present your statement in a way that does not invite your spouse to become defensive. An easy way to do this is to remember to start your statements with "I" instead of "you." (Communication specialists often call these "I statements.")

This doesn't mean you can never say anything about your spouse or your spouse's behavior, but by speaking about yourself first, you will lessen the risk of triggering a defensive reaction from your spouse.

Lester says to Moeesha, "You ran up the credit card bills and you should pay for them. I'm having enough trouble just keeping up with the mortgage payment."

Moeesha is likely to hear nothing but Lester's criticism of her credit card charges, which she may feel were valid family expenses. The discussion will turn into an argument about whether the charges were valid instead of focusing on how the bills will get paid. Lester can easily avoid this result by starting with an "I" statement.

"I'm concerned about how we're going to pay the monthly bills. We've got the mortgage payment of $1,000, plus the credit card payments."

Lester has identified the problem without pinning blame on Moeesha. The discussion of the credit card charges will then have a more neutral context when Lester and Moeesha begin negotiating a solution.

Avoid words like "always" and "never." Words like these give a statement an accusatory overtone.

Shaleh says to Kamel, "You never pick up Nadio on time to get him to his little league games. His next game is at 4:00

p.m. tomorrow, and you'd better not be late."

Kamel is likely to argue that he is not always late, and the problem of who will take Nadio to his little league game tomorrow will not get solved.

Instead, Shaleh could bring up her concern about Kamel being late by beginning with an "I" statement and ending with a request.

"It bothered me that you picked Nadio up late last week and he was late to his game. His game tomorrow starts at 4:00 p.m. Will you be able to get him there on time?"

Even if Kamel doesn't agree that he was late, the point of contention is only one incident, not all of Kamel's behavior. Kamel is less likely to get sidetracked by feeling wrongly attacked, and the main point of the communication—getting Nadio to his game on time—won't be lost in the shuffle.

Avoid finger-pointing and name-calling. This ought to go without saying, but a surprising number of us find ourselves literally and figuratively pointing our fingers at each other and calling each other names when we're in conflict. In a word, don't. Remember, your objective is to convey accurate information about certain facts or a problem. Finger-pointing and name-calling will only close your listener's ears and prevent real communication from happening.

State just the problem, not your solution. Most of us already have in mind a solution to the problem we're bringing up. It's tempting to include our suggested solution in our statement of the problem, especially if it seems obvious to us. Don't do it. As we'll discuss more in the next section of this chapter, you'll greatly improve the chances of coming up with an agreed solution if you first get agreement on the problem, and then jointly come up with the solution.

Tips for Listeners

Discussion about problems will go more smoothly if the listener follows these tips.

Remember that listening and understanding are not the same as agreeing. One of the hardest things to do when you're a listener is continue to listen and pay attention when you disagree with what is being said. It is human nature to want to register your disagreement. But if you interrupt the communication in order to disagree or you tune out, you may miss an important point in the communication. You will have a chance to express your own opinion after the speaker is finished and after you use feedback to make sure you've understood. Meanwhile, remind yourself that listening and demonstrating that you understand does not mean that you agree with what is being said.

Avoid self-listening. Self-listening is thinking of what you want to say next instead of paying attention to what the speaker is saying at that moment. It is a common problem in communications. Maybe you don't strongly disagree with what is being said; maybe you just see things differently. Or perhaps what the speaker is saying reminds you of a point you want to make. Whatever the reason, you are self-listening—silently interrupting the speaker with your own thoughts—and communication is no longer taking place.

Don't assume you know what the speaker is about to say. When we've known people for a long time, and especially if we have negative feelings about them, we tend to assume we know what they're thinking and feeling as soon they open their mouths. This is likely to be true of you and your spouse. You may see your spouse get a certain look or use a certain phrase, and you think to yourself, "Here we go again!" In your mind, you have already imagined the statement your spouse is about to make. Resist the urge to be a mind reader. Set aside your assumptions and listen to the actual words your spouse says. Then when you demonstrate your understanding using feedback, you'll be able to do it accurately.

Handling Strong Emotions in Communication

If you follow the tips we've outlined above, the odds of having a clear communication are very good. The final step is to make sure any emotions accompanying the communication are handled appropriately so they don't get in the way.

Not every communication is accompanied by strong emotions; but some are, especially in the midst of a marital separation. This is most likely to occur when you're communicating with your spouse, but you also could have strong emotions when you are in discussions with your collaborative attorney. When a communication includes an emotional element, it is important to recognize it to avoid getting sidetracked.

The emotional content of a communication is like an ocean current at the beach. If it is recognized and well-marked, swimmers can safely enjoy the surf. They can even use the current to swim further and faster. But if the emotion in a communication is ignored, it can be like a riptide pulling unwitting swimmers out to sea.

Depending on whether you are the speaker or the listener, you can "swim" with the emotional currents by following these guidelines.

Speakers: Alert Your Listener to Your Emotional State

Be aware of what you are feeling and decide whether it is important to communicate it. If you feel strongly about a specific topic, you will probably express how you feel nonverbally. If your words don't include some acknowledgment of your emotional state, you risk confusing or alarming your listener into a reaction that prevents true listening.

How do you know you're feeling strongly about something? Check for physical signs. Is your jaw clenched? Are you fighting back tears? Is your face flushed and hot? Are you fidgeting in your chair? These are just a few examples of the nonverbal signals (body language) you experience yourself and send to your listener when you are in the grip of some strong emotion.

You may not feel comfortable or safe saying how you feel. If that's the case, take a little time to breathe and calm down. See if your feelings subside before you speak. If not, try to let your listener know, in words, that the subject under discussion evokes some strong feelings for you. You don't have to talk about your feelings if you don't want to. But because your body language is bound to be saying that something is going on, you'll keep the communication clear by making your verbal statement consistent with your nonverbal one. If even this is impossible, ask for a break before you continue. Take a walk, sip some water, see whether you can settle yourself down. If it's still difficult to continue after a break, you might need to stop the mediation session and reschedule for another time. Consider also working with a counselor to find ways to make the emotional part of the process more comfortable for you.

When Emotions Get in the Way

If you find that your emotional reactions consistently interfere with your communications with your spouse, you'll probably benefit from spending some time with a professional counselor. Working with a counselor can help you resolve the emotional aspects of your situation so that you'll bring less emotional baggage to the mediation. A counselor can also help you strengthen your communication skills and develop techniques to handle your emotional reactions during mediation. (For suggestions on locating and working with a counselor, see Chapter 8.) If you are mediating and the problem continues, you might want to consider switching to a collaborative process instead of mediation, where the added buffer of having a lawyer working with you might help. Chapter 11 has more about figuring out whether the process you've chosen is the right one for you.

If you're comfortable telling your listener how you're feeling, try to use a word or phrase that accurately describes the quality and intensity of your emotion.

Lester tells Moeesha, "I'm concerned about ... [the bills]."

He's indicating a feeling of moderate anxiety. If his feeling is more intense than that, he might say:

"I'm alarmed about … [the bills]."
Shaleh says to Kamel, "I'm irritated … "
If she's really angry she might use
"furious." Picking a descriptive word that
fits will help her make her point without
being misunderstood.

Tell It Like It Is: A Vocabulary of Emotions

Communicating clearly about emotions is a two-step process. The first step is noticing the feeling. The next one is finding a word that accurately describes the emotion. It can help to think of emotions as falling into four main categories: happiness, sadness, fear, and anger. Within these categories, emotions may be more or less intense. Within the category of happiness, for example, a feeling of contentment is less intense than the feeling of exhilaration.

It helps to find a word that most closely matches the intensity of the feeling you are trying to express, if you are the speaker, or describe, if you are the listener.

Here's a brief sampling of some words in each category, going from mild to intense. We also include some umbrella words at the end of the list. Umbrella words are general enough to cover more than one category of feeling as well as a larger zone of intensity and are useful if you can't quite put your finger on what the emotion is or its intensity.

Happiness	Sadness	Fear	Anger
Content	Nostalgic	Concerned	Irritated
Satisfied	Blue	Insecure	Annoyed
Pleased	Discouraged	Anxious	Offended
Cheerful	Hurt	Worried	Resentful
Enthusiastic	Unhappy	Suspicious	Disgusted
Happy	Sad	Afraid	Angry
Excited	Inconsolable	Alarmed	Shocked
Exhilarated	Bereft	Panicked	Outraged
Ecstatic	Grieving	Terrified	Furious
Overjoyed	Miserable	Hysterical	Enraged

Umbrella words: Uncomfortable, Restless, Agitated, Bothered, Upset, Moved, Touched.

Listeners: Be an Active Listener

Just as it's important to check your understanding of the informational content of a statement, it is also critical to verify your assessment of the emotional content. Including your understanding of the emotional content in your feedback is what communication specialists call active listening. Active listening has a dual benefit. It ensures that there is no misunderstanding in the communication, and it promotes respectful and constructive dialogue by demonstrating understanding of the speaker's feelings.

If the speaker has told you expressly what he or she is feeling, it may be easy to include the feeling expressed by the speaker in your feedback.

Lester says, "I'm concerned about … [the bills, etc.]."

Moeesha might ask, "Are you worried that … [the bills won't get paid]?"

If the speaker seems to be expressing an emotion, not in words, but in body language, you'll need to proceed more carefully. No one wants to be told how they feel by someone else, even though most of us want to be understood and accepted. So the trick is to:

- put your feedback about the emotion in the form of a question
- pick a word you think will accurately describe the emotion being expressed without understating or exaggerating it, and
- accept the speaker's correction without argument.

Put your feedback about the emotion in the form of a question. Putting your feedback in the form of a question lets you tell the speaker what you heard and saw while allowing for the possibility that you got it wrong. When Moeesha asks "Are you worried that … ," Lester can confirm or correct Moeesha's perception. This is especially important if Lester hasn't given Moeesha any verbal clue that he is worried about the situation, and Moeesha is guessing based on her observation of Lester's body language. Using a statement instead of a question under those circumstances could turn the communication into an unproductive argument, while a question that accurately describes the emotion that the speaker is feeling can enhance communication by making the speaker feel understood.

Pick a word that you think will accurately describe the emotion being expressed without understating or exaggerating it. If your feedback about the speaker's feelings is based on body language and other nonverbal clues, it is important to be as accurate as you can about the quality and intensity of the feeling you've noticed.

If Shaleh is frowning slightly and Kamel gets the sense that she is annoyed, then he might ask her whether she is annoyed or irritated. If he instead asks her whether she is furious when her emotion is the milder feeling of annoyance, it may anger her further that Kamel isn't even perceptive enough to notice the difference. The same can be true in reverse. If Shaleh is obviously seething and Kamel grossly understates the intensity of the feeling by asking whether Shaleh is annoyed, he risks triggering an unproductive reaction.

If you are in doubt about the intensity of the feeling expressed, you might pick a word that describes a midrange intensity, such as resentful or angry for a feeling in the anger category, or worried or afraid for a feeling in the fear category. (See "Tell It Like It Is," above.)

If you think something is going on, but you're not sure what the feeling is, you can try using an umbrella word, such as uncomfortable, restless, bothered, agitated, or upset. For example, if Shaleh is flushed and fidgeting with papers as she talks to Kamel, and Kamel isn't sure what's going on, he could ask:

"Are you upset about … [the little league game]?"

Accept the speaker's correction without argument. A fundamental principle of active listening is respect for the speaker's autonomy. The speaker is the final word on how he or she feels and what he or she is trying to express. If you include a feeling in your feedback that the speaker denies, you must accept the speaker's correction without argument. Otherwise, you will turn the communication into an unproductive debate.

Suppose Shaleh brings up the subject of Nadio's little league games. Kamel, noticing her flushed and frowning face, says:

"You seem to be angry … "

Shaleh replies, "I'm not angry! I just want to get this situation handled."

If Kamel follows up with:

"Of course you are angry! Look at your face … "

the conversation can easily degenerate into the classic "No I'm not," "Yes you are" exchange that goes nowhere.

The temptation to insist on the accuracy of your perception of the other person is especially strong in a longstanding relationship. In these situations, we assume that we know each other so well that we can tell what's going on with the other person even if they don't admit it. It's important to resist this temptation and remember that the goal of the communication is to understand what is being said and to demonstrate your understanding, not to jump to conclusions based on your own assumptions.

 You must want to be able to communicate. All of these communication techniques assume that you sincerely desire to communicate in an honest and respectful manner. If you are trying your best to understand and be understood, using these techniques should help you do that. If you just go through the motions without making an honest attempt at expressing and understanding, then all the technique in the world won't necessarily help.

The more you understand about communication, the better you will be at negotiating for yourself. Here are some good books that go into detail about communication skills and give helpful explanations and examples.

The Tao of Negotiation: How You Can Prevent, Resolve, and Transcend Conflict in Work and Everyday Life, by Joel Edelman (HarperBusiness).

Taking the War Out of Our Words: The Art of Powerful Non-Defensive Communication, by Sharon Ellison (Bay Tree; www.pndc.com).

Messages: The Communication Skills Book, by Matthew McKay, Ph.D., Martha Davis, Ph.D., and Patrick Fanning, 2nd Ed. (New Harbinger Publications).

Non-Violent Communication: A Language of Life: Create Your Life, Your Relationship and Your World in Harmony with Your Values, by Marshall Rosenberg, 2nd Ed. (PuddleDancer Press).

Don't Be Hard on Yourself

If you make a sincere effort to practice these communication techniques, you'll find they make a difference, even if you are less than perfect at it and even if the history of communication between you and your spouse is less than ideal. For one thing, the mediator is there to coach you through the hard parts. For another, communication tends to build on its own momentum. One good communication, no matter how small, leads to more confidence in the next one, and so forth. By practicing good communication about small things, you build up a bank of confidence and goodwill that you can draw on when the communication is about more challenging issues.

Don't be too hard on yourself in the process. Nobody is perfect at communicating, but if you keep practicing, you'll get better. And don't be too hard on your spouse, either. As long as your spouse is making the effort, he or she will get better at it, too. In this way, you'll be setting the stage for a productive negotiation leading to an acceptable settlement agreement.

Concepts to Consider

Tips for Good Communication

Tips for Speakers	Tips for Listeners
1. Figure out whether you want to communicate facts, a problem, or both, and state your intention clearly at the outset.	1. Give the speaker your full attention.
	2. Use feedback to double check your understanding. Ask "Are you saying … ?" or "Do you mean … ?"
2. Be specific and accurate.	

Tips for Communicating About Problems

Tips for Speakers	Tips for Listeners
1. If you are communicating about a problem, remember it's *your* problem. Say, "I have a problem," or "I'd like to discuss what to do about … "	1. Remember that listening is not agreeing.
	2. Avoid self-listening.
	3. Don't assume you know what the speaker is about to say.
2. Avoid blaming: Start statements with "I" instead of "you."	
3. Avoid words like "always" and "never."	
4. Avoid finger-pointing and name-calling.	
5. State just the problem, not your solution.	

Tips for Handling Strong Emotions in the Communication

Tips for Speakers	Tips for Listeners
Alert your listener to your emotional state.	Be an active listener—use feedback to confirm what you've heard, and accept corrections without argument.

Chapter 13

Negotiating in Mediation and Collaborative Divorce

As we've said throughout this book, every mediation and every collaborative divorce is a negotiation. Your mediation or collaboration is no exception. With the help of your mediator or the collaborative attorneys, you and your spouse will be negotiating a settlement agreement.

In this chapter, we give you a crash course in basic negotiation theory and techniques. When you've finished reading, you'll be prepared to do your part in successfully negotiating a solid settlement agreement.

Use your mediator or collaborative lawyer. Remember, mediation and collaboration are flexible. Whether a mediator or two collaborative attorneys are directing the process, they will have their own approaches to negotiating and may even vary the approach depending on what's needed. If you get to a place in the process where you're unsure of what to do, ask your mediator or attorney. As long as you feel you're making progress, follow his or her lead, and use what we're saying here to get a better understanding of what's going on.

You may be able to skip material. You may be pretty comfortable with your ability to negotiate, your mediator or collaborative lawyer may have already taught you what you need to know. If so, skip all or parts of this chapter.

If you are using a collaborative divorce process, you are still likely to engage in negotiations with your spouse. Most of the time, your lawyer will be present at negotiating sessions (four-way meetings). The only exceptions will be if you and your spouse meet together with an expert like a child specialist or custody mediator, which might involve just the two of you and not your attorneys, working on negotiating a parenting plan. Other than that, though, your lawyers will usually be present for negotiations. This means that you can turn to your lawyer for advice and help at any time during the negotiations. In fact, you and your lawyer will probably agree in advance on ways for you to let your lawyer know if you want to take a break and talk separately about how things are going.

We Negotiate All the Time

You may think that skillful negotiation is something reserved for diplomats, politicians, and Fortune 500 executives, not for the likes of you. But the truth is, we all negotiate in our daily lives. All of us can be good at it, if we keep some simple principles in mind.

What is negotiation? Any time we try to get someone to cooperate with us in accomplishing something we can't do on our own, we are negotiating. When we respond to another person's request for our cooperation by specifying the conditions for our agreement to cooperate, we are also negotiating.

If you think of a time when you engaged in negotiation, what comes to mind? For most of us, we first think of when we negotiated some major issue in our lives, perhaps buying a house or a car, taking on a new job, or asking for a raise—stressful and not always successful events. But the truth is that we conduct other negotiations on a regular basis with much more ease and success.

If you have children over the age of two, you have undoubtedly engaged in countless daily negotiations over everything from food—"If you eat your vegetables, you can have dessert"—to bedtimes—"Okay, you can stay up late just this once if you" do x, y, or z.

At work, we negotiate with coworkers and business colleagues. Subra asks Connie for an extension on a project. Connie agrees, after obtaining Subra's promise to provide an interim report for the client. Martha offers to cover Rolando's phone calls while Rolando looks up some information for Martha on his computer.

The list goes on. We negotiate with friends and family about social events, with repair people over scheduling, with other volunteers and citizens over priorities and activities in our community and civic organizations.

For the most part, we conduct these daily negotiations with overall success

and without a great deal of thought about *how* we are negotiating.

In your mediation, you will use the same basic techniques you've developed in your daily negotiations. In mediation, you'll have the help of your mediator to keep the negotiations on track, but you'll do the actual negotiating. In a collaborative process, who does the negotiating may be different at different times and when you are dealing with different topics, but you will still be very much an active participant.

Let's take a look at what generally makes for a successful negotiation, so that you can consciously build on the skills you've already developed.

What Makes for a Successful Negotiation?

In your mediation or collaborative divorce, the negotiation will be successful if it results in a mutually satisfactory agreement that both you and your spouse can live with. That is, the substance of the agreement—what the agreement says— has to be based on what's important to each of you.

Getting to this result requires a constant balancing act between sticking up for what's important to you on the one hand and accommodating what's important to your spouse on the other. This is no easy task, and there will be times in when you'll feel yourself pulled one way or the other. Fortunately, there are some simple things you can do to help maintain the proper balance. And, of course, your mediator or lawyer will be there to help.

You have an excellent chance of success in negotiating if you keep these four basic principles in mind:

- balance assertiveness and attentiveness
- adopt a collaborative bargaining style
- use interest-based negotiation (expand the pie), and
- use an effective bargaining method (divide the pie).

Balance Assertiveness and Attentiveness

Probably the single most important thing you must do to be an effective negotiator is to maintain a healthy balance between asserting what's important to you—your interests—and attending to what your spouse tells you is important to her or him. This requires you to build on the communication skills we discussed in Chapter 12 as you explore how to settle the issues in your mediation.

Assertiveness really describes a two-part process. First, you must get very clear on what's important to you: your needs, goals, and concerns. These are what negotiators call "interests." (See the section below, called "Use Interest-Based Negotiation," for more on how to get clear about your interests.) Second,

you must speak up about your interests at each step of the way during the mediation. This means being specific and accurate about your interests, and it means being persistent in standing up for them, especially when you feel pressure not to.

Attentiveness also involves a two-part process. First, you must be able to listen carefully to what your spouse has to say about his or her interests. Second, you must be open to settlement options that address your spouse's interests while not conflicting with your own important interests.

Maintaining the proper balance between these two modes—asserting your interests and attending to your spouse's—isn't easy. It can be especially hard if one of you has initiated the divorce against the wishes of the other, setting up a leaver-leavee syndrome. (See Chapter 1.) If you are the leaver, you may feel pressure to assert your interests less and attend to your spouse's interests more. If you are the leavee, you may resist being attentive to your spouse's interests in favor of asserting your own.

The best way to make sure you stay in balance during the negotiation is to pay attention. Make a mental inventory from time to time: Am I asserting my important interests? Is something being overlooked? Do I understand what's important to my spouse? Am I willing to consider my spouse's interests in this?

If you pay attention, and if you ask for help from your mediator or lawyer when you need it, you'll find that you can keep a balance. The result will be well worth the effort: an agreement that both you and your spouse can live with.

Gender and the Negotiating Balance

Some scholars have noticed a correlation between a negotiator's gender and his or her approach to negotiating. While we should be careful to avoid generalizations that lead to stereotypes, it is probably fair to say that more women tend to be attentive and more men tend to assert themselves.

You may find it helpful to consider this when looking at your own approach. However, it is important to remember that the best negotiators, male or female, combine assertiveness and attentiveness in equal parts. This is something that simply takes consciousness and hard work. Neither gender has a corner on either market. So, whether you tend to be more assertive or more attentive, you can and should start training yourself to move toward a more balanced approach. For more on gender and mediation, see Chapter 17.

Adopt a Collaborative Bargaining Style

Using a collaborative bargaining style will increase your chances of success in reaching a lasting agreement. What are bargaining styles? These are the ways negotiators express themselves during the negotiation. Different negotiators use different bargaining styles in pursuing their objectives. Some negotiators affect a hard or competitive style. Others use a soft or cooperative style. Still others employ what we call a collaborative style.

The collaborative bargaining style consists of respectful but firm expressions and language. By contrast, the competitive bargaining style is manifested in aggressive, in-your-face expressions and language, and the cooperative bargaining style is characterized by willingness to listen and consider opposing points of view.

Research shows that negotiators who use a competitive style are ineffective. Even if they are prepared to consider opposing interests, they don't show it in their attitude. Their hard style makes other negotiators defensive and reluctant to disclose information that would lead to a meaningful settlement. On the other hand, a negotiator who uses a soft, cooperative style may not be taken seriously by the other party, and so opportunities for meaningful settlement discussions can be lost.

If you maintain a collaborative style that is consistently respectful but not self-effacing, your spouse is likely to listen to you, trust you, and take you seriously during the negotiation. This is more likely to lead to a satisfactory settlement. And by the way, this is true in both mediation and collaborative divorce. Just because the word "collaborative" is used here, it doesn't mean this style is limited only to that method of settling your divorce.

Use Interest-Based Negotiation

The best negotiators use communication and problem-solving skills to engage their counterparts in a mutual search for settlement options that would be acceptable to all parties. This is known as interest-based negotiation, also called principled negotiation or win-win negotiation. Most experienced mediators encourage some form of interest-based negotiation in their mediations.

Interest-based negotiation was popularized in the early 1980s by Roger Fisher and William Ury of the Harvard Negotiation Project in their best-seller *Getting to Yes: Negotiating Agreement Without Giving In* (Penguin Books). At the heart of their method is the distinction between positions—offers and counteroffers—and interests—concerns and needs underlying each party's position. Fisher and Ury found that focusing on positions will at best result in compromises not entirely satisfactory

to either party and, at worst, result in impasse. In contrast, shifting the focus to interests allows the negotiators to develop options that meet those interests, regardless of the starting positions of the parties.

Settlement agreements developed by focusing on interests are often more creative than the result achieved in position-based negotiation. In this sense, interest-based negotiation is sometimes said to "expand the pie," whereas position-based negotiation (bargaining) "divides the pie." Almost every negotiation involves a certain amount of pie-dividing. Interest-based negotiation ensures that the pieces will be as big as possible.

Fundamentals of Interest-Based Negotiation

Although every negotiation is unique, interest-based negotiations follow certain basic steps:

- defining the problem
- identifying underlying interests
- prioritizing interests
- coming up with options that address the interests
- combining options into proposals, and
- using objective criteria to define and evaluate options.

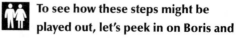 **To see how these steps might be played out, let's peek in on Boris and Natasha's mediation.** Boris and Natasha have been married for ten years. Their two

sons, age seven and nine, have been living with Natasha since she and Boris separated. Boris owns an auto repair business. Natasha is a sales clerk at a department store.

Define the Problem

Interest-based negotiators begin by clarifying the problem (issue) to be addressed in the negotiation. Sometimes, several problems or issues need to be negotiated. This is often the case in a divorce negotiation, where property must be divided, debts paid, support agreed upon, and, if there are children, arrangements for custody and time-sharing made.

The mediator—or the collaborative lawyers—help the spouses define the problem without assigning blame. This requires good communications skills like those we describe in Chapter 8.

Boris and Natasha: As we come in on Boris and Natasha, they are at the end of their second mediation session. They have spent time listing their assets and debts, assembling monthly budgets, discussing the time-sharing arrangements for the children, and giving the mediator other background information. They agree that the children should live with Natasha, but they don't seem to agree on much else, especially finances. One of the issues is the value of Boris's auto repair business, which according to state law is considered a marital asset—meaning its value is to be equally divided between the parties

at divorce. Boris believes the business is worth $80,000. Natasha says its value is at least $250,000, after its potential profitability and location are considered. Each of them claims to have information about sales of comparable businesses to back them up. In a heated discussion, Boris tells Natasha she doesn't know what she's talking about and Natasha calls Boris a cheat. After a pause, the mediator says, "It seems that you disagree about the value of the business. Each of you believes that you have a firm basis for your opinion of the value, but we need to figure out a way to decide what value to use, if we are going to come up with a financial settlement that is acceptable to both of you."

Notice how the mediator states the problem—a difference of opinion over what value to place on the business in the financial settlement—in a way that accepts the positions of Boris and Natasha without attacking either of them.

Identify Underlying Interests

This is a critical stage for interest-based negotiators. At this stage, the negotiators look behind each party's stated position in order to determine what interests of the party are met by that position. These interests will help shape the agreement without depending on positions.

Boris and Natasha: Fast-forward to the third mediation session. Once again, Boris and Natasha are discussing the value of the repair shop. The more they talk, the more entrenched they become in their positions.

In order to help Boris and Natasha make progress on this issue, their mediator tries to discover their underlying interests. Obviously, both Boris and Natasha have financial interests at stake. The lower value brings a financial benefit to Boris; the higher value benefits Natasha. There are other interests at stake here, too.

Through a series of questions, the mediator learns that Boris is afraid that he can't afford buyout payments to Natasha if the value is higher. Also, Boris is planning to take out a business loan in order to purchase new equipment for his shop. The new equipment will allow him to expand his shop's capacity to repair certain import vehicles. Boris is concerned that he will be turned down for the loan if his obligations to Natasha are too high.

For her part, Natasha is afraid that Boris will buy her out for a low value and then turn around and sell the business for a quick profit. She is reluctant to agree to a lower value that lets Boris make more money to keep for himself, while she struggles to pay her bills, including daycare expenses, and save up money for contingencies or to go back to school.

By uncovering Boris's interest in manageable buyout payments and preserving his ability to obtain business financing, and Natasha's interest in receiving a fair share of any profits from a sale or new financing so she can pay bills and go to

school, the mediator sets the stage for an exploration of options that might address those interests.

Prioritize Interests

Often, several interests underlie a party's position. Some interests are more important to each party than are other interests. To make sure that the most important interests of each party are met in the settlement, it is helpful to prioritize the interests.

Boris and Natasha: In addition to the interests already discussed, Boris wants to work fewer hours so he can spend more time with the children. He also wants to have enough money in his budget to do more skiing. He might prioritize his interests as follows:

- qualify for a new business loan
- maintain buyout payments at an affordable level
- spend more time with the children, and
- go skiing more often.

Natasha's additional interests include buying a new car to replace her old clunker and cutting back work hours in order to go to college. Her prioritized list reads:

- pay monthly bills
- avoid being cut out of profit from sale or financing of business
- buy a new car
- build up savings for contingencies, and
- go back to school.

Prioritizing Boris's interests and Natasha's interests in this way allows them to weigh settlement options. They can then pick the options that are most likely to meet the interests that have been given top priority, even if it is not possible to find a way to meet all of the interests.

Suggest Options That Address Interests

Interest-based negotiators strive to come up with as many options as possible. The more options under consideration, the more likely a settlement addressing the interests of the negotiating parties will be reached.

To get a list of as many options as possible, many mediators use the technique of brainstorming. In brainstorming, you agree to list any idea that comes to mind, without judging the idea as good or bad. (See "Brainstorming: A Creative Way to Expand the Pie," in Chapter 2.) Once all possible options are on the table, you can narrow them down to the most promising ones.

Boris and Natasha: In their mediation, Boris and Natasha come up with these options:

- Pick Boris's value ($80,000).
- Pick Natasha's value ($250,000).
- Split the difference ($165,000).
- Sell the business.

The mediator adds this option:

- Get a neutral appraisal.

The mediator then asks, "Can you think of any other options?" Boris suggests this one:

- Give Natasha a share of future sales proceeds.

Then Boris thinks of this option:

- Include in the business refinance extra money for Natasha's education and/or a new car.

After a pause, Natasha suggests this one:

- To cut down on Natasha's day-care expenses, Boris adjusts his schedule so he can have the children after school until Natasha gets off work.

The first three options just repeat Natasha and Boris's positions, or a compromise between them, and address only their direct financial interests in the value of the business. But as the mediator encourages them to continue to think of other options, they start thinking of possible ways to address other interests, too.

Combine Options Into Proposals

The next step involves weeding out clearly unacceptable options and grouping the remaining options into combinations that meet multiple interests. The initial list of options may contain some that are too far-fetched or one-sided to merit further consideration. Those are eliminated. Of the ones that remain, some are mutually exclusive. Some can be combined with others into a single settlement proposal. Some options get modified as they are considered. As this happens, proposals that address important interests of both parties begin to emerge.

Boris and Natasha: With help from their mediator, Natasha and Boris begin to consider their list of options. The options of valuing the shop at Boris's value of $80,000 or Natasha's value of $250,000 are discarded as too extreme. The split-the-difference approach is attractive to them, but it seems a little arbitrary. They don't want to spend the money on a formal appraisal if they don't have to, and selling the business is not something either of them really wants. Neither if them is crazy about the idea of giving Natasha a future share of any sales proceeds, either. They consider the rest of the list.

Boris tells Natasha and the mediator that he needs a loan of about $40,000 to refinance his current debts and still have $20,000 for new equipment. Looking at the list of options, he says he could probably afford to borrow additional cash of $25,000 for a reliable used car and contingency money for Natasha. But with the payments on that size loan, he can't afford more than about $1,000 per month in buyout payments to Natasha.

Natasha expresses doubts about a used car, because she needs safe, reliable transportation. Plus, she can't afford repairs on a used car. Boris replies that he would be willing to check out the car and make repairs free of charge.

Slowly, piece by piece, they put together this proposal: Value the business at $150,000. This means Natasha's share

would be $75,000. Boris will borrow $25,000 extra to enable Natasha to buy a used car for somewhere between $15,000 and $20,000, leaving her $5,000 to $10,000 for contingencies. Boris will pay Natasha the balance of $50,000 plus 5.5% in monthly payments of $955.06 for five years, in addition to the child support they have already agreed on. Boris will help Natasha pick out a car and will make any necessary repairs on it for five years. He will also be responsible for after-school care for the children when Natasha is at work or in school.

In discussing their options, Boris and Natasha say more about their specific interests, such as Boris's cash needs for the business and Natasha's concern about the reliability and cost of maintaining a used car. This helps them think of ways to make the options more specifically tailored to their interests. Gradually, they come up with a proposal that seems to address most or all of the interests they've identified.

Evaluate Proposals in Light of Each Party's Interests and Practical Concerns

After a viable proposal is on the table, an interest-based negotiator will test it by comparing it to the parties' prioritized interests and by asking whether it can realistically be accomplished.

Boris and Natasha: After summarizing the proposal, Natasha and Boris's mediator asks them to think back to their lists of prioritized interests. As they consider each one, they confirm that the proposal will meet their top three interests.

Looking at his number four interest, Boris grumbles, "Looks like it'll be a few years before I can do much skiing." Natasha retorts, "Well, I'm going to have to save up for school at this rate, so don't complain."

This prompts the mediator to ask, "How important is it to each of you to find a solution that also meets these last interests?"

Boris: "I'd love to ski several times a year, but I just don't see how that's going to happen anytime soon. As long as I can pay the bills, have some good times with my kids, and keep the shop going, I'll be satisfied. It's more important to get this settlement done without an ugly court battle."

Natasha: "I know I can't really expect Boris to pay me more than what we're talking about. And if he really does take the boys after school, it will help a lot. I might even be able to enroll in one or two classes at the community college next semester. It'll take a little longer to get my degree, but that's okay."

The mediator then focuses on the practical aspects of the proposal: Is Boris sure he can qualify for a loan in the amount they're talking about? What happens if Boris can't make a payment? Boris agrees to get a loan commitment and to discuss with his accountant some options for giving Natasha collateral for the buyout payments. At a later session

they firm up these details and the mediator writes up the agreement.

This last step may seem like a new negotiation, but it is actually an essential part of their negotiation. If the proposal will be of any use to Natasha and Boris, it must be workable, and it must meet the interests that each of them has identified as important. Only when the proposal meets this standard can it actually be written down in a binding agreement that both Boris and Natasha will sign.

Overcoming Obstacles in Interest-Based Negotiating

Not all interest-based negotiations go as smoothly as the theory suggests. Usually, this is because one party is unwilling or unprepared to follow an interest-based approach to the negotiation. To deal with this problem, negotiation theorists have identified the following four strategies:

- Use objective criteria.
- Be aware of available alternatives to a negotiated settlement.
- Adopt a patient, firm, and open manner.
- Recognize and counter unfair tactics or disruptions.

Use Objective Criteria

A common technique for overcoming, or at least narrowing, differences between the parties is to agree to use objective criteria.

Boris and Natasha: At some point, Natasha and Boris might agree to obtain a neutral opinion on the value of the auto repair business to break a deadlock between them, if they can obtain a reliable appraisal at an affordable cost. They might agree that the neutral opinion will be advisory only, or they might agree to make it binding.

Using objective criteria can help Natasha and Boris narrow the difference between their positions while still allowing for discussion of satisfactory options for buyout arrangements.

Be Aware of Available Alternatives to a Negotiated Settlement

Interest-based negotiators recognize that there will be no settlement unless all parties agree. Experienced negotiators begin the negotiation with a realistic idea of what will happen if no agreement is reached—in other words, what is their alternative to agreeing. Fisher and Ury refer to this as a party's BATNA (Best Alternative To a Negotiated Agreement). In other words, if you can't reach an agreement, what is the best result you are likely to get in a court, and what will it cost you (in money as well as intangible costs such as time or the goodwill of your spouse) to get there?

It is also helpful to examine the worst-case scenario. Borrowing from Fisher and Ury, some negotiation experts refer to this as the WATNA (Worst Alternative To a Negotiated Agreement). Understanding the realistic alternatives to an agreement helps the negotiator evaluate the relative attractiveness of offers from the other side. If the best you can expect in court—

your BATNA—is worse than what the other side is offering, you may want to seriously consider the offer being made. On the other hand, if you know the worst-case scenario—your WATNA—is more favorable than what is being offered by the other party, you'll be able to negotiate for concessions from a position of firmness and strength.

Boris and Natasha: Natasha and Boris have learned from legal advisers, the mediator, and their own research that if they can't agree and they have to take their case to court, they would each need to hire an expert witness to state an opinion of the value of the shop, and the judge would choose the opinion that seemed most reasonable. Boris would have to pay Natasha one-half of the value picked by the judge. Because the expert witness and legal fees could cost $25,000 or more each, here are Boris's and Natasha's BATNA-WATNAs:

Boris	Natasha
BATNA:	BATNA:
$65,000 ($40,000 + $25,000)	$100,000 ($125,000 − $25,000)
Boris	Natasha
WATNA:	WATNA:
$150,000 ($125,000 + $25,000)	$15,000 ($40,000 − $25,000)

Boris can see that the best he can expect, after factoring in the legal fees and costs, is to pay out a total of $65,000. And Natasha realizes that her best outcome would be $100,000. In addition, they are both aware of the intangible costs of having to litigate their case. Because they also see that they could come out worse than what's being offered, this exercise makes it easier to consider something in between.

Adopt a Patient, Firm, and Open Manner

If the other party to a negotiation seems immovable or uncooperative, an interest-based negotiator will attempt to go around the other party's resistance rather than increasing the resistance by pushing back.

In this mode, the negotiator maintains a consistent tone of respectful engagement with the other party. Rather than arguing against the other party's statements, the negotiator uses questions and good listening techniques to find openings for collaborative problem solving.

Boris and Natasha: Natasha and Boris start out the mediation with rigid and reactive attitudes toward the issue of the shop value. (Think back to where we came in on them.) As their mediator guides them through the six steps of interest-based negotiating, they begin to engage in real problem solving.

Notice how the mediator sets the tone of respectful engagement, which makes it easier for them to communicate and negotiate.

Recognize and Counter Unfair Tactics and Disruptions

Sometimes, a negotiator will engage in behavior that disrupts the progress toward a mutually satisfactory settlement. For professional negotiators who are paid to negotiate on behalf of someone else, this behavior can be deliberate and is usually referred to as a tactic. Typical tactics include intimidation, deceit, bluffing, and delaying.

Divorcing spouses often engage in similar disruptive behavior. But unlike professional negotiators, divorcing spouses are not usually intentionally engaging in tactics. More often, they are reacting emotionally to feeling defensive. A natural response to feeling put on the defensive, especially when emotions run high, is to become aggressive. Then, despite our best intentions, we do something that disrupts the progress of the mediation. Because this kind of disruptive behavior is unintentional, we'll call it a "negotiation blooper" instead of a tactic.

Interest-based negotiators use two related strategies to counter and minimize the disruptive effect of tactics or bloopers.

The first strategy is preventive. Before beginning the negotiations, the parties agree upon the manner in which the negotiations will be conducted. All parties are asked to make a commitment to follow through with the interest-based approach to negotiation, and not to engage in disruptive behavior.

The second strategy involves recognizing disruptive behavior for what it is, and either quietly but firmly refusing to be swayed by it or, if necessary, negotiating additional ground rules to deal with it.

These two antidisruption strategies help to prevent and then contain the disruption by separating it from the problem being negotiated, much as a fire lane will prevent and contain a forest fire.

Boris and Natasha: By the time Natasha and Boris start to discuss the value of the shop, their mediator has probably already helped them agree on some formal or informal ground rules that will help prevent disruptions. They might have agreed to take turns, for example, or to listen without interrupting each other, or they may have adopted these procedures simply by following the example of the mediator.

In this way, Boris and Natasha are already implementing the first antidisruption strategy.

Boris and Natasha: Now let's suppose that during a discussion about the value of the shop Boris angrily calls Natasha a jerk (or worse) and storms out of the room, slamming the door loudly. This doesn't have to mean the end of the mediation, but it needs to be addressed firmly and calmly so that it doesn't have an impact on the decision about the value of the shop.

The mediator might respond in a number of different ways. One simple approach is to sit quietly and wait for Boris to come back (he probably will) and then say something like this: "It seems like you [looking at Boris] reached the end of your patience in that discussion. I wonder if we can figure out a way for you to let us know you're getting to that point so this kind of disruption doesn't happen again."

By labeling the behavior as a disruption and inviting Boris to help come up with a better approach without blaming him, the mediator helps keep the behavior from derailing the negotiations over the value of the shop.

How to Deal With Common Negotiation Bloopers

 Ask your mediator or collaborative attorney for help. Your mediator or the collaborative attorneys will set up the process so that you and your spouse are less apt to commit negotiation bloopers and will monitor the negotiations so that if a blooper is committed it can be dealt with effectively. Use the following list for a general idea of what to look for and how to respond, but remember to ask your mediator or attorney for help whenever you need it.

Below is a list of the more common negotiation bloopers occurring in divorce negotiations and suggestions for responding to them. To use this chart, copy and take it with you to the mediation or four-way meeting.

Concepts to Consider

Common Negotiation Bloopers	Suggested Responses
Intimidation and threats. This can take one of two forms: • Threatens to break off the negotiations and resort to litigation. ("I'll see you in court.") • Threatens action other than breaking off the negotiation. Depending on the threatened action and how vulnerable you are to it, take this type of threat more seriously.	If you have carefully analyzed your BATNA-WATNA, this kind of threat should not be too troublesome. It is best countered with a simple statement acknowledging your spouse's right to terminate the negotiation and reaffirming your willingness to continue. In response, you might say something like, "I hear what you're saying as a threat. Unless you withdraw your threat and agree not to threaten me again, I may have to withdraw from this mediation."
Deceit. This involves a statement of fact about something important that is inaccurate or misleading.	The best counter is to insist firmly upon objective verification of the alleged facts before continuing.
Add-ons. This involves raising a new issue or demanding a new concession after an agreement has been reached.	The best way to deal with this is to let your spouse know that you will expect something in exchange for the additional concession.
The smoke screen. This is also known as the red herring, a term derived from the practice of training fox hounds to ignore false scents by dragging a smelly fish (a red herring) across the trail. In this one, your spouse distracts you from what is of value to you in the negotiation by bringing up something irrelevant or unimportant.	The best way to counter this is to avoid getting sidetracked by unimportant matters and return to the ones you've identified as critical.

Concepts to Consider

Common Negotiation Bloopers	Suggested Responses
Bluffing. This is a variation of the threat.	If you've paid attention to the discussion of your spouse's interests, and if you're aware of your BATNA-WATNA, you should be able to recognize a bluff for what it is and treat it similarly to a threat.
The ultimatum. This is another variation on threats and bluffs.	It is best countered in the same manner as threats and bluffs.
Delays and cancellations. Sometimes delays are inevitable. If your spouse is having a tough time adjusting to the reality of your separation, the process may need to go slowly. Delays can also be caused by unavoidable events. On the other hand, delay is sometimes deliberate.	Because it can be difficult to tell when a delay is deliberate, be somewhat tolerant at first, as long as you are not adversely affected by the delay. Start by talking about the problem. Maybe there's a good explanation for the delay. If you're concerned about the effect of the delay on you, ask to negotiate some consequence. For example if your spouse is late for a session, and your mediator charges for the full time allotted, you might negotiate an agreement that your spouse will pay for the unused time. Or, if you will have to wait longer for your spouse to pay child support, agree that whatever is negotiated will be retroactive. If delays become a pattern, there is a greater likelihood that your spouse is delaying deliberately. In that case, you will need to set a firm limit on further delays and let your spouse know what action you intend to take if the delays continue.

More About Negotiation

The study of negotiation has mush-roomed in the last 20 years. If you are interested in reading more about negotiation theory, especially interest-based negotiation, here are some excellent texts on the subject:

Getting to Yes: Negotiating Agreement without Giving In, by Fisher, Ury, and Patton (Penguin 2d Ed. 1991). This classic is still the bible of interest-based negotiators. It is short, written in plain English, and is still in print in an edition revised in 1998, with coauthor Bruce Patton. If you could read only one book about negotiation, this is the one we would recommend, although *Getting Past No* is a close second.

Getting Past No: Negotiating Your Way From Confrontation to Cooperation, by William Ury (Bantam Books). This short, practical, and read-able follow-up to *Getting to Yes* is well on its way to becoming another classic. The focus of this book is on anticipating and overcoming barriers to cooperation in negotiation. If you think your spouse is going to be a tough negotiator, you might want to read this book.

Between Love and Hate: A Guide to Civilized Divorce, by Lois Gold, MSW (Plume Books). This excellent book on all aspects of divorce includes a section in which the author applies the principles of win-win negotiating to the divorce context. See Section IV, "The Fundamentals of Negotiating," Chapters 12 to 14.

There are a number of other popular books about negotiating (not in the divorce context) that you may have seen in bookstores or libraries. They are generally oriented to business negotiations, but many contain useful catalogues of common negotiation techniques and tactics. Among the best is *Negotiate Like the Pros*, by John Patrick Dolan (Perigee Books).

If you are interested in more scholarly works on negotiation, here are a couple of suggestions:

Negotiation, by Lewicki, Litterer, Minton, and Saunders, 3rd ed. (Irwin).

The Mind and Heart of the Negotiator, by Leigh Thompson (Prentice-Hall).

Use Bargaining Techniques

It may seem that there is no place for bargaining in a mediation or collaboration using interest-based negotiation. After all, if an agreement is to be based on the interests of the parties, why engage in what we think of as bargaining—that is, compromising, dickering, splitting the difference, and so on?

The fact is that in just about every divorce negotiation there are some things to be divided up: money, property, even time with your children. Interest-based negotiating helps you make the pie as big as possible before dividing it. Effective bargaining helps you divide the pie as fairly as possible.

Common Forms of Bargaining

There are many different bargaining techniques. Here are some of the more common ones.

Distributive bargaining. This is probably the most commonly used form of bargaining. In it, the parties to the negotiation arrive at a compromise between two extreme positions through a series of offers and counteroffers. For example, Boris and Natasha would engage in distributive bargaining if they exchanged offers and counteroffers to arrive at the value of the shop. It is called distributive bargaining because it focuses on how to distribute the dollar value or other item in dispute between the parties.

Exchange bargaining. In trade or barter bargaining, something valued by one party is exchanged for a different item valued by the other party. A variation is log rolling, in which an item that has little or no value to Party A but great value to Party B is offered in exchange for something that does have value to Party A.

Other. Other common forms of bargaining include taking turns at choosing, auctioning, and having Party A divide and Party B choose.

Bargaining Etiquette

Each form of bargaining has its own rules. Often the rules are based on tradition and custom, much like rules of etiquette. Unwary bargainers can find themselves at a disadvantage if the rules aren't made clear at the beginning.

For example, many people engaged in distributive bargaining expect to start with offers that leave room for concession and compromise, gradually arriving at a midpoint acceptable to both sides. Because of the predictability of these steps, distributive bargaining is sometimes referred to by negotiation experts as a dance. You can sit out the dance by using a different bargaining technique, but if you decide to take the floor, knowing the dance steps can keep you and your spouse from stepping on each other's toes.

Talk About How You Will Bargain

Bargaining will go most smoothly if everyone involved has the same idea about the method of bargaining you'll use at any given point. You may use a variety of bargaining methods during mediation or collaboration, depending on the nature of the problem being resolved.

To start the discussion, say something like, "I'd like to talk about how we're going to decide among various options." Then proceed to sort through the possible methods until you find one that works.

A Dance Lesson

It is possible that you and your spouse will decide not to engage in the dance of distributive bargaining. If you do, however, you need to know the basic steps.

First, assess your bargaining range. What is the most you are willing to give on this issue? What is the least you are willing to take?

Second, start at a point that leaves you room to move. Be a little vague if you can, to leave even more room. Don't start out with your bottom line. If you do, you may have a hard time convincing your spouse that this is, in fact, your first and only offer. Unless you and your spouse have agreed in advance to dance straight to the bottom line, avoid making an offer that leaves no room for compromise.

Third, say why you think your offer is fair when you make it. Each time you make a new offer or counteroffer, give your reasons for it.

Fourth, expect concessions to become smaller and take more time to ponder as you reach the point of resistance. Be aware that a large concession granted with little time to consider sends a message to your spouse that there's plenty of room still left for compromise. Conversely, a small concession made after a lengthy period of consideration indicates that very little room for compromise remains. Don't misinterpret your spouse's moves or make moves that can be misinterpreted by your spouse, if you want the dance to go smoothly.

Finally, once you commit to a position, try your best to not change your mind. For instance, if you offer to settle a dispute over a family heirloom by saying you'll accept $200 for your share, don't decide that you really want $300 and withdraw your first offer. It will almost certainly be taken as a sign of bad faith, which will undermine the negotiations.

Remember that there are a lot of choices. Ask your mediator or collaborative attorney to help you select an approach that feels comfortable to you. Don't assume that you have to engage in a particular form of bargaining if you don't want to. Many couples discover that neither one of them wants to do the distributive dance, for example. But they only find this out when one of them says, "Look, if I tell you what I think would be a reasonable amount and why I think it's fair to both of us, can we agree that you won't expect to go back and forth with offers and counteroffers after that?"

Dos and Don'ts of Effective Bargaining

Even though bargaining techniques vary, certain principles are universal. Here are some dos and don'ts to keep in mind. We list them first, so you can copy the list and take it with you to the mediation or collaborative meeting. Then we explain each one in detail.

Concepts to Consider

Bring this chart with you to the mediation or four-way meeting.

Dos

❑ Do begin with a cooperative move.
❑ Do counter a competitive move with a firm response.
❑ Do maintain your sense of perspective.
❑ Do make credible offers that include your reasons and address your important interests.
❑ Do offer incentives.
❑ Do counter tactics firmly but respectfully.

Don'ts

❑ Don't make outrageous demands.
❑ Don't use add-ons.
❑ Don't overreact to tactics.

Dos

Do begin with a cooperative move. Start out the bargaining process by demonstrating your intent to conduct the bargaining in a cooperative, noncompetitive fashion. This does not mean that you need to begin by conceding on the issues, but only that you indicate your willingness to consider a reasonable compromise. For example, you might say, "I'm prepared to find a common ground here. What do you think would be fair?" This does not commit you to any particular position, but lets your spouse know that you are open-minded on the subject.

 Do counter a competitive move with a firm response. Suppose during the bargaining your spouse does something he or she has every right to do, but it clearly runs counter to your interests. For example, Amika and Wayde are negotiating about the amount of support Wayde will pay to Amika. Wayde informs Amika that he's just bought a new car with a big monthly payment. This results in less money available to pay support, and makes the issue harder to resolve in a way that will address Amika's interests.

If you're confronted with something like this, you need to choose a response that discourages your spouse from doing similar things in the future. You should try to match the level of competitiveness used by your spouse without escalating. If your spouse then resumes a cooperative mode, you can do so as well, and the bargaining is back on track.

In Amika's case, she might discuss her option of going to court on the support issue to let Wayde know she can choose this if his behavior remains competitive.

She can then attempt to secure Wayde's agreement that the new car payment will not be a factor in negotiating support. If he does agree, then the bargaining can resume on a more collaborative note.

Do maintain your sense of perspective. Bargaining can be intense. It is easy to get swept up in the moment and lose all sense of perspective about what you are trying to accomplish and why. If you feel this start to happen, take a break, step back, and think about where you are and what is happening. The idea is to leave the action momentarily to take stock of the situation from a slightly different angle. You can then resume with a clearer sense of purpose.

Do make credible offers that include your reasons and address your important interests—and, if possible, the important interests of your spouse. Regardless of whether you're following the predictable steps of the dance of distributive bargaining or engaging in some other method of bargaining, it is important that any offer you make be credible. That is, your offer should be one that is within the reasonable realm of possibility. Also, state clearly why you think the offer is fair. Doing this demonstrates respect for your spouse and the process and encourages cooperation on your spouse's part. Be sure to make the offer consistent with your important interests. Don't leave out something because you think you can bring it up later—that won't be easy.

Do offer incentives. If you reach a point of impasse during the bargaining, look for items of value to offer to your spouse in exchange for further concessions on points that are important to you. Use the information you've gleaned about your spouse's interests to identify these items.

Do counter tactics firmly but respectfully. Negotiation experts counsel that competitive tactics must be countered directly and firmly in order to bring the bargaining back into a cooperative mode. How to do this depends on the circumstances, the relationship between you and your spouse, and the nature of the tactic itself. For specific suggestions, refer to the list of common negotiating tactics (or negotiation bloopers) and how to counter them, above.

Don'ts

Don't make outrageous demands. Keep your proposals and counterproposals within the realm of reasonable possibility. Making an outrageous demand will almost certainly be viewed with mistrust by your spouse. This puts the entire bargaining process at the risk of being shut down.

Don't use add-ons. An add-on is a demand for an additional concession or an introduction of new conditions after the bargaining is completed. It will almost certainly be viewed by your spouse as a bad faith move and can cause the unraveling of the agreement you just reached. If you've prepared well for the negotiation, you can avoid this pitfall by getting clear about your interests before beginning. If you really need to bring up something new, apologize for the oversight and make it clear that you understand that some terms already agreed to may need to be renegotiated.

Don't overreact to disruptions. If you are on the receiving end of a tactic or negotiation blooper, you may have a visceral response. Your face may become flushed, your blood pressure might rise, or your jaw might clench. It's natural to have this kind of reaction, but it's important not to give in to the temptation to overreact and blow the negotiations out of the water. Instead, use the methods we've outlined above to get the bargaining back on track. When you're in this situation, humor can be a very effective way of defusing your own anger and making your point. Think of a way to turn your response into a joke. You'll find it works wonders.

Prepare for the Negotiation

Most negotiation experts agree that an essential key to successful negotiation is preparation. Good planning and preparation tremendously increase your odds of negotiating an agreement that truly addresses your interests. This section suggests things you can do in advance.

 Listen to your mediator or collabora-tive lawyer. Your mediator or lawyer will be helping you prepare, and he or she may do things in a different order from what we offer here. These are just general guidelines. Use them if they're helpful and ignore them if they're not. If you're in a collaborative process, it's particularly likely that your lawyer will have ideas about how the two of you should prepare for the four-way meeting(s) with your spouse and his or her lawyer. Follow your attorney's instructions.

Inventory Your Personal Negotiation Skills

Whether we know it or not, most of us have engaged in effective interest-based negotiating at some point or another in our lives. Parents use interest-based negotiating with their children all the time. Mealtime is a good example of this. If you're a parent, you have probably engaged in a negotiation over food more than once. Your interest is in seeing that your child eats nutritious food. Your child may not perceive good nutrition as an interest, but agrees to eat the food in question because doing so meets some other interest of your child's, such as having dessert, going out to play, or just pleasing you.

We also engage in interest-based negotiating with family members, coworkers, and neighbors. Every time we make an agreement with someone else that takes into account what both sides need, we are engaging in interest-based negotiation.

Exercise: Think of two or three examples from your own life in the last year. Write down what was agreed on. Try to think of what interest of yours was satisfied by the agreement and what interest of the other person's was satisfied by it. Then trace the negotiation back to its beginning. What role did you play in the discussion that led to the agreement? Did you initiate the discussion? If not, how did you respond when the subject was brought up? Were you able to assert your interests? Were you able to attend to the other party's interests? What aspects of the negotiation did you do well? What aspects could have been improved? Jot down your answers on a blank piece of paper or on Worksheet 10 in the appendix.

Completing this exercise will help you to become aware of your personal negotiation skills. You can make a conscious effort to build on skills you already have as you successfully negotiate a settlement agreement in your mediation.

Consider a Negotiation Coach

Learning to be a good negotiator is a little like learning a new sport. Even if you have the basic skills for the sport, working with a professional coach will help you hone those skills and develop your confidence.

In the same way, working with a negotiation coach can help you learn to negotiate in the mediation with ease and confidence. If you're in mediation, your mediator will be actively coaching both you and your spouse during the mediation sessions—but working with an outside coach can decrease the learning curve during mediation. If you're in a collaborative process, your lawyer will probably act as your negotiation coach, so unless you feel like you want extra support and training, you probably don't need an outside coach to help you negotiate.

If the idea of working with a negotiation coach is appealing to you, take a look at Chapter 8.

Identify the Issues to Be Resolved

Start your preparations by making a list of the problems that you think have to be addressed in the negotiation. (Another term for problem in this setting is "issue.") Write down a list of these problems in Section A of Worksheet 12.

Be specific. In most divorces, the issues fall into the broad categories of property and debt division, child custody and time-sharing, child support, and alimony. For a more complete list, see the section of Chapter 16 that relates to preparing the final settlement agreement. Your case may involve problems in some or all of these categories. Identify the specific ones that apply to your situation, such as what to do with the house, how to divide the pension, who gets the new car, how to pay the credit card debts, what the custody arrangement will be during the school year, and so on.

Practice listing each problem in neutral, nonblaming language. For example, Boris might first think of writing, "How to keep Natasha from ripping me off." He can make this more neutral by writing something like, "Reasonable buyout for shop."

Identify and Prioritize Your Interests

Once you have a list of the problems that need to be solved, take a few moments to identify your interests that need to be addressed in resolving each problem. Use Section B of Worksheet 12 to do this. Interests usually consist of long-term goals and short-term needs and concerns—fears or worries about the future.

For examples of what we mean by interests, go back and look at what Boris and Natasha came up with in Step 2 of their negotiation. To get at your own interests, ask yourself questions like, "Why is this problem important to me?" or "What will I get out of having my way on this issue?" or "What am I worried about when I think of this issue?"

After you've identified each set of interests, try to prioritize them in order of importance to you, with 1 being most important, 2 being slightly less important, and so on. Use the space to the left of each interest on the worksheet.

Make a Hypothetical List of Your Spouse's Interests

While you should not assume you know exactly what your spouse's interests are in each situation, you can probably guess some of them. Making a hypothetical list of these interests gets you started thinking about possible settlements that might appeal to your spouse. It also gets you in the right frame of mind to attend to your spouse's point of view during the mediation. As you come up with ideas, jot them down in Section C of Worksheet 12.

Compare and Match Up Interests

During the mediation or collaborative negotiation, your mediator or the two attorneys will help you move toward a settlement by matching up interests that you and your spouse share, like concern for your children's education or saving money on taxes. Focusing on shared interests helps build momentum toward settlement. Other interests are independent—not shared. Independent interests are different for each spouse, but they don't conflict with the other person's interests, so focusing on them can be another way to generate attractive settlement options. Conflicting interests are ones that appear to be in direct conflict with the other party's interests. The mediator or collaborative lawyers will work with you to narrow down the number of truly conflicting interests.

You can get a start on this process by comparing your list of your prioritized interests with your hypothetical list of your spouse's prioritized interests. To the right of each interest on Worksheet 12, put "S" for shared, "I" for independent, and "C" for conflicting.

Determine Your BATNA and WATNA

Once you've identified and prioritized the interests relating to each issue, spend some time assessing the strengths and weaknesses of your alternatives to an agreement. What is the likely range of outcomes available to you if you can't settle? What is the best result you can expect, or BATNA (Best Alternative To a Negotiated Agreement)? What is the worst possible outcome, or WATNA (Worst Alternative To a Negotiated Agreement)? Don't forget to factor in the cost of

obtaining these results—attorneys' fees, expert witness fees, appraisals, and other costs. Use Section E of Worksheet 12 to jot down your BATNA and WATNA on each issue, as well as the estimated costs of taking the issue to court.

Use a consulting lawyer. If you are in mediation and you haven't yet consulted a lawyer, this is a good time to do so. Make sure you find a lawyer who is knowledgeable about the law and who understands and supports mediation. (See Chapter 8.) The law is rarely black-and-white, so your lawyer probably won't be able to predict with precision what the outcome would be in court. However, he or she should be able to give you a good idea of the range of probable legal results and the expense you can expect to incur if you don't reach an agreement.

Realistic opinions are what counts. When you ask your lawyer to help you develop your BATNA and WATNA, make sure you stress that you want a *realistic* opinion, not a theoretically possible but highly unlikely outcome based on the most extreme adversarial position that could be taken. For example, Natasha's lawyer could tell her that her best-case scenario is one where the shop is valued at $250,000 and Boris is ordered to pay Natasha cash of $125,000 to buy her out, plus all Natasha's attorneys' fees and costs, child support, and alimony for four years while Natasha goes back to school. But what Natasha's lawyer doesn't tell her is that while there is a legal basis to ask for all of this, it is unlikely that she'd get it. This is not her BATNA, and it won't help her negotiate a realistic settlement.

Develop a Settlement Spectrum

Imagine at least three different settlement agreements covering all the issues that would be acceptable to you. All three hypothetical settlements should be in the range of realistic possibility—that is, ones that would work for you and that your spouse might consider. These hypothetical settlements should span both ends of the spectrum, from most desirable ("I'd be very happy to get this") to least desirable ("I don't like it, but I can live with it"). One should be in between.

As you formulate these settlement possibilities, compare them to your BATNA and WATNA and analyze how well they meet the interests you've identified for yourself and your spouse.

Doing this ahead of time will make it easier for you to tell whether the actual settlement proposals generated during negotiation fall within your settlement spectrum. Use Section F of Worksheet 12 to write down your ideas for settlement.

Be Prepared to See Things in a New Way

It's not always easy to know what your interests are or how important they are to you until you start considering different settlement options during the actual mediation or collaborative negotiation. It's even harder to be entirely accurate about what is important to your spouse. So be prepared to learn new things about yourself and your spouse as the process unfolds. Being flexible will help you stay on top of the negotiations. And, you can always ask for a break if you feel a need to step back and consider the impact of any new information.

Be Willing to Accept a Settlement That Satisfies Your Spouse

The final step in preparing is to answer honestly the question whether you are ready to work on creating a settlement agreement with which your spouse will be satisfied.

The expectation of interest-based negotiation is that each party will come away with an agreement that meets his or her main interests.

Some divorce negotiations get to the brink of settlement and then break down because of one spouse's desire for revenge. The desire is so strong that it prevents the spouse from committing to a settlement that satisfies the interests of the other even though it meets his or her own interests.

Test your own motivation. Imagine that you have just negotiated a settlement with your spouse. The settlement is within your settlement spectrum. It also satisfies your spouse. Do you find this impossible to accept? If so, you may need to work on reconciling yourself to the idea of a mutually satisfactory agreement before embarking on the actual negotiations.

Negotiate Clearly, Firmly, and Respectfully

Good preparation will go a long way to enhancing the success of your negotiation, whether it's a mediation or a collaboration. Bring your completed Worksheet 12 with you to refer to during the negotiation. In addition, keep in mind the simple principles listed below while you are doing the actual negotiating. Because these are things we've already touched on in this chapter or other parts of the book, we just list them for you here.

 Follow your mediator or collaborative lawyer. Remember that your mediator or collaborative lawyer is there to help you be an effective negotiator. When in doubt about what to do or say, ask for help. If your mediator or lawyer suggests something different from what we say, go with their advice, unless it is clearly wrong.

Copy this list and bring it to the mediation or four-way collaborative meeting.

- ❏ Communicate clearly.
- ❏ Agree on the negotiating approach and ground rules.
- ❏ Begin with the problems, not your solutions.
- ❏ State your interests clearly and concisely.
- ❏ Show respect for your spouse's interests.
- ❏ Be open to all options.
- ❏ Keep speaking up for what's important to you.
- ❏ Negotiate in a firm but cooperative manner.
- ❏ Remember the dos and don'ts of effective bargaining.

Final Note

Now that you've studied how to sharpen your skills as a negotiator, you're ready to try your hand at the real thing. Don't worry if you still feel shaky about your abilities. The mediator or your collaborative lawyer will be there to help you. If you approach the process with goodwill, you'll probably find it's easier than you think.

Chapter 14

Court-Sponsored Mediation

This chapter is for anyone considering mediation through a court-sponsored program or who knows court-sponsored mediation will be required as part of the divorce.

Court-sponsored mediation presents some unique opportunities and problems, especially if the mediator has the power to testify or make recommendations to the court.

This chapter describes some typical court-sponsored mediation programs, how they work, and what the benefits and risks are. We'll talk about how to prepare for court-sponsored mediation and how to get the most out of it without doing something that can later be held against you.

Since the early 1980s, a growing number of courts all over the country have offered mediation services to divorcing couples as an alternative or a prerequisite to going to court, especially for issues involving child custody and visitation and related issues such as school placement, medical care, and travel restrictions. These court-sponsored programs are based on the theory that it is better for children to have their parents decide custody and other parenting issues with the help of a trained mediator than to have these matters decided by a judge after a lengthy and expensive court case.

Some courts extend their mediation services to financial issues, but most are limited to parenting matters.

 You can skip this chapter if you know you won't be sent to court-sponsored mediation. If you expect to handle every aspect of your case in private mediation or collaboration, you probably don't need to read this chapter. However, if the court *requires* you to use its mediation service or if you and your spouse want to handle certain issues in court mediation rather than a private process, you'll find it helpful to read the parts of this chapter that apply to your situation,

Types of Court-Sponsored Mediation Programs

The types of court-sponsored mediation programs available vary from state to state, and even from court to court. The options include the following:

- **Mandatory or voluntary.** Some courts require parents who can't agree on custody or visitation arrangements to participate in mediation. Other courts offer mediation but do not require it.
- **Free or fee-based.** Some court-sponsored mediation is free in the sense that once a case is filed and court fees are paid, there is no further charge for the mediator's services. Other programs charge a fee, sometimes on a sliding scale, for all or part of the mediation.

- **Recommending versus confidential.** In some programs, often called "recommending" or "reporting" programs, the mediator is expected to make a report to the court at the end of the mediation. The mediator's report may be written, oral, or both. In addition, the mediator may testify about the mediation and the mediator's recommendations if there is a contested court hearing.

Confidential, or nonrecommending, programs limit what the mediator may disclose to the court following the mediation. And the mediator is not permitted to testify about the mediation.

In both kinds of programs, there can be exceptions: If during the mediation the mediator learns of any instance of child abuse, spousal abuse, or elder abuse, or a party who is a danger to himself or herself, the mediator may be required by law to report this information to the local child protective service or other appropriate law enforcement agency.

- **Parenting issues only versus expanded issues.** Most programs are set up for parenting issues only. The mediator is not permitted to assist with the financial issues. In some places, courts are experimenting with programs that allow mediation of the financial issues, but this is not common.
- **Limited time versus open-ended time.** Almost all programs limit the length of time and the number of sessions

for each divorcing couple. Rarely will you have the opportunity to attend multiple sessions over an extended period of time.

- **Assigned mediator versus choice of mediators.** Many programs assign a mediator to your case, either on a rotating basis or by matching the mediator's expertise to the issues in your case. Occasionally, a program will let you select from a panel of mediators.

How Court-Sponsored Mediation Works

If you end up in court-sponsored mediation, it will be because you and your spouse or partner have agreed to participate or because you have been required to attend by court policy or court order. Ordinarily, court-sponsored mediation services are only offered to people who have some court case pending, such as a divorce, legal separation, dissolution of marriage, or paternity action.

Learning About the Mediation

If you already have a legal adviser or have selected a mediator, you can ask that person whether the court that will be processing your divorce has court-sponsored mediation and, if so, how it works. If you haven't got that far in the process yet but want to know whether your court offers mediation, stop by the court clerk's office—or visit the court's website—and find out how to get a copy of any rules, brochures, or other printed information concerning the mediation program. This should be public information. Because anything you tell the court personnel about yourself or your case could end up in your file, don't go into any details about your case when requesting this information in person.

Who Are the Mediators?

Mediators in court-sponsored programs must meet standards set by the state or the court. Many court mediators are full-time employees of the court system. Some are in private practice and work for the court part-time. Some courts maintain a list of qualified mediators to whom parents are referred. Although it was common to use volunteer mediators when court-sponsored mediation first began, this is now the exception rather than the rule. Most court mediators must meet stringent standards of education, training, and experience. They are usually subject to ongoing continuing education requirements as well.

Where Mediation Is Held

The mediation sessions can take place at the courthouse or at some other building designated by the court. When mediation is conducted by a private mediator to whom the court refers a case, the mediation may be at the mediator's office.

Before the Mediation Session

Many court-sponsored programs require divorcing spouses or unmarried parents to attend an orientation or a coparenting class before meeting with a mediator. In addition, they may require the parties to fill out a questionnaire ahead of time. Sometimes, the questionnaire is the only paperwork the mediator will see prior to meeting with the parties. In other cases, the mediator may review the court file in advance as well.

Attendance Requirements

Normally, both parties are expected to attend the mediation at the same time. Many programs have procedures for holding separate sessions, however, if allegations of domestic violence have been made.

Mandatory court-sponsored programs may require completion of a minimum number of mediation sessions. In other programs, it may be enough just to show up for one session.

If the Mediation Is Successful

If you reach an agreement in a court-sponsored mediation, the mediator will probably write up the agreement.

Sometimes, the agreement is written up while you are still present so you can sign it before you leave. In that case, you often have a rescission period—a few days for you to change your mind—before the agreement goes to the court. Depending on the court, the mediator may also recommend follow-up court orders, such as an order to attend parenting classes or counseling or to submit to drug testing.

The mediator will send the agreement to the court for approval as a court order. This is usually a mere formality, because judges rarely reject agreements worked out by the parties.

If You Do Not Reach an Agreement

If you do not reach an agreement during court-sponsored mediation, the mediator will report this to the court.

If your mediation is part of a recommending program and you don't reach an agreement, the mediator will prepare a report recommending how the judge should rule on disputed issues. The mediator's report may also include information about what was said and how cooperative you were during the mediation. The mediator may even be called to testify about the mediation if there is a contested hearing.

In a confidential program, the mediator's report may simply note that you attended the mediation and did not reach

an agreement, or the mediator may be allowed to comment on your cooperation or suggest further investigation, evaluation, or counseling. Some confidential programs allow the mediator to refer the case to a second mediation with a new mediator who has the power to make a recommendation.

Of course, any recommendations made by the mediator must be approved by the judge. This means that you can go to court and argue for a different outcome. Judges generally give great weight to the mediator's opinion of what should happen, however. So, with few exceptions, the mediator's recommendations are likely to be adopted by the court even if you object.

Voluntary Mediation: To Try or Not?

If your court offers a voluntary mediation program, you'll need to decide whether to take advantage of this service. Hopefully, you'll consult with a legal adviser on this question, because he or she can guide you about the specifics of your court system. But here are some general considerations to keep in mind.

Advantages of Court-Sponsored Mediation

There are several advantages to court-sponsored mediation.

Cost

Court-sponsored mediation is probably going to be less expensive than private mediation. Usually it is free, or, if not, it is offered at a significantly lower rate than what a private mediator would charge. So if the issues between you and your partner are pretty simple and fit within the parameters of what can be mediated, and if you just need a little help in getting things worked out, this option may make sense for you.

Experienced Mediators

Mediators in court-sponsored programs are sometimes more experienced in helping divorcing parents reach agreement than many of their counterparts in private practice, because of the high volume of cases they deal with and their focus on parenting issues. If you live in an area where your choices of private mediators are limited, you might find yourself better off with an experienced mediator in a court-sponsored program, assuming that your issues are ones that can be handled by the court program.

Physical Security

Another advantage to court-sponsored mediation is the physical security it can offer. If there has been violence in your relationship, but you need to get some arrangement worked out for child custody and time-sharing, the court may have special procedures for separate meetings to ensure your safety. If this is a concern

of yours, be sure to ask about what is available.

Authoritative Structure

If there are other serious problems in your relationship, a court-sponsored program can provide an authoritative structure in which to resolve things without having to litigate a contested case. The fact that the mediation is being conducted under the supervision of the court and perhaps in the courthouse building may be enough to keep your spouse on his or her best behavior in a way that private mediation might not. Again, this assumes that your issues are ones the mediation program will handle.

Disadvantages of Court-Sponsored Mediation

There are some definite disadvantages to court-sponsored mediation.

Beware of Recommending Programs

If the program you are considering is a recommending program, you'll need to be very careful about what you say and how you present yourself in every interaction with the mediation office, including during the mediation sessions, because the mediator will be making a report to the court if no agreement is reached. If the mediator thinks you've been uncooperative or disrespectful, this could influence what the mediator recommends, which could cause a judge to decide against you.

Even in a confidential mediation program, the mediator may comment to the judge about how you approached the mediation and how cooperative you were. This might influence the judge's decision if your case ends up in court.

And the mediator may be legally required to report any accusation of child abuse, even if the accusation turns out to be false.

Limited Scope and Time

Court-sponsored mediation is limited in scope and time. If you need to negotiate financial issues as well as parenting issues, a program that limits itself to parenting issues will do only half the job. Furthermore, because these issues are often intertwined, it may be hard to get a resolution of the parenting issues without discussing the financial ones. Time limits can also be problematic. There will be more pressure on you and your spouse to cut to the chase without thoroughly exploring all of your options.

Mandatory Mediation: Opting Out

By definition, a mandatory program requires your attendance for at least one session. If you have assessed your situation and have concluded that it would not be in your best interests to attend mandatory mediation sponsored by the court,

you still may be able to avoid the process or limit your participation in it.

Negotiate an Agreement With Your Spouse

The most obvious way to avoid mandatory mediation is to negotiate an agreement with your spouse on the issues that would otherwise be sent to mediation. You can do this in private mediation, or on your own, or with the help of lawyers—collaborative or consulting—or other advisers. You can then submit your agreement to the court instead of going through the court's regular mediation program.

History of Domestic Violence

Even if you can't reach an agreement, some mandatory programs will excuse attendance in certain circumstances. Some court programs excuse attendance if there is a history of domestic violence or child abuse. Others still require you to attend but will arrange for separate meetings with confidential appointment times to minimize the risk of further violent incidents.

History of Drug or Alcohol Abuse

If your spouse has a history of, or current problems with, drug or alcohol abuse or other inappropriate behavior, this may excuse you from mandatory mediation in some programs.

Other Ways to Opt Out

Participation in mandatory mediation might be difficult because of geographical distance or language differences. Many programs will arrange for telephonic participation by a parent if that person lives too far away for in-person attendance to be feasible. Other court programs will excuse participation altogether. Similarly, many programs provide translation services, or bilingual mediators, to couples who speak a language other than English. If that is not possible, they will excuse participation.

If you think the circumstances of your case might warrant an excuse from participation, find out the program's guidelines, either by asking the court mediation office or by checking with a legal adviser.

Valid reasons to excuse participation or offer accommodation in court-sponsored mediation:

- ❑ domestic violence in your relationship
- ❑ drug or alcohol abuse by your spouse or partner
- ❑ child abuse by your partner
- ❑ you live too far away to attend mediation
- ❑ you or your spouse/partner does not speak English
- ❑ you or your spouse/partner has a physical or mental disability

- ❑ you are intimidated by your spouse/partner
- ❑ you can't get off work to attend, or
- ❑ other hardship factors.

Find out in advance. Be sure to find out ahead of time whether your request to be excused from mediation is likely to be granted. Going into mandatory mediation after unsuccessfully requesting to be excused could backfire if the mediator thinks you're coming in with a negative attitude toward the mediation.

If You Can't Opt Out of Mandatory Mediation

If it looks like there's no alternative to participating in the mediation, you'll need to decide whether to do the minimum necessary or participate more fully. This decision is best made with the help of a knowledgeable adviser or coach.

Here are some factors to consider in making that decision:

- **Find out what the program requires as a minimum.** Some programs simply mandate that you show up for one session. Others require you to attend a number of times. Still others require you to make an effort to agree, but do not specify the exact criteria for determining when your effort is enough.

- **Consider whether doing just the minimum will be held against you in court.** If you're dealing with a recommending program, this is a real risk. Most mediators have a more positive attitude toward someone who makes the extra effort to reach an agreement. In fact, in some states, a parent's willingness to find ways for the other parent to spend time with the children is considered a legal factor in deciding child custody. Even in a confidential program, there is some risk that a strategy of doing the minimum might come to the attention of the judge. On the other hand, if you know from your research that it is in your best interests to limit your participation as much as possible, then you may decide to do only what is legally required, and nothing more.

Preparing for Court-Sponsored Mediation

There are some steps you can take to prepare for court-sponsored mediation.

Learn the Court Rules and Procedures

If you haven't already visited the court clerk's office or court website, now is the time to pick up any information the court has on its court-sponsored mediation program. Your legal adviser, if you have one, should also be of help.

Find Out About the Mediator in Advance

In court-sponsored mediation, you may not have your choice of mediator. But if you are given a choice, try to learn what you can about each mediator available to you and apply the principles discussed in Chapter 6 in making your selection.

If you are not given a choice, see whether you can find out who has been assigned to your case, and then try to find out about that mediator. For example, does she tend to favor joint custody? Is he known to be biased for or against certain groups of people? Does she have a particular format she follows? Does he work hard to get you to agree, or does he take a more laid-back approach? Knowing these things in advance will help you prepare for the mediation session.

If there is no way to find out in advance who your mediator will be, try to learn this kind of information about each of the mediators who might be assigned to your case. The more you know what to expect, the more comfortable you will be in the mediation and the greater your chances of successfully reaching agreement.

The people to ask for information about the court-sponsored mediation program and the mediators who work in it include your legal adviser, your counselor, other professionals who may have experience helping people go through the court mediation program, and friends or neighbors who have had experience with the program.

Be Positive in Your Contacts With the Mediation Office

Before the mediation session, you will probably have one or more interactions with people in the mediation office, such as when you schedule your appointment or when you attend an orientation session or arrange to complete a questionnaire in advance.

It is important to be polite and positive in all your interactions with the mediation office, even when speaking to a receptionist, clerk, or secretary. If you have a negative encounter with one of these people, there is a good chance it will be reported to the mediator or noted in your file. You don't want to go into the mediation session with one strike against you.

Conversely, a pleasant encounter with someone in the mediation office will help ensure that your next encounter will go smoothly as well and that you will start off on the right foot going into the mediation.

Be Flexible in Scheduling Appointments

Most court-sponsored mediation programs are juggling schedules for several mediators and dozens of mediating couples at any given time. Consequently, they may offer you an appointment at an inconvenient or impossible time. Try to be as flexible as you can in scheduling. If you cannot come to a mediation session on a particular day or time due to your work schedule or other commitments, inform the person scheduling the appointment of your conflict and find out what other options are available. But don't reject an appointment time merely because it is inconvenient.

Once you've scheduled the appointment, try not to change it unless an emergency arises. Notify the mediator's office immediately if an emergency will prevent you from attending. Many programs will fine parents who don't show up for a scheduled appointment without notifying the office in advance.

Find Out What and Whom to Bring

You'll probably receive a notice from the mediation program indicating your appointment time and telling you what to bring with you to the mediation session. If not, or if the instructions are not clear, check with the mediation office and find out whether you should or should not bring any documents or other materials, such as school or medical records, with you.

If you are supposed to bring something, assemble what is needed at least a few days in advance so that you are not scrambling around at the last minute trying to locate documents. If you've been instructed not to bring documents other than your notes with you, follow these instructions.

Some programs will want you to bring your children. Others will ask you not to. Be sure to find out. If you are to bring your children, ask for suggestions on what to tell the children to prepare them for the appointment. You can ask the mediator's staff for help with this or a counselor or mediation coach. For more resources on talking to your children, see Chapter 1.

If you want to bring someone else with you to the mediation, arrange this in advance with the mediation office. Most mediation programs will not object if you bring a neutral support person with you. That person may be expected to wait outside, however, unless he or she is a language interpreter. And never plan to bring someone who would trigger a defensive or angry reaction from your spouse.

Be Prepared to Negotiate Effectively

During the mediation, the mediator will try to help you negotiate an agreement. You will have limited time to do this, so it is especially important that you be well-prepared and focused. Reread the parts of Chapters 9 and 10 that apply to your situation. If it's been a while since you have read Chapter 12 on communicating or if you haven't read it yet, read the parts of it that apply. Then, assuming that the mediation will primarily or exclusively involve parenting issues, use the following approach to prepare for the mediation. If you will be mediating only financial issues instead of parenting issues, you can substitute the interest-based approach outlined in Chapter 13.

Concepts to Consider

When mediating parenting issues in court-sponsored mediation:

☐ identify the problems (issues) to be resolved.

   List all the issues that need to be addressed during the mediation. Examples: regular time-sharing schedule, holiday schedule, ground rules for choosing doctors or day care providers.

☐ look carefully at each issue.
   For each issue, try to come up with one or more specific solutions that are in your child's interests. When doing this, keep these points in mind:

☐ Be sensitive to when you might be pushing for your own interests instead of your child's. This is a common tendency, and one to be avoided.

☐ When in doubt, pick the option that maximizes the other parent's time or involvement. Doing this sends a message that you are willing to put your child's interests ahead of your own.

☐ Be specific. If the issue is time-sharing, don't just list a percentage of time (like 50/50). Look at a calendar and figure out a specific schedule of when your child could be with each parent that makes sense when you look at it from your child's point of view.

☐ Be realistic. If you know from consulting with a lawyer or doing your own research that the court is unlikely to go along with something you want to propose, be prepared to back off if your spouse does not agree. For example, you might believe that your child should be raised in a certain religion. If the court won't order the other parent to go along, you may have to live with that.

☐ Imagine yourself in the other parent's shoes and think of what she or he might propose. Honestly evaluate it from your child's point of view. Be prepared to accept any option that seems to meet your child's interests.

☐ Avoid viewing the mediation as a power struggle between you and your spouse in which you "lose" if your spouse "wins." If you're having trouble doing this, remind yourself how much better it will be for your children if you and your spouse can agree without going to court.

Attending the Mediation Session

Here are some tips on how to handle the mediation session itself.

Go Into the Session by Yourself

Even if you have arranged with the mediation office to bring a neutral support person, do not expect to bring that person with you into the session. It is especially important that you not expect a new girlfriend or boyfriend, fiancé, or significant other to help you negotiate. Mediators like to see parents take responsibility for negotiating their own agreements. Involving a stepparent or new mate in this process can be seen as inappropriate.

Don't bring your children to the session, either, unless the mediator has requested you do so. If you need day care during the session, find out in advance whether the mediation office provides child care and, if not, make other arrangements.

Be Prompt

Be on time for the mediation session. Don't make the wrong impression on the mediator by being late.

Dress Simply and Conservatively

Wear clothes that are comfortable but that let your mediator know you take this process seriously. Dressing too casually can indicate a lack of respect for the mediator or the process. On the other hand, don't overdo it with attire that is too formal for the occasion. Simple, conservative clothing is best.

Do not wear sunglasses during the mediation unless it is medically necessary. The mediator will want to be able to look you in the eye.

Participate Fully

Plan to give the mediation your full attention. Turn off your watch alarm and your cell phone. Leave your pager in your car or at home, and make other arrangements for covering emergencies. Allow enough time in your schedule to be present for the entire session.

Listen and Learn

Good communication skills are important in every mediation. As you know from Chapter 12, listening attentively is an important part of effective communication. In court-sponsored mediations, good listening skills are even more important.

Even if you can't reach an agreement with your spouse during the mediation, listening carefully will give you valuable information about your spouse's attitudes toward the issues. Hopefully, this information will allow you to work toward a settlement without going to court. But, if you end up in court, the information will serve you well there, too.

Listening is also important because it will demonstrate to the mediator your willingness to hear your spouse's side of the story, even if you don't agree. This will make a favorable impression on the mediator.

Finally, and most important, listening attentively will let your spouse know that you are interested in his or her input. This will encourage your spouse to engage in constructive negotiation and, hopefully, with the mediator's help, you will reach a complete agreement.

Maintain a Firm and Cooperative Tone

Mediating successfully requires a cooperative but firm approach throughout the negotiations.

Doing this in a court-sponsored mediation is often a challenge because of the limited time allotted to each case. You will probably feel pressure to make decisions in a shorter period of time than is comfortable or ideal. This is why advance preparation is so important. If you are well-prepared, it will be much easier to maintain your poise during the mediation session.

If you are having trouble, ask the mediator for help or ask to take a short break so you can regain your composure. Whatever you do, resist any temptation to engage in a shouting match or name-calling contest with your spouse in front of the mediator.

Don't Worry If the Mediator Seems Sympathetic to Your Spouse

Many people come out of court-sponsored mediation sessions with the feeling that the mediator was on their spouse's side. In fact, the opposite is often true. It is important to remember that the mediator wants to help you reach an agreement. The mediator has limited time in which to try to make this happen and may well focus more time and attention on the spouse who is less prepared and less able to negotiate without help. If you've done your homework and have come to the mediation session ready to negotiate, but your spouse has not, your mediator may pay more attention to keeping your spouse going than to you. This may feel like the mediator is siding with your spouse when that is not true.

Clarify Any Agreement Reached Before Leaving

Hopefully, you and your spouse will be able to agree on most, if not all, issues during the mediation. If your mediator writes up the agreement while you're still there, be sure to read it carefully and discuss any questions you have at the time. Don't sign the written agreement unless you are sure that you are willing to abide by it. If you need a little more time before committing to the agreement, say so. Many court programs give you a certain number of days to change your mind after you have signed the agreement.

If the mediator is not going to write up the agreement while you wait, ask the mediator to go over each point agreed upon with you and your spouse before you leave, and make some notes for yourself at the time.

If You Don't Reach an Agreement

If the mediation session comes to an end and you have not reached an agreement, find out the next step from the mediator. Make it clear to the mediator that you are willing to continue looking for options and areas of agreement. Find out whether another session is possible. If not, ask the mediator for recommendations on what to do next. This will let the mediator know that you are motivated to reach an agreement. Additionally, if this is a recommending program, the mediator's answers to your questions may give you some idea of what the mediator intends to recommend to the court.

After the Mediation Session

After the session, make some notes for yourself of what transpired while your memory is still fresh. You can use Worksheet 10 in the appendix.

Be sure to check in with your adviser or coach as soon as you can. Your notes will help you make an accurate report to your adviser. Depending on whether or not you reached an agreement at the mediation, you will need to decide your next steps.

If you receive any follow-up report or other information from the mediation office, read it carefully. If you are working with an adviser, pass along a copy. If you think there are errors in the report or other document prepared by the mediation office, find out whether there is a procedure for calling it to the attention of the mediator; if you have an adviser, discuss how to do this in a constructive way.

If you agreed during the mediation to do something in particular, be sure to follow up. If you will be attending another session, confirm the appointment, date, and time in advance to avoid any possible misunderstanding.

Final Thoughts

Because of its close connection to the courts and its possible impact on a future contested case, court-sponsored mediation requires a careful approach. Most people who attend have a positive experience. The mediators involved in court-sponsored programs are generally experienced, well-trained professionals who sincerely care about children and their divorcing parents. They are usually skilled at cutting through the dispute and orienting parents to a child-oriented perspective.

If you follow the pointers we've outlined in this chapter, there is a good chance that you too can use court-sponsored mediation to negotiate a sensible parenting plan for you, your spouse, and your children.

Chapter 15

Encountering Difficulties in Mediation and Collaboration

We've talked before about mediation as a journey and the mediator as a guide. The same metaphor can apply to collaborative divorce. And for either process, it's important to remember that most journeys involve difficulties somewhere along the way: Delays, changes, and unexpected obstacles can challenge even the most seasoned traveler.

Encountering a difficulty doesn't have to mean the end of the mediation or the collapse of the collaboration, as long as the problem can be pinpointed and dealt with. Some problems can be easily resolved through discussion or minor adjustments in the process. Others may take longer to figure out and solve. Occasionally, the problem is serious enough that the mediation or collaboration must be temporarily suspended. And sometimes you are forced to end the process you're in, and resort to a contested divorce.

This chapter gives specific examples of types of problems that may arise during mediation or collaboration and provides tips on how to:

- bring a problem to the attention of the mediator, collaborative lawyers, and your spouse
- avoid contributing to the problem, and
- get back on track.

We also explore some ways to deal with persistent problems, including the option of suspending or ending the mediation or collaboration. If the mediation or collaboration must end, we show you how to use what you've learned in the course of the process to get a settlement as quickly and inexpensively as possible, hopefully without going to court.

Four-Step Approach to Dealing With Difficulties

You'll deal with difficulties somewhat differently depending on whether you are mediating or collaborating. Some of the suggestions below are mainly designed for a mediation process that runs into difficulties, but most will apply to either process. However, if you're in a collaborative process, you should talk with your collaborative lawyer before any problems arise about what you are going to do in the face of difficulties. You and your lawyer should make an agreement about whether you will bring up whatever is on your mind right away, ask for time out to talk to your lawyer, or make a note and discuss it with your lawyer after the collaborative meeting. Then follow whatever plan you make. You'll probably end up using the first three steps described below, and then taking some other kind of action, like having your lawyer talk to the other collaborative lawyer and see whether the issue can be resolved.

On the other hand, if you're mediating, then no matter what kind of difficulty you encounter, first try dealing with it in the mediation. Only if that fails should you take more drastic action such as ending the mediation. Try these four steps to handling the problem in the mediation.

Whichever process you are using, be sure to review the rest of this chapter.

When to Say Something

In any mediation, you are bound to hit some rough spots. But not every difficulty warrants action. Some are so minor or temporary that you can let them pass and move on. If you feel that what is going on is preventing real progress, however, it is time to take action.

Diagnose the Problem

Different problems have different causes and can require different solutions. (The rest of this chapter covers the most common kinds of problems that can arise.) Once you know what the problem is, it will be much easier to decide on the next step.

Evaluate Your Options

After you've diagnosed the problem, you'll need to decide what, if anything, to do about it. Before making that decision, you'll want to consider all of your options.

Take Action

Most of the time, the first step we suggest is to bring up the problem with your mediator. Tell the mediator you have a concern about a problem, and state the problem in nonblaming language. There may be times, however, when you'll want to consult an outside adviser before talking to the mediator. Hopefully, these steps will get the mediation back on track.

Discrepancies Between This Book and Your Experience

One problem you might encounter that is easily fixed: What is happening in your mediation or collaboration does not match something in this book.

Possible Explanation

Your mediation is shaped by your unique circumstances and your mediator's assessment of what will work for you. Also, mediators tend to have different styles. We have tried to give you a complete approach to the most common aspects of divorce mediation, but there are bound to be variations. The same is true of collaboration, where practices vary by location and individual lawyer.

What to Do

As long as you are satisfied with the progress you are making in your case, don't worry if it doesn't fit the mold of what we describe as typical. In fact, you should be relieved if your mediation looks at least a *little* different from what we describe. After all, one of the great things about mediation is that it is custom-designed by you, your spouse, and your mediator to fit your needs.

Delays and Disconnects

Sometimes the problem is what is *not* happening. Everything seems to take forever: Your spouse shows up late, cancels appointments, won't commit to rescheduling, or doesn't respond to a proposal. It can also happen that one or both collaborative lawyers seem to have frequent conflicts or scheduling problems. If this happens once or twice, it may be only a minor glitch. If it continues to happen to the point where the mediation or collaboration has come to a standstill, then it may call for some action.

Possible Explanations

There are several possible reasons for delays.

Normal part of the process. Some delays are a normal part of the process. Perhaps a piece of missing information is needed

before you can move forward. Maybe one or both of you need some time to consult with advisers before committing to a settlement. Delays of this nature are a necessary part of the mediation process.

Denial. If your spouse is the one who seems to be causing the delays, it may be that he or she has not faced the reality of your separation and divorce. If your spouse is in the denial stage of the emotional divorce, it may be very difficult to get him or her moving. (See Chapter 1 for a more complete discussion of the emotional divorce and its stages.)

Mediation is going too fast. Some people simply need more time than others to process important decisions. If the mediation is moving too quickly for your spouse, he or she may be trying to slow the process down to a more comfortable pace that allows for enough time to reflect and consider each decision.

Motivation. Your spouse may not be motivated or committed to settling with you. Perhaps your spouse is motivated by a desire for revenge. Maybe your spouse is afraid that settling is a sign of weakness. Perhaps he or she feels intimidated or pressured in the mediation and is passively resisting your efforts to make progress in order to feel more in control of what is happening.

Tactic. Occasionally, delay is an intentional tactic designed to get an advantage in the negotiations. If your spouse is using delay as a tactic, he or she may be hoping to wear you down so you are willing to make concessions just to get finished. More often, the tactic is unintentional—a defensive reaction to something going on in the mediation—even though it can have the same effect as an intentional tactic.

One or both collaborative lawyers are too busy. If it's one or both of the lawyers who seem to be causing the delay, first check in about whether that's really the case. Just as you and your spouse could be waiting for information from advisers, the lawyers could need time to gather or process information. Check in with your lawyer about the time frame. It is also possible that your lawyer, or your spouse's lawyer, has taken on too many cases and simply isn't able to give your case the attention it needs.

What to Do

Because of the wide variety of possible explanations for delays, proceed cautiously in responding. Don't compound the problem by issuing ultimatums or idle threats ("I'll see you in court"). Instead, the first step is to bring your concern to the mediator, either in a separate session or telephone call or in a joint session or conference call. Ask to have an honest discussion with the mediator and your spouse about the delay and what's causing it. In communicating about this problem, use the tips outlined in Chapter 12. Try to use the discussion with the mediator and your spouse to get as much

information as you can about the reasons for the delay. If you need help bringing up the subject, consult with a counselor, mediation coach, or mediation support person first. (See Chapter 8 for more on working with advisers.)

Perhaps the explanations offered will reassure you that the delay is a normal part of the process or only temporary, and nothing further will need to be done.

If the discussions reveal that your spouse is in denial or is uncomfortable with the pace of the mediation, you might negotiate a timetable for the rest of the mediation that builds in more time for your spouse to adjust. You may find this means that things go maddeningly slowly from your perspective, but as long as you are making forward progress, your patience will pay off in a divorce agreement that will stand the test of time.

If it comes out that your spouse has reservations about the mediation, then the mediator's job is to address the concerns and get the mediation back on a normal pace.

If delaying behavior doesn't seem to have any reasonable explanation and you suspect that the delay is an intentional or unintentional tactic—perhaps your spouse has canceled several appointments or has repeatedly not followed through with agreed tasks—ask your mediator to help you negotiate an agreement for specific consequences if the cancellations or lack of follow-through continue to occur. (For more on tactics, see Chapter 13.)

If you are concerned that your lawyer isn't following through, make an appointment to discuss the problem. Tell your lawyer what your expectations are and ask whether he or she can meet them. In most cases the lawyer will promise to be more available. And if not, you may need to find someone else to help you—hopefully at an early stage in the process.

Taking one or more of the steps outlined above should get things moving again. If not, consider the suggestions in the section titled "Dealing With Persistent Problems" below.

Tantrums and Other "Bad" Behavior

Some of the discussions you have in the process of negotiating your divorce settlement will evoke strong feelings and expressions by you or your spouse. Angry words and gestures, tears, and awkward silences can be normal, even healthy, occurrences during mediation as well as four-way meetings in collaboration. But if this kind of behavior occurs so frequently or with such intensity that it prevents you from making headway, it may be time to address the behavior, regardless of whether it is you or your spouse engaging in it.

Possible Explanations

Most disruptive outbursts have one of the following causes:

- lack of ability to recognize and handle strong emotions
- pattern of reactive interaction that has developed during the course of your relationship, or
- conscious or unconscious attempt to exert control over the outcome of the mediation—that is, a tactic.

What to Do

Different people have different levels of tolerance for emotional outbursts. You'll need to decide for yourself when things have gone past your limit. If they have, don't escalate the intensity level with outbursts of your own. Instead, take whatever time you need to calm down, and then address the problem in a constructive manner.

If you recognize that your own behavior is contributing to or causing the problem, acknowledge your responsibility for the problem to the mediator or collaborative lawyers and your spouse. Apologize, and offer to negotiate a ground rule, such as no interruptions, that you feel you can abide by. If you're unable to stick to the ground rule no matter how hard you try, you'll probably benefit from working with a counselor on constructive ways to handle your feelings.

Even if the disruptive behavior has been mutual, acknowledge your responsibility; negotiating ground rules should go a long way toward correcting the problem. If you make the first overture, chances are your spouse will follow suit. Sometimes, that's all that's needed.

If the disruptive behavior is all on your spouse's side, consider trying one of the techniques for responding to tactics and negotiation bloopers (unintentional tactics) found in Chapter 13. If that doesn't work or you need help, review the communication tips in Chapter 12. Get help with your communication style from a counselor if you feel you need it.

Ask your mediator or collaborative lawyer to help you negotiate a plan for addressing the problem. That might consist of a ground rule to which both you and your spouse can agree, such as that neither of you will leave the room without first asking for a time out. Or one or both of you might agree to consult a counselor for help with the disruptive behavior. Solving this kind of problem may also involve adjusting the timetable for the mediation or collaboration if one of you needs extra time between sessions, or shorter sessions, in order to be more composed during the mediation or four-way meeting.

Another approach to disruptive behavior in mediation is to ask to meet with the mediator in separate sessions or caucuses. Although this can end up being more time-consuming and less direct than joint sessions, it may allow you to make progress even when feelings run high.

If you've tried all these things, and nothing seems to work, consider our suggestions for dealing with persistent problems, below.

Extreme Discomfort in Mediation

You find yourself dreading each mediation session. You can hardly bring yourself to go. When you are there, you become increasingly irritated—at the mediator or your spouse or both. Or you feel overwhelmed and find it hard to pay attention. Perhaps you feel criticized and ganged up on, or pressured into agreeing to what your partner proposes.

Possible Explanations

Many reasons may exist for feeling intense discomfort with the mediation process. Here are some of the most common ones:

- unresolved feelings about your relationship—lack of trust, feelings of betrayal, or desire for revenge
- power imbalance—you feel you have no power in the mediation, you are too intimidated to speak up, or you feel you have no choice but to agree, or
- the mediator—your mediator is doing something that annoys

or offends you, or you feel the mediator is biased against you.

What to Do

Depending on what is causing your discomfort, you may want to consider different approaches. The first step is to look honestly at what is causing your discomfort. A counselor or other adviser can help you do this.

Unresolved feelings about your relationship. If your feelings of anger, mistrust, or betrayal are getting in the way, you probably won't make any real progress in mediation until you begin to deal with them. Getting help from a counselor is the most efficient way to accomplish this. (See Chapter 8.) This may mean postponing the next mediation session while you get it together emotionally. In that case, let your mediator and your spouse know the reason for the delay. Don't invite misunderstanding about your motivation by simply refusing to meet with no explanation.

Power imbalance. If the problem is a power imbalance, it may be beneficial to get some help from one or more advisers. If you experience your spouse as emotionally abusive or intimidating, you may want to work closely with a counselor. You may also want to have a mediation support person help you stand up for yourself in the mediation sessions. If you feel intimidated by your spouse's superior knowledge of financial or legal matters, then work with advisers who have expertise in those areas. (See Chapter 8.)

In addition to lining up advisers to help you address the power imbalance, discuss the problem with your mediator. Let him or her know if you want to bring a mediation support person to the session. Your mediator can help your spouse understand how the mediation support person can benefit both of you by helping you to participate in a meaningful way. You can also negotiate ground rules such as taking turns talking, taking breaks, or limiting the length of the sessions in order to increase your comfort level during the sessions.

You can also request separate sessions. This may be less efficient than joint sessions, but it can be worth the extra time if meeting together is too hard.

Problems with your mediator. If your problem is with the mediator, bring it up. If at all possible, have a frank conversation with the mediator about your reservations. Or, ask an adviser to speak to the mediator for you or with you. If the mediator has been doing something that bothers or offends you, such as laughing at your spouse's jokes, looking at you too intently, or talking too fast, your mediator may be unaware of the effect of this behavior on you and might gladly change it. If you think the mediator is biased against you, discussing your concern with the mediator can often clear the air.

If talking about the problem doesn't help, or if you can't bring yourself to talk to the mediator even with an adviser, then consider changing mediators.

If none of our suggestions alleviate your discomfort, consider the steps we suggest below for dealing with persistent problems.

Impasse: Negotiation Hits a Brick Wall

You've reached a standoff in the negotiation stage of the mediation or the collaborative process. You've made a proposal that your spouse won't even consider accepting, or vice versa, despite lengthy discussions in the mediation or the four-way meetings. Perhaps the standoff is over just one issue, such as whether to sell your house or let one of you stay in it. Perhaps it is a combination of several issues. In any event, the negotiations have come to a grinding halt.

Possible Explanations

Here are six explanations for impasse in mediation or collaboration:

- You and your spouse disagree about essential facts.
- You and your spouse disagree about the law that applies to your case.
- You and your spouse disagree about fundamental values, such as what

is best for your children or what is morally or spiritually right.

- You or your spouse has a powerful wish for revenge.
- You or your spouse is engaging in the win-lose syndrome—equating agreeing to something the other person wants as a loss for you and a win for the other person.
- You and your spouse are making different assumptions about how to negotiate.

What to Do

If you reach an impasse, don't despair. Your mediator or collaborative lawyers are all specially trained in methods for loosening the logjam and getting things moving again. Your job is to let the mediator or lawyers know if you think you've reached an impasse and then do your best to follow the mediator's lead in getting out of it.

Depending on the nature of the impasse, here are some things the mediator or collaborative lawyers might try.

Factual disagreements. If the impasse is caused by a disagreement about the facts, your mediator or collaborative lawyers may suggest a review of the information to see if there are any misunderstandings or missing pieces. If the information is all there and the disagreement persists, the mediator may suggest using an objective standard to settle the disagreement.

For example, if you and your spouse disagree about the value of a car, you could agree to refer to a published list of average values, such as the *Kelley Blue Book*. Or your mediator or collaborative lawyers might suggest having a neutral third party—for example, an appraiser or accountant—give an opinion on the factual question.

Usually, clarifying the information or getting a different perspective from an objective source will break the impasse and allow you to move ahead.

Legal disagreements. Disagreements about the law can be a major stumbling block in mediation. If you're in a collaborative process, it's a lot less likely that there will be major disagreements about the law unless the issue is one in which the law does not provide a clear answer. Otherwise, the lawyers will probably have worked out the legal issues and discussed them with you and your spouse already. And in a mediation, there are a number of ways to deal with disagreements about the law. The first step is to get an opinion about the legal options from a competent legal adviser.

If you do that and still get conflicting information, consider going back to your legal adviser and having your spouse do the same. Tell them that you and your spouse are being told conflicting information about the law, and ask for realistic reassessments of the positions. Maybe your or your spouse's adviser was unnecessarily optimistic the first

time around, or maybe one of you misunderstood something your adviser said.

Your mediator might also suggest getting a second opinion from a neutral legal adviser retained by the mediator solely for the purpose of the mediation. Or you and your spouse might be encouraged to bring your legal advisers to a joint mediation session where each one can explain his or her legal opinion. Sometimes this can produce an agreement between the advisers on the range of potential legal outcomes, which can jump-start the negotiations again.

Conflicting legal opinions often mean that you are operating in an unpredictable area of the law. Sometimes the range of possible legal outcomes is so broad that the law isn't much use as a standard for measuring a settlement by. In that case, your mediator may encourage you and your spouse to give less emphasis to the possible legal outcome in evaluating the settlement, and more emphasis to whether a proposed settlement balances the interests on both sides, regardless of what might happen in court.

Conflict in values. If the impasse seems to derive from a conflict in values, the first thing to do is double check for any misunderstandings. If you've done that, and if you still disagree about values you hold dear, your mediator or collaborative lawyers may try some different approaches to looking for solutions that don't involve compromising your values. For example, your mediator or the lawyers might invite each of you to look at the problem from your spouse's point of view, not in order to agree with it, but simply to understand it. Or your mediator or collaborative lawyers might encourage you to try to think up options for settlement that are less controversial. Sometimes the best way to deal with a conflict in values is simply to agree to disagree.

One spouse wants revenge. Sometimes, an impasse is the result of a desire for revenge. If one spouse feels wronged by the other's actions during the marriage or at the time of the separation, the aggrieved party may find it hard to agree to any settlement. If you experience this kind of resistance in yourself, you'll need to deal with it, preferably with the help of an able counselor, before resuming negotiations. If your spouse is the one who wants revenge, your mediator or collaborative lawyer may be able to get this fact out in the open in a nonjudgmental way. It will then be up to your spouse to decide whether he or she wants to take the steps necessary to deal with those feelings so that the negotiation can continue.

One spouse engages in win-lose syndrome. Sometimes, it's hard to agree to something the other person wants because it feels like that person wins and you lose. This can be especially true for someone who has felt taken advantage of during the marriage or betrayed at the time of the separation. If you start to feel this way, remind yourself that the goal is an agreement that works for you *and* your spouse. Focus on whether a proposal works for you. If it does, and if it works for your spouse, then you both win and neither of you loses.

If your spouse is the one with the win-lose attitude, be patient but firm. Don't concede more than is good for you in an effort to help your spouse feel better about the settlement, but don't overreact by withdrawing proposals, either. Let your mediator or collaborative lawyers carry the ball in getting your spouse to focus on a win-win solution. Your spouse's own collaborative lawyer should be a good ally in this effort, if the proposals on the table are in a reasonable range.

If the impasse persists despite everyone's efforts, consider our suggested steps for dealing with persistent problems, below.

Different assumptions about how to negotiate. For the negotiation to move forward to a satisfactory conclusion, you and your spouse need to be following the same rules of negotiation. Sometimes, an impasse is the result of conflicting negotiation strategies. Ask your mediator or collaborative lawyers to review with you the basic procedure for negotiating. Discuss whether both of you are adhering to those same procedures. Perhaps one of you is expecting to proceed by bargaining while the other is applying interest-based negotiating procedures. If you uncover different assumptions, talk about how to coordinate the negotiating process better to get things moving again. For more on negotiating strategies and how they operate, see Chapter 13.

Last-Minute Changes and Demands

You've spent hours in mediation or four-way meetings and have finally come up with an agreement. You've compromised some things you wanted, but you're glad to have matters settled. The mediator or one of the collaborative lawyers drafts an agreement. Your spouse responds by raising new demands and asking for changes.

Again, this is less likely to happen in a collaborative process, though it's not impossible. Generally, the involvement of a lawyer in the process makes it more difficult for a spouse to go back on agreements that were already made, but it does happen.

Possible Explanations

Sometimes, the process of putting a proposed agreement in writing causes one or both of you to see things in a new light. This can mean rethinking the terms of the agreement. Other times, a minor but significant item was forgotten during the settlement discussions. Occasionally, the eleventh-hour change is a conscious

or unconscious tactic designed to gain an additional advantage. Sometimes, a well-meaning but uninformed friend challenges the agreement ("You agreed to what?"). And every once in awhile, the spouse demanding the change is not emotionally ready to complete the divorce process.

What to Do

Whatever the reason, last-minute demands for changes need to be dealt with. It won't help to make counter-demands and threats. Instead, approach the problem by noting that it could mean an adjustment of other terms of the proposed settlement and reserving your right to request something in return. It can help to discuss what caused the change. If you can get to the real reason, you'll have an easier time figuring out a fair resolution of the new issue.

Dealing with a last-minute change usually requires some backtracking in the process. This can be very frustrating if you aren't the one who requests the change. You may be concerned that reopening the negotiations will only encourage your spouse to ask for even more concessions. If that is the case, you'll need to decide for yourself what your limits are. Until you reach that point, remind yourself that any agreement reached in mediation or collaboration must be completely understood and accepted by your spouse as well as you.

The process assumes that each of you can have as much time as you need to be satisfied with any agreement reached. So take a deep breath and assure yourself that in the long run, a little backtracking is worth it if you end up with a solid agreement.

On the other hand, if you've reached your limit with last-minute changes, consider our suggestions in the next section for dealing with persistent problems.

Dealing With Persistent Problems

What if you encounter a problem that doesn't seem to be fixed by anything you, the mediator, or the collaborative lawyers try? Short of issuing ultimatums and threats that could backfire, what can you do? After trying again with one of the techniques we've discussed in the previous sections, here are some possible steps you can take.

Take a Break From the Process

See if the passage of time changes things. Don't do this without carefully assessing the consequences of waiting. Are you setting a precedent that is detrimental to you by maintaining the status quo for a longer period of time? For example, if you are paying certain bills that both you and your spouse are responsible for, will you

get credit for continuing to do so? Are you legally entitled to more child support than what your spouse is paying? Questions like these are best answered after carefully reviewing your legal options. If it is possible to maintain a holding pattern, however, the passage of time can often put things in a different perspective. Sometimes this makes it easier to come back and mediate more effectively.

Try a Different Mediator

Although this is not a step to take lightly, it may be that a different mediator can be more effective in moving you along toward a mediated agreement. Most mediators will understand and support you in making a change if you think it might help. While it will cost you a little more time and money to familiarize a new mediator with your case, it will still be a lot less expensive than a contested trial.

Inform Your Spouse of Your Next Steps and Timetable

Develop a plan of action and time frame for what you will do if mediation or collaboration is unsuccessful. This might include actions such as discontinuing voluntary payments, hiring a lawyer (if you're in mediation without one), or going to court. Communicate your plan and timetable to your spouse in mediation. This may motivate your spouse to make a more serious effort to get past whatever problems have been plaguing the mediation. Get some input from a legal adviser when you formulate your plan.

Hire a Lawyer to Negotiate for You or Move Into a Collaborative Process

If you aren't getting anywhere in mediation, you may still be able to negotiate an agreement without going to court. A good lawyer can help you try to do that. On the other hand, hiring a lawyer definitely raises the ante. Depending on how your spouse responds, you could be looking at the beginning of a contested court case. To minimize that risk, see whether your spouse will agree to shift into a collaborative divorce process

Hire an Arbitrator

Ask your spouse to agree that the two of you will hire a private judge, or arbitrator, to decide what you can't agree on. This can be faster and less expensive than full-blown litigation in court, because it is usually more informal and streamlined. It is also private, whereas court is a public proceeding. You'll be stuck with the arbitrator's decision, however; there is no right to appeal an arbitration result unless you agree in advance that the decision

will be nonbinding or unless your state laws allow the arbitrator to be appointed by the court as a pro tem, or temporary, judge. Be sure to get advice from a lawyer before deciding to submit your case to an arbitrator.

Go to Court

This is obviously the most drastic option, and not one you want to undertake lightly. If you're convinced that no other resolution of your case is possible, however, then the emotional and financial costs of contested litigation may be worth it. If you're in mediation, give collaboration some serious thought before you move on to a contested court case. If you're in collaboration and you really feel that no other options exist, then it's time to get yourself another lawyer and move on to the contested divorce.

What to Do

Once you've reviewed your options, you'll need to decide which course of action makes sense for you. You may find it helpful to work with an adviser who can assist you in weighing the costs and benefits of each alternative.

If you choose a course of action that keeps you in the negotiation process, even if it involves a suspension of me- diation or collaboration or a change of mediators or lawyers, it is important to communicate your intentions to your spouse and the mediator or lawyers. Ironically, a discussion of this nature can sometimes have the effect of jump-starting the negotiation into a more productive mode. Even if that doesn't happen, it is important to be clear about what you are doing and why. Taking unilateral action without explaining why can undermine the ultimate success of the negotiation process.

Leaving Mediation Without Burning Your Bridges

If you come to the conclusion that mediation is getting you nowhere and you have to do something else, make your exit consistent with the principles of fair play and cooperation. Be firm, but make it clear that you are still interested in a negotiated settlement. Just because you are leaving mediation, it doesn't mean you are necessarily going to end up in court. You may have to spend more money on lawyers and legal papers before you reach a settlement, but chances are good that your case will eventually settle. Your chances of reaching a settlement with a minimum of time and expense are enhanced if you consistently signal your willingness to entertain reasonable settlement proposals.

Sometimes, a little exposure to the legal system can be what's needed to give your spouse a new perspective on the benefits of returning to mediation.

If you've kept the door open for your spouse by indicating a willingness to return to mediation, it is more likely that this will happen.

Also, be aware of the possibility of leaving mediation with a partial agreement. There are probably some things that you and your spouse did agree on during the mediation. Before you leave, ask your mediator to help you identify these things. They might be facts, such as values of certain items, or they may be decisions on certain issues, such as who will keep a particular asset or pay a certain bill. Anything you can do to limit the number and scope of facts and issues that have to be negotiated between lawyers or decided by a judge will make the rest of the process less costly, both financially and emotionally. And the process of listing the agreements reached can sometimes get the mediation moving in the right direction again.

Where There's a Will, There's a Way

The success of your mediation or collaborative process will depend primarily on two things: capacity and motivation. If you and your spouse have the emotional capacity to assess your own needs clearly and to treat each other respectfully, and if you are both motivated to work out an agreement rather than go to court, you should be able to overcome any obstacle you encounter on your journey to a settlement agreement. When you encounter a problem, it is an opportunity to reexamine and reinforce your own capacity and motivation. If you can do this, there is probably no obstacle so big it can't be overcome.

Mediation Troubleshooting Checklist

Remember to use your mediator as your guide in dealing with problems.

Steps to solving problems that come up in mediation:

❶ Assess the seriousness of the problem.   ❷ Diagnose the problem.
    If it is preventing progress, go to Step 2.   ❸ Evaluate your options.
    If it is not preventing progress, let it go.   ❹ Take action.

Possible Problems	Suggested Solutions
Discrepancies between this book and your experience.	Ignore parts of this book inconsistent with your mediation.
Delays and disconnects.	Discuss with your mediator or lawyer. Adjust the timetable; be patient. Negotiate ground rules, consequences.
Tantrums and other "bad" behavior.	Take responsibility for your behavior. Discuss with your mediator or lawyer. Negotiate ground rules, consequences.
Extreme discomfort in mediation.	Get professional help if needed. Use a mediation support person. Discuss with your mediator or lawyer. Meet separately (caucus).
Impasse.	Discuss with your mediator or lawyer. Cooperate with mediator's suggestions.
Last-minute changes and demands.	Be patient. Reserve the right to request something in return.

Suggestions for persistent problems:

• Take a break from mediation.   • Try a different mediator.

Use a collaborative process instead of mediation

• Inform your spouse of your next steps and timetable.   • Hire a lawyer to negotiate for you

• Hire an arbitrator.   • Take your case (or the contested part of it) to court.

Writing Up the Agreement

The ultimate goal of every divorce mediation or collaboration is to negotiate a binding agreement. Sometimes, a series of temporary or partial agreements culminates in one overall agreement. In other cases, you will negotiate the whole agreement as a single package. Either way, you will come to a point when your agreements must be put into writing in a mutually acceptable document suitable for submitting to the court in the uncontested divorce.

How do you get there?

The mediation sessions or four-way meetings are over. You and your spouse have settled everything. It hasn't always been easy, but you are glad that you hashed out the issues and came to an agreement. The next step consists of putting all your agreements in writing, then reviewing and revising the written document until you are both willing to sign it and submit it to the court.

The written agreement that goes to the court is often called a divorce agreement, marital settlement agreement, or marital termination agreement. It might also be known as a property settlement agreement, separation agreement, stipulated judgment, concurred-in judgment, or decree. For convenience, we'll just call it a divorce agreement.

If you mediate and if you are using a mediator who is not a lawyer, writing up the divorce agreement will probably be a two-step process. First, your mediator will prepare a written summary of the terms agreed upon, often called a memorandum of agreement. Then you and/or your spouse will hire a lawyer who will use the mediator's summary to prepare the divorce agreement. You could write up your own divorce agreement instead of using a lawyer, but unless you are prepared to teach yourself a lot about legal rules and requirements, this isn't advisable.

If you are using a lawyer-mediator, he or she will probably write the divorce agreement for you, and you won't need a separate person to do this.

Once the mediator puts your agreement in writing, you will look at it carefully to make sure it is accurate. This can often involve new negotiations over details that weren't clearly spelled out when you agreed on everything in the mediation.

The review process may involve using a consulting lawyer or another adviser. An adviser may suggest additional revisions. This, too, can mean more negotiations.

If you are using a collaborative process, you, your spouse, and the lawyers will designate one of the lawyers to prepare an initial draft of the agreement for circulation. Then you, your spouse, and the other lawyer will review the draft and make suggestions for changes, and those discussions will continue until you have a final document with which everyone is satisfied.

As we discuss in this chapter, reviewing, revising, and the accompanying negotiations are a normal part of the mediation or collaboration process. If you're prepared, it will be easier to deal with what can otherwise seem like an endless ordeal.

Interim or Temporary Agreements

Before you get to the point of the final settlement, you and your spouse may negotiate one or more interim, or temporary, agreements. These agreements cover short-term arrangements on a variety of issues, from initial separation issues like who will move out of the house, how the bills will be paid, and scheduling time with the children, to ongoing arrangements for child support and alimony. If you haven't set up satisfactory interim arrangements before you come to mediation or meet with your collaborative lawyer, getting an agreement on these matters may be the first order of business for the divorce process.

Later during the mediation or collaboration, as you seek more permanent solutions, you may revisit some of these issues and negotiate changes to the interim agreements.

As we discuss below, it is a good idea to put interim agreements in writing.

Partial Agreements

Occasionally, spouses settle one issue before deciding the rest of the issues. For example, you may decide to sell a piece of property and divide the proceeds, even though you haven't figured out what to do with the rest of the assets.

If you reach a partial agreement, write it down, even if it will be included in the overall settlement agreement at a later date.

Why Put Interim and Partial Agreements in Writing?

Unless the subject of the interim or partial agreement is so minor that it doesn't warrant the time and expense of writing it down, any agreement you negotiate during the mediation or collaboration should be put in writing. As with the divorce agreement, if you're in a collaborative process the lawyers will draft any written documents you need. In mediation, writing up an interim or partial agreement may involve having a summary memorandum prepared by your mediator and then taking the memorandum to a lawyer to prepare the actual agreement, unless your mediator is a lawyer who can prepare the agreement for you. There are lots of good reasons for taking the time to do this.

Avoids Misunderstandings

Putting the agreement in writing avoids any potential misunderstanding about the terms of the agreement. If an agreement is to be of any use to you, there must be a meeting of the minds on what you've agreed to. Putting the terms of the agreement down on paper will often catch any misunderstandings so you can clear them up at the outset.

Ensures Follow-Through

Having a written agreement also helps ensure follow-through. If you've had a problem in the past with your spouse not abiding by agreements, writing the agreement down will minimize this problem. It's hard to wiggle out of a clearly written agreement.

Helps Advisers

Writing down interim or partial agreements also helps you get input from your advisers. By looking at the written agreement, your adviser gets an accurate account of what you agreed to—the same account that your spouse's advisers are seeing. You can even ask your adviser to review the agreement before you sign it. He or she may have suggestions for improving the wording of the agreement to make it clearer.

Helps When Third Parties Are Involved

If your agreement involves a third party, having a written agreement may be important or even essential. For example, if you have agreed to set up a direct deposit of support money, you may need to show the bank a copy of the agreement. Or, if you've made agreements about your children's day care or medical care, you may want to be able to provide the day care provider or doctor with a copy of the agreement.

Helps With Tax Concerns

If your agreement concerns child support or alimony, you will need to put it in writing for the IRS. Alimony cannot be deducted by the payer unless it's paid pursuant to a written agreement. And if a parent who does not have the children 51% or more of the time wants to claim them as dependents, he or she will need written authorization from the other spouse. A written support agreement also avoids any potential future problems about the money that gets paid, such as why it was paid and what it was used for.

Helps If Court Approval Is Required

Sometimes, an interim or partial agreement needs to be approved by the court. If so, the agreement will need to be in writing so you don't have to make a personal appearance in court before a judge.

Helps If Agreement Must Be Proved

Finally, in some states, agreements reached in mediation are confidential unless they are in writing and designated as nonconfidential. This means you couldn't prove what your agreement was or have it be legally enforceable later unless you put it in writing.

Writing Up the Final Settlement

Regardless of whether you have made any interim or partial agreements, your negotiated settlement will have to be written up in a divorce agreement.

Memorandum of Agreement

The first step in completing a final agreement may be preparing a memorandum of agreement. If your mediator is not a lawyer, the settlement will be summarized in a written memorandum prepared by your mediator. If you're in a collaborative process or working with a lawyer-mediator, there may not be a need for this—the mediator or the collaborative lawyers will just keep track of your agreements and then, when all the issues have been resolved, prepare a draft agreement for you to review. Even in these situations, though, a mediator or collaborative lawyers may use a memorandum of agreement to refer to in preparing the draft.

Read the memorandum carefully and make sure it contains a clear and accurate description of everything you agreed to. If it is unclear or incomplete, or if reading it raises new questions for you, bring these up with the mediator. This may mean having another mediation session to clear things up, but doing this is well worth the trouble. An incomplete or inaccurate memorandum will only cause more problems.

If you are using mediation, it is especially helpful to have the memorandum reviewed by a good consulting lawyer. (See Chapter 8.) In addition to reviewing the terms with you, the lawyer can spot missing details that should be cleared up before the divorce agreement is prepared. These details can then be worked out with the help of your mediator.

Divorce Agreement

The divorce agreement should address all matters negotiated between you and your spouse in mediation or during collaborative meetings. The agreement should be written in clear language that you can understand. It should say what you intend it to say, and it should be in a format that meets the legal requirements for an uncontested judgment or decree of divorce.

Most often, the divorce agreement is prepared at the end of the negotiations after everything has been agreed upon. Occasionally in a mediation, the mediator will suggest writing up a proposed agreement that's still under consideration as a way of moving the negotiations along.

Who Prepares the Divorce Agreement

If you are using a lawyer-mediator, he or she will probably prepare the divorce agreement for you. If you're using a collaborative process, the lawyers will definitely prepare the written agreement.

If your mediator is not a lawyer, she or he probably will not write up the divorce agreement, because this ordinarily requires a license to practice law. This is beginning to change in some states, where paralegals and legal document preparers are authorized to write up certain documents.

If your mediator does not prepare the divorce agreement, you have several choices.

Hire a Lawyer to Prepare the Divorce Agreement

You and your spouse can agree to hire one lawyer who works for both of you to write up the divorce agreement. If you do this, the new lawyer is essentially a second mediator, because she or he is working for both of you, not as an advocate for one of you. You may want to find someone who is experienced in helping couples work through disagreements that come up during the process of preparing and approving the written agreement. It also helps if the lawyer has an established working relationship with your mediator so new issues can be handled smoothly. You can ask your mediator to help you find someone who fits this description.

Alternatively, you can agree that one of you will hire a lawyer to prepare the agreement. That lawyer's job will be to prepare an agreement that protects the spouse who hired him or her and not necessarily to look out for the other spouse. So, if you go this route, it is best that the other spouse get a lawyer too. In essence, each of you then has a consulting lawyer involved: one to write the divorce agreement for one of you and one to review it for the other spouse. It also helps to hire consulting lawyers who are known to work well together in this context. Your mediator can probably help you find lawyers who fit these criteria.

Do It Yourself

You can write the divorce agreement yourself, either on your own or with your spouse. You should not choose this option unless you are willing and able to do whatever legal research is necessary in order to write the agreement properly on your own. (See Chapter 8.)

Asking your consulting lawyer to help you write your own agreement isn't usually cost-efficient. By the time your lawyer tells you what to do and reviews your efforts for legal accuracy, the hourly fees for the lawyer's time could easily exceed the amount you would pay to have the lawyer prepare the agreement for you. In the same vein, writing up your own agreement can save a few hundred dollars now, but you may end up paying far more later to correct problems that could have been avoided.

If you have access to a book such as *How to Do Your Own Divorce in California*, by Charles Sherman (Nolo Occidental), you may be able to write an agreement that is clear and problem-free, but this is not an option in many states. Some commercial divorce websites also offer divorce agreements for a fee, but the quality of these products varies greatly.

Do It Yourself With the Help of a Legal Typing Service

If you are using a legal typing service—a paralegal or other legally savvy person who provides resources and secretarial assistance to customers who are handling their own cases—to do your own divorce, the typing service may have materials and sample divorce agreements that you can use to construct your own. But because you will be living with your divorce agreement for a long, long time, you will want to make sure that the agreement is legally valid and covers all important issues. And the only people who are legally authorized to render an opinion on this point are lawyers licensed to practice in your state.

Contents of the Divorce Agreement

Divorce agreements can have many different formats. Yours will depend on the legal requirements of your state and the preferences of the person writing it up.

Most mediators, lawyers, and legal typing services have their own forms. Self-help divorce books also provide forms. The form will have two kinds of information. First, there will be a certain amount of standard language that goes in every divorce agreement. Lawyers often call such language "boilerplate" (a newspaper term referring to preset or syndicated features). Typical boilerplate in a divorce agreement is likely to include some or all of the following:

- definitions
- warranties (promises)
- disclosures and what happens if a spouse later learns that something important wasn't disclosed
- release of claims, except for the agreed terms
- waiver of inheritance rights or other rights that married people have
- other legal language required by law, and

- noncompliance—what happens if a spouse fails to abide by the agreement.

In addition to the boilerplate, the agreement will contain custom terms that are unique to your case. These terms will include some or all of the following:

- essential facts—such as names, addresses, date of marriage, date of separation, names of children, and children's birthdates
- property division—who gets what
- debt allocation—who is responsible for which bills
- equalizing payments and reimbursements—whether one of you will owe money to the other, and how much
- alimony—will it be paid and, if so, how much, for how long, whether it can be modified, when it will end
- child custody and visitation—sometimes called time-sharing
- parenting agreements and ground rules
- child support and sharing of special expenses for children
- responsibility for children's college expenses
- insurance concerns—life insurance covering support obligations, medical insurance coverage for children or each other
- tax matters—whether alimony will be taxable/deductible, who gets the dependency deduction, who will be responsible for filing a joint return

- payment of mediation costs, lawyers' fees, and court expenses, and
- modification—whether anything in the agreement is subject to being modified in the future; if so, under what circumstances and how (of course, we suggest mediation).

Reviewing the Divorce Agreement

A divorce agreement is an important legal document. It will be submitted to a judge as part of your uncontested divorce. Once you sign it, you will be expected to live up to it. So review it carefully before signing.

If you use the two-step process of having a memorandum prepared and then a divorce agreement, you'll need to review the divorce agreement carefully even if you already reviewed the memorandum, to make sure the final agreement accurately reflects what you intend. If the lawyer who prepares the divorce agreement brings up issues that weren't discussed in the mediation, you'll have to decide whether to go back to your mediator to iron out the details or use the lawyer who is writing the agreement to do that.

This is why many people prefer to use a lawyer-mediator who can bring up as many details as possible during the negotiations and who already has experience working with the couple if new details come up when the divorce agreement is prepared.

But even with a lawyer-mediator, the process of going back and forth dealing with the little issues that come up can be very frustrating. So be prepared and try to maintain a sense of perspective. You really are in the home stretch. If you persevere, you will soon find your efforts rewarded.

Revising and Finalizing the Divorce Agreement

Even the most carefully prepared divorce agreement may contain typographical errors or blanks that need to be filled in. And, occasionally, putting the agreement in writing raises a new question that nobody thought of. If changes are proposed, you and your spouse must agree to them before they are made. Sometimes, this can be done through phone calls or notes among you, your spouse, the mediator, and the lawyer preparing the agreement. Other times, you may need to attend an additional mediation session or four-way meeting to hammer out the last details of the agreement.

Once all agreed-to changes have been made, you may want to have a final meet-ing with the mediator or collaborative lawyers to sign the agreement. Meeting to sign the agreement is often a good way to bring a sense of completion to the process. If you don't find it necessary to meet, the agreement can be circulated by mail, email, or fax, or hand-carried and signed in stages. Regardless of how you decide to do this, be prepared for the moment of signing to be a solemn one that may stir deep feelings in you. It's a good idea to think ahead about how to mark this important passage in your life in a meaningful way.

Once the Divorce Agreement Is Signed

In most states, the original divorce agreement is submitted to the court as part of the uncontested divorce. The judgment or decree of divorce often has the agreement attached to it or refers to it without attaching it.

Keep a copy of the signed divorce agreement before it goes to the court. Ask the person filing the court papers for a file-stamped copy showing the date on which the agreement was signed by the judge and filed with the court.

Chapter 17

Women and Men in Mediation and Collaborative Divorce

When divorce mediation began to gain widespread use in the late 1970s and early 1980s, it was hailed as a humane and empowering alternative to litigation in court. This was also a time when the women's rights movement of the 1970s led feminists to criticize social institutions, including the legal system, as male-dominated power structures in which women had little or no real power or voice. Mediation was seen by many feminist critics as more amenable to women's ways of thinking and expressing themselves, and was believed to hold the potential for better divorce experiences for women.

But no sooner did mediation begin to take hold than some scholars and critics began to question whether it could deliver on its promise, particularly for women. They argued that there is an inherent power imbalance between women and men that creates a serious risk that a woman in mediation will be unduly pressured or coerced into settling for less than she should.

This chapter examines the debate on this issue and its implications for you. We talk about assessing the impact of any gender-based power imbalance and offer some suggestions for minimizing the risk of an unfair process or result in your mediation.

Because both parties in a collaborative process are represented by lawyers, the possibility of power imbalances coming into play is greatly reduced. This chapter is focused almost entirely on mediation for that reason. If you're using a collaborative process, you may still find the chapter of interest, especially the section about gender-related obstacles.

Historical Background

In 1991, the prestigious *Yale Law Journal* published an article entitled "The Mediation Alternative: Process Dangers for Women." In the article, law professor Trina Grillo argued that mandatory court-sponsored mediation might in fact be more disadvantageous to some women than going to court. She identified several interrelated areas of concern:

- Moral and legal principles may be sacrificed to more practical, future-oriented considerations that lead to an agreed settlement regardless of fault or past conduct. In mediation, a woman may give up her ability to seek vindication of legal or moral rights from a higher legal authority.
- Mediation places a value on cooperation. Expressions of anger are often discouraged as not productive. This reinforces the stereotype of the bad angry woman. It can cause a woman to revert to submission and disconnect her from constructive anger that could help her stand up for herself.
- One of the main benefits of mediation is that it allows parties to

control the process and the decisions for settlement. When mediation is compulsory, the principle of self-determination is undermined. If a woman is already dominated by her spouse or partner, being required to attend mediation with an assigned mediator who controls the process, who pushes for agreement, and who may even use what is said and done in mediation as a basis for a recommendation to the court, keeps the woman in a submissive role in the mediation. This concern is amplified where the domination of the woman is accompanied by physical violence and threats.

The article set off a firestorm of debate among professional mediators and others. Professor Grillo, herself a mediator, had intended her critique to apply to mandatory court-sponsored mediation. But many women's advocacy groups began to question the advisability of mediation in general for women. Pointing to some studies showing that women tended to fare worse economically than their male counterparts following divorce (such as *The Divorce Revolution: The Unexpected Social and Economic Consequences for Women and Children in America*, by Lenore Weitzman (Free Press, 1985), and *Women in Poverty Revisited*, by the Canadian National Council on Welfare), they argued that mediation would reflect the uneven playing field of society in general and, therefore,

women would be better off fighting for improvement in the courts. Advocates of mediation, on the other hand, cited studies showing a high level of satisfaction among women participating in mediation as compared to women bearing the enormous emotional and financial costs of litigation.

The debates and discussions about this issue continue, and a growing body of research focuses on this issue and others in mediation. Most of the research so far indicates that at least when it comes to *voluntary* mediation, most women are not at a disadvantage either in the process or the outcome, especially in comparison to the alternative of court. Some critics, however, remain skeptical.

Despite the continuing controversy, the debate has had a positive effect on the development of mediation. Most mediators are now much more sensitive to the concerns raised by Professor Grillo and others. Better techniques have been developed for identifying and addressing any power imbalances between mediating couples. And strategies for dealing with gender-related problems in mediation are a regular feature of mediation trainings.

There have also been changes in court-sponsored mediation programs. Some programs allow victims of domestic violence to opt out or at least meet with the mediator in a safe environment without their spouse present. Mediators and court-sponsored programs are also trained to deal effectively with gender-related problems.

Gender and Mandatory Mediation

In some ways, the term mandatory mediation is an oxymoron. The strength of mediation lies in the fact that it is voluntary; any settlement must be voluntarily agreed to by both parties and not imposed upon them by the third-party mediator. Being required to attend mediation certainly undermines the voluntariness of the process, even if the mediator does not directly control the settlement. And where the mediator has the power to make a recommendation to the court, the parties may be even less in control of the outcome. Any bias on the part of the mediator and any power imbalance between the couple can further tilt the scales toward an unfair agreement.

There are many dedicated and exper-ienced mediators in court-sponsored programs who conduct their mediations in a way that minimizes the risks posed by gender-related issues. The compulsory nature of court-sponsored mediation, however, and its close ties to the adversarial legal system, create some risks for women and many men that cannot be completely eliminated. If you are faced with the prospect of attending court-sponsored mediation, be sure to do

it in a way that protects your rights. (See Chapter 14.)

Gender and Voluntary Mediation

If mediation is voluntary, you can decide *not* to mediate if the gender-related obstacles appear too great. Of course, a risk remains that, as a result of a power imbalance in the relationship, you may feel coerced into agreeing to mediate, so the mediation itself is not truly voluntary. Or you may voluntarily begin the process only to feel coerced into a particular settlement.

Mediators are trained to look for signals of a power imbalance between the spouses. The signals are sometimes so subtle, however, that they are easy to miss. And there is a chance that a particular mediator may exhibit some form of gender bias himself or herself. If you are in a situation where a gender-related problem could undermine a truly voluntary mediation and settlement, it will help if you can pinpoint the problem and ask your mediator for assistance in addressing it.

Common Gender-Related Obstacles

Most research and theory regarding gender-related problems in mediation focus on male-dominated relationships. This is especially true if domestic violence has been a part of the relationship, where men are statistically more likely to be perpetrators of violent acts than women. Reverse situations do arise, however, and the suggestions we make in the following sections can apply equally to male- or female-dominated couples. And, in some situations, the power balance may shift depending on the issue being discussed. For example, some studies have shown that men are more likely to feel intimidated when their wives have superior knowledge of parenting matters; in the same couple, the wife may feel at a disadvantage when it comes to finances. So regardless of whether you are a man or a woman, or are feeling one-up or one-down, you may find the suggestions in this chapter useful for your situation.

Communication Problems

Over the past 20 years, research into the patterns of male-female communications has led to the development of various theories about gender-related communication patterns. Sometimes, the patterns emerge in mediation. Fortunately, the very fact that a third party—the mediator—is present and participating in the communication can keep you from getting bogged down in these patterns. Additionally, most mediators are trained to recognize and deal with gender-based communication patterns so you don't get stuck in them.

One theory, advanced in 1982 by Carol Gilligan in a book titled *In a Different Voice: Psychological Theory and Women's Development* (Harvard Univ. Press, 1993), suggests that men often view disagreements in terms of rights and entitlements, while women are more likely to be concerned about finding solutions based on interests and relationships.

Take Tom and Alexa. They are negotiating an agreement about their family home. Tom sees the house primarily as an investment in which he is a half-owner. Alexa's focus is on her emotional connection to the house and the neighborhood, as well as the house's historical role and future potential as a home base for her and the children.

Without the mediator's intervention, Tom and Alexa may continue to insist upon their own points of view, without ever finding a mutually acceptable solution. By using the techniques of interest-based negotiating (see Chapter 13), the mediator can help Tom and Alexa find a way to settle their case that addresses Tom's interest in his financial investment in the house and Alexa's interest in a comfortable home base for her and the children.

A second theory, popularized by Deborah Tannen in her book *You Just*

Don't Understand: Women and Men in Conversation (Quill, 2001), posits that men use language, or silence, to assert power or position themselves, while women's conversation is directed toward forming or maintaining relationships.

Now let's visit Lucy and José. Lucy tends to express her every passing thought and feeling; for her it is a way to connect with other people. José is often confused by Lucy's apparent lack of focus and he frequently feels intruded upon when she insists that he respond in kind. José often resorts to silence as a way to hold his own in discussions with Lucy; when a decision has to be made, José will announce his position and is reluctant to engage in discussion. Without the mediator's help, Lucy and José could quickly reach an impasse on almost any subject. The mediator avoids this by taking turns talking to each of them about how they see the facts and the issues.

A third theory is based on research indicating that men talk more than women, interrupt more, control topics, and withhold feedback. This behavior is seen as arising from and reinforcing traditional sex roles of male dominance.

Consider Mel and Rose. At the first mediation session, Mel is quick to answer the mediator's questions, and he follows up with questions of his own. When the mediator asks Rose a question, Mel

either answers for her or interrupts her after a few short sentences. Noticing this, the mediator takes steps to make sure Rose has time to express her point of view and get answers to any questions she has, even if Mel continues to take more air time. The mediator may remind Rose and Mel that both of them need to participate fully in the mediation in order for it to be successful, and may suggest to them that they proceed by taking turns speaking without interruption.

If you see yourself and your spouse falling into a communication pattern like one of the ones described, first ask whether it seems to be interfering with communication during your mediation. Are you getting your points across? Are you able to get answers to your questions? Does your spouse seem fully engaged in the discussion? If your answer to any of these questions is "no," then point out the problem to your mediator. You can say something like, "It doesn't seem like we're communicating," or "I don't feel like I'm getting a chance to talk." Anything along these lines will get the ball rolling so that the mediator can help you find a more productive way to communicate.

Negotiation Problems

The gender differences noted by Gilligan, Tannen, and others are sometimes seen as playing a role in male-female negotiations.

Take the case of Mina and Ed. They are trying to agree on how much child support Ed will pay. Mina looks at her budget and figures she can get by if Ed pays her $500 per month. Even though she knows she might be able to ask for more, she thinks this is fair. So she says to Ed, "Why don't you just pay me $500 a month?" Ed views the negotiation completely differently. He is expecting to engage in competitive bargaining. Even though he was originally prepared to agree to child support of $500 per month, he will now expect Mina to compromise to a lower figure.

By emphasizing interest-based negotiation, mediation minimizes the chances of this kind of miscue. If, however, it seems to be happening, or if you think it might, a simple thing you can do is to talk about the negotiation method to be used. If you are like Mina and you want to present a reasonable proposal without the usual dance of back-and-forth bargaining, say so. You may be surprised to find that your spouse will welcome such an approach.

Power Imbalance

Mediation can work only if both spouses can speak up for themselves and negotiate for what they want and need with a realistic and well-informed understanding of their alternatives. If one spouse feels so dominated or controlled by the other that he or she is unable to speak and act autonomously in the mediation, you have what mediators call a "power imbalance."

Women's advocates have pointed to the general power imbalance between men and women in society and suggested that the same power imbalance would lead to unfair agreements in mediation.

Fortunately, this has not turned out to be the major problem it was once feared. First, like all generalizations, there are many exceptions. Second, research seems to show that for couples who stay in mediation, the process of mediation itself often operates to correct any power imbalance. This is because the mediator always looks for signs that both parties are able to speak for themselves and are capable of understanding the information being discussed as well as the consequences of potential agreements. When in doubt, a mediator will use one of several techniques, such as caucusing, taking turns speaking, or suggesting independent review to double check whether both spouses are actively participating in the process. Or the mediator may suggest a mediation support person for the spouse who is feeling less powerful. (See Chapter 8.)

If you believe that there is a power imbalance between you and your spouse, let your mediator know what you think is happening. Talk with the mediator about what steps can be taken to address the power imbalance and to level the playing field between you and your spouse.

From the Frying Pan Into the Fire

Sometimes, the legal system seems biased against one gender. For example, men often feel at a disadvantage in requesting custody or visitation rights and in paying child support, and women often perceive the legal system as favoring husbands when it comes to financial settlements. People often enter mediation in the hope that it will allow them to negotiate a more favorable agreement than what they could get through the courts. When they find that their spouse will not agree to give them more than a court would order without asking for something in exchange, they often feel forced into accepting less than what seems fair and just.

If this happens to you, remember that you do have choices, even if they aren't great. If you choose to accept a settlement proposed in mediation, do so only after considering the potential costs and benefits of settling your case some other way, such as hiring a lawyer to negotiate for you or taking your case to court. You may conclude that you would do better with the added bargaining power (and expense) of having a lawyer represent you. Or you may feel that it is important to take a principled stand in court and perhaps make changes in the law through your case. Or you may simply decide that, for your own sense of self-respect, you would rather have a judge make an order than voluntarily agree to something you consider unjust. The point is, you have a choice. It may not be a perfect choice, but it is one you have the right and the power to make.

Domestic Violence

If your relationship has included acts or threats of physical violence or sexual coercion, this can indicate a continuing power imbalance between you and your spouse. Depending on how recent, frequent, or extreme the incidents have been, and depending on how vulnerable you feel to the possibility of new incidents, you'll need to decide whether it's a good idea to mediate.

Most experts agree that you should not even attempt to mediate if you are currently in a violent relationship and have not obtained professional help to prevent future violence, with appropriate court sanctions such as restraining orders, if necessary. If the violence is in the past, and if you have taken steps to prevent or address the underlying causes with professional assistance, however, then mediation may be possible. But experts do not agree on where to draw the line, and some believe that mediation is never appropriate if there's been a history of domestic violence.

To make the best choice for yourself, take an honest look at your situation. It is best to do this with the help of a counselor or legal adviser. Whether you are the perpetrator or the victim of violent acts or threats, the support of a professional adviser is critical.

If your mediator will meet with you in a separate session, ask the mediator to help you assess whether mediation is appropriate for you in your circumstances. You may find it hard to disclose your circumstances to the mediator, knowing that the mediator will be communicating with your spouse, even if the mediator agrees not to divulge what is said. If you are concerned about any possible repercussions of sharing this information with the mediator, start instead with your own adviser.

If you decide to try mediation, it must be structured to ensure safety and a balance of power, or you may be better off not mediating at all. Here are some possible safeguards to consider requesting:

- Ask to have the mediation conducted in separate sessions or caucuses. As discussed in Chapter 2, there are pros and cons to this, but it does have the advantage of ensuring physical safety and limiting destructive interactions.
- Have a mediation support person attend all sessions, joint or separate, with you. This person can help you clearly state what is important to

you and keep you from backsliding into submission or aggression. For more on working with a mediation support person, see Chapter 8.

- If you attend joint sessions, arrange to arrive and leave separately, with the perpetrator arriving first and leaving last, to avoid encounters without the mediator present.
- Ask for specific ground rules limiting inappropriate conduct during mediation—such as no interruptions, taking turns, and no threats.
- Agree to have no contact with your ex between sessions.
- Insist on an independent review of any proposed agreement.

These are just a few suggestions. Your mediator may have other thoughts about how to make the mediation safe and productive. Anything that will let each of you express what you want and need and negotiate without fear of recrimination is worth considering.

Finally, if a court case has already been filed and restraining orders prohibit contact between you and your spouse, you may need to obtain a modification of the order if you decide to mediate in joint sessions. If you use separate sessions, this may not be a problem, but be sure to check.

Mediator Bias

As mentioned, most mediators are trained to be sensitive to gender-bias issues, not only between the divorcing couple, but relative to themselves. You may, however, encounter a situation in which you feel that your mediator is exhibiting gender bias. If so, the best thing is to let your mediator know what you are experiencing.

Often, an honest discussion can clear the air and allow the three of you to continue with the mediation. If talking about it doesn't help, or if you don't feel comfortable bringing it up to the mediator, consider asking an adviser—such as a financial or legal adviser or a mediation support person—to talk to the mediator about the problem. Finally, you can always start over with a new mediator. Depending on how far along in the process you are, changing mediators may be your best option.

Final Thoughts

This issue of gender and how it affects mediation is a complex one. No doubt, debate and research about this subject will continue. In the meantime, it may help to remember that at its best, mediation is a voluntary process in which progress can be made only if both spouses and the mediator feel comfortable enough to work together toward mutually acceptable solutions. So pay attention to the interactions between you and your spouse, ask for help when you need it, and cooperate with your mediator's efforts to balance the power between you. If you do, the odds are good that your mediation will be a success.

Chapter 18

Unmarried Couples in Mediation and Collaboration

The terms "married" and "unmarried" have taken on new meanings since the publication of *Using Divorce Mediation*, the first incarnation of this book. Then, same-sex couples could not marry in any U.S. state. Now, Massachusetts permits same-sex marriage and, naturally, same-sex divorce as well. In addition, four other states now have domestic partnership or civil union laws that require same-sex couples to dissolve their legal relationships in court. The chart below lists U.S. states that have legal relationships for same-sex couples, and notes whether court proceedings are required in order to dissolve those relationships.

Unmarried heterosexual or same-sex couples. If you aren't married and haven't registered as domestic partners or entered into a civil union, you won't need a court document like a divorce judgment in order to end your relationship. If the two of you agree on who owns what and how everything you have together gets divided up, and if you don't have any children together, you probably will have no contact at all with a court. This is also true for same-sex couples registered as domestic partners or reciprocal beneficiaries in Hawaii or Maine.

Consider mediation or collaborative law if you have disputes. Even if you don't have a legal relationship, you may still have legal entanglements, such as children or a house that you own together.

If you don't agree about how to deal with child custody or visitation, or about how to divide your property, you can still go to civil court—as opposed to family court—to ask a judge to resolve your disputes. And you still have the opportunity to try mediation or collaborative law before you go the litigation route. In fact, mediation is a great way to keep this type of dispute out of court.

Registered domestic partners and partners in civil unions. Except in Hawaii or Maine, if you are a same-sex couple that has registered or entered into a civil union, you'll be required to use the courts to dissolve your relationship. You can use mediation or collaborative law to help you resolve any disputes you have. Some of the legal issues will be different, however, because the federal government doesn't recognize same-sex relationships of any kind and this may affect your financial and tax situation. Make sure that you find an attorney, mediator, or collaborative lawyer who is up to date on these issues.

Same-sex couples who are married. If you have a Massachusetts marriage license or have married in Canada, you will be required to use the courts to dissolve your relationship. And like partners in domestic partnerships or civil unions, you'll need to make sure that any professional you hire is well familiar with the legal complexities of same-sex relationships of all kinds.

State	Relationship Designation	Court Required to Dissolve?	More information
California	Domestic partnership	Yes	www.ss.ca.gov
Connecticut	Civil union	Yes	www.cga.ct.gov (text of law)
Hawaii	Reciprocal beneficiaries	No	www.state.hi.us/doh/records/rbrfaq.htm
Maine	Domestic partnership	No	www.state.me.us
New Jersey	Domestic partnership	Yes	www.state.nj.us/health
Vermont	Civil union	Yes	www.sec.state.vt.us

For more about same-sex relationships, check out the *Legal Guide for Lesbian & Gay Couples,* by Denis Clifford, Hayden Curry, and Frederick Hertz (Nolo).

For those same-sex couples who are married, registered as domestic partners, or in a civil union relationship, the legal aspects of a heterosexual marriage will be present in the mediation. For unmarried heterosexual and same-sex couples, the mediation experience will be somewhat different because of their different relationship with the law and the courts.

The legal rules used in an unmarried couple's case will be different from the ones used in divorce cases. The laws regarding property rights and legal responsibilities for debts are different from the laws applied to married people. Your nonmarital relationship is governed by general civil contract laws, and any court case involving property and debt issues will be handled just as if you were business partners ending your association. However, laws covering child support, custody, and other parenting issues will usually be similar to the laws for married couples.

Mediation or collaborative law are still ideal options for unmarried partners who hope to reach an agreement without going to court but who want some help understanding their options.

This chapter explores some of the unique characteristics of nonmarital breakups and what makes them easier in some ways and harder in others to negotiate than legal divorces. We also offer tips on ways to make your mediation or collaborative process successful.

Untying the Nonmarital Knot: Opportunities and Pitfalls

As long as laws and social attitudes treat marital and nonmarital relationships differently, unmarried couples will need to weigh their options somewhat differently from married folks when ending their relationships.

The Law and Your Relationship: Friend or Foe

When married people divorce, state laws give both spouses a specified share—either equitable or equal, depending on the state—of the property accumulated during the marriage. These laws also provide for payment of alimony to a spouse under certain circumstances. Knowing that legal divorce has some predictable legal outcomes and is not a winner-take-all proposition helps many married couples evaluate their settlement options in a mediation or collaborative process. In other words, they can negotiate within a reasonable range of their BATNA-WATNA (best and worst alternatives to a negotiated agreement). (See Chapter 13 for more on BATNA and WATNA.)

Negotiating within a range of BATNA-WATNA is hard for unmarried couples because of the uncertainty of the laws that apply to them. Historically, the American legal system has reflected its puritan roots by frowning on nonmarital

relationships altogether. A relationship between two adults cohabiting together without being married (what some people now call a domestic partnership) was considered morally reprehensible, even illegal, if sex was in any way involved. If the relationship ended, a partner wanting to collect a share of the property or make good on a promise of support might be barred from pursuing a legal claim against the other.

More recently, courts in many states have come to terms with the reality of modern lives by allowing unmarried couples to sue for division of their jointly acquired property or for support or other compensation when the relationship ends. But the old attitudes toward nonmarital relationships are often still evident in laws that require more stringent proof of an agreement to share property or pay support. Most unmarried couples don't sign written agreements, so proving an oral agreement or, even worse, an implied agreement based on behavior will come down to one partner's word against the other. This makes the legal result more unpredictable and potentially more one-sided.

When it comes to same-sex relationships, many judges can be downright hostile, limiting partners' rights to share property or make financial claims. This often means that one partner has a huge advantage over the other, even if both partners know this isn't fair. For example, if the property accumulated during the relationship is all in one person's name, the deck may be stacked in favor of the partner whose name is on the property.

To see what we mean, consider these examples.

Howard and Sarah have lived together for 15 years. During this time, Howard has developed a reputation as a portrait artist. He owns his own gallery, and his work is in much demand. Sarah has helped in all the business aspects of Howard's career: running the gallery, marketing the portraits, and keeping the books. They have always talked about the gallery as "ours," but they never wrote up a formal agreement. Now that they are separated, Howard wants Sarah out of the gallery business. Sarah's name isn't on the lease or any other official papers for the gallery.

When Javier and Bob started living together in Nevada eight years ago, they moved into a house that Javier had just bought. Bob used his carpentry skills to convert the basement into a bedroom and bath, and he used some of his savings to pay for the materials for the conversion. He also paid half of the monthly house payments. Javier agreed many times to put Bob's name on the deed but somehow never got around to it. Now that Bob wants to end the relationship, Javier sees no reason to give him any share of the equity in the house, which has doubled since he bought it.

If these couples were married, Sarah and Bob might have legal claims to a share of the property built up during the relationships—in Sarah's case, the portrait business and gallery, and in Bob's case, the home equity. As it is, both Bob and Sarah will have to convince a judge that they and their respective partners had an agreement to share the property. Without any written proof, the legal outcome is uncertain because it depends on whose testimony the judge believes. Because Bob is in a same-sex relationship, he may encounter a disapproving judge who throws the case out of court without even giving Bob the chance to prove an agreement.

Differences between marital and nonmarital legalities are less extreme in questions of child support and child custody, if both partners are the legal parents. Law reforms over the last generation have done away with the legal concept of illegitimacy: A child born out of wedlock has the same legal status as a child born to a married couple. Custody and time-sharing decisions now tend to be measured by the same legal standards in cases between unmarried and married parents. Child support laws are also applied without regard to the parents' marital status.

But if one partner is not the biological or adoptive parent of the child, he or she may have no legal right to spend time with the child after the separation and no legal responsibility to support the child, even in states where married stepparents would have a legally recognized status.

While Judy and Lanita were together, Judy used a sperm bank (with an anonymous donor) to become pregnant with Matty. Judy and Lanita lived in a state where no domestic partnership is available, and did not use an adoption to make Lanita a legal parent. During the five years Judy and Lanita stayed together, they raised Matty together. As the biological mother, Judy is legally Matty's parent, but Lanita has no legal relationship with Matty. Now that Judy and Lanita have separated, Judy is refusing to let Lanita see Matty. In all likelihood, Lanita will not be able to convince a court to give her court-ordered visitation or custody rights.

Mediation and collaborative law offer a way to make separation decisions in an environment that is supportive of the situation faced by you and your partner. But because laws can be unpredictable or one-sided, you will have a hard time evaluating settlement options using the BATNA-WATNA approach. This presents both an opportunity and a challenge. Not having a good or predictable legal outcome to fall back on frees you and your partner to emphasize nonlegal considerations when coming up with a fair settlement. On the other hand, you may not be inclined to propose or accept a fair and equitable settlement if the legal odds seem to favor one of you over the other.

The Alternative: The High Cost of Going to Court

Whenever you evaluate settlement options under the BATNA-WATNA approach, you have to consider the likely cost of going to court.

Any contested court case will be expensive. Yours would be no exception. In fact, the cost of litigating a nonmarital separation is likely to be higher than the cost of taking a divorce to court, even if exactly the same issues are involved. This is because of the different legal processes involved. Married partners don't have to prove an agreement or other legal basis for their financial claims against each other. They can simply rely on the laws of their state regarding property sharing and other financial issues. In contrast, unmarried partners must prove the legal basis for their claims; this usually means their lawyers will spend more time building the case before trial and presenting the evidence at a trial. More time spent by lawyers translates to higher legal fees.

You must also consider other, less tangible, costs of going to court. Like married couples, you and your partner may ruin any chance of ever having a friendly or even respectful relationship if you go through a contested court case. And the risks to your children's emotional well-being are great regardless of your marital status. But unlike married partners, you may already be living a life that lacks societal approval or support. Exposing yourself to more public scrutiny by taking the case to court can intensify any sense of social isolation you already experience.

These factors, as well as the legal differences discussed earlier, present both opportunities and challenges in your mediation. The high cost of going to court can motivate you and your partner to use greater persistence in trying to put together a reasonable settlement. At the same time, you may feel pressured into accepting less than you think you deserve.

Getting Help: Look in the Right Places

If you and your partner want to negotiate a settlement but cannot do it on your own, finding a mediator or collaborative lawyer and advisers with knowledge and experience in handling nonmarital breakups is going to be crucial to a successful experience. This isn't always easy.

Most separating couples are married, and most mediators, collaborative attorneys, legal advisers, and other professionals who help separating couples are used to dealing with cases involving married folks. Getting help from someone who is only familiar with the

legal and nonlegal considerations that apply to marital relationships can have unfortunate consequences for you. The adviser or mediator who lacks experience with your kind of case can't help you develop a realistic idea of your settlement alternatives and may be less sensitive to the unique aspects of your case. This can make it harder to negotiate a mutually acceptable agreement.

 Research your options. Even if you find a good adviser to help you, and especially if you don't, it's a good idea to read up a little on your situation before you begin mediating. The more prepared you are, the more smoothly things will go. One of the best guides around for heterosexual unmarried couples is *Living Together*, by Ralph Warner, Toni Ihara, and Frederick Hertz (Nolo). Two good books for same-sex couples are *A Legal Guide for Lesbian & Gay Couples*, by Hayden Curry, Denis Clifford, and Frederick Hertz (Nolo), and *Legal Affairs: Essential Advice for Same-Sex Couples*, by Frederick Hertz (Owl Books).

All three books cover issues for couples both in ongoing relationships and who are separating. The latest editions of the two Nolo books have been expanded to include extensive information for couples "going separate ways."

Successful Mediation or Collaborative Separation

In addition to the general suggestions we've covered in this book, there are a few specific things nonmarital partners can do to improve their chances of a successful mediation or collaborative process.

Get Good Advice

One of the most important ways to work toward a successful resolution is to find one or more qualified advisers who can help you realistically evaluate your options—legal, financial, and emotional. Look for someone with expertise and experience in dealing with nonmarital breakups. This is in addition to finding someone who supports the mediation process and meets the other criteria discussed in Chapter 8,

Remember Howard and Sarah? After they separate, Sarah finds a mediation-friendly lawyer who helps her to assess her legal options realistically, and who encourages her to try reaching an agreement in mediation. Meanwhile, Howard's accountant is able to help Howard see how a lawsuit could hurt Howard's reputation and business, even if Howard wins. Getting competent and realistic advice helps Sarah and Howard mediate a satisfactory agreement and avoid a nasty and expensive court case.

Defuse the Emotional Issues Before Mediating

Separation and divorce are emotionally wrenching experiences for married and unmarried couples alike. The uncertainties and lack of social support surrounding a nonmarital breakup, however, can intensify the emotional volatility of your mediation. Minimize the risk that strong emotions will sidetrack your mediation or collaborative process by working with a counselor (either with your partner or separately) to learn how to handle your feelings about the relationship and your separation before you begin the process. (See Chapter 1 for discussion of the emotional divorce, and Chapter 8 for advice on how to find a counselor.)

Remember Javier and Bob? Since Bob left, Javier has been furious and devastated. No way is he going to let Bob add insult to injury by taking a share of his home. For his part, Bob can't understand why Javier is being so vindictive. After all, the relationship had been dying, if not dead, for a long time. Fortunately, Javier and Bob both have the good sense to spend some time in counseling, where each of them gets a more balanced perspective on their breakup. With their counselors' support and encouragement, they each hire collaborative lawyers with experience in unmarried breakups. Ultimately the lawyers work with them to come up with an agreement for Bob to be bought out on terms affordable to Javier.

Gender-Related Obstacles and Same-Sex Couples

Partners in same-sex couples sometimes find themselves enmeshed in stereotypical gender-related patterns of communication or negotiation. Recognizing these patterns can help you communicate or negotiate more effectively. If this is the case in your relationship, take a look at "Common Gender-Related Obstacles" in Chapter 17, where we discuss common gender-related obstacles and how mediation can help address them.

Pick a Qualified Mediator or Collaborative Lawyer

Just as it is important to find advisers who have experience with nonmarital breakups, you'll need to find a mediator or collaborative lawyer who understands the unique challenges of your situation. On the other hand, don't ignore all the other important criteria discussed in Chapter 8. Experience with cases like yours is essential, but it is not the only consideration in picking a good mediator or collaborative lawyer. Before you make your final decision, review Chapters 6 and 7. Then adapt Worksheet 1— Questions for Potential Mediators to your circumstances.

Remember Judy and Lanita? After looking around, Judy and Lanita find a mediator with a strong background in child and family issues who also has experience working with lesbian couples. With the mediator's help, they begin focusing on Matty's needs in the situation instead of their own and eventually develop a plan for Matty to spend regular time with Lanita.

Hone Your Communication Skills

If you've already read the rest of this book, we may be starting to sound like a broken record. Nevertheless, this bears repeating: Good communication is essential to a successful mediation or collaborative process.

Review the communication tips in Chapter 12. Work with a counselor to refine your communication skills, and practice good communication whenever you get the chance. This will pay off during your mediation.

Get a Commitment to the Process

Because going to court is a decidedly undesirable option, you have a great incentive to make and get at the outset a firm commitment to mediate your solution or enter into an agreement to collaborate.

Once the introductions and preliminaries are done, let your mediator know that you would like a commitment to the mediation process and to working out an agreement rather than going to court. Of course, there's a chance that your partner won't make such a commitment. In that case, go ahead and give the mediation a try, knowing that you won't be completely surprised or disappointed if your partner bails out at some point. If you and your partner do negotiate a specific commitment to the mediation, that could help you get through rough spots down the road.

In most collaborative cases, everyone involved will sign a commitment to the process at the outset. It's pretty much expected, so if that's something you want for sure, it's a point in favor of collaborative process over mediation.

Plan a Realistic Negotiation Strategy

The key word here is "realistic." Use whatever suggestions your mediator or collaborative attorney gives you, or follow the approach we outline in Chapter 13. In particular, when evaluating your settlement options, be as practical and realistic as possible. This may be hard to do. The likely legal outcome and high cost of going to court can make it hard to develop your settlement spectrum of most-to-least-desirable options. Nevertheless, it is important to be as clearheaded about this as possible so you will have a firm base to operate from when you negotiate.

Consider confidentiality issues.
Before you mediate the breakup of a nonmarital relationship, consider whether any information disclosed during the mediation needs to be protected by confidentiality laws or a confidentiality agreement. For example, if you will need to provide sensitive financial statements from your business in order to negotiate a settlement, you may want to ask your partner to sign an agreement that the information won't go outside the mediation room or the offices of the attorneys you're working with. If you're at all concerned about confidentiality, consult a legal adviser about whether it's necessary and how to ensure it.

A Word of Encouragement

We have tended to emphasize the difficulties presented by your situation in order to help you understand how to address them. We would like to end on a more positive note, however. Most unmarried couples settle their cases without going to court. You probably will do the same. Use our suggestions as you approach the mediation to help you increase your chances of success. Good luck!

Chapter 19

Mediation and Collaboration After Divorce

In most legal cases, once the settlement is reached, the case is finished once and for all. In divorce cases, some issues are settled for good but others can be revisited when circumstances change—most notably parenting (custody) issues, child support, and alimony.

Whether or not you used mediation to settle your divorce, mediation is often the most productive and cost-effective way to negotiate changes to the divorce agreement.

Mediation can also help you negotiate a property and financial agreement with a fiancé or new partner after your divorce, if you decide to have a written agreement. Mediation allows you and the new person in your life to agree on ground rules about money and property without becoming entangled in adversarial posturing between lawyers.

In this chapter, we discuss how to use mediation or collaboration effectively to negotiate changes in your divorce agreement. We also touch briefly on using mediation to negotiate a viable agreement with a new partner or fiancé.

You can use mediation or collaboration to deal with postdivorce issues whether or not you used it to settle your divorce. However, if you went through a contested case instead of mediation or a collaborative process, you will probably need to find new lawyers to help you set up either a mediation or a collaborative process.

If you did use mediation or a collaborative process for your divorce, you'll turn first to your mediator or collaborative lawyer if you find that changes in your agreement are necessary. You may be able to resolve the issue through a brief mediation session or a consultation, perhaps followed by a single four-way meeting.

Dealing With Changes in the Divorce Agreement

Usually, mediation is worth a try when you want to negotiate changes to the divorce agreement. And, if the changes have to do with child custody or other parenting issues, your state or local court may require you to mediate these issues if you can't reach agreement on them on your own or with the help of a private mediator. (For more on court-sponsored mediation, see Chapter 14.) If you are not comfortable mediating but want to try a collaborative approach, then consider consulting a collaborative lawyer to get things started.

Should You Mediate or Collaborate?

There may be some circumstances for which mediation or collaboration simply isn't a viable option. If you've lost contact with your ex-spouse, or if the animosity between you means there is no hope of working together to negotiate the changes, you may not be able to mediate or collaborate. Other circumstances that can undermine the chances of success include a history of domestic violence in your relationship with your former spouse, alcohol or drug abuse, an extreme power imbalance, or mental illness. There also may be some situations in which it is better to choose one process instead of the other.

We've covered most of these considerations in Chapter 4. If you are in doubt about whether to mediate or collaborate in negotiating changes to your divorce, review that chapter.

Agreeing to Mediate or Collaborate

If you and your former spouse successfully mediated your divorce, you shouldn't have too much trouble convincing him or her to mediate issues that arise later. In fact, you may have already agreed, either informally or as part of the written divorce agreement, to return to mediation to negotiate any changes. Similarly, if you used a collaborative process, you may have already laid the groundwork for a return to the collaborative table.

If you did not mediate or collaborate in your divorce, you'll need to consider how best to propose mediation or collaboration to your ex-spouse. Unless the divorce was so bitter and expensive that your ex no longer even speaks to you, she or he may be quite receptive to

the idea, especially if you emphasize how much the process will save you both in legal fees and emotional rancor. For tips on how to approach your ex-spouse with a suggestion to mediate or collaborate, see Chapter 5.

If You Decide to Mediate

Selecting the Mediator

If you and your former spouse have already been through mediation, you may want to return to the same mediator. He or she will already be familiar with your case and with your communication patterns, so you will be able to pick up where you left off with a minimum of preliminaries.

If you need to change mediators or you haven't mediated before with your former spouse, then you need to select a mediator. Because you are probably thinking about modifying only certain aspects of the divorce, such as parenting issues, look for a mediator with specialized expertise in that area. In this example, you can concentrate on selecting a mediator with expertise concerning children and parenting. Conversely, if the change relates solely to financial matters, such as alimony, you can focus your search on mediators with financial expertise.

Before selecting a mediator, you may find it helpful to review Chapter 6. If you consider voluntarily using a court-sponsored mediation program, be sure to look at Chapter 14.

Preparing for Mediation

Careful preparation will improve your chances of a successful mediation. If you've already been through mediation, this section will mostly be a review. If you have not been through mediation, you may find it helpful to read parts of Chapters 9 through 12.

In general, there are three things to do to get ready for the mediation:

- Ask your mediator what you should do in advance or bring with you to the mediation session.
- Consider whether to get any advice about your rights and options before the mediation. This could include legal advice, financial or tax advice, or parenting advice. (See Chapter 8.)
- Plan your negotiation strategy. (See Chapter 12.)

At the Mediation

The mediation itself may take only one or two sessions, because it will be focused on a limited number of changes rather on an entire divorce. Still, the structure of the mediation will probably follow the same five stages outlined in Chapter 2, only in much more abbreviated form. If you've prepared well for the mediation and you focus on clear communications and a collaborative negotiating approach, you'll probably have little trouble reaching an agreement. If you hit a snag, or if you can't come to an agreement, you may find it helpful to take a look at Chapter 15.

At the end of the mediation session, make some notes of what transpired. If you are coming back for another session, list any steps to be taken by you, your former partner, or the mediator before the next session. You can use Worksheet 10—Mediation Progress Notes, found in the appendix.

After the Mediation

If you reach an agreement in mediation, you'll want it written up and signed by you and your ex to avoid any misunderstandings. You may also need to have the agreement filed with the court. For information on preparing a written agreement, including who prepares it and how to meet any legal requirements such as filing, take a look at Chapter 16.

If you don't reach an agreement in mediation, you'll need to consider your options. If making a change in the divorce agreement is important to you, consider other options, such as using a lawyer or other representative to negotiate for you, hiring a private judge or arbitrator, or taking the issue to court. (See Chapter 15.)

If You Decide to Collaborate

The most important thing you'll need to do is find a good collaborative attorney. If you need suggestions for how to go about locating and selecting a collaborative attorney, read Chapter 7. Once you have found an attorney with whom you are comfortable, your attorney will undoubtedly help you prepare for the process. You can use parts of this book to supplement your attorney's guidance. For example, in Chapter 3 you'll find a description of what happens in a collaborative divorce. Even though you will be negotiating a finite issue rather than a whole divorce settlement, you can fill in your lawyer's description of what might happen in your situation by skimming that chapter.

Mediating New Relationship Issues

Your divorce experience may have convinced you of the wisdom of having a clear written agreement *before* making a commitment to a new relationship. If so, you will need to figure out how to go about negotiating the agreement with your new partner in a constructive way that avoids putting undue pressure on your new relationship.

Just deciding to have a written agreement with your new partner can be a big step. It can seem pretty antiromantic, and you may even worry that it will do in your relationship. If you don't own much going into the relationship, and you like what the laws of your state have to offer in the way of protections if you separate or when one of you dies, maybe you don't need a written agreement. On the other hand, having a written agreement can cut down on misunderstandings during the relationship. And it can prevent major hassles with heirs when one of you dies or with each other if you separate.

There are some excellent resources for couples who want to draft an agreement themselves, but if you need more help, mediating the agreement can be an ideal way to proceed.

 Suggested reading. Below we list a number of books to help you negotiate your own agreement with your new partner. Even if you plan to use a mediator or other adviser, you would do well to familiarize yourself with the subject in order to make good use of the time spent with your mediator or adviser.

Love, Marriage and Money, by Gail Liberman and Alan Lavine (Dearborn Financial Publishing)

Living Together, by Ralph Warner, Toni Ihara, and Frederick Hertz (Nolo)

A Legal Guide for Lesbian & Gay Couples, by Hayden Curry, Denis Clifford, and Frederick Hertz (Nolo)

Legal Affairs: Essential Advice for Same-Sex Couples, by Frederick Hertz (Owl Books)

Unmarried to Each Other: The Essential Guide to Living Together as an Unmarried Couple, by Darian Solor and Marshall Miller (Marlowe Company).

Premarital, Postmarital, and Living Together Agreements

If you are contemplating remarriage, the contract you negotiate might be called a "premarital agreement," "prenuptial agreement," or "antenuptial agreement." We refer to it as a premarital agreement. If you're going into a domestic partnership or civil union, you may also want to prepare a prepartnership or preunion agreement.

Sometimes couples enter into the contract after the wedding. In that case, the contract might be called a "marital" or "postmarital agreement." We'll use postmarital agreement here.

If you intend to live together rather than marry, the contract would be known as a "cohabitation" or "living together agreement." We'll refer to it as a living together agreement.

Why Mediate or Collaborate Premarital, Postmarital, and Living Together Agreements?

There are two reasons why you might want the help of a mediator or collaborative lawyers in coming up with a premarital, postmarital, or living together agreement: First, if

negotiating the agreement on your own isn't working very well, a mediator or two good collaborative lawyers can help the discussions go more smoothly. Second, if you want help writing up your agreement, involving a neutral mediator or collaborative lawyers who have both participated in the discussions can help ensure that the written agreement will reflect your intentions.

Mediation and collaboration offer a distinct advantage over the more traditional approach of using independent lawyers to prepare and draft the agreement. In the traditional scenario, one partner-to-be asks his or her lawyer to prepare the agreement. This is often done even before the partners have had any meaningful discussions about what will go into the agreement. The draft agreement is likely to be slanted in favor of the partner whose lawyer prepared it, even if that wasn't the partner's intention. The other partner may be surprised and hurt when presented with the document. This can set in motion a series of unnecessarily adversarial negotiations that ultimately produce an agreement that nobody feels very good about. Worse yet, the first draft gets signed with no changes, but with a lingering resentment that can threaten the relationship for months and years to come. Or, even worse yet, the relationship that had so much promise ends before it's begun, with hard feelings all around. Of course, not all premarital or living together agreements negotiated by lawyers have such disastrous results, but the adversarial nature of the traditional approach increases the risk.

In contrast, mediation and collaboration offer a way to discuss your common values and your differences to come up with mutually satisfactory decisions in a setting that supports your love and respect for one another. If you mediate, the mediator is working for both of you and is not an advocate for one side or the other. As points of agreement are reached, the mediator can keep track of them. Ultimately, the mediator will prepare a draft agreement or a written summary to serve as the basis for the written agreement. If you collaborate, the attorneys are committed from the very beginning to finding solutions that work for both of you, and to writing up an agreement that is not one-sided, no matter who does the initial drafting.

Using mediation does not mean you should forgo independent legal advice. Getting separate legal advice and review of the written agreement is often advisable. In fact, it is sometimes legally required, especially with premarital agreements. But using mediation to provide a neutral, mutually supportive context for your negotiations allows you to use independent legal advisers as supporters, rather than advocates engaged

in a tug of war. And of course, if you collaborate, the independent advice of your collaborative attorneys is built into the process.

 For more information on premarital agreements, see *Prenuptial Agreements: How to Write a Fair & Lasting Contract,* by Katherine E. Stoner and Shae Irving (Nolo).

Selecting a Mediator or Collaborative Attorney

When choosing a mediator or collaborative lawyer to help you negotiate an agreement for your new relationship, try to find someone who has experience in the field. Because some of the toughest issues will probably be financial ones, make sure the mediator or attorney has expertise in financial matters. If you mediate and want the mediator to write up the agreement, you may need to use a lawyer-mediator. For more on this question, see Chapter 16.

For a general overview of the qualifications to look for in any good mediator, see Chapter 6. Take a look at Worksheet 1 in the appendix and modify the questions there to apply to your situation. For tips on finding a collaborative attorney, use Worksheet 2 in conjunction with Chapter 7.

Using Advisers

While getting separate legal advice may not be required for your agreement to be legally valid, most lawyers in most states will tell you that a premarital agreement may not hold up in court unless each partner received separate legal advice about the agreement before signing it. This logic applies to postmarital and living together agreements, too. Getting legal advice before committing to the agreement you mediate is sort of like an insurance policy for the agreement. If you can afford the premium, it may be worth the extra money. And the laws of your state may even require it.

If you decide to use a collaborative process, your collaborative lawyer will advise you about the legalities of all aspects of the agreement.

If you mediate, read Chapter 8 before you begin mediating., It explores how to select a mediation-friendly consulting lawyer. Then use your mediator as a resource in finding a legal adviser who will support you in negotiating a fair agreement without turning the process into a stressful, adversarial tug of war.

Preparing for Mediation or Collaboration

As with all mediations, preparation is a key to success. And because this mediation is about building a relationship rather than ending it, you can do a lot of the preparation with your spouse- or partner-to-be.

One important element in preparing is to allow enough advance time. Don't wait until days or even weeks before the wedding or move-in date to begin your discussions. Not only does waiting until late in the game put added stress on your relationship, but it increases the risk that any agreement you sign could be challenged on the basis of duress—undue pressure placed on one party to an agreement.

Brush up on your communication skills if you haven't already done so. (See Chapter 12.) Familiarize yourself with the basic principles of interest-based negotiating. (See Chapter 13.)

Next, make an inventory of your property. Include all assets and debts. Consider making up a budget of projected monthly expenses. You can use Worksheets 3–6 in the appendix. Also check with your mediator or collaborative attorney regarding any suggested or required advanced preparation.

At the Mediation or Four-Way Collaborative Meeting

Depending on how much preparation you've already done and the number of decisions you need to make, the mediation or collaboration itself could take one or more sessions or meetings.

If you haven't been through a mediation or collaboration before, take a look at Chapter 2, which describes what happens in a divorce mediation, or Chapter 3, which describes a collaborative divorce. While your situation is decidedly different from that of a divorcing couple, much of the process will be similar, so you can get an idea of what to expect in the process.

During meetings, work on clear communication and maintaining a collaborative negotiating approach, using the suggestions in Chapters 12 and 13. If you seem to reach an impasse, consider some of the techniques described in Chapter 15, or consider working with a marital counselor. (See Chapter 8.) Most of the time, what appears to be an impasse can be overcome. In rare cases, the process of negotiating uncovers a true incompatibility that is so significant, it causes the couple to reconsider their relationship. While this can be a big disappointment, finding out the bad news at the outset is better than discovering the incompatibility later on down the road.

Realize that you may have to respectfully disagree on some matters. At the same time, make a commitment to your partner to value the relationship and your love for one another even when you disagree.

At the end of a mediation session or collaborative meeting, jot down some notes of what was accomplished and any follow-up steps to be taken. You can use Worksheet 10.

What to Include in the Agreement

Just what to include in your agreement is too large a subject to cover adequately in this book. To get you started, here are some key issues you are likely to include in your written agreement. For more detailed suggestions, look at one or more of the resources listed above.

Issues to include in your agreement:

- ❑ property rights, separate and joint
- ❑ pensions and retirement plans
- ❑ responsibility for debts
- ❑ how living expenses will be paid
- ❑ support payments following a separation, if state law permits
- ❑ wills and inheritance rights, and
- ❑ process for negotiating future changes or settling disputes.

Silver Linings

Many mediators and collaborative professionals believe that one of the best things about mediation or collaboration is that it teaches people problem-solving skills that they can use again and again, in old relationships and in new ones. It is our hope that your experience of mediation or collaboration after your divorce will be just that for you: a silver lining bringing a promise of sunnier days ahead whenever new clouds appear on the horizon.

Appendix

Worksheet 1—Questions for Potential Mediators

Worksheet 2—Questions for Potential Collaborative Attorneys

Worksheet 3—Assets (Parts 1, 2, and 3)

Worksheet 4—Debts (Parts 1 and 2)

Worksheet 5—Your Income

Worksheet 6—Your Monthly Expenses (Parts 1 and 2)

Worksheet 7—Exercise: Assessing Your Children's Needs

Worksheet 8—First Session Checklist

Worksheet 9—Sample Agreement to Mediate

Worksheet 10—Mediation or Collaboration Progress Notes

Worksheet 11—Inventory of Personal Negotiation Skills

Worksheet 12—Negotiation Notes

Worksheet 13—Notes of Consultation With Adviser

Your Name: _____

Worksheet 1—Questions for Potential Mediators

Make several copies of this form. Use one for each mediator or mediation agency you contact. Skip any sections or questions that don't apply.

Who referred you to this mediator or agency? _____

Basic Information

Name of mediator or agency: _____

Address: _____

Telephone number: _____

Fax number: _____

Email: _____

Will send brochure or other printed information: ❑ yes   ❑ no

Basic Qualifications of Mediators

Agencies or Court-Sponsored Mediators Only:

Does the agency provide divorce mediation? ❑ yes   ❑ no

Percentage of agency caseload devoted to divorces: _____

Minimum qualifications of the divorce mediators:

   Professional background: _____

   Years of mediation experience: _____

   Hours of training: _____

   Other: _____

How is a mediator assigned to a case? _____

Do you have a choice of mediators? ❑ yes   ❑ no

If so, list names and contact information: _____

_____

_____

_____

Private Practice Mediators Only:

Mediator's professional background (lawyer, accountant, therapist, etc.): _____

Professional degrees or licenses held: _____

Mediator's experience with divorce law/court system: _____

Years of experience as mediator: _____

Percentage of mediation practice devoted to divorce mediation: _____

OR

Number of divorce cases mediated in past year: _____

Any other field in which the mediator practices or does business: _____

Your Name: _____

If yes, percentage of professional practice devoted to mediation: _____

Hours of professional training in mediation (should be at least 35): _____

Hours of training in divorce mediation: _____

Hours of continuing professional education in past year: _____

In mediation: _____

In other related field (specify): _____

Membership in any mediation associations: _____

Experience in divorce law: _____

Special Issues

Mediator's training or experience in:

Child development issues: _____

Tax and finance issues: _____

Legal issues: _____

Power imbalance issues: _____

Domestic violence issues: _____

Substance abuse/recovery issues: _____

Other (specify, such as religious or cultural background, language services, teleconferencing, etc.): _____

Fees

Basic mediation fee: _____

Fee for the first session: _____

Charges for agreement: _____

Charges for other paperwork: _____

Advance deposit fee: _____

Sliding scale fee available? ❑ yes   ❑ no

Monthly payments accepted? ❑ yes   ❑ no

Credit cards accepted? ❑ yes   ❑ no

How spouses will allocate the fee: _____

Mediation Process

Will the mediator speak separately to each spouse before the first session? ❑ yes   ❑ no

How to make an appointment for the first session: _____

How to prepare for the first session: _____

What to bring to the first session: _____

Length of first session and what happens at it: _____

Your Name: _____

Are mediation sessions confidential? ❑ yes   ❑ no

Will the mediator meet separately with each spouse? ❑ yes   ❑ no

Will statements spouses make in separate meetings be shared with the other party? ❑ yes   ❑ no

Will spouses sign a written agreement to mediate covering confidentiality, fees, and other matters? ❑ yes   ❑ no

Is copy of agreement available in advance? ❑ yes   ❑ no

How long (how many sessions) will the mediation last? _____

Will the mediation be conducted by a single mediator or with a comediator? _____

Qualifications of any comediator: _____

Additional charge for the comediator: _____

How long have the comediators worked together? _____

Does the mediator subscribe to voluntary standards of practice? _____

Paperwork Preparation

Mediator will prepare agreement: ❑ yes   ❑ no

Consulting lawyers will review agreements: ❑ yes   ❑ no

Mediator will prepare the court paperwork: ❑ yes   ❑ no

My Impressions of Mediator or Agency

_____

_____

_____

_____

Your Name: _____

Worksheet 2—Questions for Potential Collaborative Attorneys

Make several copies of this form. Use one for each attorney you contact.
Skip any sections or questions that don't apply.

Who referred you to this attorney? _____

Basic Information

Name of attorney: _____

Address: _____

Telephone number: _____

Fax number: _____

Email: _____

Will send brochure or other printed information: ❑ yes ❑ no

Basic Qualifications of Attorney

Professional degrees or licenses held: _____

Years of experience as divorce attorney: _____

Years of experience as collaborative attorney: _____

Percentage of law practice devoted to collaborative divorce: _____

Number of collaborative divorce cases handled in past year: _____

Any other area of law in which the attorney practices: _____

Hours of professional training in collaborative divorce (should be at least 12): _____

Hours of training in mediation or dispute resolution: _____

Hours of continuing professional education in past year: _____

In collaborative divorce: _____

In other related field (specify): _____

Membership in any collaborative associations: _____

Special Issues

Attorney's training or experience in:

Child development issues: _____

Tax and finance issues: _____

Legal issues: _____

Power imbalance issues: _____

Domestic violence issues: _____

Substance abuse/recovery issues: _____

Other (specify, such as religious or cultural background, language services, teleconferencing, etc.): _____

Your Name: _____

Fees

Basic hourly fee: _____

Fee for the first consultation: _____

Other charges: _____

Advance deposit (retainer) fee: _____

Sliding scale fee available? ❑ yes ❑ no

Monthly payments accepted? ❑ yes ❑ no

Credit cards accepted? ❑ yes ❑ no

My Impressions of Attorney

_____

_____

_____

_____

Your Name: _____

Worksheet 3—Assets (Part 1)

- Use one or more copies of the attached pages to list assets known to you in the order of the categories below.
- Use one space for each asset. Include in the "Description" space the information indicated below.
- In the "Joint or Separate" space in Part 2, put your initials (or your spouse's initials) if you consider the asset to be your sole property (or your spouse's), and put "Joint" if it belongs to both of you.
- Values of assets in Part 3 are your best estimates of current market value; if you don't have an estimate, write "Unknown."
- Check off each category as you finish it, or, if it doesn't apply, write "N/A" or "None" above the box.
- Attach copies of documents indicated below, if available.

Asset Category	Include in Description on Worksheet	Attach to Part 3 of This Worksheet
❑ Real estate	Address and assessor's parcel number	Copy of deed(s), property tax bill
❑ Household furnishings, appliances, tools, and equipment (see Part 3)	Write in one of the following: "Already divided on our own" "To be divided on our own" "See Part 3 for list of items"	
❑ Art, antiques, and collections (see Part 3)	Same as above	
❑ Vehicles	Year, make, and model	Copy of title certificate or registration
❑ Boats and trailers	Make, model, and size	
❑ Bank and credit union savings, checking, certificate of deposit accounts	Name and branch, type of account, name of account holder	Copy of latest statement(s)
❑ Other cash	Location	
❑ Tax refunds	Tax year and whether state or federal	
❑ Life insurance	Name of insured, insurance company, face amount, any cash value	

Your Name: _____

Worksheet 3—Assets (Part 1) cont.

Asset Category	Include in Description on Worksheet	Attach to Part 3 of This Worksheet
❏ Stocks, bonds, mutual funds (nonretirement)	Name of investment and account number	Copy of latest share certificate
❏ Retirement plans, pensions, IRAs, Keoghs, 401(k) plans	Name of owner, type of plan	Copy of latest statement
❏ Money owed to you (notes, accounts receivable)	Name of debtor and purpose of loan	Copy of note, invoice, etc.
❏ Partnerships, other business	Business name, form of ownership interests, and percentage owned	
❏ Other		

Your Name: _____

Worksheet 3—Assets (Part 2)

Make extra copies if you need them. List in order of categories shown in Part 1.

Asset Category	Asset Description	Date Acquired	Joint or Separate	Estimated Current Value	Balance Due on Mortgage or Lien

Your Name: _____

Worksheet 3—Assets (Part 3)

Household Goods, Art, Antiques, and Collections

❑ We have divided these items to our satisfaction.

❑ We plan to divide these items between us without help. If we need help later, we will complete this worksheet.

❑ We can't agree on who gets some items, or we can't agree on values. The items we can't agree on are listed below.

Group items when appropriate—for example, Dining Room Set, Flatware, etc.

The value is your best estimate of what this item would sell for in its current condition. If you prefer to use the cost paid, put "C" beside the cost, or, for replacement cost, put "R."

Make extra copies of this page if you need them.

		VALUES	
	Who Gets This Item (If Agreed)	**Furnishings, Appliances, Tools and Equipment**	**Art, Antiques, and Collections**
SUBTOTALS (THIS PAGE)			
TOTALS (LAST PAGE ONLY)			

Your Name: _____

Worksheet 4—Debts (Part 1)

- Use one or more copies of the attached pages to list all debts owed by you or your spouse in the order of the categories below; skip the categories that are not applicable.
- Use one row for each debt.
- If you don't know the balance due on a debt, put "Unknown."
- Check off each category as you finish it, or, if it doesn't apply, write "N/A" or "None."
- Attach a copy of the latest statement for each debt showing current balance due, if available.

Debt Category	Include in Description on Worksheet (Part 2)	Attach to Worksheet
❑ Taxes owed	Tax years	
❑ Secured debts (debts tied to collateral such as mortgage, car loan, 401(k) loan, home equity loan)	Account number and description of collateral securing the debt (such as 19xx Ford)	Copy of latest statement
❑ General unsecured debts (including personal loans from friends or family members)	Creditor name and reason this debt was incurred	Copy of promissory note or latest statement
❑ Credit card debts	Account number	Copy of latest statement
❑ Student loans	Account number	Copy of latest statement
❑ Support arrears (child support or alimony/spousal support)	Names of child/children, if child support	
❑ Overdue bills (not monthly household bills that are current)		Copy of invoice or statement
❑ Other debts (not included above)		

Your Name: _____

Worksheet 4—Debts (Part 2)

Debt Category	To Whom Owed	Description	Date Incurred	Balance Owed at Separation	Current Balance Owed

Your Name: _____

Worksheet 5—Your Income

List gross (before-tax) income earned or received by you in previous calendar year. Specify source of income: wages, self-employment, interest, dividends, commissions, annuities, etc. Do *not* include your spouse's income.

Your Gross Taxable Income   **Annual Amount**

_____ $ _____
_____ $ _____
_____ $ _____
_____ $ _____
_____ $ _____

| **Total Taxable Income** | $_____ ÷ 12 = $ _____ |
| | Monthly Amount |

Your Gross Nontaxable Income
Specify source: tax-free interest, disability, etc.

_____ $ _____
_____ $ _____
_____ $ _____

| **Total Nontaxable Income** | $_____ ÷ 12 = $ _____ |
| | Monthly Amount |

| **Total Monthly Gross All Income** | $ _____ |
| Add taxable and nontaxable amounts. | Total Monthly |

If different from the above, your *current* gross (before-tax) monthly income (use an average if you need to).	$ _____
	Taxable
	$ _____
	Nontaxable

Do you pay: State income tax? ❑ yes ❑ no   FICA/Medicare? ❑ yes ❑ no

Regular monthly deductions from your paycheck (attach a copy of a current pay stub):

Federal Tax: _____   Mandatory Retirement: _____

State Tax: _____   Voluntary Deductions: _____

FICA/Medicare: _____   Health Care, Day Care: _____

Health Insurance: _____   Other: _____

Union Dues: _____   Total Deductions: _____

Your Name: _____

Worksheet 6—Your Monthly Expenses (Part 1)

Names of all persons in your household whose expenses are included on this worksheet:

_____

- List the average monthly expenses for the household in which you live. Do not include your spouse's expenses if you are living separately. Do not include any special expenses for your children (see below).
- Include all expenses that apply. Refer to your records to be as accurate as possible.
- If monthly amount varies, indicate annual amount and divide by 12 for monthly average.
- Put an * next to expenses on which you've had to cut back since your separation.

Item	Annual	Monthly	Item	Annual	Monthly
rent or mortgage			life or disability insurance		
property taxes			your education		
owner/renter insurance			entertainment		
maintenance			car registration/insurance		
cleaning/yard service/pool			car gasoline and oil		
water softener/bottled water			car repairs/auto club		
food and household supplies			car parking		
food: eating out			car payment		
utilities			gifts, donations		
telephone			dues/subscriptions		
laundry/dry cleaning			vacations		
clothing (yourself)			haircuts, personal hygiene		
health insurance			pets (food, vet, etc.)		
unreimbursed medical			accountant		
unreimbursed dental			unreimbursed business exp.		
unreimbursed psychotherapy			installments (Part 2)		
unreimbursed prescriptions			other (specify)		
			Total Monthly		

Does anyone else contribute to the above expenses? ❑ yes ❑ no

If so, who and how much? _____

Your Name: _____

Worksheet 6—Your Monthly Expenses (Part 1) cont.

Special Expenses for Children

Names of Children: _____

Item	Annual	Monthly	Item	Annual	Monthly
health insurance			day care		
unreimbursed medical			tuition		
unreimbursed dental			school lunches, supplies		
orthodontia			activities/lessons		
clothing			other (specify)		
			Total Monthly		

Does anyone else contribute to the special expenses for children? ❑ yes ❑ no

If so, who and how much? _____

Your Name: _____

Worksheet 6—Your Monthly Expenses (Part 2)

Installment Payments Paid by You: Creditor's Name/Account Number	Payment for	Balance Owed at Separation	Balance Owed Now	Monthly Payment
Total Monthly Installment Payments				$

Enter this total on Part 1

Your Name: _____

Worksheet 7—Exercise: Assessing Your Children's Needs

For this exercise, make enough copies of this page so that you have a separate sheet for each child, as these questions require you to answer about each individual child. You don't need to make extra copies of pages 2–4, as those questions ask more generally about all of your children. Later, you can share your answers with your spouse or the mediator if you want to, but that's optional. Completing this exercise will help you prepare, mentally and emotionally, to have a productive discussion with the mediator or collaborative attorneys and your spouse about parenting issues.

Step 1: Name of child: _____

What makes this child unique? Describe this child's personality, talents, and troublesome traits. If this child has special tutoring needs, medical requirements, or other special needs, include them.

_____

_____

_____

As honestly as you can, describe this child's relationship with you.

_____

_____

_____

_____

Now, with equal honesty, describe this child's relationship with your spouse. (If you are angry with your spouse, this can be hard to do, but remind yourself that your child is not getting a divorce from your spouse, and try to be as objective as you can.)

_____

_____

_____

_____

Your Name: _____

Step 2: You as a Parent:

List your skills and talents as a parent. What are your strengths? What are the core values you want to impart to your children?

List your weaknesses as a parent. Be honest. (Remember, this exercise is for you, and you don't need to share it with anyone else.)

_____   _____

_____   _____

_____   _____

_____   _____

_____   _____

_____   _____

_____   _____

_____   _____

_____   _____

_____   _____

_____   _____

_____   _____

_____   _____

_____   _____

_____   _____

_____   _____

_____   _____

_____   _____

_____   _____

_____   _____

_____   _____

_____   _____

_____   _____

Your Name: _____

Step 3: Your Spouse as a Parent:

List your spouse's strengths as a parent: skills, talents, strengths, core values you see your spouse trying to impart. Are you having a hard time thinking of anything but your spouse's weaknesses? Keep trying. If you keep your focus child-centered, you'll think of at least a few positive attributes. (Remember, you don't have to share what you've written down.)

After you've got a list of strengths, list your spouse's weaknesses. Try not to be petty. The point of this exercise to see your children's situation as objectively as possible.

_____   _____

_____   _____

_____   _____

_____   _____

_____   _____

_____   _____

_____   _____

_____   _____

_____   _____

_____   _____

_____   _____

_____   _____

_____   _____

_____   _____

_____   _____

_____   _____

_____   _____

Your Name: _____

Step 4: Time-sharing

Days and times the children usually spend with you and with your spouse. Even if you and your spouse still live together, see if you can identify a pattern of time with each parent. Refer to a calendar for the last couple of months if you aren't sure.

_____

_____

_____

_____

Anything about the pattern of time-sharing you'd like to change. Why?

_____

_____

_____

_____

List all holidays and special days (like birthdays) in the year.

_____	_____
_____	_____
_____	_____
_____	_____
_____	_____
_____	_____
_____	_____

Put your initials beside the days that have special significance to you.

Put your spouse's initials next to the days that you think have special significance to your spouse.

List three times in the last year when you and your spouse saw eye-to-eye on something involving your children. Reminding yourself that the two of you have agreed about what's best for the children in the recent past can help put things in perspective as you prepare for the mediation.

_____

_____

_____

_____

Worksheet 8—First Session Checklist

Read through this checklist. Add your own questions and comments. Check off each item as you discuss it in the session. Jot down your notes in the space given.

Confidentiality

❑ Are statements made in mediation confidential? ❑ yes ❑ no

❑ By state law? ❑ yes ❑ no

❑ By written agreement? (see Sample Agreement to Mediate) ❑ yes ❑ no

Questions to Ask the Mediator

These are intended to give you an idea of how this mediator works. There are no right or wrong answers.

❑ What is mediation? _____

_____

❑ What is your role in the mediation? _____

_____

❑ How do you avoid conflicts of interest? (Do you know of any conflict of interest in our case?)

_____

❑ How will you stay neutral and avoid taking sides? _____

_____

❑ What do we do if we feel like you are taking sides during the mediation? _____

_____

❑ Will you tell us your opinion of what is the best settlement? _____

_____

❑ Will you discuss our legal options with us? ❑ yes ❑ no

❑ How do you feel about us working with legal advisers? _____

_____

❑ Will we meet together, separately, or both? _____

❑ Will things we say to you in separate meetings be kept private? ❑ yes ❑ no

❑ How do we decide what is the best settlement? _____

_____

❑ What do you do if we can't agree on something? _____

_____

❑ What happens next if we reach an agreement? _____

_____

❑ Do you prepare a written settlement agreement for us?   ❑ yes ❑ no

❑ Does our written settlement agreement need to be reviewed by lawyers? ❑ yes ❑ no

❑ Will you help us with the divorce paperwork? ❑ yes ❑ no

❑ What happens if we don't reach a complete agreement? _____

_____

❑ If the mediator is a lawyer: What if one of us wants you to represent him/her after the

mediation is over? _____

❑ Other:_____

_____

_____

_____

Fees

❑ What are your fees and how are they billed? _____

Agreement to Mediate

❑ Will you prepare a written agreement to mediate? (Compare to Sample Agreement to Mediate.)

❑ yes ❑ no

❑ Is the written agreement to mediate clear and acceptable? ❑ yes ❑ no

❑ Additional questions about the agreement: _____

_____

_____

_____

_____

Things to Watch For

❑ On a scale of 1 to 10, how much does the mediator control the discussions during mediation?

_____

❑ How does the mediator handle interactions between you and your spouse? _____

_____

❑ Do you think the mediator will give you enough/too much guidance on what the settlement should be? _____

❑ On a scale of 1 to 10, how much weight does the mediator give to legal rules? _____

❑ On a scale of 1 to 10, how comfortable are you with this mediator's style? _____

Other questions and observations:

_____

_____

_____

_____

_____

Next Step

❑ Date and time of next session: _____

❑ Other:

_____

_____

_____

_____

_____

Worksheet 9—Sample Agreement to Mediate

The people ("parties") and the mediator agree to mediate subject to the following terms and conditions.

Parties: The parties participating in this mediation are _____

and _____

Mediator: The mediator(s) is (are) _____

Subject: The subject of this mediation is _____

Mediation Defined: Mediation is a private, voluntary process in which a neutral mediator assists the parties in reaching an agreement on the subject of the mediation.

Mediator's Role and Responsibilities

General Role. The mediator will facilitate the negotiations of the parties and assist them in reaching an agreement. However, the mediator will not make any decisions for the parties.

Neutrality. The mediator is neutral. She/he will not side with either party. If the mediator becomes aware that she/he has any bias on an issue under consideration, the mediator will immediately disclose that bias to the parties, and will either obtain the parties' consent to continue the mediation or terminate the mediation.

Conflict of Interest.

1. The mediator has no prior relationship with either party or any related person that would create a conflict of interest for the mediator.

OR

The mediator has the following prior relationship with a party or related person: _____

_____

The parties to this mediation knowingly waive any conflict of interest created by the above relationship.

2. The mediator will not enter into any future relationship with a party to this mediation that would be adverse to any other party or that would otherwise be a conflict of interest.

Legal Advice. The mediator will not give legal advice to any party to the mediation. Each party is encouraged to obtain separate legal advice about the subject of this mediation.

The mediator ❑ will ❑ will not assist the parties to understand the possible legal outcomes on issues and to compare them to alternative options under consideration.

Use of Experts. During the mediation, the mediator may consult with experts in order to obtain necessary information about issues under consideration, but only if the parties agree in advance to the consultation and to payment of the experts' fees.

Confidentiality.

1. This mediation, including all statements by the parties and the mediator, and all written notes, memoranda, or other documents prepared during the course of the mediation, is confidential under the law of the state of: _____

   A copy or summary of this law is attached to this Agreement.

OR

   All statements by the parties and the mediator, and all written or electronic records provided or prepared during the course of the mediation, are confidential. Unless both parties sign a written consent authorizing disclosure, the mediator will not disclose to any person other than experts or consultants retained by the mediator with the parties' consent any confidential information provided to the mediator during the course of the mediation. Neither the mediator nor a party can be compelled to testify in any adversarial proceeding regarding any statements made during mediation or other confidential records provided or prepared during mediation, nor to produce any confidential records provided or prepared during the course of mediation. If any party tries to compel such testimony or production of records, that party will pay the reasonable expenses, including attorneys' fees, of the person or persons opposing the testimony or production of records. Note: The confidentiality of this mediation may not apply to criminal prosecutions, depending on applicable law.

2. Each party authorizes the mediator to disclose confidential information provided or prepared during mediation, by that party only, to that party's lawyer, therapist, or other (specify):

   _____

3. Because of the sensitive nature of the information to be disclosed in this mediation, neither party shall disclose confidential information provided or prepared during the mediation to any third person not participating in this mediation, except for the following people:

Each party's advisers and counselors

Other(s): _____

Recording of Sessions

A party may electronically record (on audiotape only) mediation sessions for his/her personal use if he/she informs the other party and the mediator immediately prior to recording. The tapes shall be considered confidential records subject to this agreement.

OR

Mediation sessions may not be recorded electronically.

Duty to Disclose Information

The parties agree to disclose and exchange all relevant information and documents available to them concerning the issues under consideration in this mediation.

OR

Each party agrees to disclose and exchange all relevant information and documents available to him/her concerning the issues under consideration in this mediation to the extent that party deems appropriate, but each party specifically reserves the right to withhold information if he/she deems that to be in his/her best interests.

Mediation Sessions

Privacy. The mediation sessions are private. No person other than the parties, the mediator, and the parties' authorized representatives may attend any session unless the parties and the mediator agree.

Separate Sessions.

1. The mediator will not have any separate contact with either party and neither party will attempt to communicate separately with the mediator.

OR

The mediator may meet separately in person, by telephone, or in writing with either party at any time.

2. The mediator will disclose to the other party the substance of any separate meeting, telephone conversation, or written correspondence with one party.

OR

The mediator shall not disclose to the other party the substance of any separate meeting, telephone conversation, or written correspondence with one party, unless the party to the separate communication has authorized disclosure.

Status of Legal Proceedings. During the course of this mediation, any adversarial legal proceedings pending between the parties will be suspended and held in abeyance, and no new adversarial proceeding will be initiated by a party to the mediation except upon written consent of the parties and the mediator.

Ending Mediation. Mediation is voluntary. The mediation may be ended by any party or by the mediator at any time for any reason. A person who wishes to end mediation will notify the others of his/her decision to end mediation. Mediation may be resumed at a later time if the parties and the mediator agree.

Preparation of Agreement

If an agreement is reached in mediation, the mediator will prepare the following written document setting forth the terms of the agreement:

❑ Memorandum of Agreement

❑ Settlement Agreement

The written memorandum or agreement will be binding on the parties to the mediation after it has been reviewed and signed by each of them. Until the agreement is signed by every party, it will be considered a confidential record prepared during the course of mediation and will be subject to the nondisclosure terms of this agreement.

Mediation Fees

The mediator's fees are as follows: _____

_____

The mediator's fees shall be paid by the parties in the following proportions: _____

_____

_____

Payment shall be made:

❏ At the time of each session.

❏ Upon presentation of a written statement.

❏ Other (specify): _____

_____

_____

_____

Additional Ground Rules

Communication rules:_____

_____

_____

Other: _____

_____

_____

Dated: _____   _____
                                             (Party's Signature)

Dated: _____   _____
                                             (Party's Signature)

Dated: _____   _____
                                             (Mediator's Signature)

Worksheet 10—Mediation or Collaboration Progress Notes

Date: _____

People present: _____

_____

Date and time of next session: _____

Things to do before next session or four-way meeting:

Item   Person responsible

_____

_____

_____

_____

What will be discussed in the next session or four-way meeting:

_____

_____

_____

_____

Agreements reached at this session or meeting:

Item   Tentative? (yes or no)

_____

_____

_____

_____

My comments, concerns, or questions:

_____

_____

_____

_____

_____

Worksheet 11—Inventory of Personal Negotiation Skills

Summarize details of negotiations you've been involved in.

Make copies of this form if you have more than one example.

Example number: _____

When did this negotiation occur? _____

Who was involved in it? _____

What was the agreement reached? _____

What interests of mine were met? _____

_____

What interests of others were met? _____

_____

What was my role in the negotiation? (initiator/responder/other) _____

How well did I assert my interests? _____

How well did I attend to the other party's interests? _____

What did I do well? _____

_____

What could I improve? _____

_____

Worksheet 12—Negotiation Notes

Bring these notes with you.

A. Problems (issues) to be resolved

_____

_____

_____

_____

_____

_____

B. My interests

Priority	My Interests
_____	_____
_____	_____
_____	_____
_____	_____
_____	_____
_____	_____
_____	_____

C. My spouse's interests

Priority	My Spouse's Interests
_____	_____
_____	_____
_____	_____
_____	_____
_____	_____
_____	_____

D. Compare and match up interests. To the right of each interest, put "S" for shared, "I" for independent, and "C" for conflicting.

E. My BATNA (Best Alternative To A Negotiated Settlement) and WATNA (Worst Alternative To A Negotiated Settlement)

Issue: _____BATNA: _____

Fees/Costs: _____WATNA: _____

Issue: _____BATNA: _____

Fees/Costs: _____WATNA: _____

Issue: _____BATNA: _____

Fees/Costs: _____WATNA: _____

Issue: _____BATNA: _____

Fees/Costs: _____WATNA: _____

Issue: _____BATNA: _____

Fees/Costs: _____WATNA: _____

F. Settlement Spectrum

Most desirable settlement: _____

_____

_____

_____

_____

In-between ideas: _____

_____

_____

_____

_____

Least desirable settlement: _____

_____

_____

_____

_____

G. Am I prepared to see things in a new way?   ❏ yes ❏ no

H. Can I accept a settlement that my spouse will be satisfied with?   ❏ yes ❏ no

Worksheet 13—Notes of Consultation With Adviser

Adviser's name: _____

Date of consultation: _____

My Questions	**Adviser's Answers**
1. _____	_____
_____	_____
2. _____	_____
_____	_____
3. _____	_____
_____	_____
4. _____	_____
_____	_____
5. _____	_____
_____	_____
6. _____	_____
_____	_____
7. _____	_____
_____	_____
8. _____	_____
_____	_____

Plan of Action

Steps to take, questions to ask, or things to say in mediation or four-way meeting.

1. _____
2. _____
3. _____
4. _____
5. _____
6. _____

Index

Remember:
Little publishers have big ears.
We really listen to you.

Take 2 Minutes & Give Us Your 2 cents

Your comments make a big difference in the development and revision of Nolo books and software. Please take a few minutes and register your Nolo product—and your comments—with us. Not only will your input make a difference, you'll receive special offers available only to registered owners of Nolo products on our newest books and software. Register now by:

PHONE
1-800-728-3555

FAX
1-800-645-0895

EMAIL
cs@nolo.com

or **MAIL** us
this registration card

— fold here —

Registration Card

NAME _____ DATE _____

ADDRESS _____

_____

CITY _____ STATE _____ ZIP _____

PHONE _____ EMAIL _____

WHERE DID YOU HEAR ABOUT THIS PRODUCT? _____

WHERE DID YOU PURCHASE THIS PRODUCT? _____

DID YOU CONSULT A LAWYER? (PLEASE CIRCLE ONE)   YES   NO   NOT APPLICABLE

DID YOU FIND THIS BOOK HELPFUL?   (VERY)   5   4   3   2   1   (NOT AT ALL)

COMMENTS _____

WAS IT EASY TO USE?   (VERY EASY)   5   4   3   2   1   (VERY DIFFICULT)

We occasionally make our mailing list available to carefully selected companies whose products may be of interest to you.

❏ If you do not wish to receive mailings from these companies, please check this box.

❏ You can quote me in future Nolo promotional materials.
   Daytime phone number _____.

DWCT 1.0

Nolo in the NEWS

"Nolo helps lay people perform legal tasks without the aid—or fees—of lawyers."
—USA TODAY

Nolo books are ..."written in plain language, free of legal mumbo jumbo, and spiced with witty personal observations."
—ASSOCIATED PRESS

"...Nolo publications...guide people simply through the how, when, where and why of law."
—WASHINGTON POST

"Increasingly, people who are not lawyers are performing tasks usually regarded as legal work... And consumers, using books like Nolo's, do routine legal work themselves."
—NEW YORK TIMES

"...All of [Nolo's] books are easy-to-understand, are updated regularly, provide pull-out forms...and are often quite moving in their sense of compassion for the struggles of the lay reader."
—SAN FRANCISCO CHRONICLE

fold here

- -

Nolo
950 Parker Street
Berkeley, CA 94710-9867

Attn: DWCT 1.0